THE NATIONAL INSTITUTE OF
ECONOMIC AND SOCIAL RESEARCH

Economic and Social Studies

XI

COLONIAL SOCIAL ACCOUNTING

T0300460

THE NATIONAL INSTITUTE OF ECONOMIC AND SOCIAL RESEARCH

OFFICERS OF THE INSTITUTE

The National Institute of Economic and Social Research, London, is an independent, non-profit-making body founded in 1938. It always has had as its aim the promotion of realistic research particularly in the field of economic. It conducts research by its own research staff and in co-operation with the Universities and other academic bodies. The work done under the Institute's auspices is published by the Cambridge University Press in two series: Studies and Occasional Papers. A complete list of these publications is printed at the end of this book.

2 DEAN TRENCH STREET, SMITH SQUARE

LONDON, S.W. I

TELEPHONE ABBEY 7665

COLONIAL
SOCIAL ACCOUNTING

BY

PHYLLIS DEANE

CAMBRIDGE
AT THE UNIVERSITY PRESS
1953

CAMBRIDGE UNIVERSITY PRESS
Cambridge, New York, Melbourne, Madrid, Cape Town,
Singapore, São Paulo, Delhi, Tokyo, Mexico City

Cambridge University Press
The Edinburgh Building, Cambridge CB2 8RU, UK

Published in the United States of America by Cambridge University Press, New York

www.cambridge.org
Information on this title: www.cambridge.org/9781107601284

First published 1953
First paperback edition 2011

A catalogue record for this publication is available from the British Library

ISBN 978-1-107-60128-4 Paperback

CONTENTS

page

Preface   xiii

PART I

INTRODUCTION

CHAPTER I.   THE PURPOSE OF SOCIAL ACCOUNTING   1
CHAPTER II.   THE BASIC ACCOUNTS   13

PART II

THE ECONOMY OF NORTHERN RHODESIA

CHAPTER III. THE COLONY AND ITS PEOPLE   17
CHAPTER IV.   THE STRUCTURE OF NATIONAL OUTPUT   34
CHAPTER V.   THE SOCIAL ACCOUNTS   59

PART III

THE ECONOMY OF NYASALAND

CHAPTER VI.   THE COLONY AND ITS PEOPLE   73
CHAPTER VII. THE STRUCTURE OF NATIONAL OUTPUT   88
CHAPTER VIII. THE SOCIAL ACCOUNTS   99

PART IV

THE RURAL COMMUNITIES

CHAPTER IX.   SOCIAL ACCOUNTING FOR PRIMITIVE COMMUNITIES   115
CHAPTER X.   COLLECTING THE DATA   131
CHAPTER XI.   EXPERIMENTS IN VILLAGE ECONOMIC SURVEYING
              (1) QUESTIONS AND ANSWERS   154
CHAPTER XII. EXPERIMENTS IN VILLAGE ECONOMIC SURVEYING
              (2) COMBINING THE ANSWERS   184
CHAPTER XIII. VILLAGE ECONOMIC SURVEY RESULTS   199

PART V

CONCLUSIONS

CHAPTER XIV. THE CENTRAL AFRICAN ECONOMY   211
CHAPTER XV.   THE EXPERIMENT REVIEWED   223

APPENDIX I.   SOURCES OF THE ESTIMATES FOR NORTHERN RHODESIA   230
APPENDIX II. SOURCES OF THE ESTIMATES FOR NYASALAND   303
APPENDIX III. NOTE AND BIBLIOGRAPHY ON VILLAGE ECONOMIC
              SURVEYING IN CENTRAL AFRICA   334

Index   343

LIST OF TABLES

PART I

INTRODUCTION

CHAPTER II. THE BASIC ACCOUNTS

page

1. The income-output-expenditure table   13

PART II

THE ECONOMY OF NORTHERN RHODESIA

CHAPTER III. THE COLONY AND ITS PEOPLE

2. The population of Northern Rhodesia   18
3. Distribution of population in 1946   18
4. Industrial distribution of the European population   20
5. European personal consumption, 1945   23
6. African subsistence and barter incomes, 1945   25
7. African personal consumption, 1945   26
8. Sources of African incomes   26
9. African average earnings from employment, 1945   27
10. Available village population, 1945, as percentage of total available in each province   28
11. Village cash incomes, 1947   29

CHAPTER IV. THE STRUCTURE OF NATIONAL OUTPUT

12. National territorial output, 1945 and 1948   35
13. The Northern Rhodesian mineral industry   35
14. Expenditure by mining industry in Northern Rhodesia   37
15. Agricultural areas of Northern Rhodesia   39
16. Municipalities and Management Boards, 1945   57

CHAPTER V. THE SOCIAL ACCOUNTS

17. (a) National (residents') income, output and outlay of Northern Rhodesia, 1938 and 1945   63
   (b) Residents' balance of payments, 1938 and 1945   63
18. (a) National (territorial) income, output and outlay of Northern Rhodesia, 1938 and 1945   64
   (b) Territorial balance of payments, 1938 and 1945   64
19. Changes in distribution of national product, 1938–48   65
20. Territorial output in Northern Rhodesia, 1938–48   67
21. Northern Rhodesia Ten-Year Development Plan   70

PART III

THE NYASALAND ECONOMY

page

CHAPTER VI. THE COLONY AND ITS PEOPLE

22. Population of Nyasaland at the 1945 Census   74
23. Population of Nyasaland since 1911   75
24. Estimated numbers of Africans in receipt of cash income in 1945 and 1948   77
25. Industrial distribution of gainfully occupied European population in 1945 and 1947   78
26. Estimated distribution of earned cash incomes received by European residents in 1945   79
27. Estimated pattern of European expenditure in Nyasaland, 1945   80
28. Estimated distribution of income among African employees of Central Government and missions, 1945   82
29. Estimates of African consumption, 1945   85

CHAPTER VII. THE STRUCTURE OF NATIONAL OUTPUT

30. Territorial output of Nyasaland, 1945 and 1948   89
31. Domestic produce exported, 1938–48   93
32. National income, output and expenditure of Nyasaland, 1938–48   98

CHAPTER VIII. THE SOCIAL ACCOUNTS

33. Territorial balance of payments for Nyasaland, 1938–48   107
34. Distribution of taxation, 1936–48   110

PART IV

THE RURAL COMMUNITIES

CHAPTER X. COLLECTING THE DATA

35. Village Economic Survey Schedule   132-5

CHAPTER XI. EXPERIMENTS IN VILLAGE ECONOMIC SURVEYING

(1) QUESTIONS AND ANSWERS

36. Provincial variations in economic conditions in Northern Rhodesia   157
37. The surveyed population   158
38. Crops grown by the Tonga   160
39. Lozi gardens   161
40. Livestock   162
41. Percentage of livestock killed or died   163
42. Summary of crops sold in three Tonga villages   165
43. Crops sold from among sixty Ngoni households   165
44. Income from livestock   167
45. Income from sales of beer   168
46. Income from miscellaneous goods and services   170
47. Income from employment and migrant labour   171
48. Receipts from damages and marriage payments   174
49. Estimated Ngoni expenditure on consumable goods and services   177
50. Expenditure on doctors and transport   177
51. Transfer expenditures   179

52. Expenditure on clothing   180
53. Comparative prices of clothing   181
54. Expenditure on household and productive equipment   182
55. Expenditure on livestock   183

CHAPTER XII. EXPERIMENTS IN VILLAGE ECONOMIC SURVEYING
                (2) COMBINING THE ANSWERS
56. Recorded income and expenditure of sixty Ngoni households   185
57. Income and expenditure of sixty-eight Tonga households   186
58. Income and expenditure of thirteen Lozi households   187
59. Estimates of average income and expenditure for 141 households   189
60. Comparison of recorded income and expenditure distributions   190
61. Estimated distribution of incomes in 141 households   191
62. Possessions of the average household in three areas   192
63. Value of property owned by three groups of households   193
64. Property distribution in fifty-four Tonga households and sixty Ngoni
    households   194
65. Relative importance of different forms of economic activity as a source
    of village wealth   197
66. Estimate of monetary and non-monetary income   198

CHAPTER XIII. VILLAGE ECONOMIC SURVEY RESULTS
67. Comparative Tonga incomes   200
68. Comparative Tonga expenditures   201
69. Tonga village budgets. Estimated average   201
70. Tonga income and expenditure. Generalized account for Mazabuka
    District (villages only)   202
71. Summary of budgets obtained from twenty-nine Lamba households   205
72. Village cash incomes and activities   205

PART V

CONCLUSIONS

CHAPTER XIV. THE CENTRAL AFRICAN ECONOMY

73. Central Africa. Area and population, 1948   211
74. Territorial incomes in Central Africa, 1948   214
75. An estimated balance of payments for Central Africa   215
76. Funds brought into Southern Rhodesia by immigrants   217

APPENDIX I

APPENDIX I. SOURCES OF THE ESTIMATES OF NATIONAL INCOME,
          OUTPUT AND EXPENDITURE OF NORTHERN RHODESIA

77. Population of Northern Rhodesia in 1945. From district estimates   232
78. Proportions of the population in Central African Censuses   234
79. Estimates of population of Northern Rhodesia based on District Com-
    missioners' Returns of Taxpayers, 1945   235
80. Distribution of adult males in 1945, Northern Rhodesia   235
81. Population available in the villages of Northern Rhodesia in 1945   236
82. European income distribution in 1945. Derived from 1946 Census   241
83. Estimated earnings of European individuals in each income group, 1945 242
84. Earnings of European individuals, 1945, classified by industries   243

		page
85.	Income distribution among Asians in 1945 according to the 1946 Census	244
86.	Estimates of earnings of Asian individuals	245
87.	Earnings of employed Africans computed for Workmen's Compensation	246
88.	Earnings of Africans employed in the mining industry, 1945	247
89.	Earnings of Africans in Northern Rhodesia on the railways, 1945	247
90.	African incomes from the Central Government, 1945	249
91.	African earnings in employment, 1945	251
92.	Africans employed by other Africans	252
93.	African incomes from migrant labour	253
94.	Distribution of African incomes from abroad	254
95.	African income from traded crops	256
96.	Quantity of output of African livestock	257
97.	African income from livestock and livestock products	259
98.	Value of Northern Rhodesian fisheries	260
99.	African incomes from independent work	262
100.	Value of income from village industries	262
101.	Estimates of African agricultural output per head	265
102.	Evaluation of agricultural output	266
103.	Volume and value of agricultural output	266
104.	Value of subsistence and marketed output	267
105.	Metal sales in Northern Rhodesia, 1945 and 1946	268
106.	Operating surplus of principal mining companies	268
107.	External production costs of mining industry	268
108.	Net output of principal mineral companies	269
109.	Analysis of output of mining industry	270
110.	Payments made by mining industry in Northern Rhodesia	271
111.	Output of the Northern Rhodesian mining industry	271
112.	Principal products of European agriculture	271
113.	Value of output of European agricultural produce	272
114.	Net value of output of European agriculture	273
115.	Summary table for European agriculture	274
116.	Trading licences issued by District Administration	274
117.	Distribution by licensed traders	275
118.	Internal trade in local produce	277
119.	Revenue and expenditure of railways, 1944–5	278
120.	Output of railways, 1945	279
121.	Net output of transport, 1945	279
122.	Output of local government service	280
123.	Output of Central Government	280
124.	Value of manufacturing output, 1945	282
125.	Income and expenditure of missions	283
126.	Output of miscellaneous services	284
127.	Imports into Northern Rhodesia, 1945, valued at entry	286
128.	Analysis of imports by destination	288
129.	European personal consumption	289
130.	Asian personal consumption. Rough estimate	291
131.	African consumption of traded goods and services	293
132.	Revenue and expenditure of Central Government, 1945	296
133.	Revenue and expenditure of European Local Government, 1945	297
134.	Revenue and expenditure of the Native Treasuries, 1945	297
135.	Combined net revenue and expenditure account for Central and Local Government, 1945	298
136.	Investment and saving	299
137.	Territorial balance of payments, 1945	299
138.	Balance of payments of the resident nation	302

APPENDIX II

Appendix II. Sources of the Estimates of the National Income, Output and Expenditure of Nyasaland, 1945

page

139. Europeans classified by industries, 1945   304
140. Incomes of European individuals, 1945   306
141. Company incomes in Nyasaland, 1945   307
142. Indian incomes, 1945   307
143. Distribution of Indian incomes   308
144. Incomes of Coloured individuals   308
145. African incomes from government service, 1945   310
146. Africans employed in agriculture   312
147. Africans in transport and distribution   312
148. Miscellaneous employments   313
149. Receipts from migrants   314
150. African output of cash crops   315
151. Miscellaneous African incomes   317
152. Estimated food-crop yields or yield equivalents   318
153. Rough estimate of value of other subsistence incomes   319
154. Net income of government   319
155. National taxable income of Nyasaland   320
156. Gross output of European agriculture, 1945   321
157. Net output of European agriculture and livestock   322
158. Net output of government   322
159. Output of distribution   323
160. Output of transport   324
161. Combined account for missions   325
162. Net output of miscellaneous services   326
163. National output of Nyasaland   326
164. Estimated pattern of European expenditure   328
165. Estimated pattern of Asian consumption   328
166. Estimate of value of African consumption   330
167. Central Government revenue and expenditure   331
168. Combined revenue and expenditure account for government and local authorities   331
169. National outlay of Nyasaland   332
170. Balance of payments of Nyasaland   333

APPENDIX III

Appendix III. Note and Bibliography on Village Economic Surveying in Central Africa

171. Agricultural areas of Northern Rhodesia   336

LIST OF ILLUSTRATIONS

Between pp. 224-5

1*a*. A corner of Nchanga Mine Compound, Northern Rhodesia

1*b*. Lusaka Municipal Compound, Northern Rhodesia

2*a*. A sanitary worker's home in a Lusaka compound, Northern Rhodesia

2*b*. A civil servant's home in the African Suburb, Lusaka, Northern Rhodesia

3*a*. An African boatman on the banks of the Luangwa River, Northern Rhodesia

3*b*. A fishing party spearing fish in the Barotse flood plain, Northern Rhodesia [*Photograph by Max Gluckman*]

4*a*. An African market in Northern Rhodesia

4*b*. African sawyers at work, Northern Rhodesia [*Photograph by Max Gluckman*]

5*a*. A Barotse woman making a pot, Northern Rhodesia [*Photograph by Max Gluckman*]

5*b*. A Tonga woman making a basket, Northern Rhodesia [*Photograph by Elizabeth Colson*]

6*a*. Small boys assisting at a fishing party on Lake Nyasa

6*b*. Sharing the catch after the net is landed, Lake Nyasa

7*a*. A grass house in the making, near Livingstone, Northern Rhodesia

7*b*. The finished product. A newly built grass house near Livingstone, Northern Rhodesia

8*a*. Women carrying harvest from the gardens [*Photograph by Max Gluckman*]

8*b*. Preparing the ground for planting, Northern Rhodesia [*Photograph by Max Gluckman*]

PREFACE

Recent developments in techniques of national income accounting, and the multiplication of national income estimates, suggest that a publication on this subject should be prefaced with a more precise indication of its place in time than is usually given on the title-page. When nearly three years have elapsed between writing and publication, as has been the case with this volume, a preliminary comment on its timing becomes a necessity.

This book had its origins in an enquiry into the national income of colonial territories initiated in 1941 by the National Institute of Economic and Social Research.[1] A Colonial Research Fellowship which I held from 1945–48 enabled me to spend eighteen months collecting first-hand material and a further period of about nine months analysing the data in London at the National Institute. The work of writing up was completed during the two years 1948–50 in the time I could spare from my researches at the Colonial Office and at the University of Cambridge Department of Applied Economics. I am indebted both to the Colonial Office and to the Department of Applied Economics for freeing me as much as possible for the task of completing this volume. The manuscript went to press in June 1950 and embodies the results of my own first-hand enquiries undertaken in 1946 and 1947, of other first-hand enquiries carried out by the Rhodes-Livingstone Institute in 1948 and 1949, and of the published data available by mid-1950.

I have tried in this volume to illustrate the ways in which national income accounting (or social accounting as it is often called) can be used to illuminate the structure of a colonial economy. Both of the Central African economies which have been chosen for purposes of illustration are European-settled colonies, and in both of them the political power and the economic initiative lies at present with the European group in the community. It is thus fatally easy for those of us brought up in the European tradition to define these economies and to measure their economic progress in terms of the European-inspired sector. The unqualified global aggregates of a social accounting system encourage this tendency, since the money measure gives European transactions an importance which is disproportionate to their welfare significance and since the changes in money-flows generated in the European sector of the economy can be so much more accurately and

[1] An interim report on this enquiry was completed in 1945 (Phyllis Deane, *The Measurement of Colonial National Incomes*, Occasional Paper XII published for the National Institute of Economic and Social Research by Cambridge University Press, 1948).

xiii

adequately measured than the changes in inter-village trade or in the volume of goods and services produced for home consumption.

In this study I have tried to use social accounting estimates as a tool of description and analysis of the Central African economy in Northern Rhodesia and Nyasaland and to examine their real implications for all sections of the community. It is for the village communities, numerically the most important section of all, that our information is least adequate, and in the belief that future economic research in Central Africa can most usefully be concentrated in this field I have described my own small experiments in village economic surveying in considerable detail.

My debt to the many people who helped me to make my enquiries in Central Africa and who discussed and advised upon the enquiry in its various stages is so great that it is impossible adequately to express it in a brief preface. In general terms I should like to thank the patient villagers and interpreters who endured my unending barrage of questions with incredible good humour, the anthropologists who introduced an inquisitive stranger to their good friends in the villages and gave up much of their precious field time to helping me with the design and the performance of the village surveys, the hard-pressed government and local government officials who answered questionnaires, opened up their files to me and took endless trouble to ensure that I went where I wanted to in search of information, and, last but not least, the farmers, business men, accountants, compound managers, missionaries and many others who spent so much time and energy in digging out data from intractable records and in answering questions and questionnaires. To all these people I am grateful not only for their practical assistance in the enquiry but also for much generous hospitality.

In particular terms I should like to give special thanks to Professor E. A. G. Robinson, Professor W. Arthur Lewis, and Mr Richard Stone, who were members of the Committee set up by the National Institute to launch and guide the enquiry in its early stages and who continued to give advice and guidance as members of the Committee set up by the Colonial Economic Research Committee of the Colonial Office. The assistance of members of the Rhodes-Livingstone Institute has been acknowledged in many places in this study, but the collaboration with them was such a happy one that I cannot deny myself the pleasure of a special word of thanks to Professor Max Gluckman, Miss Elizabeth Colson, Mr J. A. Barnes and Mr J. C. Mitchell, whose knowledgeable advice and practical assistance made the village surveys possible. Professor Gluckman and Miss Colson also provided some of the photographs for this volume. Among others who wrestled with the manuscript in its early stages Professor I. Schapera was particularly constructive and suggested many improvements for which I am grateful.

Finally, I must acknowledge a debt of many years' standing to the staff of the National Institute, particularly to Miss H. M. Rogers who in correcting the proofs removed many inelegancies of style and to Mrs F. S. Stone whose lively interest and active encouragement have been a valued inspiration since the beginning of the enquiry

PHYLLIS DEANE

Cambridge, 1952

PART I

INTRODUCTION

CHAPTER I

THE PURPOSE OF SOCIAL ACCOUNTING

One of the most striking characteristics of the economic problem of the twentieth century has been the great increase in the accepted responsibilities of government. It is generally assumed, at least in the more developed economies, that the structure, direction and tempo of a country's economic activity are subject to government control, whether through direct intervention, or through its influence on private enterprise, or indeed through its failure to exert any influence. The extent to which the government should intervene directly in the economic system, and the ways in which it might take action to guide the economy, are still political issues, but its basic responsibility for economic development is now taken for granted. The overriding economic needs of war, and the practical experience of wartime controls, have accelerated this process, and have increased government direct responsibility in the sphere of economic policy. The wartime experience helped particularly to emphasize the necessity for regarding the economy as an organic whole rather than in terms of a collection of separate economic problems.

This in its turn brought with it the need for new kinds of information as well as for a wider range of data on economic conditions. The economic policy-maker needed a method of making a rapid analysis of the economic situation, of assessing the significant current trends, and of appreciating the probable effects of a given policy. In some countries, where the need for total economic planning for war purposes stimulated a drastic overhaul of the available economic policy-making tools, the concept of national income has proved a fruitful avenue of development. The nation's total income, like the individual's total income, is some reflection of the total value of its economic activity. It is the aggregate, expressed in money terms, of all the needed goods and services produced by the mass of individuals and institutions which constitute the nation. On the face of it, this lump sum should provide a useful index of total national economic activity considered in relation to its own past (and potential future) activity, and to the total activities of other nations.

Unfortunately, in its crude form it is far from being a true reflection of the value of economic activity. A money index is not a satisfactory measure of real values, largely because the value of money is not itself fixed through time and space. The yardstick is not standard. A general rise in prices (which is a symptom of a fall in the value of money) could increase the apparent value of the national income without there being any change in the volume of goods and services produced or consumed or in their value relatively to each other. Alternatively, an attempt to compare one country's national income with another's, or even national income at one point of time with national income at another point of time, is vitiated by the fact that the different money totals represent different combinations of goods and services for different epochs. This can be illustrated within the relatively narrow sphere of individual experience. A man who emigrated from the United Kingdom to, say, Nyasaland, would find that to maintain in colonial conditions the standard of living to which he was accustomed would demand a higher rate of earnings than he would need in the United Kingdom. Oddly enough, the converse may also be true, and the cost of buying that combination of goods and services which the European inhabitant of a Central African colony takes for granted may be higher in the United Kingdom than it is in the colony. Similarly, the difference in standard of living for a family earning at the rate of £500 a year to-day and the same family earning £500 a year before the war cannot be measured simply by taking account of the change in prices. The whole content has changed and the two quantities are barely comparable.

Nevertheless, in spite of serious difficulties (and some allowance can be made in practice for the distorting factors) national income estimates do provide a useful first approximation to a kind of economic thermometer. Like a clinical thermometer, however, it is only a relative indication of the health of the patient and must be read in the light of essential additional data on case history and current symptoms. It is a tool which can be dangerous if it is made the basis for hasty conclusions, but it is a tool which even the layman can use as a pointer, provided that he is sufficiently well informed on the general background of the case to interpret its significance. Unless the administrator knows more about the economy than the figure for national income (plus the data necessary to correct it for price changes) he is not much better equipped than he was before to frame economic policy. The patient's temperature may be moving up or down, but no diagnosis is possible until it is known what causes it to move and no intelligent action can be taken until it is known what effects the movement is producing or is likely to produce and what they signify in real terms.

To take another analogy, the business man does not plan his policy on the strength of an enterprise's profits only. He requires a set of accounts, a summary of all the transactions of the enterprise over a significantly long period of time, so consolidated as to give him a clear picture of the main dynamic factors involved. Similarly the administrator requires information on the share of different groups of individuals in the national income, on what goods and services they produce in return for their incomes, and what goods and services become available for their consumption and investment when they lay out their incomes. He ought to be able to trace economic relationships between different individuals and industries. If a tariff would relieve unemployment in Industry A by protecting it from foreign competition, will it by increasing prices diminish the amount that purchasers can spend on the products of Industry B and so merely shift the incidence of unemployment without reducing it? If a reduction in income tax would raise the standard of living of earners in the higher income groups, would it be at the expense of the standard of living of other income groups, by reducing the funds available to maintain or extend social services? What would be the nature of the redistribution of income which would be effected by an inflationary or a deflationary policy? These are examples of the many practical questions to which the policy-maker tries to find a definite answer. He wants to be able to see each of the constituent items in the network of national economic activity not only as a separate feature of the national accounts, but also as a factor influencing and influenced by other activities.

It is in response to this kind of need that the system of social accounting which is now in international use has been developed. In its essentials the system is officially accepted in the majority of the independent countries of the world, and has received the official blessing of the United Nations Organization. In principle it involves a complete census of transactions and their systematic consolidation into a national, balancing, income and expenditure account. The resulting national or social accounts are designed to show in what directions, from what sources, and in what form the flow of money income courses through the national economy. Each transaction appears at least twice in the accounts—once as a debit item when the money is paid out, and once as a credit item when the money is received. It may appear more often if the accounts are presented in more than two different ways as they may well be in order to illustrate different aspects of the economy. Thus if the basis of presentation is a triple entry account showing in the first column by what groups of individuals or institutions the incomes are earned, in the second column in what industries they are earned and in the third column how they are consumed or invested, each transaction would appear three times, once as it became part of income received, once as it represented the value of a particular kind of good or service produced, and once as it entered into some form of consumption or investment. In any case, the final tables would group the transactions under each main heading in what seemed to be the most significant way from the point of view of the country concerned and its current problems.

A complete census of transactions on a double entry basis is a formidable undertaking for any national economy. The basic form of accounts, however simplified, is an overwhelming mass of detail and it is open to the objection that a great many of the individual entries are insignificant from the point of view of economic policy. In practice it is generally necessary, since records are inadequate, to have recourse to estimates over a large part of the field and to estimate net balances rather than to find the balances by aggregating the constituent transactions. The purely mechanical difficulties of the complete census of transactions should not be given undue importance in designing the basic accounts, however. The more detailed the basic accounts, the easier it is to eliminate the difficult problems of definition by considering each concept as the sum of its simplest constituents. In the last analysis it is the conceptual problems that are the chief stumbling blocks to the effective use of national income estimates for policy purposes. If an accountant were forced through lack of basic records to draw up the accounts of an enterprise by estimating profits, operating costs, replacement costs, etc., the chief problem in using the accounts would be that of knowing exactly what was meant by profits or operating costs without being able to reduce these concepts to their meaning in terms of particular transactions. In the same way, it is not the margin of error arising from inadequate statistical data that hinders most the application of national income estimates to practical policy purposes, it is the fog that surrounds the concepts themselves.

It seems necessary to emphasize this point because it is often maintained that a detailed system of social accounts is inappropriate for an economy where the degree of economic planning from the centre is limited, or where the pattern of economic development is relatively simple. The belief that a set of social accounts with very few items is a 'simple' set of accounts is completely fallacious. It is unfortunately true that for the less developed economies this is the sort of national income table one is often forced to construct because the records are so few that a sufficiently detailed approach is impossible. All that can be distinguished by the 'simple' approach is a few large shapes in a thick fog, and the fact that the attempt to make more precise observations reveals often ludicrously uncertain results is a reason for putting less rather than more reliance on the appearance of the large shapes. The national income investigator who is not prepared to adopt a semi-mystical attitude to these indistinct visions will welcome any opportunity of checking them by giving precision to particular points, however trivial these points may be in themselves. Except in so far as his results are derived from the systematic observation of all the available evidence, they have less claim to be accepted as a basic factor in economic policy than the quantitative hunches of the experienced administrator.

In the last analysis the basic set of accounts is no more than a frame of reference, and the end result must be to produce as brief an account of the economy as is necessary to illustrate all its most significant characteristics for economic policy purposes. Ideally therefore, the accounts should be designed in such a way that they can readily be consolidated into the few most useful concepts sought by the administrator. What these concepts are will be determined in part by the nature of the economy and its problems, and in part by the nature of the role which government assigns to itself. In an economy which is going through a phase of rapid economic change—for example, a change-over from dependence on agriculture to dependence on mining or secondary industry—with a government which aims at maintaining standards of living throughout the community, the need is for a system of accounts which will illustrate not only the rate and direction of the changes in industrial structure and productivity, but also the social and economic costs as well as the advantages of change. Similarly, in an economy with two or more communities at different stages of economic development and a government which aims at effectively pursuing the interests of them all, the need is for a design of accounts which shows up the distribution of the national income among the different groups, the nature of each one's contribution to it, and the characteristic composition of each group's standard of living.

The development of the role of government in the economy, which has been such a conspicuous feature of the twentieth century economic history of Europe and the Americas, has not been paralleled to the same extent in the British colonies. There the tendency has been, on the one hand to keep government direct intervention in the economic system to the minimum, and on the other to pursue a policy in line with the current economic policy of the United Kingdom in the international sphere. Thus, during and since the war the international trade of the colonies was put into the same kind of straitjacket as the United Kingdom trade, although the willingness and ability of colonial governments to pursue the implications of a policy of control throughout the domestic economies was weak. As a result of these conflicting tendencies —one could hardly call them policies—government intervention in the colonial economies was indeterminate. The characteristic approach of the colonial government has been to resist the adoption of any form of economic planning until the political pressure from its own articulate groups or from the United Kingdom government has forced it into action on a particular issue. Yet on the other hand the very looseness of government control in the economic sphere and the lack of a strong directive from the centre has sometimes meant that localized action by administrators or technical officers or entrepreneurs has been permitted to cause considerable local upheaval in the life of the community.

Although these tendencies still persist, colonial governments have in recent years been consciously assuming new responsibilities in the sphere of economic policy. The first Colonial Development Act was passed avowedly with the aim of relieving unemployment in the United Kingdom. The last, the Colonial Development and Welfare Act of 1940, passed in time of war when the physical shortages of capital and skill were such as to make it difficult rather than advantageous to export them, had as its aim the raising of the standard of living of colonial peoples and their emancipation from economic dependence on the United Kingdom. Before the funds were allocated the colonial governments were called upon to present ten-year plans of development. It is fair to say that the majority of them produced not plans of development, but plans for expenditure, and that the process was simply one of inviting the various government departments to submit supplementary estimates covering a ten-year period. In the event the allocation was made before all the plans had been framed, and those that had drawn up their plans were forced to think again with a definite ceiling in mind. The departmental heads pruned their supplementary estimates and the plans were again sent forward for approval.

If there was a philosophy behind the development plans, it was that the government's role in the economy was to spend money in the socially desirable directions neglected by private enterprise. Since no attempt was made to assess the priorities for the system as a whole, government departments competed with enterprise and with each other for scarce factors of production. Prices rose and most of the plans that had been ready early had to be entirely revised and re-costed. Since little attempt has apparently been made to assess the impact of the government expenditure on each colonial economy it is not clear whether the result of the expenditure will be to raise the level of amenities which the community can afford or to increase the cost of maintaining the administration.

What will happen in 1956 when the ten-year period of the Development and Welfare votes comes to an end it is difficult to say. Most of the colonies will be better off in real terms as a result of the expenditure, although it will not be possible to measure how much better off, and the improvement may well be partly offset by the increased recurrent costs of the annual budget. Some of them will be unable to go forward without grants in aid from the United Kingdom and all of them would experience a marked setback if the flow of aid were cut off. For these reasons it seems reasonable to assume that there will be a new Colonial Development vote, and that then, if not before, the colonial govern-ments will be required to embark on development plans which involve a more conscious direction of the economic system and which are based on a more continuous and systematic assessment of the needs of each colonial economy as a whole. Such a development would be facilitated by the construction in each case of a system of social accounting that was both appropriate to the colonial economy concerned, and capable of being adapted for intercolonial comparisons.

In principle there is no reason why each colonial government should not be able to design for its own purposes a useful set of social accounts which fulfils both these qualifications. The difficulty in practice is one of collecting and evaluating the data. It has never been possible to conduct the complete census of transactions required for the ideal system of accounts, and probably the most significant difference be-tween a system of social accounts and the accounts of a firm or an individual is that the social accounts are not records but estimates based on inadequate records. In an economy such as the United Kingdom or the United States, where the statistical reporting system reaches into the heart of the economy, the coverage of the systematically collected information is such that the main totals can generally be relied upon to be within, say, about 5% of the truth. The constituent items—including some of the most important constituents for certain policy purposes—may, of course, be much less reliable. On the other hand, since the degree of economic planning is limited in a democratic society, the need for absolute accuracy is less than it would be if all transactions were regulated.

In a less developed community, however, and particularly in a colonial community, the problem of the inaccuracy of the estimates is a more serious limitation on the value of a system of social accounts. Where—as is true for most African colonies—the total population figures are little more than guesses, there are no reliably complete figures showing the distribution of persons between occupations, there is no satisfactory census of agriculture (the main industry), and no systematic survey of the volume of internal trade, then the construction of a system of national accounts tends to be a highly subjective pro-cedure. Even leaving aside the special problem of measuring and evaluating the significant volume of *subsistence* output (i.e. the produc-tion of goods and services for personal or family consumption), the problem of drawing an objective account of income, output and expenditure out of the totally inadequate basis of statistical data

8 COLONIAL SOCIAL ACCOUNTING

that is available for the majority of colonies is extraordinarily difficult. Until the fundamental basis of statistical information in the colonies has been reorganized and established on an improved basis the compilation of colonial national income accounts must remain a process involving a wide margin of error. In many cases it is not possible to rely on obtaining from this process more than a general indication of the principal orders of magnitude involved. On the other hand, it is possible to be too despondent about the results of such a calculation. Where the available data consists of a variety of details covering a wide range of activities, often in qualitative rather than in quantitative form, the process of organizing the many incoherent details into a systematic whole on the basis of deductions derived from all the existing evidence serves a useful purpose.

The triple-entry balancing account provides a convenient means of organizing the miscellaneous data. It permits the effective utilization of every scrap of economic information by providing a considerable number of cross-checks. It thereby reduces the area of unconfirmed estimate to the smallest possible range and presents in a single account the sum of the available data and of the deductions that can be drawn from that material. Being in an internationally agreed form its items conform to a standard set of definitions and, within the limits of comparability of data over time and space, can be compared with the corresponding items in the accounts of other territories. The process of completing the account constitutes a searching examination of the adequacy of the statistical data for purposes of economic analysis.

In brief, the construction of national income accounts involves digesting and assessing the existing supply of facts about the economy and illustrates the nature of the major inadequacies in the data. A colony which has processed its economic data by producing a system of social accounts has marked out the chief outlines of its economy and made it possible to observe the structural content and changes therein as a connected picture, even though the uncertainty of some of the outlines may leave parts of the picture rather blurred. It has not thereby eliminated the unknowns or justified the institution of a more rigorous form of economic planning, but it has made it possible to draw the fullest significance from the known factors and to take more intelligently the policy decisions which have to be made.

The initial stages of putting the mass of disconnected data through the mill, and setting in train the regular collection of essential statistical material needed to keep the accounts up to date are among the most difficult parts of the process. For the shape of the basic accounts, the type of data available, and the methods of estimate, will tend to vary from one country to another. It is not to be expected that a framework which meets the needs of the administrators and economists concerned with the United Kingdom economy is likely to satisfy the administrators of an African colony, or even that the design of accounts suitable for an African colony is necessarily the kind that would effectively reveal the significant features of a West Indian colony. The division of income into rents, profits, interest, wages and salaries, for example, a classification which has positive significance for an industrial economy, introduces concepts which are largely inappropriate to one consisting largely of peasant producers. Or again, it is generally necessary to rely more heavily on one column in the triple-entry account than on another. The official national income accounts for the United Kingdom, for example, depend primarily on completing the income column, because income and wage data are better on the whole than output and expenditure data: the outlay column contains substantial residual features particularly in connection with investment. For a colonial economy on the other hand, largely because income tax and wage data cover such a small fraction of the total population, it may be more fruitful to concentrate on completing the output column and to use it as a support for the other weaker columns.

For the undeveloped economy, however, as for the more advanced economy, the conceptual problems are the most fundamental. To some extent the data problems are temporary and the establishment of adequate statistical departments in all colonies will provide the solution to many difficulties which are now so prominent. It is true that all the data problems are not so superficial that a strong statistical reporting system will eliminate them. The problem of obtaining adequate statistical data on the real income of subsistence farmers, for example, is as much a political as an administrative one. However, it is probable that an improved system of statistical reporting will make the margins of error less rather than more limiting for colonial national income estimates than for national income estimates compiled in a more complex economy. The conceptual problems, on the other hand, will continue to be peculiarly intractable. How is it possible, for example, convincingly to compare the real income of an African working on the mines with that of his family producing subsistence crops in the villages? Two different scales of value are involved. Yet this is the kind of assessment which is required if the social costs or advantages of new large-scale development are to be adequately appreciated.

This study, which considers some of the practical problems, is the final report on an enquiry into the problems of building up social accounts for the two Central African territories of Northern Rhodesia and Nyasaland. The interim report was based on an analysis of the 1938 material available in the United Kingdom and was an exercise in the manipulation of a severely limited set of facts about the economies concerned. This final report is based on a compilation of material on record in official and other documents in the colonies concerned, together with a number of personal *ad hoc* enquiries into some of the more significant aspects of the economy where there was little or no existing documentation.

Inevitably the ground that could be covered systematically by one person working alone was limited, and although the generous expenditure of time and labour by government officials, anthropologists and many private individuals enabled me to bring together very much more information than I could have collected otherwise, there remained important gaps in the information. The deficiencies in the data are on a grander scale than the available data themselves in these African colonies and the problem of making them good requires a complete reorganization of the whole system of fact collecting, by a properly equipped and qualified statistical department. The problem of assessing the volume of production of people who grow the bulk of their own food, who make their own homes and furniture, and who in fact spend the greater part of their working lives in the production of goods and services which are of vital importance to the national standard of living but which never enter into the stream of trade, is the principal obstacle in the way of producing satisfactory social accounts for African territories. Next in importance to this is the problem of estimating the volume of the inter-village and inter-neighbour trade in locally produced goods and services. Much of the local trade, for example, never flows through an organized market: some of it is barter trade which often seems to contradict the 'laws' of economic theory evolved on the basis of money economy analysis.

These problems are both practical and theoretical. They are practical in that, for example, an effective and reasonably inexpensive system of regularly measuring output for a community dependent largely on subsistence production has yet to be devised. They are theoretical in that we have still to establish any firm conclusions of the mainsprings of economic behaviour in African rural communities, on the motives for work and leisure, and on the relevance of the money values of an incomplete price system to the system of values of a community living in semi-subsistence conditions. These are subjects which require more intensive research. All that I was able to do was to reveal one aspect of them by considering the kind of problems which arose from an attempt to apply a modern accounting technique to the available facts, and to fill some of the gaps in the basic data.

Thus, although it would have been impossible for one individual to collect enough data to provide the basis for reliable estimates of total agricultural output or of the volume of village trade, it was possible to make brief experimental enquiries in a number of spheres which were very poorly documented. I compiled acreage and yield estimates with the help of the Agricultural Departments, attempted first-hand budget surveys in the rural areas with the advice of the Rhodes-Livingstone Institute anthropologists, and sent several series of questionnaires to companies and institutions in the private sector of the economy. The resulting estimates, although not based on accurate records, were relatively broadly based, and to that extent less likely to be seriously distorted. By making these experimental enquiries it was possible to form a subjective impression of the relative weight of various factors in the economy which it was impossible to measure systematically.

Some comment on the arrangement of the material of this study may be useful here. This chapter and the one that follows it are introductory in nature. Chapter II is a brief note on the accounting framework used. A more detailed description can be found in the interim report on the enquiry which was published in 1948 in the series of Occasional Papers issued by the National Institute of Economic and Social Research.[1]

Parts II and III discuss in turn the economies of Northern Rhodesia and Nyasaland on the basis of the material yielded by their social accounts. The methods of estimate are described in Appendices I and II respectively. Broadly speaking, the approach was on the same lines as that already described in considerable detail in the interim report, except that the material for estimate was a great deal fuller. For the reader who wants to be able to assess the weight which can be placed on particular items in the completed accounts, a lengthy description of the method and bases of estimates is unavoidable. I have tried to keep the description as short as possible without losing any of the essential points, but since it is unlikely that there will be many who want to read it consecutively I have relegated it to an appendix where it can be used as a background of reference as required. Appendix I goes step by step through the estimates for Northern Rhodesia, and Appendix II covers the Nyasaland estimates in a similar way. In both cases the description follows the course of the detailed estimates for 1945: the 1938 estimates have been described in the interim report and the 1948 estimates are

[1] Phyllis Deane, *The Measurement of Colonial National Incomes*, Occasional Paper XII, published for the National Institute of Economic and Social Research by Cambridge University Press, 1948. A more comprehensive account of social accounting method can be read in *Definition and Measurement of the National Income and Related Totals*, the Appendix by Richard Stone to the Report of the Sub-Committee on National Income Statistics of the League of Nations Committee of Statistical Experts (Studies and Reports on Statistical Methods No. 7), Geneva, United Nations, 1947.

simply the result of using the published records to adjust the 1945 estimates.

In Part IV some of the most fundamental of the social accounting problems encountered in the attempt to apply these modern techniques to the Central African economies are discussed at length in terms of the experiments in village social accounting which the anthropologists of the Rhodes-Livingstone Institute helped me to make. It cannot be claimed that these problems have been solved, but it is hoped that the more important issues have been sufficiently well ventilated and discussed in these pages to permit an assessment of their importance in relation to the social accounts which were eventually constructed. More research is needed in this field if a more fundamental treatment of the theoretical problems is to be possible, and if this section of the accounts is to be reasonably free from distortion. Appendix III gives an annotated list of published and unpublished budget surveys made for the Central African region and consulted in connection with Part IV.

Part V consists of two chapters embodying the main conclusions of the enquiry—one summarizing the conclusions for the Central African economies, and the other commenting briefly on the general results of the enquiry.

CHAPTER II

THE BASIC ACCOUNTS

The Occasional Paper which was published as an interim report on this enquiry contains a chapter on the logic of the fundamental tables describing in detail the principles on which the triple entry income-output-expenditure table is constructed.[1] The bulk of the interim report is concerned with a practical application of these principles of construction. I do not propose to go over this ground again, but for the convenience of those who have not read the Occasional Paper a brief note on the accounting framework which has been treated as basic to this enquiry may not be out of place here.

The fundamental table is the income-output-expenditure table which consists of three balancing columns. In its simplest form it looks like this:

TABLE 1. The income—output—expenditure table

Net national income	Net national output	Net national expenditure
1. Wages and salaries	Net output of:	13. Expenditure on goods
2. Profits	6. Agriculture	and services for current
3. Interest	7. Mining	consumption
4. Rent	8. Manufacture	14. Net investment
	9. Distribution and transport	
	10. Government	
	11. Other goods and services	
5. Total national income	12. Total national output	15. Total national expenditure

Since the net output of an industry is definable as the sum of the wages, salaries, profits, interest and rent earned by the factors of production engaged in it, the second column of the table is essentially a rearrangement by industries of the information contained in the first column. The third column shows how the incomes earned in the first column were laid out. Hence, by definition each of the three columns should, when fully compiled, produce the same total. These are the three ways of arriving at an estimate of the aggregate value of goods and services produced (or received) in the country during the period under review.

[1] Deane, op. cit., chapter 11, pp. 7–20.

What the fundamental table might look like for any particular economy depends on the structure of that economy and on which of its problems seem to require illustration. Thus Table 18 on p. 64 shows a completed version of the table for Northern Rhodesia. Table 32 on p. 98 shows a version for Nyasaland. In both of them, for example, the distinctions between rents, profits, interest, wages and salaries has been replaced or overlaid by the more significant distinction between incomes earned by the different sectors of the economy—Africans, Europeans, Asians, companies and Government. These distinctions have been carried through into the expenditure column because the sectors are so sharply defined that overall aggregates seemed relatively insignificant.

The fundamental table is a source for all other income and expenditure tables which might be drawn up for the economy. Thus the entries required for a table of receipts and payments on international account can be derived from a detailed income-output-expenditure table. Indeed, the process of constructing the fundamental table involves the construction of all the smaller balancing accounts of which it is made. In this way the inevitable discrepancies between the estimates for total incomes in the first place, total output in the second and total expenditure in the third are not dealt with residually in the final consolidated table but are traced to their sources in the constituent sectors of the economy. A separate account is drawn up for each sector, for Africans, Europeans, Asians, companies and Government, for international receipts and payments, for each industry, and for each type of expenditure.

One result of this method of approach is that the implications of each estimate are considered and adjusted where necessary in the light of all the other factors which might bear on it. The fundamental table is thus fully articulated and an improvement in the data available for a particular entry produces a consequent chain of improvements in other entries throughout the system. The chances of a serious distortion of the truth are effectively reduced by automatically subjecting each estimate to a minute series of cross-checks. The more varied the data available on the economy, the more chance is there of constructing each column separately on the basis of an independent series of estimates. The greater the degree of independence the more effective are the cross-checks. In practice the data are generally such as to make it necessary to rely most heavily on one approach and to derive large parts of the other two from it. Thus for the United Kingdom the quality of the income data is incomparably better than the case for output information or expenditure material. In most colonial territories it is the output column which must form the mainstay of the table. To the extent that it is necessary to rely on one column the potential cross-checks are less effective and the danger of distortion is greater. Essentially this is an accounting framework and presupposes the use of money. It measures money flows at different points in their progress through the economy—it measures them as receipts, for example, and it measures them as payments. Subsistence output (i.e. output produced for home consumption, which never enters into the stream of trade and hence never involves a money receipt or payment) only appears in the fundamental table because we decide to impute a money value to it and enter it in each column—as a form of income, as a form of output and as a form of consumption. Similarly, incomes received in kind, the imputed rents of owner-occupied houses and other forms of non-monetary income have to be given an artificial status in the accounts. As we shall see, these 'strangers' in the accounts raise all sorts of logical difficulties and even throw some doubt on the significance of the final aggregates. However, an aggregate which excluded them would lose so much of its value as an index of total economic activity that it seems worth while including them in spite of the logical difficulties.

Finally, it is possible to contemplate more than one set of values for the fundamental table because it is possible to postulate more than one definition of national income. On the one hand we may decide to draw the line between economic and non-economic activities in different places and thus to measure different totals of goods and services. On the other hand we may decide to draw the boundary round the economy at different points and to measure the incomes of a different universe of people or institutions. Tables 17 and 18 on pp. 63 and 64 show two different fundamental tables for Northern Rhodesia, one based on a definition of the national output which covers all economic activity carried on within the territorial borders, the other based on a definition which confines attention to the activities of residents. We might equally decide to exclude the remittances of migrants because they were earned from activity carried on outside the country's borders or to include even that part of migrants' income which is spent abroad on the grounds that all the economic activities of the country's nationals are of interest. It is not necessary to be dogmatic about definitions. The solutions eventually adopted depend partly on what information we want to find in the accounts and partly on the kind of economic analysis we hope to undertake. It may prove convenient—as for Northern Rhodesia —to consider more than one definition. Alternatively, if inter-colonial comparisons were a prime motive, it might be thought appropriate to adopt one definition and to stick to it rigidly. The set of definitions which are ultimately adopted should be framed with a view to local conditions as well as to inter-colonial comparisons.

PART II

THE ECONOMY OF NORTHERN RHODESIA

CHAPTER III

THE COLONY AND ITS PEOPLE

The Protectorate of Northern Rhodesia lies on the plateau of Central Africa between the longitudes 22° E. and 33° 33′ E., and between the latitudes 8° 15′ S. and 18° S. It is thus placed well within the tropics and fairly centrally within the African continent. Except in the sparsely populated lower reaches of the three great river valleys—the Zambezi, the Luangwa and the Kafue—the territory's elevation (varying from 3,000 to 5,000 ft. above sea level) relieves it from the high temperatures and humidity of the tropics.

In area, Northern Rhodesia is about 290,000 sq. miles or roughly three times the size of the United Kingdom. Its neighbouring territories are—on the west, Angola (Portuguese West Africa), on the north, the Belgian Congo and Tanganyika, on the east, Nyasaland, and on the south, Portuguese East Africa, Southern Rhodesia, and the Caprivi strip of south-west Africa. Its rail links with the sea are through Belgian territory to Lobito Bay on the west coast, through Southern Rhodesia, Bechuanaland and South Africa to Cape Town in the south, and through Southern Rhodesia and Portuguese East Africa to Beira on the east coast. The last named is the usual outlet for the mineral exports, but it involves a rail haul of roughly 1,500 miles.

Three different racial groups live in the colony. The indigenous population is of Bantu origin and has been classified into seventy-three different tribes. It has never been properly counted and estimates of African population are derived from the registers of taxpayers (i.e. adult males of the apparent age of eighteen years or over) corrected where possible by sample counts.[1] It is believed that the African population is in the region of 1.7 million but the suspension of district touring during the war years and the constant shifting of population, not only between districts in Northern Rhodesia but across its borders, makes it difficult to arrive at a reliable estimate. The European and Asian peoples were numbered at the time of the Census in October 1946 and were found to be 21,809 and 1,115 respectively. There is also a 'coloured' population estimated at 789 persons. Since the Census was taken in

---

[1] See Appendix I, pp. 230–302.

18   COLONIAL SOCIAL ACCOUNTING

1946 roughly 16,800 Europeans and 800 Asians have entered the colony as immigrants, but as no record is kept of emigration no reliable figures are available for present European or Asian population, which is officially estimated to have been 36,000 in 1950.

The changing pattern of the Northern Rhodesian population is illustrated in the following table:

TABLE 2. The population of Northern Rhodesia

	European	Asian	Coloured[2]	African	Total
1926	5,581	n.a.[1]	n.a.	1,199,000	1,204,581
1931 (Census)	13,846	176	425	1,372,235	1,386,682
1936	10,588	342	604	1,366,425	1,377,959
1946 (Non-African Census)	21,809	1,115	789	1,700,000	1,723,713
1950 (estimated)	36,000	3,000	n.a.	1,850,000	1,889,000

It will be seen that the immigrant population has increased considerably over the past twenty years or so but is still relatively small in numbers. The census data for the African population are so very poor, however, that it is impossible to make any reliable statement about its trend, except to note that it appears to be increasing. The 1950 estimate is a provisional figure based on the results of the Sample Survey of African Population carried out in 1950 by the Central African Statistical Office.

Each of the racial groups in the population has its own distinct standard of living and its own characteristic pattern of economic activity. Even their distribution over the country varies as will be seen in the following table:

TABLE 3. Distribution of population in 1946

	Area %	European %	Asian %	Coloured %	African %
Outer Provinces	59	8	18	51	66
Railway Provinces	41	92	82	49	34
Total	100	100	100	100	100

In effect, therefore, while over 90% of the immigrant communities live in the provinces through which the single railway line passes, nearly two-thirds of the Africans and roughly half of the coloured peoples live in the outer provinces through which no railway line passes and in which there are no large towns. This has an important bearing on the nature of the development generated by the immigrant

[1] In this and the following tables n.a. is used to indicate that no figures are available to support an estimate.

[2] The term Coloured is used throughout this study to indicate persons of mixed race.

communities. For the vast majority of the inhabitants of the outer provinces the cost of transport between their homes and a market in which they could trade their produce is prohibitive. It is generally cheaper, in terms of effort, to transport themselves and sell their services as labour in the towns of the railway line or of Southern Rhodesia and the Union, than to carry their produce on foot or by bicycle over many miles of poor road to an uncertain market. More than a third of the able-bodied adult men in Northern and Barotse Provinces and more than half of those in Eastern Province were working away from home in 1945. The working population available in the villages, the population on which the standard of living of the majority of the African people depends, consists largely of women, old or infirm men, and children.

The majority of the Europeans in the territory are temporary residents employed by the mines or the government. An increasing proportion of them are South Africans. In the past ten years, 1940 to 1949, well over half of the European immigrants from all sources have been born in South Africa or Southern Rhodesia. In the war years the rate of influx was particularly high, reaching over 80% in 1943. The pace slackened immediately after the war, but more recently there have been signs of an increased movement to the north from southern Africa. In 1949, 74% of the immigrants reported that their last place of permanent residence was the Union or Southern Rhodesia. The white South African element in the community lends weight to the political movement towards responsible self-government.

Table 4 gives the industrial distribution of the gainfully occupied population at the time of the 1946 Census and at the two previous Censuses, and makes use of immigration data to estimate the relative position at the beginning of 1950. This table is a concise illustration of the colony's history over the past thirty years. In 1921 the chief occupation was agriculture with public service, transport and communication, and commerce and finance in second, third and fourth places respectively. This whole group accounted for more than 80% of the European occupied population and it is interesting to compare a very similar composition in present-day Nyasaland (see especially pp. 77–8 below). Between 1921 and 1931 the mineral discoveries were made which completely reversed the relative positions of agriculture and mining in the territory, and almost quadrupled the gainfully occupied European population. The 1931 figures also reflect the growth in the building industry attendant on the new mining development and the cut in government expenditure due to the world slump. By 1946 the building industry, which was naturally reduced by the ending of the main construction period on the mines and was artificially hindered by war and post-war shortages, had fallen to under 3%. Manufacture and other industries (mainly professional services) were also artificially cramped by world shortages, especially shortages in capital equipment. By the beginning of 1950, however, manufacture (5.2%) and building (5%) and the other (mainly professional) industries had shot ahead, building with particular vigour, as the post-war boom gathered momentum. The total number of gainfully occupied persons in January 1950 is not known because no record is kept of emigrants and the rate of turnover is high in Northern Rhodesia. It seems likely, however, on the basis of the information which does exist on employment that the total was between 13,000 and 14,000.

TABLE 4. Industrial distribution of the European population

Industrial group	1921 %	1931 %	1946 %	1950 (estimate) %
1. Agriculture and forestry	33.9	7.3	7.4	6.5
2. Mining and quarrying	6.3	35.1	38.2	36.1
3. Manufacture, building and construction	5.4	13.4	6.5	10.2
4. Transport and communication	14.5	10.0	10.2	10.9
5. Commerce and finance	12.2	11.0	12.5	12.1
6. Hotel and personal services	2.6	3.0	3.8	2.9
7. Public services and other services of general interest	23.1	14.1	20.8	18.3
8. Other industries	2.1	6.1	0.6	3.0
9. Total gainfully occupied:				
Percentage	100.0	100.0	100.0	100.0
Numbers	2,110	8,102	8,729	n.a.[1]
10. Total adult population (i.e. over fifteen)	2,682	10,752	15,251	n.a.
11. Total population	3,634	13,846	21,907	n.a.

Comparatively few Europeans retire in Northern Rhodesia. At the time of the 1946 Census there were only 121 retired persons in the colony of whom nine were women. In general, therefore, the European adult population consists of employed individuals who spend their working life or part of their working life in the territory and retire with their savings or their pensions to other countries. Most of them maintain close personal contact with their country of origin and with Southern Rhodesia or the Union throughout their lives. They take their holidays abroad, do much of their shopping abroad, often educate their children and support dependants abroad, and maintain continuous links with commercial and financial institutions (department stores, banks, insur-

[1] The estimated percentages employed in each group at the beginning of 1950 are based on immigration data, assuming a common rate of turnover for each industry. Since there are no emigration records it is impossible to make a reliable estimate of the actual totals.

ance companies, etc.) outside the colony. Many of them come to Northern Rhodesia for a few years only, to take advantage of the high rates
of wages in the copper belt before buying property in the Union or
Southern Rhodesia, or to serve some years as members of the Colonial
Service before going elsewhere for promotion or a change of scene.
Some indication of the turnover of the European population can be
deduced from the fact that although 2,766 persons immigrated to mining
jobs in the three years 1947–9, the increase in the number of Europeans
employed on the mines over that period was less than 1,000. There is,
however, a growing stable population. At the 1931 Census, less than
3,300 residents (or about 25%) either had been born in the territory
or had lived there longer than ten years. In 1946 the proportion was
over 40%, or nearly 9,000 persons.

Like the Europeans, the Asians too, are temporary immigrants. Less
is known of their patterns of behaviour, but it is believed that most of
them aim to make their money in the colony and to retire elsewhere to
enjoy their savings. All but a negligible proportion are engaged in
trade, largely in retail trade for the African market. Some of them come
without capital and live very poorly as shop assistants in the store of a
friend or relative until they can save enough to set up in business for
themselves. Others come with the necessary capital in their possession.
They build small stores, either in the so-called 'second class trading
estates' which are attached to most of the larger towns, or in the rural
areas, although there are a few who cater for the European trade and
build their shops in the main shopping centres. They live as a society
apart, both from the Europeans and from the Africans.

The vast majority of the African population are engaged in agriculture, but as has already been noted, the agricultural work is largely
done by women, by old or infirm men and by children. To these must
be added the men who are resting between trips to the areas where
employment can be found. In 1945 there were about 379,000 registered
male taxpayers in Northern Rhodesia. Of these about 34,000 were at
work outside the country and about 64,200 were resident in urban
locations within Northern Rhodesia. A further 78,000 or so were at
work in the rural areas and probably the majority of these were in
reach of their villages and could return to them for harvesting or planting periods when their labour was urgently needed. It is estimated that
out of a total population of about 1,454,000 actually available in the
villages in 1945 only 653,000 were adult and only 18% of them were
adult men: if we assume that men in employment were not available
for other work then the number of men available for work in subsistence
agriculture amounted to only about 15% of the rural population.

The proportions vary widely from one area to another. In the maize belt of Southern Province along the railway line where the African farmer can find a ready market for all the cash crops he can produce, the percentage of men away at work is estimated at 14% or less. This, however, is an exceptional area. In parts of Eastern Province and Northern Province, three days' journey or more by lorry from the railway line and far from any sizeable market 60% to 70% of the adult males are estimated to be normally absent from their homes. The average for the whole territory is certainly over one-third.

It is not possible to draw up for Northern Rhodesia an African occupational table in which all or most categories are mutually exclusive, since there is no hard and fast specialization of labour. What we can say, however, is that out of a total adult population of about 850,000 there are about 450,000 women who are principally engaged in subsistence agriculture and whose trading activities are confined to interpersonal or inter-village transactions on a very small scale; over 200,000 men are in employment at home or abroad; and of the remaining men probably not more than about 70,000 draw their main cash incomes from independent production of crops, fish, village industries or independent sale of services. In effect, therefore, somewhere in the region of 130,000 men are neither employed nor engaged full time in independent economic activity; these obtain their cash incomes from past visits to the employment centres, or from relatives, or by engaging in intermittent trade with their near neighbours: their main current work is assisting the women in the production of subsistence food crops.

Each of the different racial communities in Northern Rhodesia maintains its own characteristic standard of living. Of the Asians and the Coloured persons one can say little, although an attempt has been made to assess their patterns of expenditure in drawing up the consumption estimates for Table 32. All that we know with any certainty, however, is that they maintain a level of consumption which falls between the Africans and the Europeans. In general, they live austerely, and so far as can be ascertained the Asian rate of saving and propensity to work are both high. Neither the Asians nor the Coloured persons form a substantial proportion of the population, however, and their role in the national economy is still fairly small.

The European sector of the community contains a fairly wide range of income groups but most earners receive more than £500 per annum. It was estimated as a result of a preliminary examination of the 1946 Census returns relating to income that the average per earner was in the region of £600 per annum, and if one allows for a number of married women and young persons living at home the average per household was somewhat higher than this.

In general, as one would expect from such a high standard of income and from the fact that there are no unskilled labour groups among the Europeans, the standard of living is high. Since, however, the European standard of living depends predominantly on imported goods and services the real consumption level is rather lower than would appear from a cursory examination of income levels. Table 5 gives estimated expenditure per head of the European population for the main categories of European outlay.

TABLE 5. European personal consumption, 1945[1]

Expenditure on:	Per head gainfully occupied population £
1. Food	125
2. Drink	55
3. Tobacco	48
4. Clothing and footwear	45
5. Fuel, light, rent, rates	36
6. Servants	37
7. Household expenses	19
8. Medical, etc., expenses	14
9. Donations, subscriptions, books and stationery	12
10. Other locally purchased goods and services	27
11. Insurance	22
12. Education	23
13. Dependants abroad	20
14. Holidays and leave, pension and gratuities[2]	99
15. Total value European personnel consumption	582
16. Direct taxation	28
17. Savings	11
18. Total European outlay	621

Too much reliance should not be placed on the details into which this table is broken down since for many items the information was not sufficient to permit a reliable estimate to be made. Nevertheless the table does give a fairly satisfactory picture of the relative weight of the different items in the European standard of living. It indicates that the European population spent more than a third of its income directly on food, drink and tobacco and about a quarter on imported goods and services other than those included in the visible trade of the territory: most of these invisible imports were bought by the individuals or their families while actually abroad, and they include many items which should properly be split up under other expenditure headings (e.g. 1, 2, 3, 4, 7, 8 or 9) if we knew their details.

For a European resident in Northern Rhodesia, in order to maintain

[1] The totals on which this table is based are given in Appendix I. See especially p. 289.
[2] This item includes the value of pensions and gratuities which can be regarded as hidden savings for the present residents of the territory.

the standard of living to which he is accustomed or which is the socially accepted minimum, it is necessary to have a level of income which is high by United Kingdom standards. Moreover, although those living in the main townships enjoy certain amenities in shopping facilities, housing, proximity to medical attention, etc., those who are in the smaller townships or who are away from the railway belt have considerable disadvantages to contend with. Except in the mining townships where cheap water and electricity is produced by the mine, waterborne sanitation is the exception rather than the rule. Outside of the main townships and off the line of rail there is no electricity and usually no telephone system. There are dangers of tropical disease and communications are not good, so that the family off the line of rail often runs considerable risks. Food supplies in the remoter districts tend to be monotonous and may be unbalanced. Holidays and children's education are expensive and small farmers and traders may have to do with a low standard of both. Indeed, for those who are not in pensionable occupations, with all the incidental amenities in housing, medical attention, etc., provided by most large employers, a slump in trade and in the value of agricultural crops would be disastrous.

In the war and post-war years, however, the standards of living maintained by most members of the European community have been consistently high by comparison with standards in other European countries. Farmers have profited from the high price obtainable for agricultural crops. Traders have shared in the general boom in incomes. In the three years since 1946, European wage rates on the mines have risen by about 40%, compared with an estimated increase of less than 15% in the cost-of-living index over the same period. The high standard of food consumption and also of drink consumption absorbed a large proportion of the European earner's total income. Taxation is low by United Kingdom standards, but although there are few reliable data on savings they were believed to be low also. In effect, although the standard of living is high the rate of individual saving tends to be low except in so far as it is saving for consumption purposes (for example, for holidays) or for insurance purposes.

The standard of living of the African population of Northern Rhodesia presents a strong contrast to that of other groups, both by reason of its low level and by reason of the variations of level and content within the group. There is a striking uniformity about the standard of living of the Europeans of Northern Rhodesia and also (so far as one can judge on very scanty evidence) about that of the Asians. We do not know a great deal about the standard of living of the Africans, but what we do know tends to confirm the view that it is unwise to rely heavily on generalizations from small samples.

Taking the African community as a whole, however, it is estimated that in 1945 the total value of its income was in the region of £10¼ millions, of which about 46% was accounted for by subsistence income proper (i.e. by output which was not exchanged for money). If we try to separate out the incomes that were received by Africans in the form of goods and services, rather than in the form of money, we have to add to subsistence income the value of the incomes in kind received by employed Africans and incomes brought back in kind by migrants. Then we get the following list of incomes received in kind.

TABLE 6. African subsistence and barter incomes, 1945

Income from:	£
1. Agricultural crops	4,044,000
2. Village industries	151,000
3. Livestock and fish	352,000
4. Migrants	181,000
5. Employment	988,000
6. Total incomes in kind	5,716,000

The remainder, or between £4½ millions and £5 millions represents African cash purchasing power. It is impossible to be more precise than this because part of items 1 to 3 in Table 6 may have entered into trade within or between the villages and so may have resulted in cash incomes.

A total income of about £10¼ millions for a population of about 1.65 millions implies an African average of £6 per head or about £27 per adult male. The cash income (including incomes received in kind from employment which are actually bought *for* the African if not by him) was probably between £3 and £3½ per head, nearly £13 per family (i.e. per adult female) and more than £14½ per adult male. By 1949 the African income probably exceeded £7 per head and approached £35 per adult male, cash income being between £4 and £5 per head.

Table 7 shows how the African community consumed or otherwise disposed of its income. According to this general picture of African consumption about 61% of income was consumed in the form of food, drink and tobacco, about 24% on clothing and footwear and the remainder on all other goods and services, taxes and saving. (See also Table 29 on p. 85.)

No attempt has been made to calculate the value of African cash saving and investment as an independent item, but it seems unlikely that it exceeded £350,000 even if we include expenditure on livestock not wanted for food. Detailed estimates made for the total value of African earnings gave a figure of £10,270,000, suggesting a net saving of about £187,000, but since the margin of error in the total is over

5%, this residual figure has no intrinsic significance as an estimate of saving.

TABLE 7. African personal consumption, 1945

	£000	£000
1. Food, drink and tobacco		
(a) Cash	1,700	
(b) Subsistence	4,402	
(c) Total		6,102
2. Clothing and footwear		2,400
3. Household, etc., expenses		
(a) Cash	400	
(b) Subsistence	332	
(c) Total		732
4. All other consumption expenditure		549
5. Total value personal consumption		9,783
6. Expenditure on livestock		150
7. Expenditure on direct taxes and fines		150
8. Total African expenditure		£10,083

However, these community averages and the pattern of consumption which has been set out in Table 7 do not throw much light on particular instances. Some idea of the variety of income levels can be gained by examining the sources of the incomes.

TABLE 8. Sources of African incomes

	£000	£000
1. Agriculture		
(a) Subsistence	4,050	
(b) Traded crops	400	
(c) Livestock	540	
(d) Total		4,990
2. Fish and fish trade		275
3. Village industries		666
4. Other independent work		375
5. Employment		3,369
6. Migrant labour		595
7. All sources		£10,270

It would appear that about one-third of all incomes was earned from employment and the bulk of this and of the earnings from 'other independent work' was earned in the urban areas where only a small proportion of the population (less than 10%) live. Most of the income from the trade in cash and livestock is derived in the railway belt provinces where most of the employed population is also concentrated.

The wealthiest group in the African community was the group employed by the mining companies. Since 1938 their wage rates have more than doubled. In 1945 they enjoyed cash receipts to the value of £23 per man employed, rations to the value of nearly £15 and housing to the value of over £3. The average rate of mine wages paid to Africans in 1949 was nearly 70% above the 1945 level. In addition they had the advantage of medical services, recreational facilities and other welfare services which were much superior to anything of the kind enjoyed by any other substantial group in the community. On the other hand, the cost of living on the Copperbelt, even for those whose essential foodstuffs were provided, was so high that the wealth of the miners was easily dissipated: the obligation to provide presents to families and numerous relations (many of whom descended on the wage earner in person to make their claims while others were waiting in the villages to despoil the returning worker) tended to distribute the income over the community more evenly than would at first be apparent.

Table 9 gives an indication of the average value of earnings from employment in each industry or group of industries.

TABLE 9. African average earnings from employment, 1945[1]

	Numbers engaged	Average annual earnings £
1. Agriculture (European)	27,000	10.3
2. Mining	33,000	41.2
3. Manufacture	9,500	19.1
4. Building and construction	6,000	10.7
5. Transport	5,400	17.1
6. Commerce	4,200	23.8
7. Professional (mainly mission employees)	9,700	11.7
8. Government	29,700	18.9
9. Personal and domestic services	17,500	19.4
10. Other (including all Africans employed by individual Africans)	24,000	6.0
11. Total employed	166,000	20.2

Generally speaking, those whose average level of earnings is relatively low among the above groups are those who live in the rural areas, who do not get free housing by virtue of their employment, and who do not get free rations (except perhaps on a very limited scale) since they have access to rural food supplies. Their food, if they have to buy it, is not as expensive as in the towns. Many of the employees of government and of the missions fall into these categories. A large proportion of the employed men in the rural areas are able to cultivate gardens and

[1] For the absolute figures see especially p. 246 in the Appendix I.

with the assistance of their wives to grow their subsistence food needs, while housing is never a problem in the villages. At the other end of the scale about 44% of the income of the miners is attributable to food and housing: and although their diet is substantially better than that of most villagers the difference in their standards of living is not so wide as would seem from a comparison of the money value of their incomes.

Nevertheless, in very broad terms it might be said that the real incomes of those in employment are more than a third above the average level for the African community as a whole and that those employed by the mining companies enjoy an average real income which is more than twice the African average.

The majority of the African population lives in the rural areas, however. The following table shows the percentages available in the villages in 1945 by excluding migrants and town dwellers from the total population as estimated from figures supplied by the District Commissioners.[1]

TABLE 10. Available village population, 1945, as percentage of total available in each province

Province	Men %	Women %	Children %
Northern	18	27	55
Central and Western	17	27	56
Southern	20	26	54
Barotse	18	27	55
Eastern	13	29	58
Totals	18	27	55

Out of a total estimated population of 1,647,000 persons, about 1,454,000 were living in the villages in 1945 and of those only 257,000 were adult men. This population earned the vast bulk of its income from subsistence activities and got its cash largely from small-scale local trade and from returned migrants, except in the limited areas where trade in maize, livestock, or fish could be carried on with urban markets.

The results of a series of village surveys carried out early in 1947, supplemented by a number of small budget collections carried out in earlier years, suggests that village cash income may vary from £1.0 per head among the Lozi of Barotseland to £2.5 per head among the Tonga. Unfortunately, no quantitative details are available on the value of subsistence income in different areas, but the total value of agricultural output was estimated to vary from £2 per head in the Chitimene areas of Northern Province to £3 per head in Western Province. No reliable details are available on the value of agricultural output in the rich flood plain areas of Barotse Province, but even taking into account the low

[1] For absolute figures see Appendix I, p. 232.

local prices of this relatively remote area it is probably in excess of £3 per head.

Generalizing the averages derived from these village surveys so that they cover whole provinces and estimating from other evidence for areas where no surveys had been made, we get the following very rough picture of the level of village cash incomes in the rural areas of Northern Rhodesia for 1947.

TABLE 11. Village cash incomes, 1947

Province	Population	Estimated cash income per head £	Estimated total cash incomes £
Northern	373,000	1.50	559,500
Central and Western	248,000	1.50	372,000
Southern	257,000	2.60	668,200
Barotse	316,000	1.00	316,000
Eastern	260,000	2.20	572,000
Totals	1,454,000	1.71	2,487,700

Using these generalizations, therefore, it is estimated that the rural cash income was nearly £1 15s. per head, a figure which includes income brought into the villages by migrants and returning labourers and earned locally by those employed in the rural areas. It includes also the value of local sales of crops, livestock, fish, beer, village manufacturing and all kinds of services. Since the surveys were carried out in early 1947, it includes also the value of 1946 demobilization receipts, which were extremely heavy for Eastern Province, and certainly raised the Provincial average above its normal, although there has always been a substantial flow of income to that province from migrant labour.

In all, therefore, if we add the value of subsistence incomes to these cash incomes it is estimated that the total income of the inhabitants of the villages was in the region of £7,000,000 or about £4 16s. per head. Of this, rather more than £3 per head was accounted for by subsistence output. This leaves a total for the urban areas of £3¼ millions or between £16 and £17 per head. These figures must be treated with some caution, but it is fair to deduce from the evidence available that the average *cash* value of total incomes per head was three to four times as much in the urban areas as in the rural areas, and although the money cost of living in the towns is high there is still a considerable disparity between rural and urban standards of living.

The quality of living standards in the villages is in fact extremely poor. The average villager has a monotonous diet of maize or millet or cassava porridge enlivened with a relish made from green leaves, groundnuts, or pulses (according to the season) and only very occasionally with meat. In the tsetse fly areas meat consumption is less than 10 lb. per man value per annum, and this includes game and poultry as well as small domestic stock. In the cattle-breeding areas it may be three to four times as much as this, but even where livestock is relatively plentiful meat remains a luxury in the rural diet. It is eaten at a funeral or other ceremonial occasion, or when animals die of disease or malnutrition, or when a hunting party makes a kill in the grassburning season, and when a migrant returns with ready cash and the inclination to celebrate. Milk and eggs are consumed, if at all, in very small quantities. In certain limited areas, for example in the Bangweulu swamps or near some reaches of the larger rivers or on the Barotse flood plain, fish is a fairly regular item of diet, and there is a small village trade in dried fish with areas too far from the fishing grounds to catch their own fish: for the majority of Northern Rhodesia villagers, however, fish is even more of a rarity than meat.

In addition to this dull diet mainly of porridge and vegetable relish, the village household brews beer once or twice a year at least and shares its brew with the other households of the village, usually on a part-sale part-gift basis. During the harvest season beer brews are frequent and lively, but in the season when maize is short they fall to a very few ceremonial occasions. In some districts beer brewing is illicit and in some others a licence is required, but there are very few where beer does not figure, at least occasionally, as part of the local diet and as a source of needed vitamins. The average value of beer sold per household is probably between 5s. and £1 per annum, the actual amount varying from district to district. Total consumption of beer is probably worth at least 10s. per rural household per annum on the average.

When we have considered the villager's food we have considered the major factor in his standard of living, and as has been seen, its quality falls very low indeed in some areas. In others, for example in the Barotse flood plain, there is sufficient variety of local resources—a wide range of crops, fruit, fish and meat—to compensate in some measure for primitive methods of agriculture, but this applies to a very small area and even here the maintenance of a reasonable standard hinges largely on the regularity of the floods.

Apart, then, from agricultural crops, livestock and fish, the range of goods and services which enters into the income of the average village household is very narrow. The villager has usually a blanket and one set of clothing (shirt and shorts or blouse and cloth) which he wears to rags and which has usually to be renewed in less than a year. He has a hut (which he builds himself with the aid of his neighbours), usually made of wattle and daub (occasionally of home-made bricks), thatched with grass. It is not intended to last more than 5–7 years, and if the thatching is not renewed it probably leaks in the rains after the first year or two. He also makes for himself one or two storehouses for his crops. Then he has a small range of essential household furnishings made by himself or his wife or by a neighbour or occasionally bought from wandering pedlars. They include a sleeping-mat or a roughly made bed (of poles slung with thongs), some clay or wooden pots and dishes, baskets, and wooden spoons, some cups or calabashes and chairs or stools. He generally buys his hoe and a knife, a mortar and a grainsifter from the local stores, but he may have his axe made by the local smith and probably fashions his own grain-pounder. Ploughs are rare except in the maize-selling area of Tonga country.

These few rough furnishings and this bare minimum of clothing together with a few additional treasures, such as a pair of scissors, a belt or some trinkets, and together with one or two small stock and some chickens, make up the total wealth of the majority of rural Africans. It is true that the 'upper ten' in this society have to share their wealth more than is usual in more developed economies. For example, bicycles, ploughs, sewing machines, water drums, even cattle, tend to be accessible to a wider group of people than the owner's immediate family. Nevertheless, the poverty of the average villager is striking. His clothing—which is next to food in urgency of needs—is particularly inadequate. Except for the fortunate few (and their beneficiaries) who returned with army clothing or who earn high wages, the number of men in possession of warm clothing of any kind is very small indeed. The average woman or child in the village has no warm garment or woollen blanket (although they may occasionally have an old inadequately cured skin), and yet the evening and morning temperature is often bitter. Relatively few villagers are able to afford soap, and even salt is a much sought-after commodity.

In short, the village standard of living, expressed in material terms, is bleak and monotonous. It is clearly reflected in vulnerability to diseases (malaria and parasitic diseases are prevalent everywhere, and venereal disease and sleeping sickness are serious problems in some areas) and a high rate of infant mortality (the exact rate is unknown, but wherever investigations have been made the incidence is shown to be high). It is probably also reflected in a low standard of productivity and a lack of enterprise.

In the towns the picture is better in some respects. The relatively high standard of living of the African miner has already been commented on. He gets a ration allowance for his wife and children, meat several times a week, and a balanced diet in other respects. He has up-to-date medical attention, lives in malaria-controlled townships, enjoys special recreational and welfare facilities, including cinemas, beer-

halls and educational centres, and usually has enough money to keep
himself adequately clothed.

Other urban dwellers are not so well off, although most of them have
access to social welfare amenities which far outstrip those available for
most villagers, and they normally have a wider range of consumption
goods. Their level of actual consumption and the urgency of their
unsatisfied wants are both high in comparison with village standards.
Families who do not have a full scale of rations often find it difficult to
make ends meet in view of the high price of food in the towns. A budget
survey carried out in the Lusaka municipal location in 1947 showed
that many of the families went hungry on the last few days of every
month and for most of them the marked difference in intake during
the first and last week of every month showed that there was a great
discrepancy between the standard of living to which they actively
aspired and the scale of living which their incomes dictated. A ration
allowance which is enough for an adult male does not go far if he has a
wife and children none of whom is in a position to assist regularly in
producing food or earning cash. On the other hand, meat and dried
fish, which are luxuries in the villages, are quite common items in
urban budgets. Similarly, standards of dress are higher in urban areas,
and while one ragged set of clothes might be good enough in the villages
it is not sufficient for the more sophisticated social standards of the
towns, where a man has also to clothe his wife and children with more
care.

Overcrowding in the urban locations results in unsatisfactory housing
conditions. Although at one end of the scale there are the attractive
bungalows for civil servants of the Lusaka African suburb, at the other
end of the scale there are the mud and grass dwellings of the municipal
locations in Ndola and Livingstone, not much better in construction
than the rural huts and very much less sanitary and comfortable in
view of the fact that they are used as permanent dwellings. Nor does
the possession of a brick house ensure comfort. The 'horse box' brick
houses condemned by Major Orde Browne during his visit in 1937 were
still in use in Livingstone ten years later. In the private compounds of
builders and farmers and in some railway and Public Works Department temporary compounds the standards of housing are often still
lower.

In sum, therefore, the conclusion which emerges most strongly from
this brief survey of living conditions in Northern Rhodesia is that there
is an urgent need to raise the standards of consumption of the African
community and more particularly of those members of it who live in
the rural areas. In spite of the considerable quantities of wealth and
skill which (as will be evident from the following chapters) have been

injected into the Northern Rhodesian economy by the immigrant communities, the standard of living of more than 85% of its population is demonstrably low, even by colonial standards. It is an inescapable conclusion that development has somehow passed these people by.

CHAPTER IV

THE STRUCTURE OF NATIONAL OUTPUT

The previous chapter has laid particular emphasis on the fact that the colony is inhabited by three different racial groups with three differing income scales and three differing standards of living. It is important, however, not to conclude from this that there is a lack of coherence in the colony's economic structure. In practice, the three groups are economically interdependent in every sense, and each forms an integral part of the colonial economy. This can be seen by analysing the colony's economic activity not in terms of the incomes earned or the goods and services consumed, but through the medium of the goods and services produced. The business of economic co-operation in a plural community as in other more homogeneous communities is thus shown to be a co-operative process. There is no such thing as a 'European economy' as distinct, say, from the 'African economy' in Northern Rhodesia, although it may be convenient to distinguish a European sector and and African sector for some analytic purposes.

The economy of Northern Rhodesia is an agricultural economy in that most of its people are engaged in agricultural occupations. In terms of gross value of product, however, the most important industry is mining which is largely concentrated in Western Province and Central Province at the Copperbelt and Broken Hill centres respectively. These two industries form the basis of the economy. To a very considerable extent the other industries of the territory depend on them, more particularly on mining.

Table 12 shows the value of the national territorial output of Northern Rhodesia (i.e. the value of the output produced, plus incomes brought within its territorial boundaries), set out according to the industries concerned. In this table the value of each industry is assessed according to its net contribution to the total value of goods and services produced in the territory and all raw materials and purchased services are eliminated or included in the net output of the industry producing them. Thus the net output of an industry amounts to the gross value of its output less goods and services purchased from other industries: which is, in effect, equivalent to the value of the wages, salaries, rents, profits and interest incurred in its output.

TABLE 12. National territorial output, 1945 and 1948

Net output of:		1945 £ millions		1948 £ millions
1. Mining			7.417	18.5
2. Agriculture and livestock			5.590	6.2
(a) European	0.600		0.9	
(b) African	4.990		5.3	
3. Fishing			0.046	0.05
4. Forestry			0.970	1.4
5. Manufacture			1.150	1.6
(a) Factory	0.300		0.7	
(b) Village industry	0.850		0.9	
6. Building			0.150	0.6
7. Distribution			2.300	4.4
8. Transport			0.920	1.3
9. Government service			1.645	2.5
10. Miscellaneous services			1.060	1.3
(a) Missions	0.188			
(b) Other professional	0.272			
(c) Personal, domestic, etc.	0.450			
(d) Services by Africans to Africans	0.150			
11. Income from abroad			0.752	1.2
(a) Migrants	0.595			
(b) Government	0.017			
(c) Missions	0.140			
12. Total national territorial output			22.000	39.0

1. MINING

The colony's most valuable industry in money terms is the mining industry. It currently accounts for over 95% of the total published value of domestic exports, is the principal single source of employment for both Africans and Europeans, and accounts directly for more than half the total revenue of government. Table 13, below, gives some indication of the recent growth in importance of the mineral industry and of its composition.

TABLE 13. The Northern Rhodesian mineral industry

Employment	1938		1945		1949	
African	25,434		32,890		36,971	
European	2,729		3,470		4,661	

Output	Quantity	Value £	Quantity	Value £	Quantity[1]	Value[1] £
Blister copper (tons)	181,664	7,445,093	132,690	7,431,857	194,889	24,253,843
Electrolytic copper (tons)	31,367	1,440,536	61,324	3,814,693	64,413	8,228,214
Zinc (tons)	10,215	141,701	15,240	696,218	22,850	1,944,974
Lead (tons)	273	4,308	1,720	63,560	13,945	1,382,595
Cobalt alloy (tons)	28,762	1,369,076	33,430	672,148	27,123	627,795
Vanadium (tons)	368	333,709	385	232,587	269	181,512
Limestone (tons)	—	20,760	75,330	32,999	106,824	48,070
Gold (oz.)	1,113	35,147	265	2,283	1,186	11,986
Silver (oz.)	88,237	5,259	2,269	251	134,920	28,257
Other metals and minerals		6,849		15,926		34,695
Total value of output		£10,802,438		£12,962,522		£36,741,941

[1] Provisional, as given in March 1950.

The bulk of this mineral output is produced by five large companies. Four of these work the copper mines clustered at the northern end of the railway in Western Province. The fifth mines lead, vanadium and zinc at Broken Hill, which is roughly 200 miles from the Copperbelt and just over 400 miles by rail from the southern border of the colony. In addition there are a few small gold mines and lime workings which account for less than one-half per cent of total expenditure on mining operations in the colony and a still smaller percentage of total output.

Since the giant mining companies are registered in the United Kingdom, the greater part of their balances are held abroad and their dividends flow abroad. Sales are also negotiated abroad. The system is for the companies to remit such moneys as are necessary to cover operating costs (including external operating costs such as railways and shipping) and to retain the balance of their proceeds in the United Kingdom. Out of this operating surplus they meet London office expenses, directors' fees, interest charges, and other managerial expenses, and pay taxation. The net profit is then available to swell reserves held in the United Kingdom or to distribute to shareholders. A detailed analysis of the financial implications for 1945 is given in the Appendix.[1] Table 14, below, shows the estimated expenditure by the industry in Northern Rhodesia for the years 1946–9 compared with the gross value of output for these years. In assessing future returns from the industry it is, of course, necessary to take account of the recently concluded agreement whereby the Northern Rhodesian government receives 20% of the mineral royalties accruing annually to the British South Africa Company for a period of thirty-seven years, after which time the mineral rights fall to the colonial government.

In recent years the mineral industry has ridden on the crest of the good world market prices for its products, but the situation has not always been so favourable. The collapse of prices in 1930–1, for example, caught the industry at a critical period of its early development. The price of copper fell from £72 to £44 per ton in eight months of 1930 and to £27 in 1931. Production and development were drastically curtailed. Complete townships were put out of work and the native labour force which stood at 30,000 in 1930 fell to 12,000 at the end of 1931 and to under 7,000 in 1932. The whole economy felt the shock of this disaster, but the European sector was particularly vulnerable. Imports, which had exceeded £5 millions in value in 1931 fell to less than £2 millions in 1932 and 1933. The total of assessed incomes from all sources fell in 1932–3 to nearly a third of its 1930–1 level. The budget deficit in

[1] Appendix I, p. 270, below.

1932–3 was 26% of revenue in 1932–3 compared with a surplus of 15% in 1930–1.

TABLE 14. Expenditure by mining industry in Northern Rhodesia

	1946	1947	1948	1949 (estimate)
	£000	£000	£000	£000
1. European salaries, wages, bonuses	2,620	3,108	3,897	4,100
2. African wages and bonuses	808	930	1,150	1,400
3. African rations	492	548	582	600
4. Payments to contractors	180	342	865	1,000
5. Payments to Rhodesia Railways[1]	1,284	1,254	1,731	1,800
6. Income tax	1,076	1,190	2,842 ⎫	3,600
7. Customs[2]	18	16	34 ⎭	
8. Total expenditure	6,478	7,388	11,101	12,500
9. Gross value of output	14,503	23,521	29,772	36,742

Revival began in 1933. Developments were resumed in those mines in which they had been abandoned, and the output of copper (which was less than 6,000 tons in 1928) had reached 213,031 tons by 1938. Output expanded during the war years, and in 1940 and 1943 it exceeded a quarter of a million tons. In recent years, however, it has been restricted by the shortage of coal, which in its turn hinges on the shortage of carrying capacity on the Rhodesia Railways. Prices, on the other hand, have remained high. By March 1947 the price of electrolytic copper was £137 per long ton, reported to be the highest ever, and although as world supplies improved it showed a tendency to fall in 1948 and 1949 (to £107 10s. per long ton in September 1949) devaluation shot it up again to the new high level of £141. As supply continues to overtake demand, the prospects are that prices will resume their steady downward trend, but there is no serious slump in sight for the industry. Meanwhile the indications are that the national territorial income (which is broadly equivalent to what is generally known as geographical product) was running at an annual rate in excess of £40 millions in 1949 and early 1950, largely as a result of the high prices ruling for minerals.

[1] This excludes freight divisible with South African Railways but includes payment for transport outside Northern Rhodesia. As Rhodesia Railways is not a Northern Rhodesian concern this is only partly a payment to the Northern Rhodesian economy.

[2] This includes only payments made direct to Northern Rhodesian customs and not payments made to South African or Southern Rhodesian customs and later received by the Northern Rhodesian Government under the terms of the Customs Agreement.

2. AFRICAN AGRICULTURE

The greater part of Northern Rhodesia is covered by poor soil cultivated by a variety of primitive African agricultural systems. Except in
the central Barotse plain (where the annual flooding permits the development of fertile gardens in grassland) bush cultivation in one form
or another forms the traditional basis of native agriculture. A garden of
3–4 acres per household is made by cutting and burning into the bush
at the rate of ½–1 acre each year, and leaving behind an exhausted
patch. In the more densely populated areas the rate of progress is
slower, but the yield tends to be less except in the few instances where
manure is used to replace the fertilizing effect of the ash and to protect
the land from exhaustion.

Crops vary from tribe to tribe and with soil conditions in different
areas. The staples (which may be maize, millet, sorghum or cassava
according to area) are planted in the bush garden, together with subsidiary cucurbits, generally under-planted, and with under-planted or
adjoining pulse crops. These bush gardens may be a mile or more
from the villages and many people also cultivate small gardens by the
villages and even within the village. Cultivation is carried out by the
hand-hoe and largely by women, although the plough and cultivator
are common in the limited area of Southern Province which regularly
grows maize for sale.

There is little reliable information on the productivity of African
agriculture which would permit generalization for a colony as large as
Northern Rhodesia. What we do know, however, as a result of the work
of the Agricultural Department, is that both acreages and yields are
low. It seems that the average acreage under cultivation is normally
in the region of 1 acre per head of the population. Even for the cash-
cropping Plateau Tonga (most of whom if they have not a plough of
their own have access to one on loan) the average acreage was found
to be in the region of 1¼ acres for the whole group and 1.1 acres for
subsistence cultivators only. Yields of most crops are poor, and it was
reported by the Land Tenure Committee that in the principal maize-
growing area of the country, in Mazabuka District, a yield of the order
of three bags of maize per acre is usually regarded as good.[1] Most
producers will generally be content with less. This compares with an
average annual yield in a good year of over six bags per acre by
European farmers in the same area.

Except in the maize-growing areas near the railway line where the
presence of the European farmer and the incentive of the cash crop

[1] Report of the Committee on Native Land Tenure, Lusaka, Government Printers,
1946.

both combine to overpopulate the native reserves there is no land hunger, although there are a number of areas where the soil has deteriorated to an extent that there is a shortage of good land. The amount of land which can be cultivated is limited by the labour involved. The use of the plough is limited both by its high cost and by the lack of draught livestock over the greater part of the colony where the tsetse fly is prevalent. When it is used it is not always an advantage to the community as a whole since it contributes to the ever-present problem of soil erosion and exhaustion, and in parts of Southern and Central Provinces the Agricultural Department is endeavouring to limit ploughed areas.

The Director of Agriculture, in presenting his Ten-Year Development Plan, divided the colony into ten main agricultural areas as follows:

TABLE 15. Agricultural areas of Northern Rhodesia

	Approximate extent 000 sq. miles	Approximate population 000 people
1. Abercorn	50	200
2. Fort Rosebery	24	200
3. Serenje	24	80
4. Fort Jameson	22	280
5. Ndola	42	160
6. Lusaka	24	74
7. Mazabuka	23	125
8. Sesheke	20	65
9. Mongu	30	210
10. Balovale	30	106
	289	1,500

The present population of Northern Rhodesia is probably in the region of 1.8 million, but the above table gives some idea of its distribution by agricultural area. The bulk of the population in Ndola District is, however, an urban and industrial population.

The problem in both of the Northern Province areas (Abercorn and Fort Rosebery) is predominantly one of deforestation and soil deterioration and hence of overpopulation. There is an almost complete absence of stock in these areas and hence no animal manure. The range of local produce is narrow, although the Fort Rosebery region carries on a flourishing fish trade. Large-scale migration of labour from Northern Province is having increasingly serious effects on agriculture in this area and until there are more opportunities for earning money locally it is unlikely that the drain of able-bodied men will be checked. The future development of this area depends on obtaining for it an economic outlet to the industrial centres around the Northern Rhodesian and Congo mines or to the Lupa goldfields in Tanganyika. Its crops are food crops and hence will not bear heavy transport burdens: it is too far from the railway line to make transport of its produce by road an economic proposition, and the alternative—unless the proposed rail link between the Rhodesian and Tanganyikan railways takes effect— is river transport, which is a slow process and unlikely to suit the bulky cheap crops.

Similar problems of soil erosion and relative overpopulation exist in the Eastern Province (Fort Jameson area). Here too, remoteness from the railway line and a tradition of migrant labour handicap agricultural development. The rural African of this area, however, has two advantages which the Northern Province African has not—he can keep cattle since most of Eastern Province is free from tsetse fly and he can obtain work locally (on European tobacco farms). The drain of able-bodied men from the villages is thus not quite so severe, since many men can earn cash wages at a tobacco farm and return to their villages at planting and harvesting seasons. On the other hand, the presence of European settlers and the apparent danger of dispossession to make room for their expansion may be something of a deterrent to local agricultural development, as it seems to be in some of the farming areas of Central and Southern Province.

In the railway-line areas of Western, Central and Southern Province (i.e. in the parts of Serenje, Ndola, Lusaka, Mazabuka and Sesheke areas which are near or at the railway line) there is considerable scope for marketing of native agricultural produce and hence the problem of labour migration is very much less. There is, however, serious land shortage in some areas, and in Lusaka and Mazabuka areas, which have considerable concentration of cattle, soil erosion aggravated by extensive ploughing is a major problem.

On the west of the railway line the remoter areas suffer to an even greater extent than those to the east from inadequate outlets. In central Barotseland, particularly in those areas around the periodically flooded Barotse plain, the land is fertile and the range of resources large: as a result an indigenous system of internal trade in local produce has developed. A wide variety of crops is grown and there are cattle, fish, fruit trees and local arts and crafts to a greater extent than anywhere else in Northern Rhodesia. There are no all-season roads to Mongu, however, and there is no economic outlet. Moreover, the steady influx of Mawiko immigrants from Portuguese territory and the congestion of population around the fertile margins of the flood plain are producing soil depletion and deforestation to an increasingly serious extent. Other areas of Barotseland (Balovale and Sesheke) are less rich in natural resources, but would also benefit by an outlet to the railway line or to centres of population.

In sum, therefore, the agricultural picture of Northern Rhodesia from the African point of view is one of soil deterioration and relative overpopulation in almost all areas, of inaccessibility in all areas away from the railway line, of overploughing and congestion near the railway line, and of a very limited range of national resources in all areas except the Central Barotse plain. In addition, five-eighths of the country is infested by tsetse fly and is therefore almost devoid of livestock, while in many areas of Northern and Eastern Province more than half of the able-bodied male population is away at work, leaving the gardens to be tended very largely by women, unfit males, the very old and the very young.

An attempt to estimate the volume of agricultural output per head on the basis of information supplied by the Agricultural Officers suggested that the amount of meal produced varied from about 400 lb. to about 600 lb. per head, and of pulses from 10 lb. to 116 lb. per head, according to area. Root crops were grown in all areas, but dependence on them varied greatly. Almost all peoples depended to a large extent on various kinds of green leaves, cultivated and wild. A rough evaluation of the output calculations for each province suggested that the value of agricultural output per head at 1945 (railway line) prices varied from £2.44 per head in Southern Province to £3.11 per head in Western Province. (See Tables 101 and 102 in Appendix I, pp. 265, 266.)

The final estimates are given in the Appendix in some detail. In general terms, what they suggest is that the total value of African agricultural output in 1945 was about £4.1 million, of which about 10% was traded and to which meal contributed rather more than two-thirds of the value and pulses about 13%. Among the traded crops, maize contributed about 45% in value in 1945 and perhaps as much as 75% in 1948, when the African maize crop yielded a cash return to the producer of about £300,000, or nearly twice as much as in 1945. It is worthy of note, however, that much of this return tends to flow to a relatively limited group of producers and that it can fluctuate violently with different harvest conditions. Budget data collected by Dr. Colson in 1948 and 1949 showed an average value for crop sales per family in one Tonga area of £22 5s. 2d. in 1948 and £4 8s. 11d. in 1949, which was a very bad year. In another Tonga area the corresponding figures were £4 11s. 3d. in 1948 and £1 15s. 9d. in 1949. The average cash income from all sources in the richer of these two areas was between £40 and £50 in 1948, which compares favourably with the average cash wage earned on the mines but covers a much wider income distribution.[1]

[1] See below, p. 202, for further details on these budgets.

So far, no attempt has been made to consider African incomes from livestock. In the tsetse-fly areas the livestock population consists at the very most of a few goats and chickens. Even in fly-free areas where it is possible to build up herds the African tendency is to regard livestock as a form of investment rather than as a source of food, and this is an important limiting factor in the growth of a native livestock industry.

Nevertheless, in the vicinity of the townships and particularly along the railway belt the demand for meat and other livestock products has been steadily growing. This is intensified by the government policy of setting down a ration scale for employees in industrial and mining establishments, which includes regular meat and which has for twenty years been obligatory on all urban employers with a labour force of any size. There is now a considerable trade in slaughter cattle, pigs, sheep and goats, and poultry drawn from native stocks. The quality of the small stock is quite good in the railway-line areas of Central and Southern Province. In addition to the beasts slaughtered for the meat markets of the urban areas and to provide the rations of the thousands of workers on the mines, an unknown quantity of animals are slaughtered in the villages each year for ritual and ceremonial purposes: a further number die from illness or old age or other causes. Animals killed for ceremonial purposes and animals which die are all normally consumed as meat. Poultry, milk and eggs are not much consumed by Africans, although in areas where there are returned migrants or rich farmers there may be occasional trade in these products within the village. Along the railway line and in the immediate vicinity of European settlements a brisk and growing trade is done in dairy products. Estimates of the total amount of home-produced livestock slaughtered in the markets and abattoirs and in the villages suggested that the total amount of meat involved was less than 20 million lb. even allowing for game. The value of output of African livestock was estimated to be about £540,000 in 1945, about 63% of this being attributable to subsistence output.[1] By 1948 the value of traded African livestock was probably in the region of a quarter of a million pounds to the producer, but it is doubtful whether the value of subsistence output increased at all.

In sum, therefore, although there is an increasing volume of food produced for the market by those Africans living in the vicinity of the railway belt, African agriculture in Northern Rhodesia is primarily the production of food for subsistence purposes. Except along the narrow belt of country within easy reach of the railway line and to a lesser

---

[1] See Tables and Appendix (below, pp. 256–9) for detailed estimates.

extent in the villages close to a major centre of European settlement, there is no appreciable trade in agricultural produce. The basic problem is one of improving the yield of the land in general and of broadening the range of food crops grown rather than of stimulating the production of any particular crop or of protecting the African farmer from the vagaries of the market. There is an urgent need to arrest soil deterioration in some areas, to relieve population congestion in others (or to increase the carrying capacity of the land) and to introduce improved methods of agriculture. Effective animal manuring in the fly-free areas, grass manuring in the fly areas, improved rotation of crops, contour ridging, and other policies which demand an adequately staffed agricultural department, should achieve significant increases in overall yield if they can be made more general.

The development of cash crops depends on adequate transport outlets which do not exist in the areas away from the railway line. Generally speaking, if cash crops are to be encouraged in a community with such a low standard of output it is desirable that they should be predominantly food crops so that in a year of bad harvest the cash crop would provide an insurance against starvation. On the other hand, food crops are low-price crops which cannot stand a heavy transport burden, while even the development of food cash crops does not necessarily ensure an adequate food consumption level. A survey of the maize-growing Plateau Tonga undertaken in 1945 (which was a good year for maize) suggested that about a third of the Tonga families, the chief cash-crop producers in the colony, retained insufficient grain to feed themselves properly.[1] There are, unfortunately, no comparable data for other groups, but it is possible that deficiencies in consumption in other areas are at least as great, probably greater, if only because they are subject to a heavier drain of able-bodied men away from the villages. The successful development of cash crops and village industries would reduce this drain to less alarming proportions and would raise the rural standard of living considerably, provided that it took the form of increased total output without diversion of output from subsistence to market channels.

3. EUROPEAN AGRICULTURE

European farming is carried on in large estates in two main farming areas: one lies along the railway belt and until recently has been almost entirely concerned with maize-growing and some ranching; the other is a tobacco-growing area around Fort Jameson in Eastern Province. There is also a handful of European farms in Northern Province and

---

[1] See Rhodes-Livingstone Paper No. 15, cited in Appendix III, p. 341.

Barotse Province. Generally speaking, Europeans in agriculture are planters rather than farmers and the more intensive farming requires considerable capital and experience. There is a great variation in the quality of the land in the European farming area of the railway line and the cultivable percentage rarely exceeds thirty and is sometimes as low as five (on a maize standard of fertility). This accounts in part for the large undeveloped portions of European farms which are a source of some friction with local African farmers who have within living memory been moved off these lands to make room for European settlement and still have a tendency to drift back.

The only significant export crop and the chief income-earner for European farmers is tobacco. Until a few years ago, after their bitter experience of the slump in tobacco prices in the early thirties, European farmers, except those in the area around Fort Jameson, were primarily dependent on maize production. Consistently high prices for tobacco, however, have recently drawn them into tobacco farming on an unprecedented scale. Since 1939, acreage under Virginia tobacco has more than doubled, and a more recent venture has been the expansion of acreage under Turkish tobacco on the railway-line farms. Tobacco growing, which brought farmers less than £100,000 in 1939, gave them a gross return of nearly half a million pounds ten years later. At the same time, however, stimulated by the prosperity of the home market, particularly by the boom on the Copperbelt, and even more particularly by a subsidy which contributed more than half the price received, the acreage under maize has also expanded, since 1939, by over 70%. In addition, European farmers produce nearly 20% of the meat bought from butchers in the territory, together with the bulk of the home-produced potatoes, butter, fruit, vegetables, etc., required for the now substantial European market.

Detailed estimates for the output of European agriculture in 1945 are given in the Appendix.[1] Since then, however, gross output has risen to something like £1½ millions in 1948, which represents more than double the 1945 value. Costs have also risen and it may be that net incomes have not increased by as much, but it is interesting to note that assessed incomes from farming increased by 140% as between assessment years 1943–4 and 1947–8.

In the short run the problems of European agriculture are more economic than agronomic, since the prosperity of the farmer depends on the world market price for tobacco, on the maintenance of a high level of employment in the mining and industrial areas and on the maintenance of the maize subsidy. The main need is for efficient market-

[1] See below, pp. 271–4.

ing and price stabilization organizations and for a broadening of the basis of European farming so that it does not rely too exclusively on one crop. Thus European farmers along the railway line are being encouraged to plant Turkish tobacco on land too poor for maize and to adopt ranching as a sideline. The long dry season, however, militates against the establishment of grass leys, and production of a large bulk of feed from small acreage and the expansion of ranching depends largely on the development of irrigation on small holdings.

Much controversy has been aroused by the high rate of subsidy for maize and the differential prices for European and African producers. At present the position is that the difference between the African and European price is—in the case of African output—held to the credit of the African community in general and devoted to measures for the improvement of African agriculture. The argument for the high rate of subsidy is that the industry of the territory must be able to rely on an adequate supply of cheap food for its labour. The African farmer cannot provide a reliable supply through good years and bad (in the 1947 drought year African output for the market dropped to about a fifth of its normal level). He only provides at best less than half of what the home market requires, and it is even doubtful whether the African community can healthily spare as much as it actually markets. To devote the African share of the subsidy to measures designed to increase long-run African output is on the face of it sound policy, although whether enough of the government's revenue is going to this purpose is another matter.

In effect, the result of the subsidy is a rather curious redistribution of income within the territory. The cost of the subsidy is met by the taxpayers, of whom the mining companies are by far the most important. The beneficiaries are: (1) the European maize producers, (2) the African farmers whose yield improves as a result of the improved farming measures financed by the subsidy or who get some direct share of the subsidy, (3) employers of labour with a low rate of profit in relation to their labour needs (since most employers have to provide the legal minimum ration it is they who are the principal purchasers of maize, rather than the actual consumers), and (4) Africans in the urban or rural areas who have to buy their own food. It should be noted, however, that only the first group and some of the second (those getting a direct share in the subsidy) benefit from the subsidy as such. The remainder benefit from the controlled price of maize or from the fact that a proportion of government revenue is devoted to improvement of their farming conditions.

In the short run, given the inadequacy of maize supplies from African sources and given the impossibility of developing a low cost and reliable source of supply outside the territory, it is difficult to see what alternative there is but to subsidize European producers. Clearly, however, it is important (a) to ensure that the subsidy is not more than is necessary to maintain production at the level required without letting price to the consumer rise faster than the consumers' ability to pay, and (b) to devote as much of the territory's resources as possible to developing low-cost production, i.e. to raising the yield of African agriculture. What these limits are cannot be determined without a study of the relevant costs of European agriculture and industry and of the economic and technical factors limiting the rapid expansion of African output. Meanwhile, however, ignoring completely the political considerations which may be involved, it can be stated that the economic situation demands a policy with three main objectives, to reduce the subsidy, to control the price and to expand African output.

For all European agricultural products, not only for maize, the demand is greater than the supply. A substantial European population and a growing purchasing power among Africans promise a solid and expanding home market for foodstuffs. Given the low standards of African farming practice and the lack of capital or skill among the African community, it would appear that the future of European agriculture in the long term depends on the extent to which it can change over from the 'planter' tradition and develop the intensive highly capitalized agriculture of advanced agricultural communities in Europe and North America.[1]

4. FORESTRY

Although more than half the area of the colony is under trees, it is estimated that less than 3% is covered by the tall forest capable of yielding heavy timber. Only two areas have so far proved suitable for commercial exploitation. In the south, in Livingstone and Sesheke Districts, there are forests of Rhodesian teak which supply hardwood suitable for railway sleepers. In the north, at the other end of the railway line, the mining companies cut timber for their own needs from the woodland in the vicinity of the Copperbelt. The remainder of the licensed timber is cut by or for native sawyers, furniture-producing firms and builders in the vicinity of the line-of-rail townships. Net output of wood and furniture by European concerns exceeded £200,000 in value in 1947 and was still increasing rapidly.

---

[1] In this connection it is significant that output of wheat, which is grown under irrigation, has recently been falling. It amounted to 25,500 bags in 1945 but had fallen to 5,000 in 1947 and in spite of an increased price and a good harvest was only 9,000 in 1948.

Since 1945, for which detailed estimates are given in the Appendix,[1] the annual licensed output of timber has increased more than sixfold. By 1948 it was in the region of 25 million cubic ft. Two factors have contributed to this. First, the boom in European industry and settlement in general, and particularly in the building industry, and secondly, the boom on the mines. The mining companies' consumption of licensed timber, which amounted to over 70% of the total by 1948, was accelerated by the coal shortage and the need to use wood as a substitute fuel on the mines.

At present the value of timber produced in the colony is probably in excess of £1½ million, the bulk of this being now attributable to commercial output. It is clear, however, that this relatively high rate of output has been reached at the expense of the national capital in basic timber resources. Although it is impossible with present data to measure the rate of depreciation, it is important to recognize that the increased output is not all real gain to the territory. Nor can this rate of output be expanded much further, or even maintained indefinitely, unless there is an appropriate acceleration in the territory's re-afforestation programme in the vicinity of the main industrial consumers.

5. FISHING

Fishing is carried on in Northern Rhodesia wherever there are swamps, rivers or perennial streams. Its importance as a contribution to economic activity varies widely from area to area. It is at its lowest near small rivers where total output is provided by occasional seasonal excursions to the streams by men and boys with spears or women with baskets; and it is at its highest in the swamp areas where men leave their villages and stay at the fishing sites for periods of months at a time with a view to obtaining substantial commercial catches.

It is probably true to say that the majority of Northern Rhodesian Africans have some kind of access to small-scale fishing at certain seasons, although many of them will not find the effort worth while. In general, therefore, subsistence fishing, except in the major fishing areas, is a small and perhaps negligible contribution to total output. In some areas, however (and this is particularly so for the Barotse flood plain areas), small-scale, seasonal, non-commercial fishing is too widespread to be so lightly dismissed. Unfortunately we know very little indeed about economic conditions in this unique area of Northern Rhodesia, and any guesses on the volume of output of its fisheries must be regarded with considerable caution.

There are five main fishing areas in Northern Rhodesia. The three

[1] See below, p. 281.

main areas are in Northern Province—the most important being in the Bangweulu swamps beside Lake Bangweulu and along the Upper Luapula: the next in importance are those in and around Lake Mweru and the lower Luapula where there are more stretches of swamp land: and there is also some lake fishing on the shores of Lake Tanganyika. More important, however, than the lake fishing is the river fishing in the lower Kafue in Southern Province and the swamp fishing in the Lukanga swamp which lies some miles to the west of Broken Hill. Finally, there are a number of areas in Barotseland where extensive fishing for subsistence purposes is possible, but which are too far from the main concentrations of population to be commercial fishing areas.

It is estimated that the volume and value (to the fishermen) of the cash trade in fish is in the region of £50,000, but its market value is probably in the region of £300,000 if allowance is made for the inflated prices of the urban areas.[1] Most of this return accrues to African traders, although there are European concerns which have some share in the produce marketed on the Copperbelt and in the Belgian Congo: the latter have freezing plants and transport facilities which enable fresh fish to be supplied to the European population. Generally, however, the output of the fishing industry is dried and carried by Africans on bicycles to the railway-line and urban townships where it is retailed in native markets. During 1947 a European concern based near Abercorn commenced fishing operations on Lake Tanganyika after obtaining a ten-year grant of exclusive fishing rights in the deep waters of the lake. The Game and Tsetse Department conducts fish-farming experiments, but there is still much research to be done in the possibilities of fish farming in Northern Rhodesia before it becomes a commercial proposition.

6. MANUFACTURE

Manufacturing industry in Northern Rhodesia is directed towards the local market and is on a small scale. In response to the post-war boom, however, it has expanded substantially. As a matter of deliberate policy the colony's factories are largely concentrated at Ndola on the edge of the Copperbelt, the chief industrial market. However, there are minor manufacturing concerns at other centres of European population —Broken Hill, Lusaka and Livingstone in particular—including a small cigarette factory at Fort Jameson. The new cement factory has been established at Chilanga, which is a few miles from Lusaka and is designed for expansion to serve the Kariba Gorge hydro-electric project, should that materialize.

[1] See Appendix, p. 260, below for detailed estimates for 1945.

The principal products of the colony's factories are milled grain, sawn timber, furniture, parquet flooring, plywood, veneer, bricks, oxygen and acetylene, ferro-concrete pipes, soap, and mineral waters, but there are also bakeries and some small sweet factories and clothing factories, and more recently a blanket factory and an iron foundry began production. It was estimated[1] that gross output in 1945—excluding smelting and extracting of non-ferrous metals, and wood and furniture industries—was about £680,000. Since then there has been an appreciable raising of the level of output and some widening of the scope of industry. The Central Office of Statistics took a census of manufacturing production in 1947 and again in 1948, but the results have not yet been published, with the exception of a few preliminary reports which appeared in the *Economic and Statistical Bulletin of Northern Rhodesia.*[2] It is thus difficult to calculate reliably the present rate of output. In 1947 the food, drink and tobacco groups alone had a gross output in excess of £700,000. This is the chief group and it is tentatively estimated that *net* output for all manufacture in 1948—again excluding smelting metals and wood and furniture—was at least £700,000.

The territory has no special advantages in skill or resources which would permit the development of an export trade in manufactures and the future of the industry depends on the expansion of other industries and of African purchasing power. An Advisory Committee on Industrial Development set up in 1945 considered a wide range of potential new secondary industry before it wound up in 1948: the general conclusion from its reports and other evidence seems to be that secondary industry will continue to expand with increasing European population and economic activity and with increasing African purchasing power, but that there is little scope as yet for any striking new developments.

So far no mention has been made of village industry which in 1945 was estimated to yield a net output worth more than twice as much as the net output of European secondary industry. The comparison is a very loose one since the activities considered under the head of village industry were a much wider group than those included in secondary industry, but as an indication of rank order of importance it was fair enough. Africans in the villages make for their own use and for trade a variety of household goods, including pots, beds, chairs, baskets, mats, etc., they make and sell a grert deal of beer, and in addition they act as smiths, shoe repairers, bicycle repairers, tailors, doctors, or leather workers, while in the vicinity of the European settlements many of tnem

[1] See below, p. 281.
[2] *Economic and Statistical Bulletin of Northern Rhodesia*, Volume II, Nos. 3, 4, 6, and 9, June, July, September, and December 1949. Central Office of Statistics, Salisbury, Southern Rhodesia.

E

devote a good deal of time to the making of curios from wood and ivory and bone. This wide variety of activities is still a recognizably important factor in the national income, although problems of evaluating the subsistence section of output make valid comparisons with other types of industry difficult. It is hard to say, for example, whether village industry is now more or less important as a source of income than European secondary industry, but it is clear that it is rapidly losing ground in relative importance.

For village industry as for factory industry the future depends on the development of local purchasing power and also to some extent on the ability of the African producer to adjust his commodity to the requirements of a European consumer. The native product in such articles as baskets, pottery, furniture, mats, skins, etc., is far less in evidence in European households in the territory than it is, say, in European households in the East. This is partly due to the fact that the African craftsman does not reach the same standard of workmanship as, say, the Indian or the Chinaman, but it can also be attributed in some measure to the fact that the African basket-maker or mat-maker or furniture-maker, for example, follows too closely the traditional African pattern in these articles to satisfy the average European consumer.

To some extent the African-made and European-made goods produced in the territory are in competition. In so far as European industry supplies a more efficient and durable product (as it can, for example, in some household utensils such as cooking pots) a fall in the price of the durable machine-made good which enables it to dislodge the shorter-lived hand-made goods would prove a net gain to the rural community. In assessing the value of village industry, however, it must be stated that those communities which are accustomed to making a large proportion of their own household goods tend to enjoy a higher real income as a result than those who rely heavily on traded goods—whether these are made by the specialist village carpenter or the European factory. The versatile subsistence producers not only enjoy a wider variety of goods and services per head, they also have more cash left to purchase the goods which only European industry can supply.

7. DISTRIBUTION

The bulk of the trade with Europeans and a substantial proportion of the trade with Africans is in the hands of Europeans. They run large stores in every township and a host of little stores in the rural areas. These smaller establishments may be one-man trading concerns or branches of a large business, or they may be stores set up by farmers for the convenience of their employees. In addition, Europeans control most of the trade in producers' goods, such as machinery, office equipment, oil, etc., and a large part of the wholesale trade.

All but a negligible proportion of the few hundred Asians in Northern Rhodesia are engaged in trade. For the most part they concentrate on trade with the Africans. They own most of the stores in the so-called 'second-class trading sites' which have been set up in several townships and which are intended for African customers. Except in the Copperbelt townships, however, where a policy of restricting the number of distributive units has operated against Indian commercial expansion in the European trading areas, the Indian traders enjoy some share of the trade with Europeans in each township.

In effect, the bulk of the retail and wholesale trade carried on in the colony, and especially of the trade carried on through fixed premises and in imported goods, is controlled by Europeans or Indians. African storekeepers are increasing in number, but their share in the total volume of trade is still very small and largely confined to the rural areas. Many of them buy retail and sell retail, sometimes because the European or Indian wholesalers are unwilling to supply small quantities or to grant them credit, sometimes because they have not a sufficient knowledge of the business to make the right sort of contacts. Standards of efficiency and profit levels are thus low among African storekeepers and prices are high.

In the markets, which handle the bulk of the organized trade in African foodstuffs and tobacco, and in the hawking which goes on continually in the rural areas, the African monopolizes the trade. For most of the marketeers and pedlars, however, this is not a full-time occupation. Many who are selling flour or fish at the market on a given day are there simply to dispose of a load of their own produce. They may return again with another consignment, but a large number of them will have disposed of their entire surplus in one visit. Even those marketeers and pedlars who are not dealing in their own produce may not be permanent traders. A man will often go on a trading expedition in the same casual or adventurous spirit in which he takes temporary employment, with every intention of returning to his village or to another occupation as soon as he has made an adequate sum for immediate future needs.

All traders who deal in imported goods are required to take out a licence. This covers all European and Indian traders, and all but a very few African storekeepers. An African may run a small store without a licence from the District Commissioner if he limits his stock to such locally produced commodities as bread, tobacco, groundnut oil, soap, and (in some cases) salt. The part played by unlicensed (or Native Authority licensed) concerns of this kind can, however, be regarded as negligible in relation to total trade. African hawkers are licensed only when they deal in imported goods, which is relatively seldom. The pedlar who hawks second-hand clothes from the Belgian Congo through the African villages requires a licence. The fish trader, the pedlar who carries claypots or baskets or mats or skins from village to village, and the man who hawks fruit and vegetables in the European townships are all unlicensed. It is therefore extremely difficult to say how many are engaged in this unlicensed trade or in the trade through the markets. It is estimated[1] that the total value of turnover by licensed traders was roughly £9 million in 1945 and that the net value of output was about £1.8 millions, of which about 96% was attributable to European or Asian concerns.

Between 1945 and 1949 the annual value of merchandise imported into the territory roughly trebled. A large part of this, of course, is due to the boom on the mines and in other forms of industrial activity, which produced considerable imports of capital goods. However, by 1948, consumer goods imports were about 100% above the 1945 level and by 1949 they were about 150% above. If the gross turnover of the licensed distributive trade increased in a similar proportion it reached about £18 millions in 1948 and about £22½ millions in 1949.

There are comparatively few organized markets for domestic produce in Northern Rhodesia. Except on the Copperbelt, where the compound markets are thriving centres of trade, such organized markets as do exist accounted for only a small proportion (sometimes a negligible) proportion of the District's trade. This was markedly so in recent years when the attempt to impose price control at the markets drove sellers to hawk their wares by the wayside or at unofficial markets where no control could be exercised. Others took their chance with the relatively lax control at the organized markets and sold there at prices above the controlled figures.

In general, therefore, and excluding the Copperbelt, the bulk of the trade in foodstuffs (and other native produce such as pots and baskets) takes place in a haphazard and unorganized fashion. Pedlars travel from one village to another. Along the main labour routes the villagers within walking distance of the route habitually sell their surplus at the side of the road. The returning migrants travelling by lorry or bus from Lusaka to Fort Jameson are tempted at many points along the road by sellers of all kinds of produce—meal, groundnuts, honey, mangoes, scones, tea, chickens, and so on. The roads around any township have their haphazard trickle of sellers ranging from the old widow who has a small basket of pounded flour which she will exchange for salt or the

[1] See below, p. 275.

money to buy salt, to the cyclist who makes several trips weekly with his load of vegetables, fruit, milk or eggs to a group of regular European customers. Even where there is no market there are always places where people gather regularly—the District Administration head-quarters, or the Chief's court, or a farm store, or a Public Works Department camp or a mission clinic—and where it is worth squatting with one's basket of goods to wait for a potential customer. Many of the sellers of small amounts of produce will never reach the market but will dispose of all they have to someone met on the way.

An attempt to assess the volume of trade conducted in these irregular ways must necessarily involve a high degree of guesswork. Some information is available on the regular markets, but about the inter-village and wayside trade very little indeed is known. Estimates made on scanty data suggested a total value of turnover of about half a million pounds for all this unlicensed and largely unorganized trade, but this may well be an underestimate although it is believed to give a fair indication of the order of magnitude involved in 1945.

The high share of the distribution industry in the national output is due in large part to the high cost of production of European or Indian concerns relatively to the standard of living of their customers. African participation in the organized and licensed trade through fixed premises is limited partly by lack of capital but more by lack of skill. Shopkeeping requires a degree of ability in book-keeping which few Africans have had a sufficient standard of education to develop. Moreover, they are already at a disadvantage in competition with more strongly entrenched European and Indian concerns. As a result, African distribution tends to involve an even higher cost for both producer and consumer than non-African distribution. The problem of high cost distribution is an important one. A reduction of retail distribution costs could release purchasing power to stimulate secondary industry and to raise the standard of living generally. Until the wholesale channels are open to the African retailer at least as readily as for the non-African (which is partly a question of providing security for credit) and until the African retailer has acquired the necessary book-keeping skill to be able to run his business on profitable lines it does not seem likely that costs of distribution will fall. What action the Government might most usefully take in order to introduce into the economy a corps of African shopkeepers with the necessary skill and economic privilege is a matter for investigation.

8. TRANSPORT

Northern Rhodesia is traversed by a single railway line which enters the territory from Southern Rhodesia at the Victoria Falls in the south and passes out of it at the Copperbelt into the Belgian Congo in the north. All the townships of any size, all the large industrial undertakings, and most of the commercial farms (European or African) lie along the railway belt, although there is a European tobacco farming area around Fort Jameson in Eastern Province which is agriculturally prosperous. Industry and commercial agriculture has tended to concentrate along the railway line and the areas through which no railway passes are generally in an undeveloped state. Along the railway goes the bulk of the territory's freight and passenger traffic. It carries the minerals consigned from the Copperbelt or Broken Hill to overseas markets on the long haul via Bulawayo, Salisbury, and Beira. It brings in the machinery, coal and other materials for the mines and the consumption goods for retail distribution. Goods and passengers are taken to the outer provinces by road, usually by European contractors operating regular lorry services. Except for tobacco from Fort Jameson district very little produce emanates from the non-railway-line provinces. The railway and the line-of-rail markets are fed by European produce from railway belt farms and by African produce brought by head-load or by bicycle from villages within reach of the line.

Communications within the outer provinces are poor. There are all-season roads from Lusaka to Fort Jameson, and from Broken Hill to Abercorn, but the lorry service from Lusaka to Fort Jameson, for example, takes nearly three days. There is a river transport service in the Zambesi operated by government and a small barge traffic into the centre of Barotse Province. For European passengers the air service provided by Central African Airways is becoming increasingly popular, but it is beyond the means of most Africans.

The railway was until June 1947 operated by the Rhodesia Railways Ltd., a company formed in the late nineteenth century under the aegis of the British South Africa Company. Rhodesia Railways, with the Mashonaland Railway Company (whose assets it acquired in 1937), linked the South African railway with the Belgian Congo in the north and (through the Beira Railway Company) with the port of Beira in the east. In 1947 the company was taken over by the Southern Rhodesian Government and Northern Rhodesia's share amounts to an undertaking to underwrite up to 20% of any losses on the working of the railway.

The Central African Airways system is operated by a public corporation financed by the three Central African governments in the proportion: Southern Rhodesia 10, Northern Rhodesia 7, and Nyasaland 3. These internal services lapsed during the war but are now fairly frequent and are carrying a growing passenger traffic. They are contributing substantially to the efficiency of administration of government and commerce by making Lusaka and Ndola readily accessible to the Central African capitals of Blantyre and Salisbury as well as to the outer province headquarters of Mongu, Abercorn and Fort Jameson. The contribution of the transport industry to the net territorial output of Northern Rhodesia was estimated for 1945 at less than £1,000,000 and its gross output at between £1¾ millions and £2 millions. Of this gross output the railways accounted for about £1.65 millions and they paid about £568,000 in salaries, wages, and rations to employees in Northern Rhodesia, and some £233,000 in tax to the Northern Rhodesian Government. These figures are based on calculations made with the assistance of the company's accountant since the operating statistics do not usually distinguish the Northern Rhodesian section of the line separately. Judging by the broad financial results for the Rhodesia Railways system, the 1948 gross output was at least 40% above the 1945 output in terms of money value.

The contribution of African carriers to the industry whether by barge, bicycle or head is impossible to evaluate at all precisely, but it is estimated that the road transport companies contributed less than £60,000 to the net value of output in 1945. By 1947 they had increased their contribution; by how much it is difficult to say. It is significant, however, that only just over 100 commercial vehicles were registered during 1946, 453 in 1947, 1,234 in 1948, and 1,428 in 1949. Much of this increased rate of registration was due to the heavy backlog of replacements that had been accumulated in the war and post-war years, but there was certainly an expansion of new investment in the road transport industry. The transport industry remains largely in European hands, and there are very few Asians or Africans who are in a position to compete with the established European concerns.

9. BUILDING

The colony's building industry is concentrated in the railway-line townships, primarily in the mining townships and their satellites. At the outstations, individual farmers or traders and mission or government stations undertake their own building, while African housing (except where provided by employers) consists of mud and pole or sun-dried brick structures constructed by the owners and their neighbours. In the railway-line townships, since employers are statutorily obliged to provide housing for their African labour and often provide it for their European employees also, the private contractors are largely engaged in building houses for both Africans and Europeans. Their most important customers for both housing and industrial building are the mining companies.

Shortages of materials hindered the full expansion of the industry in the war and immediate post-war period. Since 1946, however, the expansion of the output of building and construction has been one of the most striking features of the Northern Rhodesian economy. At the Census held in October 1946, 232 persons were reported to be gainfully occupied in building and reconstruction, i.e. a little over 2%. Since the Census and up to the end of January 1950, 698 persons have entered the colony to assured employment in building and construction. The flow started at the end of 1947 when the quarterly intake leapt to twenty-nine after an average for the past year of seven a quarter. During 1948 the average was sixty-one a quarter, in 1949 eighty-nine a quarter, and in the single month of January 1950 there were forty. It cannot be assumed that all these builders stayed in the territory and that the building labour force increased fourfold in a little over two years, but the figures are a convincing indication of a vigorous expansion. The evidence from other sources confirms this. In 1945 it was estimated that the gross output of private builders was less than half a million pounds. In 1948, building permits to the value of about £2.7 millions were issued, 44% of them being to the mining companies. Over 70% of the total was in respect of dwelling houses.

10. OUTPUT OF GOVERNMENT

Partly as a result of the 1945 Colonial Development and Welfare Act and of the increased public interest in development and welfare schemes which that Act helped to render effective, the rate of government expenditure has shown a marked increase throughout the major colonies. In Northern Rhodesia the trend towards increased government expenditure was accelerated by the rapidly increasing revenues which the post-war boom put at the disposal of the Central Government. In 1945 the total expenditure of all government authorities in Northern Rhodesia was approximately £2.9 millions, of which about 12% was attributable to local government. By 1948 Central Government expenditure was £6.2 millions, and by 1950 it exceeded £14 millions.

Local government in Northern Rhodesia falls into two main categories. First of all there are the Municipalities or Management Boards which deal with the administration of the European townships. There are two Municipalities, one at Livingstone and one at Ndola, and these have elected councils. Elsewhere the European townships are administered either by a small Management Board (some of which are elected but most of which are largely nominated) or directly by the District Commissioner. Both the Municipalities and some Management Boards levy rates and conduct trading services. All Municipalities and Manage-

ment Boards have their own budget and are assisted in part by government grant. Table 16 lists the Municipalities and Management Boards
together with their revenue and expenditure for the year 1945. This
gives an indication of the relative strength of these agencies. Full figures
are not available for a later year, but those which are available suggest
that local authorities had doubled the 1945 rate of expenditure by 1948.

TABLE 16. Municipalities and Management Boards, 1945

	Revenue £	Expenditure £
1. Livingstone	55,417	51,827
2. Ndola	56,419	52,194
3. Lusaka	33,974	29,389
4. Broken Hill	21,451	20,397
5. Luanshya	30,400	25,600
6. Chingola	17,121	13,271
7. Mufulira	21,052	18,690
8. Kitwe	44,728	39,682
9. Mazabuka	3,669	2,552
10. Kafue	1,860	1,434
11. Other railway townships	1,700	1,560
12. Fort Jameson	2,620	2,294
Total	£290,411	£258,890

The second category of local authority covers the Native Treasuries.
There were forty-five of these in 1945, spending a total of £77,000.
Most of their funds are derived from Government Grant (through
which they get a share of the poll tax levied on Africans), but there is a
certain amount of locally collected revenue, such as court fees and fines,
and local licences and levies (e.g. dog and fishing licences).

The total value of government's contribution to the national territorial output was estimated at £1,330,000 in 1945 and was probably
between £2½ millions and £3 millions in 1948. This includes the value
of the incomes received in government service (including incomes in
kind) by all government employees, established and casual, and the
value of government's own earnings in respect of interest, rent and other
income from property, profits from trading services, and miscellaneous
fees and receipts from the sale of goods and services.

II. PROFESSIONAL AND PERSONAL SERVICES

In 1945 there were relatively few professional people in Northern
Rhodesia except those employed by government, the missions and the
banks. Those working on their own account were very few indeed. In
part, of course, this was due to the shortage of skilled professional people
caused by the war, a shortage which persisted at the time of the 1946
Census, but which, judging by the figures of immigrants, has been

greatly reduced since. A large number of insurance companies do business in the territory, but generally through agents for whom it is a part-time occupation rather than through permanent employees.

The missions are a sufficiently important sector of the economy to be considered separately. They provide services of an educational, medical and religious nature throughout the colony and are financed partly by contributions from charitable institutions abroad and partly by government grant. In addition all of them rely to some extent on their ability to produce goods and services for their own consumption and occasionally for local sale.

It is difficult to put a value on their activities largely because many mission stations are not centrally administered or controlled. There are a large number of stations where no cash incomes as such are paid to the European staff, but where members are maintained partly by their own economic activities and partly by contributions from Mission headquarters towards their maintenance. It was estimated, however, on the basis of the replies to a questionnaire sent round in 1947, that the total value of mission income, including income from abroad, government grant, local contributions and sales and subsistence output, was at least £275,000. The net contribution of missions to national territorial output can be defined as being equivalent to the salaries, wages, and rations received by their members and was estimated at about £188,000 for 1945. It does not seem likely that there has been much increase since 1945, and the present net annual value of mission output is probably not more than about £200,000.

The total value of personal services rendered in Northern Rhodesia consists largely of services rendered by Africans in the capacity of domestic servants to Europeans, and to a lesser extent to Asians and Africans. The hotel industry is very inadequately developed and for some years now there has been an acute shortage of hotel accommodation. A new hotel is to be built in Lusaka, but there is need, especially with the increase in air traffic, for an expansion of the hotel trade in most towns. Estimates of the total net value of personal services provided by the hotel and boarding-house trade in 1945 suggested that it was between £60,000 and £70,000, which is not much more than the net value of services provided by clubs, cinemas and sports associations.

CHAPTER V

THE SOCIAL ACCOUNTS

The two preceding chapters contain a fairly detailed description of economic conditions in Northern Rhodesia in the post-war period. At this stage it may be of some use to consider the economy as a whole by presenting in a more systematic fashion the basic quantitative data which was used to illustrate this description.

Tables 17 and 18 set out the main features of the economy for the years 1938 and 1945 in the form of two consolidated sets of social accounts. They are designed to show as fully but also as concisely as possible, how the nation's income was earned, by whom it was earned, and on what it was spent. Both sets of accounts contain (*a*) a triple-entry income-output-expenditure account covering the whole economy, and (*b*) a double-entry balance of international payments account covering the transactions of the economy with the world outside its borders. The two sets, however, draw the boundary round the Northern Rhodesian economy in two different ways. One of them (Table 18) would define it on a geographical basis and would account for all the economic activity carried on within the territorial borders of the colony. The other (Table 17) defines it on a 'national' basis and would measure all the economic activity carried on by residents of the colony.

Some explanation is necessary for this double system of accounts. In most countries the national income is defined as the sum total of the goods and services produced by a country's nationals. This (see Table 17) is the definition of national income that is generally used for the purposes of international comparison. Meaningful reduction of national income estimates to a *per capita* basis, for example, depends on the possibility of relating them to a definable population. Their measurement and arrangement in the form of a double-entry account showing, on the one hand, the origins of the incomes (in the form of goods and services produced), and, on the other hand, their destination (in the form of goods and services consumed or accumulated), is in principle possible only if the transactions are performed by individuals or institutions whose behaviour is generally observable; hence, other things being equal, each government would normally prefer to measure the economic activities of its own nationals.

In an independent developed economy such as that of the United Kingdom, the difference between the two definitions is largely a formal one. For some analytical purposes it is convenient to think in terms of net geographical product, and for some in terms of net national income. Generally speaking, however, the value of the goods and services produced within the country's borders is not likely to differ greatly from the value of the goods and services produced by the country's nationals. This may not be so for a dependent economy where the economic boundaries coincide less closely with national boundaries, and where economic resources can only be exploited with the substantial aid of factors of production drawn from outside its own geographical borders.

Northern Rhodesia is a particularly striking example of this kind of dependent economy in that its principal industry—mining—demands a high rate of capital investment which cannot be financed from sources within the colony's borders. Thus the share of 'foreign' factors of production (shareholders in the United Kingdom or the United States) in the net output of minerals produced in Northern Rhodesia is almost as much as the share of 'nationals'.[1] In times of high prices—in 1948 for example—the profits earned by the providers of capital may exceed the reward earned by the providers of labour.

Since the two definitions differ so widely in content and magnitude it is important to recognize the distinction between them from the outset. In drawing welfare conclusions (e.g. when comparing average income per head over time or between colonies) it is the total income of residents which provides the most convenient concept. In studying the productivity implications (e.g. when assessing the rate of development of the colony's resources) the net geographical product is the most useful indicator. For some purposes (e.g. in measuring the potential tax yield of the colony or its investment capacity) it may be necessary to take both concepts into account.

It would be unnecessarily complicated to carry each piece of analysis through two definitions and two sets of accounts, and it is therefore inevitable that some kind of choice should be made between the two concepts for everyday purposes. Since welfare analysis is still the least satisfactory (although the most popular and desirable) of the uses to which national income estimates can be put, it is probably wise to regard the net geographical product as the most acceptable working

---

[1] The use of the term 'foreign' in this context is as arbitrary as the use of the term 'national'. The former covers British firms registered in the United Kingdom which would certainly not be regarded as politically foreign in the colonial context; the latter covers those Europeans and Asians who would regard themselves as essentially temporary residents of the colony.

definition for most purposes. It is more important than ever, however, not to attempt welfare analysis with this most unsuitable definition. What it amounts to is that for most purposes we treat mining companies registered in the United Kingdom and operating in Northern Rhodesia as if they were, with the exception of their London head office, wholly within the Northern Rhodesian economy. Their undistributed profits, incomes earned by their shareholders, and royalties, are regarded as part of the annual product of Northern Rhodesia, a part which is remitted abroad for an unspecified purpose. We value the minerals inclusive of the interest, profits, and royalties accruing in the course of production, but exclusive of railage and realization or other purchased materials and services obtained from other industries or from abroad. If we are tempted to compare, say, incomes per head in Northern Rhodesia with incomes per head in Nyasaland, or income per head in 1938 with income per head in 1945, we must remember to restrict our attention to the incomes actually accruing to the persons we have in mind and to eliminate those incomes which flow to non-residents.

Attention will be largely concentrated in the following pages on the set of social accounts summed up in Table 18, bearing in mind that discussions of standards of living (as opposed to standards of productivity) are more effectively illustrated by Table 17.

Tables 17 and 18 show in skeleton form the structure of the Northern Rhodesian economy as it was in 1938 and 1945. The 1938 estimates were made during the years 1941–5 on the basis of published and unpublished material available in London. They were published and described in detail in an interim report on this enquiry.[1] The 1945 estimates were based on material collected in the colony in the course of enquiries made under the terms of a Colonial Research Fellowship in 1946 and 1947. They are described in detail in an Appendix to this volume.[2]

A comparison of the 1938 figures given in Tables 17 and 18 with the corresponding tables in the interim report reveals certain differences in the two sets of figures. Lest this should give the second thoughts the appearance of being wiser than they are, it is important to emphasize that no major changes have been made in the original estimates. The only change of substance was an upward revision of about 50% in the estimates for African village industry and forest products. This put up the estimate for total territorial income by about 1% and the estimate

---

[1] *The Measurement of Colonial National Incomes*, by Phyllis Deane, Occasional Paper XII, published for the National Institute of Economic and Social Research by Cambridge University Press, 1948. Especially pp. 64–7.

[2] See below, pp. 230–302.

for national (residents') income by nearly 2%. The other differences are due to rearrangements of the material or a change in the definitions for certain items to bring them more into line with the definitions adopted in making the 1945 estimates.

Unfortunately, apart from this minor and still fairly arbitrary change relating to village industry, it was not possible usefully to revise the estimates originally made for 1938. I should not therefore wish to add to or detract from any of the warnings made about their reliability in the course of the interim report. They are certainly not as satisfactory as those made for 1945—and even these must be treated with considerable caution, particularly in their finer breakdowns. I found no evidence when in the colony to suggest that they gave a distorted picture of the economic situation in 1938.

In view of these warnings it would be unwise to place much weight on detailed comparisons between the 1938 and 1945 figures, although very broad comparisons are attempted below. Similarly, 1948 estimates, based on the 1945 figures brought up to date with the aid of published material available in the United Kingdom in early 1950, will not support detailed comparisons. However, the estimates do provide a broadly reliable reflection of the changes which have taken place in the economy over the past decade.

It would seem that the aggregate incomes of residents increased by nearly 118% between 1938 and 1945 and by a further 40% between 1945 and 1948. It cannot, of course, be assumed that real incomes increased in anything like the same proportion, but as there are no reliable price indices it is impossible to attempt a quantitative measure of the changes in real income. Even if there were adequate price data and the totals could be deflated accordingly, they would throw very little light on the change in real incomes for the rural communities since there is insufficient information on the content of their standard of living in 1938. More will be said in Part IV about the content of the rural standard of living and it may be possible at some future date to attempt some measure of comparison with the 1947 level described there. At present comparisons can be made only in terms of the consumption of imported goods. In normal times a study of the territory's imports would be an incomplete but nevertheless significant indication of changes in the standard of living. Over the war and immediate post-war period, however, when imports were artificially restricted and purchasing power was driven into other channels, the trade statistics are a very unsatisfactory guide to trends in real incomes. It is nevertheless interesting to note that imports of cotton piece goods increased from 11 million yards in 1947 to 19.4 million yards in 1948.

Territorial incomes (geographical product) also increased, but at a

TABLE 17. (a) National (residents') income, output and (b) ...

(In thousands of pounds)

Residents' incomes	1938	1945
Incomes of:		
1. European individuals and local companies	4,071	5,916
2. Other non-Africans	74	325
3. Africans	3,529	10,270
4. Government (including receipts from foreign taxpayers)	820	1,989
5. Total national income	8,494	18,500

Residents' output	1938	1945
Net output of:		
6. Mining	2,484	3,908
7. Agriculture and livestock	2,000	5,590
8. Manufacture, building, forestry	321	1,400
9. Distribution and transport	1,304	1,659
10. Government	627	1,645
11. Income from abroad (including income tax)	784	2,397
12. Other goods and services	974	1,901
13. Total national output	8,494	18,500

Residents' outlay	1938	1945
Personal consumption:		
14. Cash expenditure at market price	4,627	9,109
15. Less indirect taxes	−465	−799
16. Plus subsidies	—	136
17. Domestic cash expenditure at factor cost	4,162	8,446
18. Subsistence consumption	1,891	4,734
19. Expenditure abroad by individuals	774	1,482
20. Total personal consumption	6,827	14,662
21. Government current expenditure at home and abroad	1,345	2,080
22. Investment and saving	322	1,758
23. Total national outlay	8,494	18,500

(b) Residents' balance of payments, 1938 and 1945

Receipts from non-residents	1938	1945
1. Exports of domestic produce	463	410
2. Sale of goods and services to non-residents in colony	3,193	4,500
3. Income from abroad	784	2,397
4. Tourists and missions	156	140
5. Residual	272	232
6. Total receipts from non-residents	4,868	7,679

Payments to non-residents	1938	1945
7. Retained imports by residents	3,244	4,815
8. Expenditure abroad	1,046	1,873
9. Investment abroad	578	991
10. Total payments to non-residents	4,868	7,679

TABLE 18. (a) National (territorial) income, output and outlay of Northern Rhodesia, 1938 and 1945

(In thousands of pounds)

Territorial income	1938	1945
Incomes of:		
1. European individuals	3,768	5,666
2. Other non-Africans	74	325
3. Africans	3,529	10,270
4. Companies	5,954	5,400
5. Government	175	339
6. Total territorial incomes	13,500	22,000

Territorial output	1938	1945
Net output of:		
7. Mining	7,353	7,417
8. Agriculture and livestock		
(a) European	197	600
(b) African	1,803	4,990
9. Forestry and sawmilling	200	970
10. Manufacture and building	121	450
11. African village industries and miscellaneous independent work	206	896
12. Distribution	745	2,072
13. Transport	1,066	1,148
14. Government	899	1,645
15. Miscellaneous services	771	1,060
16. Income from abroad	139	752
17. Total territorial output	13,500	22,000

Territorial outlay	1938	1945
Personal cash expenditure on:		
18. Food, drink and tobacco	1,937	3,781
19. Clothing, footwear, etc.	1,079	2,835
20. Other local produce	1,611	2,493
21. Total at market price	4,627	9,109
22. Less indirect taxes	−465	−799
23. Plus subsidies	—	136
24. Total at factor cost	4,162	8,446
25. Subsistence consumption	1,891	4,734
26. Government current expenditure	973	1,689
27. Expenditure abroad by		
(a) Individuals	774	1,482
(b) Government	272	391
28. Investment, saving, and remittances abroad by non-resident companies	5,428	5,258
29. Total territorial outlay	13,500	22,000

(b) Territorial balance of payments, 1938 and 1945

Receipts from abroad	1938	1945
1. Value of domestic merchandise at border	9,340	12,285
2. Expenditure by tourists and missions	156	140
3. Income from abroad	139	752
4. Total receipts from abroad	9,635	13,177

Payments abroad	1938	1945
5. Value of retained imports at border	7,023	9,000
6. Expenditure abroad	1,046	1,873
7. Net commercial remittances and expenditure abroad	1,566	2,304
8. Total payments abroad	9,635	13,177

different pace. Thus the value of the geographical product increased by a greater amount in the three years 1945 to 1948 than in the seven years 1938 to 1945, thereby reflecting the post-war trend in world mineral prices. The increase was 63% between 1938 and 1945 and 77% between 1945 and 1948. Real geographical product rose a great deal less rapidly than its money value; it was probably slightly smaller in 1945 than in 1938 and was less than a third higher in 1948. Output of copper—the principal contributor to the money product—fell in 1945 to about 75% of its 1938 volume and by 1948 was only 22% above the pre-war level.

The following table shows the estimated change in the distribution of residents' and territorial incomes over the period.

TABLE 19. Changes in distribution of national product, 1938–48

(In percentages)

	1938 %	1945 %	1948 %
(a) Residents' incomes			
1. European individuals and local companies	48	32	40
2. Other non-Africans	1	$1\frac{1}{2}$	2
3. Africans	$41\frac{1}{2}$	$55\frac{1}{2}$	44
4. Government (including receipts from non-resident taxpayers)	$9\frac{1}{2}$	11	14
5. Total national income	100	100	100
(b) Territorial incomes			
1. European individuals	28	26	26
2. Other non-Africans	$\frac{1}{2}$	$1\frac{1}{2}$	$1\frac{1}{2}$
3. Africans	26	$46\frac{1}{2}$	$29\frac{1}{2}$
4. Companies	44	$24\frac{1}{2}$	42
5. Government	$1\frac{1}{2}$	$1\frac{1}{2}$	1
6. Total geographical product	100	100	100

It will be seen that the war changed the shape of the Northern Rhodesian economy but that it has since shown a tendency to revert to its 1938 pattern. The net change, over the whole period, amounted to a small increase in the share of the African community at the expense of European individuals and companies: this is the more significant in that the European population increased faster than the African population. The Asian share has remained small and has tended to increase, but not faster than the Asian proportion of the population. Government's share in the incomes retained in the colony is a good deal higher—largely as a result of the new double taxation arrangements which permit the colonial government to retain the full value of its company rate of tax, leaving only the difference between the colonial and United Kingdom rate to flow to the United Kingdom. This has

F

tended to offset the decline in the proportion of the national income over which Government has command, a tendency to decline which must inevitably result from a shifting of the balance in favour of the African community unaccompanied by a progressive rate of tax on Africans.

The shape of the balance of payments account seems to have changed relatively little over the period. A fall in the value of exports of domestic produce (other than minerals) between 1938 and 1945 reflects the greater effective demand of the home market. By 1948, tobacco exports, stimulated by high world prices, had provided an important source of income, and domestic exports other than minerals exceeded a million pounds in value. The increase in the value of income from abroad in the residents' balance of payments between 1938 and 1945 is mainly due to the relatively high government receipts from taxation, an inward flow that continued to increase after 1945. However, it illustrates also the inward flow of army remittances and gratuities which reached their peak in 1945–6, and the increased rates of pay in Union and Southern Rhodesian mines, which continue to rise.

In 1945 the industrial economy was cramped and confined by war-time shortages of skilled labour, capital equipment and materials. Since then it has burst most of the bonds which held it at the end of the war, although industrial expansion is still hindered by lack of basic resources, which—in conjunction with the colony's relatively inaccessible position —keeps it chronically short of some essentials, such as skilled labour, some types of heavy equipment, coal, etc. Table 20 shows the position in 1948 when easier supply conditions enabled industry to respond more effectively to vigorous world demand. Wartime distortions which gave an overweighted importance to agriculture and government were disappearing.[1] Secondary industry, building, distribution and transport were advancing in step with the expanding mining industry. In rela-tive, although not, of course, in absolute, terms, the African share of the territorial product was falling to the 1938 level.

Apart from the increase in the relative importance of secondary industry and building which accompanied the increase in the European population, there is a striking similarity about the structure of the Northern Rhodesian economy in 1938 and in 1948. Once again, the picture is one of an unbalanced economy in which roughly half the value of the geographical product is due to one industry and in which the development of other industries is geared to the dominating one. In terms of the value of capital invested, and of product arising within

---

[1] Both agriculture and government maintained a new high absolute level of output compared with 1938. It is in relative importance that they have recently fallen towards the 1938 levels.

its borders, the development of the Northern Rhodesian economy has been considerable. In rather more than ten years the geographical product has almost trebled. By 1949, gross investment in private building was at the rate of between £2 and £3 millions per annum. Imports of mining, electrical and industrial machinery in 1949 reached over £3¼ millions, with a further £1 million for motor vehicles. In addition, Government, financed in part by Colonial Development and Welfare Funds, but even more by the immense tax revenue it can obtain from the mining industry, is operating a ten-year development plan estimated (in 1948) to cost £17 millions. By colonial standards and for a population of about two millions, all this adds up to an astonishingly high rate of investment.

TABLE 20. Territorial output in Northern Rhodesia, 1938–48

	1938		1945		1948	
	£m.	%	£m.	%	£m.	%
Mining	7.4	54.8	7.4	33.6	18.5	47.4
Agriculture and livestock	2.0	14.8	5.6	25.5	6.2	15.9
Forestry, manufacture, building, etc.	0.3	2.2	1.4	6.4	2.7	6.9
African village industry, etc.	0.2	1.5	0.9	4.1	0.9	2.3
Distribution and transport	1.8	13.4	3.2	14.5	5.7	14.6
Government	0.9	6.7	1.6	7.3	2.5	6.4
Income from abroad	0.1	0.7	0.8	3.6	1.2	3.1
Other	0.8	5.9	1.1	5.0	1.3	3.3
	13.5		22.0		39.0	

The most striking feature of it all is the localized nature of private investment. Development has been development in the Copperbelt, or on a narrow belt of country along the railway line, following the mining industry's channel of communication with the outside world. The velocity of this development is a function of the world market price for minerals, for copper in particular. Beyond the railway belt Northern Rhodesia was in 1948, as in 1938, an underdeveloped area. The problem of developing this backward hinterland in which the bulk of the population live is the most important and most difficult of the problems facing the colony.

In 1945 it was estimated that the resident community was saving under 10% of its annual income. If we assume that the African contribution to this investment was negligible, which is a reasonable assumption,[1] the non-African community (including government) was saving at the rate of more than 20%, a proportion which approximates to the current target for the United Kingdom. Bearing in mind that

[1] African expenditure on bicycles, ploughs, sewing machines, etc., has been treated as consumption expenditure, because it would be impossible to distinguish investment expenditure by Africans without a special enquiry devoted to the purpose.

the non-African community is partly composed of temporary residents who may well prefer to invest in their country of origin or retirement rather than in the colony, it seems unlikely that there can be any substantial increase in investment from this source. An increase in the rate of investment over the underdeveloped mass of the country depends either on increasing the proportion of African income which can be diverted to investment purposes, or on increasing the rate of government investment. Since in any case the only Africans who have an appreciable surplus over current consumption needs are likely to be those who are living in or near the railway belt, the prospect of financing investment in the underdeveloped areas from this source depends on the extent to which government is prepared to channel the resources.

In sum, therefore, we can conclude that the future economic progress of the colony depends primarily on the adequacy of the resources at the disposal of government and on the effectiveness with which it uses them. This is true for most colonies, but it is in danger of being overlooked for a territory where the rate and magnitude of the spontaneous development tends to obscure the fact that it is an insignificant factor in the lives of the majority of the population. It is doubtful whether this spontaneous local development benefits the remoter areas of the territory any more than the developments which take place in Southern Rhodesia or the Union of South Africa. The migrants who leave their Northern Rhodesian villages for the railway line have less distance to cover than those who go to the Rand gold mines, but they earn less. The urban markets provide a market for cash crops produced by Africans within reach of the railway belt, but with the present levels of yield and the tendency for soil to deteriorate through overploughing, the existence of a ready and profitable market is not an unmixed blessing for the community as a whole.

The poverty of the mass of the people reflects a fundamental poverty of resources. Again, if we exclude the mineral wealth of the territory, whose benefits tend to be concentrated in a relatively small area, and the European tobacco industry, the colony has no resources which could immediately be put to good account on the world market. Its soil is poor and is afflicted in many areas by soil erosion and tsetse fly; its indigenous peoples have no special skills and are retarded by malnutrition and malaria; its immigrant peoples are for the most part temporary migrants and the community already shows a tendency to divide against itself to the detriment of the national productivity—as for example when the European workers oppose training of Africans for responsible jobs and when African farmers defend their backwardness with reference to the better lands on European farms.

The most urgent need is to effect an improvement in the productivity of the indigenous peoples. To some extent this must await the long-term results of an intensive policy of improvement in the social services— by improved education, by vocational training, and by better medical services. The problem which stands in the way of any short-term improvement in productivity and standards of living, however, is the problem of improving the yield of agriculture in its broadest sense.

The Northern Rhodesia Ten-Year Development Plan[1] lays special emphasis on the development of agriculture and of the rural areas. In the review of the revised plan approved by the Legislative Council in June 1948 it was stated that the prime objectives in their order of importance were:

(1) increased food production
(2) more housing, European and African
(3) improved roads

and the report added: 'By way of explanation of the above immediate priorities it should be stated that the Territory is at present a net importer of *all* foodstuffs, African and European: that the recruitment of essential technical, scientific and professional staff required for the development of the Territory, particularly for increased production, has had to be postponed or curtailed for lack of housing (and office) accommodation: that the main roads of the Territory are in most cases incapable of carrying efficiently and through all weathers the present traffic, let alone the increase expected from development.' An additional argument in favour of pursuing road development as a primary objective was the fact that it could be tackled immediately 'thanks to the availability in the Territory of civil engineering contractors equipped with modern mechanical road plant, and that roads represented a lasting and visible physical asset which was at the same time essential to development'.

Table 21 gives a summary analysis of the revised ten-year plan and compares it with the original proposals made in 1946–7. Revision of the plan was part of the process of adjustment to a situation in which net geographical product had risen from about £22 millions to £39 millions. It thus reflects the inflation in costs and revenues produced by the post-war boom already described.

The main changes introduced into Northern Rhodesia's Ten-Year Plan by the revised proposals lie in the increased allocation for buildings and road development. This represents a further shift of emphasis in favour of the railway belt. In so far as it represents concessions to the increased prices and the shortages which affect railway-belt develop-

[1] See *Ten-year Development Plan for Northern Rhodesia*, Government Printer, Lusaka, 1947, and *Review of the Ten-year Development Plan*, Government Printer, Lusaka, 1948.

ment more than rural development it is perhaps inevitable. In spite, however, of the avowed emphasis on agricultural and rural development, the financial provisions show a tendency to perpetuate the bias which is already a pronounced feature of the economy.

TABLE 21. Northern Rhodesia Ten-Year Development Plan

	Original (1946) allocation £ millions	Revised (1948) allocation £ millions
1. Social services	3.50	3.70
2. Economic services	2.10	2.00
3. Rural development	1.50	1.50
4. Communications	1.80	2.90
5. Water development	1.00	1.00
6. Economic development	0.50	0.50
7. Loans to local authorities	0.50	0.50
8. Buildings	2.20	3.80
9. Unallocated	0.15	1.10
10. Total	13.25	17.00

If the Zambesi hydro-electric schemes that are now being investigated are approved there will be some shift of emphasis from the northern part of the territory to the southern part, but development will still be largely concentrated within the vicinity of the present railway belt. The rail link between Kafue and Salisbury will open up a wider area of Southern Province and probably increase the cash cropping area, but will not greatly change the economic map of the territory. On the other hand, the proposed link with the East African railway system or with the groundnut areas would bring a railway line through the backward areas of Northern Province. It is difficult to see precisely how much spontaneous advantage could be taken of this outlet in view of the apparently poor resources of the area, but it seems likely that it will help to check the drain of able-bodied men out of the area and thereby increase local output and consumption. It may also be possible to establish a trade in the export of dried fish to the development areas of Tanganyika if the proposed rail link materializes.

The proposed developments leave Barotseland still very much a backwater. The Province has always been starved of agricultural officers. This is unfortunate, for the area of the Barotse flood plain is probably the richest in resources and variety of resources in the whole territory. Even now there is a flourishing internal trade and the Lozi are well known to be keen and lively traders. It would seem well worth while conducting a special investigation into the potentialities of this area, which might prove a more effective starting-point for indigenous development than any other and would certainly offer an interesting site for an experimental rural Development Centre of the type suggested in the Plan.

More will be said about the rural communities in Part IV and the concluding chapters. At this stage it seems sufficient to emphasize that in terms of the numbers involved the rural areas constitute the most important sector of the economy, that rural standards of living are exceedingly low, and that their rate of improvement over the past decade or so has been imperceptible by the admittedly scanty data available for their measurement. Nor indeed are the resources now being devoted to their improvement large in relation to the total disposable or potentially disposable resources of government.

PART III

THE NYASALAND ECONOMY

CHAPTER VI

THE COLONY AND ITS PEOPLE

Nyasaland is a narrow strip of landlocked territory some 520 miles long and 50 to 100 miles broad, which lies along the eastern border of Northern Rhodesia. At the north-east it borders on Tanganyika, and in the east, south-east and south-west its neighbour is Portuguese East Africa. Its total area is only 37,000 sq. miles, and of this about a third is accounted for by Lake Nyasa, which is 360 miles long and 10 to 50 miles wide. This lake, the colony's most striking natural feature, is almost an inland sea. It has a maximum depth estimated at about 2,300 ft., and a variable level over a range of nearly 20 ft. At the southern end of the lake the River Shiré runs south to join the Zambesi in Portuguese territory.

In the early days of missionary and trading enterprise the normal means of access to the Colony was by steamer on the River Shiré. When Livingstone was in Nyasaland the water route from the extreme south of the territory to the extreme north was interrupted only by a sixty-mile stretch where porterage was necessary to skirt the Murchison Rapids. Since then, however, the level of the River Shiré has been steadily falling. By 1889, when the discovery of a navigable route through the Zambesi delta linked Nyasaland to the Indian Ocean by international waterway, the Lower Shiré had fallen so low that the steamer could not go beyond Chiromo. Now the level of the Upper Shiré has also fallen, to such an extent that steamer traffic is impossible outside Lake Nyasa.

From the lake, which is 1,500 ft. above sea-level, the sides of the Great Rift Valley rise steeply to high plateaux of 3,000 to 4,000 ft. on the west and 8,000 ft. in the far north. The country south of the lake, the Southern Highlands, is the richest and most thickly populated part of Nyasaland, with an average elevation in the region of 3,000 ft., rising to 7,000 ft. on Zomba mountain and more than 10,000 ft. on Mlanje mountain. In the extreme south the Shiré is only 120 ft. above sea-level. If, however, the 3,000 ft. contour is accepted as the limit of health or habitability for Europeans, then over 70% of the country is healthy enough for white settlement.

The climate varies widely with height and humidity. On the lake shore the temperature is normally not above 100°, but the humidity makes it trying to live in. In the extreme south, in the Shiré valley, the temperature rises to 115° in the hot season. Over most of Nyasaland, however, the temperature is equable enough, and even those who have to work in the hot valleys can take periodic refuge in higher country not many miles away. The day temperature in the uplands is rarely very high, and on winter evenings fires are generally a necessity. There is a well-defined summer rainy season which is expected to occur from November to April, but the start of the rains is often uncertain and the colony suffers in the wet season from locally violent storms, sometimes of a catastrophic nature. In the Southern Highlands the normal summer rains are supplemented by winter rain in the form of heavy scotch mists (locally known as Chiperonis) lasting several days at a time.

In this little country, which is only about three-quarters the size of England and whose cultivable area is reduced by 11,000 sq. miles of water and by stretches of mountainous country, there are roughly two and a half million people. This is a dense population by African standards. There are more people in Nyasaland than in the whole of Northern Rhodesia, which has more than ten times its land area. At the time of the 1945 Census the density of population in Southern Province was about eighty-three persons per square mile.

As the following summary of the results of the 1945 Census shows, Nyasaland is predominantly a country of Africans. The small communities of Europeans and Indians, however, exert an influence on the political economy of the Colony which is large out of all proportion to their numbers. In this table 'adult' means Africans over eighteen years of age and Europeans and Asians over twenty.

TABLE 22. Population of Nyasaland at the 1945 Census

(excluding absentees)

	Adult males	Adult females	Children	Total
African	387,861	567,426	1,089,420	2,044,707
European	898	691	359	1,948
Asian	1,186	427	1,191	2,804
Other non-Africans	60	67	328	455

Until the present century the colony lay in the track of many migrating tribes and of the Arab slave traders. Nineteenth-century Nyasaland was described in the Bell report as 'a whirlpool of migrant tribes, war and slave trading'. A certain amount of movement is still going on. It is estimated that in the past twenty-five years the population has nearly doubled, largely as a result of immigration from Portuguese East Africa of labourers and their families attracted by the opportunities of employment on the tea estates. There has also been a small increase in the immigrant populations of Europeans and Asians. Table 23 gives some indication of the pattern of population change since the beginning of the present century.

TABLE 23. Population of Nyasaland since 1911
(excluding absentees)

Census year	Europeans	Asians	Africans
1911	766	481	969,200
1921	1,486	563	1,199,900
1931	1,975	1,591	1,599,900
1945	1,948	2,804	2,044,700
1949 (estimate)	3,500	4,300	2,300,000

The chief African tribes in the territory are the Chewa (28%), Lomwe (19%), Nyanja (15%), Yao (14%), Ngoni (9%), and Tumbuka (6%). There has been a marked tendency to intermarriage, however, especially in the Shiré Highlands of Southern Province, which has tended to blur the tribal distinctions. The Director of the 1945 Census reported that 'Nyasaland Askarai, who in the past were referred to as Yaos, are now popularly known in East Africa as the Wa Nyasa, whereas no such territorial nomenclature is heard of in speaking of African peoples in other East African Colonies and Dependencies.'

The Nyasaland African is a wanderer by tradition and necessity. It is estimated that about 140,000 men were away from the colony in 1948 and if we allow for a seasonal migration to European agricultural estates within the colony at times of harvest and other heavy pressure of work, the numbers of men away from their homes at any given time must approach an average of 50% over the territory as a whole. In the far north, often called 'the dead north' because there are few local opportuniites for economic advancement, the proportion is even higher.

The European population, most of which is resident in the Southern Highlands, has shown little change in size over the past twenty years, although there has been a noticeable increase since the end of the war. It is not certain, however, that this recent increase reflects a significantly higher rate of European immigration or settlement, for it can be largely attributed to the overdue recruitment of staffs after the lean war period. Of the 259 immigrants between May 1945 and December 1946, for example, only thirty-seven were definitely classified as concerned with agriculture and 123 were government servants or missionaries. Of the remainder, most filled the backlog of vacancies in commercial concerns, although there was a certain amount of immigration to new concerns. It is still true that most Europeans in Nyasaland aim to retire abroad, a feature which is reflected in the relatively high proportion of people of working age. Two-thirds of the Europeans are between twenty and sixty years old. Nevertheless there is a growing nucleus of permanent settlers. Fifteen per cent of the Europeans are Nyasaland born, rather less than half come from the British Isles and of the remainder most originate in the Rhodesias or the Union.

The Asian population, like the European population, is an immigrant community which has maintained strong ties with its homeland. There are signs, however, of a marked tendency to settle permanently. It is estimated that more than a third of the 1947 population is Nyasaland born, and it is significant that of the 275 new arrivals in 1947 over 60% were females.

Generally speaking, the population of Nyasaland is a rural population. There are no large towns, although there are four European townships with several hundred Europeans and Asians—Blantyre, Limbe, Zomba (the administrative capital) and Lilongwe. These, however, are small concentrations of people rather than genuine towns. It can fairly be said that there are no urbanized Africans in Nyasaland, for even those who live and work in the European townships normally have a small garden on which the worker's family can supply its and his major food needs. Nearly 14,000 Africans were classified as urban in this limited sense at the 1945 Census, and of these over 70% lived in Blantyre or Limbe. In addition, about half the European and Asian population lived in the four main 'towns', giving them a total population in the region of about 18,000.

At the 1945 Census it was estimated that there were 390,000 African adult males in Nyasaland and a further 123,000 at work outside the territory. By the end of 1948 there were probably about 430,000 adult males in the colony and 140,000 men at work abroad. As in Northern Rhodesia, the African man tends to be the chief earner and the woman is mainly engaged in subsistence agriculture. She earns some cash income through sales of beer and food crops such as groundnuts, and in the harvesting and tobacco-grading seasons women and children work for wages in the fields and in the grading sheds. Women and children also take short-term jobs at brickmaking, building and other unskilled manual work in the farming areas.

Since no African labour census has been taken it is difficult to obtain a clear picture of the occupational distribution of the working population. In any case the majority of the people are engaged for a large part of their working lives in subsistence agriculture, and for many of them cash-earning activities tend to be temporary occupations in which they neither specialize nor settle. By building up details of numbers engaged from a variety of sources we get a picture of the industrial distribution on the following broad lines.

In interpreting Table 24 it must be remembered that there is some overlap between the items because these are gross employment and not average employment figures, i.e. they include people in short-term occupations who may have gone from one occupation to another within the year. They also include child and female labour engaged in seasonal agricultural work. The totals leave roughly 100,000 adult males unaccounted for. Most of these would be in receipt of some cash income from the sale of minor produce and livestock, and many would be migrant labourers 'resting' between visits to areas of employment abroad or returned soldiers.

TABLE 24. Estimated numbers of Africans in receipt of cash income in 1945 and 1948

	1945	1948
European agriculture (including tobacco and tea factories)	64,000	74,000
Government	29,000	25,000
Distribution	16,500	18,000
Missions	14,000	15,000
Transport	5,500	7,000
Domestic service	5,000	9,000
Other	1,000	2,000
Total employed in Nyasaland	135,000	150,000
Employed abroad (including armed forces)	142,000	140,000
Tobacco growers	89,000	94,000
Cotton growers	43,000	47,000
Others engaged in sale of goods or services (e.g. fishing, hawking, livestock, etc.)	35,000	38,000
Total (including seasonal and child labour)	444,000	469,000

Table 24 suggests that the majority of Africans in Nyasaland obtain their cash incomes from some kind of agricultural activity. Indeed, the picture presented there understates the dependence on agriculture, for the majority of those who have been counted as engaged in some kind of employment are primarily concerned in subsistence agriculture. Most even of those who are employed full-time in non-agricultural activities have families fully occupied in agriculture.

The small European working population in Nyasaland consists of a group of relatively highly skilled people. Of the 1,948 who were in the colony at the time of the 1945 Census 359 were under the age of twenty. There were almost 500 married households in the community and probably as many as 550 single households. The number of gainfully occupied Europeans was 1,162 of which 305 were women. In addition there were estimated to be thirty-eight individuals who were either away on leave or on active service but who continued to draw salaries from the colony. The summary of industrial distribution of the gainfully occupied European population of Nyasaland shown in Table 25 includes persons away on leave or active service. The 1945 figures are based on the Census returns, but Table 25 also includes an estimate of the industrial distribution in 1947. By 1949 it is estimated that over 2,000 Europeans were gainfully occupied in Nyasaland.

TABLE 25.   Industrial distribution of gainfully occupied European population in 1945 and 1947

	1945			Estimated total 1947
	Working on own account	Employed	Total	
1. Agriculture	87	170	257	300
2. Government service (including forces)	—	348	348	350
3. Missions	—	275	275	330
4. Trade and other industries	70	250	320	420
	157	1,043	1,200	1,400

The majority of those recorded in the Census as engaged in 'trade and other industries' were in the transport and distributive trades. Very few are engaged in manufacture (fifteen at the time of the 1945 Census) or in mining (two at the time of the Census). In effect, the bulk of the European community is engaged in supplying services. More than three-quarters of the gainfully occupied Europeans are in the so-called tertiary industries.

This is also true of the Asian population. Most of the Indians in Nyasaland are engaged in the distributive trade. They have shops in all the main townships and there are small Indian stores serving rural populations throughout the territory. In addition there is a small group of Indians engaged in professional and clerical occupations and another small group in agriculture. Eighty-eight Indians were engaged in road and rail transport undertakings in 1945: most of the railway station staffs are Indian.

Apart from the three main racial groups there is a small community of Coloured people, i.e. persons of mixed racial origin, estimated at about 2,000 persons in 1945. Of these about half are above marriageable age and it is estimated that only about a third maintain a European mode of life. Only 455 were recorded at the Census as non-African, but this is simply the number of Coloured persons in families of mixed origin where the head pays the non-African poll tax. The majority of the Coloured population was counted with the African population. The Coloured men are mainly engaged in trading, transport and agriculture, and some of the women are employed as children's nurses. At the time of the 1945 Census sixty-four Coloured persons were recorded as 'gainfully occupied'. Those who were not recorded separately as Coloured at the Census were probably primarily engaged in agriculture.

In Nyasaland as in other parts of East and Central Africa the three main racial groups live at different standards of living and within different cultural patterns. The smallest of the three groups, the Europeans, is the most influential within the framework of the money economy. With the exception of some missionaries whose standards of life are austere in the extreme it can be said that the majority of European individuals in Nyasaland live at a uniformly high standard of living in most material respects. Table 26 gives an estimated income distribution for European earners in Nyasaland for the year 1945. Since most European earners are assessed for income tax purposes these figures, although not accurate, can be taken as a fair reflection of the level and distribution of European earnings in 1945. The level has almost certainly risen since 1945, but there is no reason to assume that the rise has been significant or that there has been a change in the broad pattern of income distribution.

TABLE 26. Estimated distribution of earned cash incomes received by European residents in 1945

Income group	Earners Nos.	Average cash earnings £
Under £400	484	248
£400 to £599	287	491
£600 to £799	169	692
£800 to £999	97	907
£1,000 to £1,499	65	1,215
£1,500 to £1,999	26	1,731
£2,000 and over	34	3,382
Totals	1,162	£607

Thus it is estimated that the earned cash incomes of European residents averaged over £600 per earner and over £670 per household. If we add to the above earned cash incomes the value of unearned incomes (i.e. pensions, interest, rent), of subsistence incomes (i.e. food produced by missionaries and farmers for own consumption and annual value of rent-free or owner-occupied houses), and of incomes paid to persons abroad on leave or on active service the average level of earnings was about £735 per European recipient of income or about £450 per head of the population. This is a high general level of earnings even for Europeans in Central Africa. It is higher than the average estimated for Northern Rhodesia although it cannot be assumed that the opportunities for earning high-level incomes in Nyasaland were more than (if indeed they were as much as) those prevailing in Northern Rhodesia. The higher average can be attributed to the smaller proportion earning low-level incomes.

Table 27 gives estimates of the way in which the European population laid out this income of about £888,000 (including the unearned incomes and the subsistence incomes) and estimates saving as a residual. By 1949 the European population was probably earning at the rate of £1½ millions per annum.

TABLE 27.   Estimated pattern of European expenditure in Nyasaland, 1945

	Value of consumption or expenditure £	Value per household of consumption or expenditure £
1. Food and tobacco	150,000	143
2. Drink	102,000	97
3. Clothing	60,000	57
4. Rents, rates, etc.	33,000	31
5. Servants	35,000	33
6. Other household expenses	60,000	57
7. Insurance	35,000	33
8. Education	32,000	30
9. Leave, dependants and other expenditure abroad (including pensions)	150,000	143
10. Other consumption expenditure	120,000	114
11. Direct taxes	78,000	74
12. Saving	26,000	25

Two qualifications should be made in considering this table. The first is that it includes under item 9 the incomes of pension holders who are not residents of Nyasaland. On the other hand their incomes can be regarded as some index of the pension rights accruing during the year to present residents and thus of an important item in their hidden emoluments. Secondly, in considering the proportion that the various items bear to total expenditure it must be remembered that Nyasaland's shopping facilities are limited and a considerable amount of expenditure on such items as clothing, household furnishings and other essential items is undertaken when on leave, so that it appears in item 9.

In terms of most material things the standard of living of the European population is high. There was no war-time rationing of clothes or food, although shortages (usually of a temporary nature) have occurred in certain items from time to time. On the other hand, prices and social commitments are also at a high level and, in fact, most Europeans appear to live up to or near the full limits of their incomes. The high cost of education, insurance, holidays, is significant. There seems to have been little, if any, margin for real saving in 1945 as opposed to saving for expenditure (e.g. leave or insurance expenditure and the saving of 'hidden emoluments' for pension purposes). Moreover, in terms of many of the amenities which communities of a similar basic standard of living elsewhere would take for granted the Nyasaland Europeans are poor. Waterborne sanitation is rare. Electricity is available only in the immediate vicinity of the main townships. Roads are poor. Until recently there was no bus service and in a territory where other facilities (for example, shopping facilities) are sparse this is a serious disadvantage. The commercial centres of Blantyre and Limbe, for example, are some forty miles or so away from the administrative capital of Zomba where shopping facilities are severely limited to a few 'general' stores. Cultural and other facilities are also of a lower quality than the European community would expect in its place of origin.

To a lesser extent, perhaps, this kind of consideration applies also to the other immigrant community in Nyasaland, the Indians. They, too, lack many of the amenities which they might expect to enjoy in their home country. On the other hand the Indian community has within itself a much wider range of variation in standards of living. In 1945–6 the young shop assistant, fresh from India, earned a net cash income in the region of £3 per month, together with food (often of indifferent quality), and lodging which generally amounted to the duty of sleeping in the store and thus of acting as a kind of night watchman. The minimum rate of wages recommended by the Indian Chamber of Commerce in 1946 amounted to an inclusive minimum gross wage of £8 per month. Since the new shop assistant is usually brought from India on a three years' contract this would amount to about £75 per annum (excluding the value of the return passage to India) for the first three years' service. At the other end of the scale there were the 139 Indians assessed to tax in 1945 who reported average 1944 incomes of nearly £1,600 apiece. Between these two extremes there are a number of railway workers (stationmasters, clerks, etc.) earning at the rate of £200 to £300 per annum, a small group of professional workers whose incomes are unknown, and a host of traders engaged in a variety of kinds and scales of trading activity.

The average income for the whole Indian community in 1945 was estimated to be rather more than £460 per annum per man earning. (Indian women's earnings are negligible.) In view of the variation in standards of income average figures of Asian expenditure are not particularly significant,[1] but it may be noted that this community is estimated to have a relatively high rate of saving and investment. It was estimated that the Asians saved or invested or remitted abroad more

[1] A rough income distribution Table is given in Appendix I. See below, p. 245.

G

than 47% of their annual income in 1945 and that they spent about 11% on direct taxation. This implies that Asian standards of consumption do not show such a wide variation as their standards of income. Unfortunately the information on Asian outlay was particularly unsatisfactory and these conclusions are merely tentative.

African standards of living vary according to area of residence and occupation of earner. In 1945 the average value of income per household was in the region of £14 per annum and per head of the population it was about £3.5. Of this £14 about £8.2 was attributable to subsistence income together with inter-village trade and barter trade. By 1948 African incomes had risen above £4 per head. Subsistence income was a substantial element in total income for almost all Nyasaland Africans, since most, even of those at work in the townships and in the higher-paid occupations, had families producing food. Thus a clerk earning £5 a month in Blantyre and having a food-producing family within walking distance has no commitments in the way of basic food or housing to meet out of his monthly wage. His standard of living compares favourably with that of the farmer or even of the agricultural labourer on a private estate.

Some idea of the pattern of income distribution in 1945 among the higher income groups can be obtained from the following table, which is a composite table for the employees of central government and missions. It covers all but a very few of the Africans in the highest income groups. The vast majority of other earners would figure in the '£12 and under' group if a complete income distribution table were compiled.

TABLE 28. Estimated distribution of income among African employees of Central Government and missions, 1945

Income group	Numbers	Average earnings £
£12 and under	19,844	7.5
£13 to £20	3,157	15.7
£21 to £30	759	25.0
£31 and over	650	46.2
Totals	24,410	£10.4

To get some idea of the true level of income in these groups we must add about £8 per household for subsistence incomes of all kinds, including crops, livestock, in some areas fish, tobacco, beer, village industries, and so on. Some employed persons were able to engage in trade of crops, livestock, beer, and other such produce and so supplemented their incomes by this means. By 1948 there had been an upward shift in all incomes and a significant increase in the proportion of those in the £13 to £20 a year group, but it was still true that the majority earned a cash total of £12 or less during the year.

Most other groups in the African community earned at a lower rate than those in central government and mission service. Domestic servants, for example, earned an estimated overall average (in cash and in kind) of nearly £8½ per annum in 1945 and £12 in 1948, and other kinds of non-agricultural employees about £7½ and £10 respectively. Not all these, however, were adult men. A number of children were in employment on a casual basis as garden boys, shop boys, messengers, etc., many being employed for less than a full year. This qualification— that the average earnings from employment is not the same as the average rate of earnings in employment—applies even more strongly to agriculture where so much of the labour is seasonal labour, where there is a high turnover and where there are many women and children in employment for the two or three months of the harvest.

Nevertheless, if we allow for the value of subsistence production, estimated at £8.2 per household in 1945, and remember that employment and, indeed, any cash-earning occupation is often a sudsidiary activity, we can form some idea of the level of incomes per household. A household which depended on migrant labour for its cash earned an average annual income in cash and in kind of about £14½ in 1945 and about £18 in 1948. If other economic activities on a small scale were possible for this household (e.g. beer or crop sales) the averages were probably about £15 and £19 respectively. An agricultural labourer's income would be of a similar level: it might be in the region of over £20 in 1948 if his wife and children could take on seasonal work. An African tobacco farmer got an average of £3.2 for his crop in 1945 and £13 in 1948, which when added to subsistence income, and after making allowance for other local trade, probably gave him a net annual income of about £12 in 1945 and £24 in 1948. The registered cotton grower got only £1.4 for his crop on the average in 1945 and £3.2 in 1948, and his average level of earnings was probably between £10 and £11 in 1945 or roughly £15 in 1948 including subsistence production and allowing for some trade in other crops.

The content of the African standard of living probably varies less widely than income levels. The family of the African clerk, earning an annual income of £50 or more on the average probably lives in the same village as the family of the shop assistant earning less than £25 per annum from all sources.[1] The clerk's family may live in a thatched

[1] A clerk in government service may earn anything from £22 to £360 per annum, but the higher income ranges (£222 and over) demand educational qualifications which are not obtainable in the colony.

roofed hut of sun-dried brick, would normally have more clothes and have more money to spend on other luxuries—beer, sun-glasses, sugar, bread, meat, furniture, etc.—whereas the shop assistant's family would have a thatched mud hut, wear their clothes till they were a good deal more ragged, make their own chairs, beds, tables rather than buy them, and go without sugar, meat, bread and similar luxury items, except on ceremonial occasions or when they obtained a gift from their richer neighbours.

The clerk's family might thus be rather better nourished, housed and clothed, but the similarities between the two families would be more obvious than the differences. Both, for example, would tend to follow the pattern of one substantial meal of maize porridge ($1\frac{1}{2}$ to 2 lb. per head) and relish (about $\frac{1}{4}$ lb. of groundnuts and green leaves), supplemented by snacks varying according to the season (roasted sweet corn, sweet potatoes, pumpkins, fruit, etc.). The clerk's relish would be more interesting, for he could afford meat or dried fish several times a week, whereas the shop assistant's family would be lucky to have it once, and the subsistence farmer who was not close to the lake or in the cattle-rearing area might not eat it more than two or three times a year and then only at a funeral or other ceremonial occasion.

One of the reasons why the standard of living in terms of consumption of material things would vary less than incomes as between one African and another, is that the richer ones pay for services that the poorer would do for themselves. The clerk might pay to have his thatch kept leak-proof whereas the unskilled labourer would mend his own. On the other hand the clerk normally works a more rigid working day. The agricultural labourer works a week of eighteen to thirty hours and usually regards himself as free not to turn up to work when he has more pressing domestic business of his own to attend to. Another factor which tends to level real standards of consumption is the responsibility of the richer members of the community to make gifts to their poorer relatives. This means in practice that cash is spread more evenly and such items as beer, sugar, clothing, etc. reach people whose earnings would not have been sufficient to buy them.

In view of these levelling factors in the economy the averages given in the following table of consumption estimates have rather more significance than they would in an economy where there were a number of sharply differing social strata corresponding to the different income groups.

It can be seen from Table 29 that the principal cash commitment is clothing and it is in respect of clothing that the standards of African consumption vary most obviously. It is an expensive item in the average budget and although even the relatively wealthy groups cannot afford a high standard of dress the poorer families are very poor indeed. It has already been observed that the plateau country has cold winter nights and the winter days when the chiperoni is prevalent in the Southern Highlands can be unpleasantly damp and cold. Only the relatively rich can afford warm clothing. The poor go about in the same ragged cotton clothes through summer and winter. At the end of the war the returned soldiers and those who had received gifts or bought clothing from them were relatively well clad in army greatcoats and pullovers, while returned migrants often bring woollen garments for themselves, but it is rare to see a woman or a child in Nyasaland with adequate clothing for the cold season. In 1947 only just over 7,000 yards of woollen piece goods were imported into Nyasaland and under 6,000 pairs of woollen blankets. Many of these were bought by non-Africans.

TABLE 29. Estimates of African consumption, 1945

	Total expenditure or value of consumption £	Average per household (516,000 households) £
Food—Cereals	1,520,000	2.95
Other local foods	1,580,000	3.06
Salt, sugar and imported goods	192,000	0.37
Beer	600,000	1.16
Tobacco	30,000	0.06
Clothes	1,880,000	3.64
Household goods and housing	419,000	0.81
Tax (direct)	183,000	0.36
All other	704,000	1.36
Total expenditure and consumption	£7,108,000	£13.77

During the war years Nyasaland was relatively short of cotton piece goods and the average annual import for the three years ending in 1945 was less than 10 million yards, i.e. under 5 yards per head of the population, so that the 1945 figure for expenditure on clothing certainly falls short of the demand. How far short can be judged by a comparison with 1938 and 1939 when the average annual value of imports was more than 12½ million yards in spite of a smaller purchasing power and a smaller population. By 1947 the volume had risen to 16½ million yards, or rather more than 8 yards per head of population, but it would seem that part of this was due to the temporary effects of the war-suppressed demand, for in 1948 imports had fallen to 14 million yards. By this time a wider range of commodities was available and increased African purchasing power is reflected, for example, in a greatly increased rate of import of footwear.

Similar considerations can be applied to the items relating to expenditure on household goods (in so far as these were European manufactures) and on 'other' items. Pots and pans were very short, for example, and bicycles and sewing machines were also scarce in relation to the demand for them. On the other hand it is estimated that the net saving by Africans during the course of the year 1945 did not exceed £96,000 in all. In 1946, when incomes were swollen by army gratuities, and goods were still in short supply, the rate of hoarding may have been, and probably was, a good deal higher; but the abundance of ready cash and the bare shelves of the trading stores would not necessarily lead to hoarding. It might equally well have led to an increase in the relative volume of village trade and it most probably did.

This conclusion conflicts with the widely held theory that a large amount of currency was lost to circulation during the war and immediate post-war years by being buried under hut floors. In the report of the Fiscal Survey of Nyasaland,[1] published in 1947, for example, it is stated that: 'Currency figures show that at the end of 1945 £524,000 were hoarded by the African community and the amount is estimated at the end of November 1946 as £933,000.' It is thus estimated from currency data that during the year 1946 over £400,000 was saved or hoarded in the form of cash by Africans, whereas income and expenditure data would suggest that £200,000 was an outside estimate for 1946. It is also estimated that from currency data at the end of 1946 a total of about a million pounds was literally buried in the form of cash hoards.

It should be emphasized that the estimates given in Table 29 are subject to a wide margin of error and are not of themselves sufficient to disprove this contention. The arguments against are qualitative rather than quantitative. It is not necessary to assume that money which was lost to circulation as far as the European and Indian monetary economy are concerned was in fact lying idle. Prices of goods entering into village and inter-village trade—meat, fish, groundnuts and beer—had all risen in sympathy with the increase in prices of exports and imports. They would therefore require an increased supply of currency to support the same volume of trade. Nor can we assume that the volume of local trade was static. On the contrary, it is fair to assume that a community living at such a low standard of living as the African community would take advantage of the ready cash (which could not be spent on imports) to increase its consumption of local produce.

The report of the Fiscal Survey, for example, quotes an estimate of £2 10s. as the average expenditure on beer of a family earning £12 per annum.

---

[1] *Report of a Fiscal Survey*, Government Printer, Zomba, 1947.

Unfortunately I did not make any systematic budget surveys while in Nyasaland and the budgets that I did collect were in no way a random sample nor even a suitably selected sample. They were sufficient, however, to suggest strongly that the returned soldier or migrant or the worker with more cash than he could spend at the stores did not normally hoard his money until such time as the stores could provide him with goods to buy. He invested in livestock whenever he could, or in a wife. He bought beer, meat, fish and other home-produced luxuries. He built himself a brick house with African-made bricks and African labour. He hired help to plant his garden. During the first year of his return from the forces, before he had planted a garden, he had to buy a large part of his food locally. He bought beds and chairs made by the local carpenter. He bought grain so that his wife could make beer for parties. He gave many gifts to relatives. All these had been influenced by the general rise in prices and were therefore expensive. So, although the shelves of the village store were bare, he had no lack of temptations to spend his money and he had to be relatively strong-minded to hold cash for a bicycle or a sewing machine when there were none in the shops to encourage him, and when the possibility of getting such things, even when he had the money, seemed remote.

Thus the conclusion is that although there was a loss of currency to the economy of traders and banks, there was an increase certainly in the value and probably in the volume of local inter-African trade. The increase in the volume of local trade could be attributed either to an increase in output or to a diversion of goods from purely subsistence channels to trade channels. Probably there was an element of both in a situation where the level of cash demand was increasing. Because money was kept overnight in African huts and not deposited in European banks there is no reason to assume that it was being hoarded.

CHAPTER VII

THE STRUCTURE OF NATIONAL OUTPUT

Nyasaland is almost exclusively an agricultural country. There are no minerals worked on an appreciable scale although small quantities of corundum (922,000 lb. in 1945) are extracted from alluvial deposits. A geological survey is in progress and coal has been found in the north-east and in the south-west, while small deposits of gold, copper, lead, iron, bauxite and other minerals have been reported. There is no prospect, however, of any significant mineral development of the territory and, although the prospects for manufacturing industry may be more promising, no spontaneous development in these directions has arisen except in industries ancillary to agriculture, e.g. tobacco and tea factories, cotton ginneries, sisal, tung oil and soap factories. There is a small commercial fishing industry and a limited timber trade.

Table 30, by setting out an estimate of territorial output, illustrates the extent of the economy's dependence on agriculture. 'Territorial output' is here used to signify total output produced within the territory, or earned and remitted to the territory by its nationals. The term is used to distinguish the concept from 'national output', which would include only that part of output accruing in the territory which was produced by its own nationals.[1] The difference between these two concepts for Nyasaland can be observed by comparing Table 30 with the output column of Table 32, which excludes all incomes accruing to companies registered outside the colony except in so far as they are remitted to local shareholders, or to the government in the form of income tax.

It will be seen from Table 30 that almost half of the net value of output produced in Nyasaland, or accruing to Nyasaland nationals, was directly derived from agriculture. Only about a quarter can be regarded as largely independent of agriculture; most of this was earned in the service of government or the missions or by migrant labour. The weight of 'services' in the total value of output is a particularly striking feature of the economy. They account for between 35% and 40% of the whole;

[1] See also Part II, pp. 59–61, where the use of this concept is described in the Northern Rhodesian context.

88

part of this disproportion may be due to relative under-valuation of primary production, particularly of subsistence agriculture.

TABLE 30. Territorial output of Nyasaland, 1945 and 1948

Net output of:	1945 £m.		1948 £m.	
Agriculture and livestock:				
1. Non-African agriculture and livestock	0.860		1.230	
2. African agriculture	3.439		5.400	
3. African livestock and products	0.122		0.150	
4. Total agriculture and livestock		4.421		6.780
Manufacture, forestry, building, etc.:				
5. Non-African factories	0.075		0.095	
6. Forestry products	0.700		0.750	
7. Fish	0.070		0.075	
8. Beer	0.600		0.600	
9. Building	0.063		0.120	
10. Village industry and handicrafts	0.093		0.100	
11. Total manufacture, etc.		1.601		1.740
Distribution and transport:				
12. Distribution	1.025		1.700	
13. Transport	0.245		0.360	
14. Total distribution and transport		1.270		2.060
Government and missions:				
15. Government	0.864		1.350	
16. Missions	0.164		0.200	
17. Total government and missions		1.028		1.550
Miscellaneous output:				
18. Migrant labour	0.901		1.200	
19. Miscellaneous services, property, etc.	0.279		0.370	
20. Total miscellaneous output		1.180		1.570
21. Total territorial output		9.500		13.700

African agriculture is predominant. The average garden acreage varies from district to district according to the nature of the soil, the number of cultivators per family, the yield of crops, the degree of pressure on the land and the possibility of supplementing subsistence output by output for trade. In the south it is estimated that the average falls as low as 2 acres per family, or even less, and where there are ample opportunities for earning cash and buying food (e.g. in the immediate vicinity of Blantyre or Limbe) it may fall to 1 acre per family or less. In the far north, in the hill country it has been estimated that the average family cultivates as much as 6 acres of land, but cropping tends to be sparse, gardens may be set at a sharp angle on the hillside, and yields are low. In terms of acreage per head it would seem—judging by the few agricultural surveys available—that the average might vary in Southern Province alone from a little under ½ acre per head to under 1 acre per head. The only evidence for Central Province is Dr Platt's Nutrition Survey for three villages, which suggested an average of about 3 acres per hut (or rather less than 1 acre per head).

On balance, therefore, the available information suggests that the average cultivated acreage per head is of the order of rather less than 1 acre (which is much the same as was found for Northern Rhodesia) except in the densely populated areas of Southern Province. Yields seem to be higher than for Rhodesia on an average, judging from the material collected from the Agricultural Departments. Conclusions based on estimates collected from Agricultural Officers in Nyasaland suggested an average yield of about 4 bags of maize per acre in Southern Province and 3 bags in the rest of the country, whereas for Northern Rhodesia the average was put at near 2½ bags and in Southern Rhodesia the average in most areas seems to be accepted at about 2 bags. So little has been done in the way of systematic agricultural surveying, however, in any of these territories that these differences in estimates cannot be regarded as significant. They may reflect degrees of optimism on the part of the Agricultural Officers from whom the estimates were collected.

The main African cash crops are tobacco and cotton, although rice, groundnuts and pulses, potatoes and maize are all worthy of note. They are generally grown either on Native Trust Land and marketed through organized produce markets or on private estates and marketed through the estate owner. The minor food crops may be sold direct to the African consumer in the villages or through native markets. Allowance must also be made for crops grown for sale to Africans and for crops grown primarily for subsistence purposes but traded in view of particular local circumstances. For the latter no estimate could be made and it must be regarded as part of the estimated volume of subsistence output. For the former—crops grown for sale within or between the villages—a very rough estimate was made. The total value of African cash crops, excluding some local trade, was estimated to be less than half a million pounds in 1945 and to have reached about £1.4 millions in 1948, the return from tobacco alone being in excess of a million pounds.[1]

Livestock is not an important source of income. Large areas are without cattle at all because they are infested with tsetse fly, and elsewhere there is overgrazing and soil erosion. It is estimated that the value of all livestock and livestock products produced by Africans in 1948 did not exceed £150,000, and of this the traded output accounted for less than half.

---

[1] See Appendix, pp. 314–315, for details of 1945 estimates and a breakdown by crops.

Tobacco and cotton between them accounted for nearly three-quarters of the value of African income from cash crops in 1945 and for over 90% in more recent years. The acreage under tobacco on Native Trust Land was estimated in 1943 at 73,417 acres and on private estates at 29,220. Both types of tobacco grower get supervision and advice from Europeans—in the former case by the Native Tobacco Board supervisors and in the latter case from the European farmers on whose land the tobacco is grown. The number of growers fluctuates, apparently in response to prices in the previous season. In 1943 there were 108,000; in 1945, 89,000; in 1947, 110,000; and in 1948, 94,000. African-grown tobacco is almost entirely fire-cured tobacco (i.e. tobacco cured over open fires) and sun- or air-cured tobacco. Fire-cured tobacco is mainly used for the production of plugs, cut plugs, twists and rolls, and is smoked widely in industrial areas in the United Kingdom. Some well-known brands are made almost entirely from this type. Sun- or air-cured tobacco is a lighter, milder type and tends to be used in chewing tobacco or in mixtures as pipe tobacco. There has been a marked increase in the average return per grower in recent years. Over the period 1927–38 the average return per grower on Native Trust Land was 33/5 in Southern Province and 38/11 in Northern Province. Excluding 1939, which was a very bad year, however, the annual average over the period 1940–5 fluctuated between 45/8 in 1941 and 74/9 in 1942. In 1945 the average was 56/11. By 1948 it was four times as great.

Cotton has been grown commercially in the Lower River since 1904, although during the first twenty years of the century the bulk was grown by European estates. The period after 1922 was characterized by an increased acreage, a dramatic fall in the proportion produced by Europeans (which was 86% in 1922 and nil in 1932), and sharp fluctuations in acreage. Since 1932 there has been a rapid expansion of African production, acreage rising from 20,000 in 1932 to 62,000 in 1935, but there have been very wide fluctuations in both acreage and yield. The general instability of the industry has extended even to time of harvesting and the proportion of first-grade cotton. There have been marked changes also in the proportion grown on floodland. Before 1922, when European production predominated, the greater part of the crop was produced on non-floodland. After 1922 the importance of the Chikwawa, non-floodland, area diminished and by 1933 seasonal floodland and dimba (or marsh) gardens comprised 66% of the Lower Shiré acreage. From 1932 onwards there has been a steady increase in the importance of the Chikwawa district and in 1939 serious flooding reduced drastically the number of dimba gardens. Since 1939, production has been almost entirely non-floodland.

With the loss of floodland following the rise of the Shiré there has been a greater tendency to inter-cropping and practically no pure stand cotton is grown to-day. Most is grown with maize, but some with millet. This has depressed the average yield of cotton, but in view of the shortage of land inter-cropping is a physical necessity. Food supplies are perennially short in the Port Herald area, for example, and the African needs a cash crop to enable him to buy food from outside the district. The average return from cotton is a good deal lower than from tobacco. Between 1938 and 1945 (again excluding the very bad year of 1939) the return per grower has varied from 16/3 to 35/5. Generally speaking, the number of growers rises and falls in sympathy with the price paid in the previous year. In 1948 there were 47,000 growers with an average return estimated to be over £3. The acreage planted has varied from not much more than 35,000 acres in 1939 to 89,000 acres in 1944.

European agriculture in Nyasaland has been on a prosperous footing for the past few years as a result of recent favourable prices. The main products are tea, flue-cured tobacco, tung oil and oil seeds. Gross output was estimated to be worth about £1,014,000 in 1945 and to exceed £1½ millions in 1948, when the output of tea was worth more than a million pounds and of tobacco a quarter of a million pounds.[1] The area under European agriculture is in the region of 50,000 acres, compared with about 40,000 acres before the war.

The possibility of expanding acreage under tea is limited by shortages of suitable land and labour. It is grown only in certain areas of Southern Province with an adequate winter rainfall and it requires a considerable labour supply. Similar considerations keep the European output of flue-cured tobacco relatively stable. There is no likelihood of any big increase in European tobacco grown in Southern Province, now the main centre, although it has been said that there is enough suitable land in the Kasungu area of Central Province to grow 10 to 20 million pounds of flue-cured tobacco. The Colonial Development Corporation has started tobacco farming on an experimental scale in this area and there is some prospect of creating an African flue-cured tobacco industry there with European assistance. At present, standards of cultivation and processing required for flue-cured tobacco are far above the normal for African producers in a post-war market which accepts all qualities of tobacco.

A promising avenue of expansion for the European farmer at present may be to increase acreage under tung, which has recently proved

---

[1] See Appendix, pp. 321–322, for details of the 1945 estimates and breakdown by crops.

a profitable sideline for the Southern Province tobacco grower. Again the chief limiting factor is the shortage of African labour—in particular the shortage of labour for manuring, which has recently exerted a depressing effect on yields. World demand is likely to continue firm; the United Kingdom alone currently required 12,000 tons per annum and the present rate of output for Nyasaland is under 500 tons. The Colonial Development Corporation is launching a large tung-growing scheme in Northern Province and Southern Province farmers are steadily increasing acreage.

Since 1945 the prices of all Nyasaland's agricultural produce have improved substantially, and the overall importance of the rising trend in prices is reflected in the following table of domestic exports.

TABLE 31. Domestic produce exported, 1938–48

	All domestic produce £000	Tea £000	Tobacco £000	Cotton £000
1938-42 (average)	1,089	488	522	50
1943	1,354	503	695	100
1944	1,472	587	717	78
1945	1,831	686	826	114
1946	2,327	750	1,253	126
1947	2,709	849	1,528	190
1948	4,162	1,350	2,243	369

In effect, the total value of produce exported was by 1948 nearly four times the value in 1938–42. Tea, tobacco, and cotton still accounted together for more than 95% of total domestic exports in 1948 (as compared with more than 97% in 1938–42), but the price of all agricultural produce has risen substantially. Provided that the prices of its major products do not fall, the agricultural industry should continue to expand, although at a steadier pace as the production of tung oil and rice is developed, and as an increasing standard of living stimulates the production of food crops for the local market. However, if the price of tobacco falls, as it may well do, the problem of improving the quality of African tobacco—and there is much scope for improvement—will become urgent.

An important limit to the expansion of European agriculture has been the acute shortage of local labour. Increasing prices have enabled European farmers to offer higher wages and the rate of agricultural wages seems to have roughly trebled over the decade ending in 1947. The drain of labour from the territory has continued, however (although the estimates for 1948 show a decline from 1947), and the remittances in cash and kind of Nyasaland Africans employed abroad was estimated to amount in 1945 to over £900,000, or nearly 10% of the national income (i.e. the income of residents) and more than 9% of the value of territorial income.

Various theories have been put forward to explain why employment abroad is often more attractive than employment in Nyasaland, but there is unsufficient information to allow a firm conclusion. It seems probable that one of the elements is a desire for travel, especially travel to the big cities of Rhodesia and the Union, and the higher money wages offered in the industrial centres are also an incentive, although their high cost of living makes the net cash return very little higher, if at all, for the Nyasaland emigrant.[1] It seems likely also that one of the principal incentives for labour to go abroad can be found in the city shops. Nyasaland stores were almost bare of essential cloth for African consumption for most of 1945 and 1947, and although supplies of essentials have increased since then the variety of goods obtainable does not compare with that to be found in the cities abroad. The village store is usually a dim-lit, unattractive hut where the scope for evasion of price control is fairly considerable and the range of goods marketed is pathetically small. Even in the main townships the stores are dreary, the goods are badly displayed (there are few shop windows), and Africans are usually discouraged, if not actually prevented, from using the main entrance. The high cost of the retail distribution industry seems to be out of all proportion to the services rendered. It is perhaps not surprising that the village beer brewers do well out of those who stay at home, and that those who have a wider range of wants are driven out of the colony to satisfy them.

Another reason for the drain of labour abroad can be seen in the relative lack of variety and opportunity for local employment. Farmers, we have seen, are short of labour, but the Nyasalander abroad works in a variety of occupations—in mines, in domestic service, as a clerk, and in factories. With the small immigrant population the opportunities of employment in domestic service are naturally limited, there are no mines, wages in clerical occupations are low, and there is very little secondary industry. There are almost no wage-earning opportunities in Northern Province from which a large proportion of the migrants come. They therefore have a choice between low-wage employment in Southern Province Nyasaland and high-wage employment abroad. Some of them do come to Southern Province. But for most of them the attraction of a new country and higher wages is stronger and this is particularly so for those who do not want to become farm labourers. For them the low wages of Southern Province are not supplemented by

---

[1] It is possible to exaggerate the level of wages outside Nyasaland. The average for Africans on the Southern Rhodesian mines in 1948 was less than £23 per annum cash, plus about £13 in rations, etc. Considering the higher cost of living for workers away from their families this is not a great incentive in itself, yet about 60% of the Nyasaland emigrants were in Southern Rhodesia.

subsistence production (unless they move with families and take semi-permanent jobs) and the high cost of living and relative unattractiveness of 'urban' conditions in Nyasaland are a definite deterrent to local employment.

In effect, a lack of variety and a tendency for the major proportion of cash-earning activities to be concentrated in the overcrowded Southern Province are characteristic of the territorial output of Nyasaland. Leaving aside the village economic activities such as house building, beer brewing, handicrafts and forestry, the only non-agricultural activities of any importance are service industries. There is a small but thriving commercial fishing industry concentrated at the south end of the lake and accounting for less than 1% of territorial output. There are a few factories (cigarettes, tobacco, sisal, soap, minerals, etc.) which together account for perhaps 2% of territorial output at the present time. The service industries, in order of relative value of contribution to territorial output, are distribution, government, transport and missions. Their importance is striking. Together they account for roughly a quarter of total output in the colony.

The distribution industry falls into three main categories. First there is the licensed retail trade carried on through stores owned by Europeans (344 stores in 1945), Asians (1,139 stores), and Africans (1,988 stores). Reference has already been made to the high cost of this industry in relation to the real value of its service. Secondly, there is the retail trade carried on by Africans in markets, in unlicensed stores (or stores licensed by the Native Authority), or as hawkers. Thirdly, there is the handling of export crops (of which the most important is tobacco), dealt with primarily by Europeans but also by some Asians. Much of this handling is carried out by European farmers. This branch of the industry seems to be reasonably efficient and accounts for probably more than a third of the total value of distribution.

The transport industry contributes surprisingly little to total national income, although the recent formation of an omnibus company and the post-war development of air traffic has raised the rate of output since 1945. These new developments, however, relate mainly to passenger traffic, and for goods traffic Nyasaland is still dependent on inadequate facilities. For a territory whose products are all agricultural and hence unable to bear a heavy transport burden this is an important limiting factor to expansion.

There is one railway, of 3 ft. 6 in. gauge, which joins the southern end of the lake to the Port of Beira in Portuguese East Africa. Construction of the railway and of the Zambesi bridge was financed by a loan from the United Kingdom Government, and the railway has never borne the whole burden of debt. Traffic density is low and railway freight rates are higher than elsewhere in East Africa. The bulk of the traffic is between Blantyre and Beira, and the so-called Northern Extension of the railway, from Blantyre to Salima, is so unprofitable that from time to time the question of closing it is raised. The railway is frequently cut by floods. The bridge over the Shiré at Chiromo, for example, was down for most of the period 1948 to 1949.

Freight transport on the lake is controlled by Nyasaland Railways Company, except for the steamer run by the Universities Mission to Central Africa and the small-scale dhow traffic. The Company runs a small steamer of 200 tons, four tugs and some barges. Development of steamer transport, however, is restricted by the variability of the lake level which makes it difficult to construct jetties for transhipment. There are only two all-weather refuges and the lake is subject to violent storms. The Murchison Rapids prevent through traffic from the lake to the Indian Ocean, but at high lake levels bulk transport from the lake to rail head would be possible. Stabilization of the lake level and the upper Shiré (which has recently been estimated to cost £¾ million to £1¾ million) may be a means of opening up Northern Province, the so-called 'dead north' of Nyasaland. The rapid development of cash crops and of industries for the processing of local crops in the north of Nyasaland might become a practicable proposition if bulk transport by water from north to south were a possibility. Alternatively an outlet from Northern Province to the sea by Tanganyika might prove practicable. The colony is relatively well served by roads, in view of its small land area, and there are 3,866 miles of road. Of these, however, only four miles are full tarmac roads, and most are of very poor quality. The cost of road upkeep is high, varying from 30s. a mile to £30 a mile for tarmac roads. Roads, like railways, suffer from the periodic flooding of the rivers, and in 1946 the road link with Southern Rhodesia was washed away. Generally speaking, the cost of road transport is heavy, far too expensive for all but the high-priced crops like tobacco and tea.

No survey of Nyasaland's output would be complete without reference to the considerable part which missions play in the economy. They provide the bulk of the educational facilities and a considerable proportion of medical and other welfare amenities in the remote areas. Because mission personnel receive such low incomes in general the money value of their services bears very little relation to the real value of their contribution. In all it was estimated that the missions spent over £200,000 in the colony in 1945, and perhaps half as much again in 1948, and that their net output, i.e. the value of wages and salaries paid and the value of subsistence production, was estimated to be about £164,000.

Government in Nyasaland is supplied (a) by the Central Government with a net revenue and expenditure of rather less than a million pounds in 1945, (b) by the European township authorities of Blantyre, Limbe and Zomba, (c) by the Sanitary Boards of the other European settlements, and (d) by the Native Treasuries. In all it was estimated that the central and local government authorities had a combined net revenue of about £981,000 in 1945.[1] By 1948, net expenditure of Central Government alone exceeded £2 millions. Over 20% of Central Government revenue, however, took the form of free grant from the United Kingdom Government, more than half of this being assistance in respect of the burden of debt which construction of the railways and the Zambesi bridge laid on the community.

For those Africans who live in the vicinity of the lakes, fishing is an important economic activity and a valuable contribution to subsistence output. Groups of men and boys fish regularly from the shore and there is a certain amount of trade and barter trade with villages farther inland. The size of the average catch is small, however, in relation to the numbers who have a claim to share in it, and the bulk of the dried fish which is carried by traders on bicycles throughout the villages of Central Nyasaland and parts of Southern Province is caught and dried by the European fishing firm which has operated at Fort Johnson for some years now. Large-scale open-water fishing requires capital and is therefore confined to non-African enterprise. A South African firm working in agreement with the Colonial Development Corporation has recently launched a ship and begun fishing operations, but there is some danger that the lake is being overfished. Certainly the evidence points to a falling yield, and investigations into this problem are proceeding. At present the contribution of fish to the territory's output amounts to less than 1% which, considering that over a third of the colony is water area, is a very small proportion.

In concluding this survey of the structure of national output it might be noted that although a high value has been put on forestry, little has been said about it. The reason is that the present output is largely output for subsistence purposes—for firewood, hut poles, etc.—and that forests containing valuable indigenous timber species suitable for commercial exploitation are very limited in area. Tea is exported largely in imported plywood chests, although more tobacco hogsheads and boxes for export are made locally from timber grown on private lands. The whole of the supply of softwood timber is taken by the Public Works Department, and the local demand for durable softwood timber such as Mlanje Cedar, the most valuable local wood, far outstrips the supply. There is no organized timber trade in Nyasaland, although mahogany and other species are cut under licence by individual native

[1] See Appendix II, pp. 330–331, for the details.

H

sawyers who use it for building construction and furniture. The local demand is such that an export trade in timber is not at present practicable, but if Mlanje Cedar (which is a durable, ant-proof softwood) is ever produced in sufficient quantities it should be easily marketed outside the colony.

TABLE 32. National income, output and expenditure of Nyasaland, 1938–48

	1938		1945		1948	
National income	£000	%	£000	%	£000	%
1. African income from:						
(a) Employment	363		1,139		1,815	
(b) Independent agriculture	2,009		3,561		5,550	
(c) Migrant labour	234		901		1,200	
(d) Other independent activities	390		1,603		1,800	
(e) Total African incomes	2,996	71.9	7,204	79.1	10,365	77.9
2. European individuals	654	15.7	884	9.7	1,250	9.5
3. Other non-Africans	202	4.9	575	6.3	1,000	7.5
4. Companies	53	1.3	87	1.0	200	1.5
5. Government	260	6.2	360	3.9	485	3.6
6. Total national income	4,165	100.0	9,110	100.0	13,300	100.0
National output						
7. Agriculture and livestock	2,347	56.4	4,221	46.4	6,550	49.2
8. Secondary industry	18	0.4	75	0.8	75	0.6
9. Other manufacture, forestry, building and village industry	342	8.2	1,456	16.0	1,575	11.8
10. Fishing	50	1.2	70	0.8	70	0.5
11. Distribution and transport	466	11.2	970	10.6	1,710	12.9
12. Government and missions	629	15.1	1,138	12.5	1,750	13.2
13. Other services, including migrant labour	313	7.5	1,180	12.9	1,570	11.8
14. Total national output	4,165	100.0	9,110	100.0	13,300	100.0
National outlay Personal consumption of:						
15. Europeans	465		566		1,000	
16. Other non-Africans	125		272		500	
17. Africans	2,859		6,925		10,000	
18. Total personal consumption at market prices	3,449		7,763		11,500	
19. Plus subsidies and less indirect taxes	−230		−277		−550	
20. Total personal consumption at factor cost	3,219	77.3	7,486	82.2	10,950	82.4
21. Expenditure abroad	230	5.5	417	4.6	650	4.9
22. Government net current expenditure on goods and services, and investment and saving	716	17.2	1,207	13.2	1,700	12.7
23. Total national outlay	4,165	100.0	9,110	100.0	13,300	100.0

CHAPTER VIII

THE SOCIAL ACCOUNTS

It is now possible to consider the economy as an integrated whole. Table 32 shows the consolidated social accounts of Nyasaland for 1938, 1945 and 1948. The 1938 figures are those already published in the interim report of this enquiry, and with two exceptions are unrevised.[1] The exceptions are (a) the return from migrant labour, and (b) the value of non-agricultural subsistence activity. Both have been revised in an upward direction because it seemed from evidence collected in the colony that they had originally been underestimated. In both cases the extent of the upward revision was arbitrarily determined, and neither the new 1938 totals nor the constituent items can in general be regarded as having more reliability than was attributed to the original estimates. They are likely to be 'of the right order of magnitude' and to provide a reasonably reliable picture of the main proportions of the economy at that time.

The 1945 figures are more reliable than either the 1938 or the 1948 estimates, being based on material collected in Nyasaland in the second half of 1946. Unfortunately, however, for Nyasaland, as for Northern Rhodesia, the two years 1945-6 covered the period when the war-induced distortions in the economy reached their peak. This means firstly that the shape of the economy in 1945 is not a particularly useful guide to its shape in more normal times, and secondly that the 1948 figures, which are the results of bringing 1945 estimates up to date in the light of published material available in 1950, may still reflect some of the post-war distortions which were no longer characteristic of the economy.

The second implication has rather more force for the Nyasaland 1948 estimates than for the Northern Rhodesia ones, since the statistical and other data were less satisfactory for Nyasaland. For Northern Rhodesia there was enough reliable material available on 1948 conditions by 1950 to make it likely that the distortions produced by using an a-typical base year were unimportant. For Nyasaland it was difficult to obtain

---

[1] Op. cit. See especially Table 70, p. 202. Other changes are due to re-arrangements of material and minor changes in definition.

from the published material available in the United Kingdom enough evidence to construct a quantitative statement of 1948 conditions or to assess the post-1946 trends in the economy. There were, for example, no satisfactory data on African employment, the information on migrant labour amounted to a very hazy estimate of the total numbers away, and there had been no attempt to estimate either the numbers of European or Asian earners or the changes in company earnings, in spite of the fact that the immigrant population seems to have increased by over 60% since 1945.

So far as can be judged from the accessible material, the conclusions which could be drawn from the figures shown in Table 32 are a fair reflection of what was actually occurring. Without adequate employment or migration data, however, and without more detailed population and immigration data for the rapidly increasing and economically important European and Asian communities, it is impossible to assess present trends with precision or confidence.[1] The following comments should therefore be read with these qualifications in mind.

It will be observed that the estimates in Table 32 are built up to national income (i.e. national income of *residents*) rather than to territorial product which was measured in Table 30 above. The difference between the national income of residents and the product of territorial economic activity is not as great as it is, say, for Northern Rhodesia, and the more normal definition of national income is convenient for most national accounting purposes. The income of companies not registered in Nyasaland was estimated to be about £280,000 in 1938, rising to about half a million pounds in 1945 and to about £600,000 in 1948, although this last figure is largely conjectural. The non-local companies are mainly agricultural and distributive, but the railway company is also included among them. The figure of about £600,000 for 1948 incomes was reached after consideration of public company reports which distinguished their operations in Nyasaland. Some firms operate throughout central and southern Africa and give no indication of their profits from activity in Nyasaland. Others are private companies and do not publish reports. However, on a combination of the available evidence it seems likely that company incomes increased by about 20% between 1945 and 1948 (rather more in the case of local companies).

[1] The Central African Office of Statistics published towards the end of 1949 a *Statistical Handbook of Nyasaland, 1949*. Although this proved a useful compendium of historical data it was not as useful as that Office's monthly bulletin of statistics of Northern Rhodesia (op. cit.) in giving data on post-war trends. Thus twenty-eight of its forty-seven Tables are summaries of or extracts from Tables in the 1945 Census published in 1946, there is no agricultural information for a later year than 1947, and apart from a summary of principal exports there is no information of economic value for later than 1947.

The economy pictured in Table 32 is an agricultural economy in which more than three-quarters of the national income is earned by Africans, about 10% by Europeans and approaching 8% by other non-Africans, the remainder being attributable to local European or Asian companies or to Government. There has been a trend towards an increase in the relative share of Africans since 1938 and a fall in the share of Europeans (in spite of an increase in population of about 60%), and an increase in the share of other non-Africans (who have more than doubled in numbers).

Between 1938 and 1945 the most significant changes have been an increase in the earnings of Africans from employment and migrant labour. Between 1945 and 1948 this increase continued vigorously and was accompanied by a still more notable increase in the reward of Africans from independent agriculture. It would seem that opportunities for earning cash in Nyasaland have improved considerably over the past decade or so, and on the face of it one would expect a corresponding fall in the proportion going abroad, although increased wages for migrant labourers would provide a counter-attraction. Unfortunately, the published data on migration is scanty, although it is interesting to note that there is estimated to have been a fall in numbers abroad between 1947 and 1948.

The geographical distribution of the new wealth is an important factor in the migrant labour situation. The chief reservoir of migrant labour is Northern Province, from which 39.3% of the adult men were absent in 1945; Central Province comes next with 24.1%; and Southern Province had 19.7% away. From one district of Northern Province more than 60% of the male adults were absent, and from Kasungu in Central Province 43.7% were away.[1] Broadly speaking, it is not in the areas of greatest migration that the opportunities for earning cash have recently increased so significantly. Central Province has benefited to some extent from the prosperity of the tobacco industry, but most of the increased return from tobacco and cotton, and most of the higher earnings from employment, have been received in Southern Province. It would be interesting to know what effect the recent developments have had in those areas in which they have had most influence, but it is significant that even in 1945, when there was a shortage of labour in Southern Province, one in five of the adult men chose to seek work elsewhere— a higher proportion than in 1937.[2]

---

[1] Both Chinteche (60%) and Kasungu had similar proportions away in 1937. For the whole country the 1937 proportion was 20.3% compared with 24.2% in 1945.

[2] The high density of population in Southern Province might have been a contributory factor.

In any case, it seems unlikely that an increase in economic opportunity in Southern Province, and to a lesser extent in Central Province, would appreciably affect the economic situation in Northern Province. Given the relatively low wages obtainable in Nyasaland (relatively that is, to the wages obtainable in the Rhodesias or the Union), and given the limited range of employments available there, it is not to be expected that there would be any great increase in the number of Northern Province migrants seeking employment in Southern Province rather than abroad. Distance does not seem to be a deterrent and it may lend some enchantment. Thus in 1948 as in 1938, in spite of a marked increase in African cash earnings, Nyasaland's chief economic problem was one of utilizing its working population within its own territorial boundaries as effectively as it could be used in neighbouring territories. The problem seems, if anything, to have become more acute since 1937. However attractive the wages obtainable in other countries, there seems to be little doubt that for the community in general and for the migrant's family in particular, much of the apparent gain in the form of cash or goods remitted or brought back to Nyasaland (estimated to account for between 9% and 10% of the national income in recent years) must be set off against a fall in rural living standards due to the absence of able-bodied males. Generally speaking, the employed man in Nyasaland— even the 'urban' employee who is more often tied to a full working day than, say, the agricultural or Public Works Department labourer in the rural areas—is able to lend practical assistance to his family at the clearing, planting and harvesting periods when adult male labour is most sorely missed.

There is a need for intensive socio-economic research into Nyasaland's migrant labour problem, designed among other things to show precisely what the community gains or loses on balance by the flow of labour abroad and the corresponding flow of incomes to Nyasaland. The problem of measuring this gain or loss is not a simple one and *a priori* comments should be received with caution. It seems at least probable, however, that for an economy where the staple necessities of life are produced by the family unit, the loss to less vital forms of production of the head of the family in the prime of his working life would have a depressing effect on the village standard of living. The depression must be particularly severe in the areas of greatest migration such as Chinteche and Kasungu: but for all areas, unless the village standard of living is high in terms of the staple necessities (and the evidence of surveys made by the Agricultural Department suggests that, on the contrary, it is too low for healthy living) the increase in the range of satisfactions which the migrant labourer can put at the disposal of his family and himself by earning cash and buying goods abroad, will be cancelled by the lower standard of living induced by his absence.

Possible solutions to this problem are of two kinds: (a) those which increase opportunities for earning cash in independent agriculture or other 'own account' activities such as fishing, village industry, etc., and (b) those which increase the range, earning power, and number of local employments. To be most effective, both types of solution require to operate in the areas from which the migrants come. The main limiting factor to the expansion of the fishing industry as of village industry in general, is the African lack of capital. As far as the fishing industry is concerned, there is some doubt whether the Lake will yield an increased output of fish, and plans for expansion would depend on the results of research into fish yields, fish farming experiments and potential local and extra-territorial markets. Similar research would be required before plans could be made to expand village industry. Expansion of the output of African cash crops would seem a more promising possibility in view of recent trends, but the present highly profitable market for tobacco cannot be regarded as a stable factor in the situation. The evidence points to a decline in world demand for the dark fire-cured tobacco in favour of the more valuable flue-cured types which require higher standards of cultivation and processing than those which are characteristically attained by the African farmer. The costs of achieving these standards are mainly to be measured in terms of the provision of adequate teaching and supervision, but there are some minor capital costs, such as those involved in the construction of tobacco barns, which are within the reach of individual Africans. Similarly, the development of new cash crops (e.g. of sugar for which there would be a good local market) or the expansion of existing food crops (e.g. rice or groundnuts) depends as much as anything on the intensive and extensive activities of an adequately staffed and qualified agricultural department.

An increase in the employment activities open to Africans in Nyasaland is to some extent a function of the prosperity and size of the immigrant population, although government and public corporations can play a part. The scope, however, is not great. There is no mining industry, and although the colony has not been fully surveyed there is no evidence that any considerable mineral developments are going to be possible. It is too far from the centres of population and purchasing power to develop a substantial secondary industry. Some minor developments, based on local products and designed for local markets, are worth detailed investigation—e.g. a fish or fruit cannery, a larger tourist industry and a corresponding expansion of hotel services and small handicrafts, a textile factory, and other small projects of this nature.

At present roughly 50% of national output is attributable to agriculture, and of the remainder over a third is accounted for by the so-called tertiary industries—distribution and transport, government, missions, personal and professional services—together with the reward from migrant labour. It seems doubtful whether much relative expansion is possible in the value of fishing, building and village or factory industries, although it is reasonable to plan for an expansion in step with agricultural expansion. Distribution and transport should expand with purchasing power in general, but it is well worth considering whether an increase in their efficiency (e.g. an improvement in the service which could act as an incentive to local earning or an increase in skilled African participation which could reduce costs) might not prove a valuable stimulus to economic advance in general. Generally speaking, however, although there are these other possibilities, a reduction in the dependence of the colony on migrant labour earnings, without a corresponding reduction in the value of the national income, requires a substantial expansion in the output of agricultural and livestock products.

On the face of it, therefore, there is a fairly straightforward solution to Nyasaland's problem, a solution which depends, not on the introduction of any new or exotic factors into the economy, but on an increased rate of expansion of existing industries. It is precisely in this problem of increasing the *rate* of expansion that the difficulty lies and the novelty appears. It implies a difference in the scale of investment.

The third section of Table 32 provides a broad picture of the way in which the community laid out its current incomes. It will be seen that the proportion of the national income which was devoted to personal consumption has tended to increase over the period 1938 to 1948. This is an inevitable result of the change in income structure already noted.[1] It illustrates a fundamental problem of Nyasaland development. The African community lives at a low standard of living, and for the vast majority of people there is no savable surplus above basic consumption needs. On the contrary, for many of them basic consumption needs are not always met. As the share of Africans in the national income increases, so the savable proportion for the economy as a whole decreases. Yet given the existing political and social framework—a small and relatively flourishing immigrant community living with a large and poor indigenous community—the only acceptable definition of economic progress is one which involves a further redistribution of income in favour of the very poor. The danger is that instead of being cumulative, such progress tends to be self-retarding.

In Table 32 government current expenditure on goods and services

[1] See above, p. 101.

has been included with the estimate for investment and saving (largely estimated as a residual) because in practice, and for an underdeveloped territory of this kind, it is difficult to draw a logical distinction between current and capital expenditure by government in such a way as to throw light on the rate of development. The current expenditure of the Agricultural Department, for example, is as much a form of social investment as the building of a new government station—and perhaps more so in terms of its income-yielding properties.

It is, of course, probable that the externally registered companies whose incomes are not included in national income as it is defined for the purposes of Table 32 will make some contribution to local investment. Unfortunately, no direct material was available on investment by non-local companies. Normally, one way of calculating investment financed from abroad would be by constructing a balance of payments table which would show investment as a residual. For a dependent economy, however, the construction of a balance of payments table becomes largely a formal exercise because there are no clearly recognizable boundaries to the economy. There is, for example, no foreign exchange transaction involved when a United Kingdom firm remits money to Nyasaland for capital development purposes. Colonial currency is freely exchangeable against sterling, and from a monetary point of view Nyasaland is merely an extension of the United Kingdom economy. What this means in effect is that a colonial balance of payments need never balance in recordable terms.[1] Thus we can draw a fictitious line round the Nyasaland economy for purposes of analysis, and in drawing up our accounts we can pretend that when a United Kingdom firm builds a tobacco barn in Nyasaland it is a split personality and that its United Kingdom office is lending to its Nyasaland office. Similarly, we can pretend that when the migrant labourer steps across the Nyasaland border with his pockets full of money and his suitcase full of goods he is transformed into another person who has just received a cash payment from a foreigner and bought goods from abroad with some of it.[2] These are convenient fictions which enable us to say that a new tobacco barn in Nyasaland is an addition to the territory's wealth and

[1] This failure to balance in recordable terms is not, of course, peculiar to a colonial balance of payments. It is acceptable practice in a European context, for example, to regard an addition to wealth which takes place within a country's borders as an addition to that country's domestic capital even if legal ownership rests with a foreign enterprise; the transaction is then set off by entering a 'fictitious' financial claim in the accounts with the rest of the world.

[2] The migrant from Southern or Northern Rhodesia does not even have to make an exchange of one kind of money for another, since the same Currency Board issues the money for all three Central African countries.

that the money and goods brought back by a migrant labourer are additions to Nyasaland's national income. But they are fictions nevertheless. They represent no claims outstanding between banking institutions in Nyasaland and banking institutions in the United Kingdom.

Thus, when we have accounted as far as possible for all sales of goods and services and all grants and gifts which create a flow of incomes to persons and enterprises now resident in Nyasaland, and on the other side for all purchases of goods and services and all remittances which represent a flow of incomes to persons and enterprises resident outside Nyasaland, the difference between is not a significant figure which we can regard as an addition to or deduction from Nyasaland's assets outside its borders, an increase or a fall in Nyasaland's power to purchase goods abroad. It means no more than that in a given year the flow of payments in one direction exceeded the flow of payments in another. Whether, when a United Kingdom firm operating in Nyasaland leaves its balances to accumulate in London this is a flight of capital or an addition to Nyasaland's foreign assets, is not a question which we can claim to answer.

Table 33 is described as a territorial balance of payments for Nyasaland. It corresponds conceptually to the territorial output of Table 30 above.[1] Item 10 of this table—Company remittances—is estimated on the assumption that the operating surpluses of the local branches of non-local firms accrue to the head office abroad (with the exception of the amount that is retained by the local central government in payment of income tax). Operating surplus, less income tax, is thus entered in full as an outgoing item of payments. Some of it will be used by head office to pay expenses incurred outside Nyasaland, some of it to pay dividends, some of it to add to reserves or balances, and some of it will be re-invested in the operating branch. It is this part which is re-invested which we should like to be able to measure because we propose to regard it, as it is for all practical purposes, as an addition to the national or domestic wealth of Nyasaland. In so far as the investment takes the form of expenditure on machinery or materials brought from

[1] To construct a balance of payments which confined itself to incomes received by resident individuals (i.e. a balance which corresponded conceptually to the economy covered in Table 32) we should require (a) to adjust the value of imports so as to exclude the value of services rendered by foreign factors of production—e.g. to re-value output produced by non-local capital so as to exclude the profits earned thereby—and (b) to adjust the value of imports so that only imports paid for by resident individuals were accounted for—e.g. to exclude machinery purchased by non-local firms and shipped to the colony. These adjustments were made for the Northern Rhodesian case because the differences were important enough in themselves to warrant special treatment. (See Table 17 (b) above, p. 63.) It did not seem, however, to be particularly useful in connection with the Nyasaland analysis.

outside Nyasaland we hope to have accounted for it in fact in the residual item 5. In so far as it takes the form of remittance of cash to Nyasaland to buy labour and materials on the spot we may have failed to account for it at all, although it should, if we were omniscient, appear either positively in the receipts from abroad side of the accounts as borrowing by the resident operating enterprises from the non-resident head offices, or negatively on the expenditure abroad side as a deduction from foreign investment, if any.

TABLE 33. Territorial balance of payments for Nyasaland, 1938–48

	1938 £000	1945 £000	1948 £000
Receipts from abroad:			
1. Domestic exports	960	1,831	4,162
2. Migrant labour	234	901	1,200
3. Tourists and missions	144	100	135
4. Colonial Development grants[1]	15	22	186
5. Residue	45	—	57
6. Total receipts from abroad	£1,398	£2,854	£5,740
Expenditure abroad:			
7. Retained imports	834	1,576	4,290
8. Goods brought in by migrants	84	321	400
9. Expenditure abroad by individuals and government[1]	230	417	650
10. Company remittances	250	320	400
11. Residue	—	220	—
12. Total expenditure abroad	£1,398	£2,854	£5,740

What it all amounts to, therefore, is that since we are not fully informed on all the company transactions between local and head offices, and since the borders of a dependent economy are not sufficiently clearly defined with respect to the economies on which it depends to make them a useful measuring point, the probability is that the balance of payments account will be incomplete. We can look at the item Company remittances to get some idea of the scale of non-local company transactions with the colony, and we can try to judge from movements in the residual item of receipts from abroad not otherwise accounted for, i.e. item 5 in Table 33, whether more goods and services have been flowing into the country than the current outflow would finance, but we cannot with this incomplete picture hope to measure borrowing from abroad in any absolute sense.

Looking at Table 33 we might conclude that there was probably some investment financed by borrowing from abroad in 1938 and 1948,

[1] Debt service payments which are financed by grant from the United Kingdom Treasury are excluded from both sides of this balance.

though not a great amount, and that in 1945 the tendency was for the Nyasaland economy to send capital abroad rather than to receive it. Further, bearing in mind that the proportion of item 10—Company remittances—which did not go to meet expenses incurred abroad or dividends, would be only a fraction of the total, the scale of capital investment which existing companies would be likely to contemplate on existing prospects is not a very weighty factor in the economy. For the most part it is likely to be located largely in the Southern Highlands with other forms of European or Asian investment. More recently the Colonial Development Corporation has taken active steps to assist in the economic development of the colony, and it will be interesting to note the effects of this activity on the balance of payments. If the Corporation's tung-growing scheme in Northern Province, its tobacco scheme in Kasungu, and the new fishing company in which it has an interest at the southern end of the Lake all have as much success as is hoped for them, there may be a noticeable shift in the geographical distribution of wealth within the next decade or so. However, unless a deliberate and successful policy of attracting new immigrants and new 'foreign' companies is adopted, it is unlikely that there will be any great increase in investment from non-native sources.

In any case, investment by non-local companies (and still more so, investment by non-local public corporations) creates its own problems of debt service charges and remittances abroad. The Public Debt charges nominally chargeable to the Nyasaland Treasury, most of which were incurred in the building of the railway and its bridge over the Zambesi, are a striking illustration of this point. They amount in all to about 13% of the total expenditure of Government and have to date been largely met by free grant from the United Kingdom Government. Effectively the community can only borrow from abroad to the extent that it expects to be able to carry the debt service charges. From this point of view, equity capital is a more attractive proposition than the fixed interest-bearing loans of public corporations. On the other hand, equity capital is made available only on the prospect of a higher commercial return than the public corporations contemplate. Much of the needed investment is so basic that no direct commercial return can be expected in the foreseeable future—investment in agricultural staff and equipment with a view to improving the yield of subsistence crops is an extreme case of this—and the possibility of financing it from abroad is practically limited to the possibility of obtaining annual grants in aid from the United Kingdom Government. Certainly it would seem that no appreciable advance in economic development can be relied upon to take place within the next decade or so except by the direct agency of government or government-inspired institutions.

At present, in addition to the experimental schemes now being conducted by the Colonial Development Corporation, the territory is operating a ten-year development plan involving the expenditure of about £8¼ millions over the ten years ending in 1956.[1] Of this, £2.3 millions are to come from the funds provided under the Colonial Development and Welfare Act, £3 millions are to be raised by loan, and £3 millions are to be provided from the Protectorate's own funds (largely from war and post-war surpluses). This represents a considerable scaling up of the plan devised in 1946 which provided for an expenditure of £4½ millions. Like Northern Rhodesia, Nyasaland was forced to do extensive re-costing on account of the high cost of development in a world of physical shortages. Roughly 18% of the planned expenditure is to be devoted to improvement of communications, 14% to economic services (agriculture, forestry, electricity, lake and river control, etc.), and rather more than 38% to social services (education, medical, health, housing, water supplies, etc.). The remaining 30% is allocated to administration, research, interest charges, and contingencies.[2]

In theory it is necessary to plan for a cessation of Colonial Development and Welfare grants at the end of the ten-year period. In practice it may be possible to take a more optimistic view of the willingness of the United Kingdom taxpayer to continue the flow of contributions to colonial development. On the other hand, it may be wise to expect a lower rate of incomes and profits for the immigrant communities if world prices fail to maintain their present level and to plan for a possible fall in income tax yields. In all events the rate of expenditure now must be limited by considerations of the level of maintenance charges (as well as debt service charges) which will be involved in the future, and the expected capacity of the colony to meet these charges. It would be unfortunate, for example, if the burden of recurrent charges on electricity plants or communications were to threaten future allocations to health and agricultural services.

To some extent this is a political dilemma rather than an economic problem. Since progress towards self-government hinges to a large extent on financial independence, it is desirable that the colony should be freed as soon as possible from dependence on the United Kingdom Treasury. On the other hand, since the most urgently needed developments are those which are unlikely to contribute much realizable financial return (the improvement of subsistence food supplies is again the

[1] See the report on the *Nyasaland Development Programme*, Government Printer, Zomba, 1948.
[2] The distinction between economic and social services is not particularly useful as it stands. Much of the expenditure in the social or research categories could fairly be called 'economic'.

best example of non-commercial progress) it may be that it is best to accept a slow rate of political progress and to concentrate in the first place on freeing the people from the more physical forms of want, with the aid of as much financial assistance as the United Kingdom Treasury will provide.

Nevertheless, whether we rest on the political or the economic horn of the dilemma, the economic problem is essentially one of ensuring that Government's share in the national income keeps pace with the expansion of national income as a whole. This need not be taken as a literally exclusive definition of the problem. It is important to investigate exhaustively the measures which might be adopted to stimulate and utilize local saving (for example, through co-operative societies, or by providing the small producer with capital or working equipment on easier terms than would be possible through commercial channels). The initiative, however, will lie with Government for some time to come, and the problem of increasing the tax revenues of Government is basic.

From this standpoint it is significant and alarming that the relative weight of government in the economy has diminished rather than increased in recent years in spite of increased Government preoccupation with development. The tendency to a fall in Government's share in the national income is a result of the tendency to an increase in the share of the African community, as can be seen from Table 34, which estimates the proportion of taxation paid by the different groups in the economy in 1936, 1945 and 1948.

TABLE 34.   Distribution of taxation, 1936–48[1]

(As percentages of total tax paid each year)

	1936 %	1945 %	1948 %
Africans	69.30	41.86	39
Europeans and companies	25.33	42.43	46
Asians	5.37	15.71	15
All groups	100.00	100.00	100

In effect, while the African share in the national income has been rising, the African percentage contribution to the public revenue has been falling. The yield of direct taxation of natives (now standing at a rate of 10s. per adult male) has increased by only 60% over the period 1938 to 1948. Over the same period African incomes have more than trebled. Indirect taxation has shown more resilience to improved economic conditions, but it also has only increased by about 150%. Over the same period, income tax has increased its yield more than sevenfold.

[1] The 1936 and 1945 estimates are extracted from the report of the Fiscal Survey, op. cit.

It may still be possible to increase the volume of tax paid by immigrant individuals, and it may be politically important to do so, but they are so few in number that this could not affect the main issue.[1] In practical terms it is a problem of devising a satisfactory system of direct taxation of Africans which will permit some redistribution of wealth *within* the African community.

The conclusion, therefore, is that Nyasaland is an African territory in more than the geographical sense. The bulk of its national income flows to its $2\frac{1}{2}$ million native inhabitants, and it follows from this that the capital resources for its economic development must be largely provided by Africans. To some extent the problem of planning for economic progress in Nyasaland is similar to the problem as it presents itself in West Africa, with the difference, however, that Nyasaland is less accessible to world centres of purchasing power and that its products compete more directly with those of the relatively highly capitalized European or Asian producers in southern Africa.

At present there are four main limiting factors to effective development in Nyasaland, apart from the poverty, political backwardness, and disease which are the hallmarks of an underdeveloped economy. The chief of these is ignorance. It is impossible to plan for the maximization of the colony's resources until it is known what these resources are. We do not know what inspires so many young men to sell their labour abroad, and what real net advantage, if any, the community gets from this sale. We do not know whether the land could carry them if they stayed in Nyasaland to farm on their own account, or whether European employers could in fact afford to pay a sufficiently high rate of wages to keep them at home. It may be that there is mineral wealth in the colony. It may be that the Lake, if properly fished and farmed, could yield a valuable return, or that new export crops could be developed, or that secondary industries could be built up to feed the local market. It is possible that development of the output of tobacco or cotton has been at the expense of food crops, and we do not know whether the volume (as opposed to the value) of subsistence output has risen or fallen in the past decade. Since we cannot measure the distribution of income we cannot assess the surplus available for investment. Without information on the present distribution of the country's manpower it is impossible to plan intelligently for its most efficient use.

The second limiting factor is accessible wealth. The majority of the population lives at a uniformly low standard of living and it is difficult

---

[1] Under the double taxation arrangements recently brought into force, any increase in Nyasaland's company rate of tax up to the United Kingdom rate would be at the expense of the United Kingdom. Any further increase would endanger the flow of capital from abroad.

to contemplate any reduction in consumption for most of them. Even for those who might be conceived to have a surplus, the problem of measuring this surplus and of directing it into the most profitable channels from the social point of view has yet to be solved. In any case it is unlikely that any spectacular increase in capital investment can be achieved in the foreseeable future, and it is the more important therefore, that the expenditure of existing resources should be planned with care.

The third limiting factor is skill. At present the skill of the community is largely supplied by the small group of immigrants. They are the agriculturists, the entomologists, the teachers, the doctors, and the artisans on whom all development plans depend. There is an absolute shortage of them and, being immigrants of a relatively high standard of living, their services are an expensive charge on a poor African community. It is possible to plan for transmission of this skill to the natives of the colony, so that in time they can provide their own professional and technical experts; this in itself, however, requires more agriculturists, teachers, doctors, etc., and the community is faced with the dilemma of using its scarce resources of skill either to create a cadre of cheaper local skill, or to get on with the practical tasks of development right away.

Finally, a fourth limiting factor is land. The density of population is high and the cultivable land in some areas—particularly in some areas of Southern Province—is too small to maintain the population living on it. Expansion of the agricultural and livestock industry beyond a certain point would demand more intensive and highly capitalized methods of production, intensified war on the tsetse fly, new irrigation and river control measures, increased re-afforestation and soil conservation programmes, and so on. Agricultural Department files provide ample evidence that this pressure on land resources has rendered many villagers hungry in the past few years. It may well have driven many African men abroad in search of a more abundant standard of life. It is now beginning to act as a brake on the relatively developed sections of the economy. In the review of 1948 which begins the annual report of Nyasaland for that year, the section describing the favourable 1947-8 agricultural season and the excellent crops of tobacco, tea, cotton and tung, contains the following ominous passage: 'The internal food situation, however, deteriorated, not because of any decrease in the production of maize (the staple food of most of the African population), but because of the increasing pressure of a growing population upon a soil of dwindling fertility and a rising material standard of living. The Maize Control Board was only able to dispose of a surplus of about two per cent of the estimated total production; major consumers including the Government, are now taking steps to produce as large a proportion as possible of their own requirements of maize, as they cannot rely any longer on surpluses from subsistence farming.'[1] In a year of bad harvest such as 1949, large sections of the indigenous population are obliged to depend on the bulk importation of foodstuffs.

In sum, therefore, there are numerous obstacles in the way of a rapid increase in incomes or output, and unless unknown resources (e.g. mineral resources) are revealed, or unless existing resources acquire unexpected new values, no spectacular advance is possible. It would seem, indeed, that the prices of agricultural products are already as high in terms of manufactured goods as they are likely to be in the foreseeable future. It may even be difficult to maintain the present level of real incomes as competitive world output improves, and as the pressure on Nyasaland's scanty resources of land-skilled labour and capital is intensified. It is certain that the need for free grants in aid from the United Kingdom will continue, and that there is much new ground to be broken and much basic research of an economic, technical and social nature to be completed before the pace of development can be regarded as satisfactory.

---

[1] *Annual Report on the Nyasaland Protectorate for the Year 1948*, H.M.S.O., London, 1949, p. 5. 'Major consumers' are, of course, major employers of labour who provide rations for their employees.

I

PART IV

THE RURAL COMMUNITIES

CHAPTER IX

SOCIAL ACCOUNTING
FOR PRIMITIVE COMMUNITIES

It has been repeatedly emphasized in the preceding pages that the problem of obtaining adequate data on the rural economies of Africa is the most serious obstacle in the way of framing satisfactory national income estimates for these territories. The importance of this problem can be judged from the fact that for most Africans the typical background of economic activity is still the village. In Central Africa, for example, the urban population is small—8% of the total in Northern Rhodesia and less than 1% in Nyasaland. Even on the assumption that all absentees from the villages have gone to towns, about 88% of Northern Rhodesian Africans and about 90% of Nyasaland Africans are actually resident in the villages. Both town-dwellers and migrants tend, moreover, to be temporary absentees from their villages, and the majority will return at intervals and eventually retire to the rural areas. Comparatively few of them take their entire families to the towns even for short periods. The economic activity of the villages is the principal determinant of the standard of living of the majority of people in Northern Rhodesia and Nyasaland.

The accounting problem is not simply that of the acute scarcity of quantitative data which is discussed below in Chapter X. It is also a qualitative problem which brings into question the fundamental validity for primitive communities of the social accounting concepts themselves. In this sphere also the difficulty of finding a solution to the practical problems is aggravated by a lack of relevant information.

An attempt to examine the structure and problems of a primitive community in the light of the existing body of economic thought raises fundamental conceptual issues. Economic analysis and its framework of generalizations are characteristically described in terms appropriate to the modern exchange economy. It is by no means certain that the existing tools of analysis can usefully be applied to material other than that for which they have been developed. In particular, it is not clear what light, if any, is thrown on subsistence economies by a science which seems to regard the use of money and specialization of labour as axiomatic. The jargon of the market place seems remote, on the face of it, from the problems of an African village where most individuals spend the greater part of their lives in satisfying their own or their families' needs and desires, and where money and trade play a subordinate role in motivating productive activity. A science which studies 'that part of social welfare which can be brought directly or indirectly into relation with the measuring rod of money' does not appear to have much contribution to make to the problems of a semi-subsistence economy.[1]

In practice, the economist's definition of the scope of economics, and of such fundamental concepts as 'economic activity', 'income', and 'wealth', tends to be vague at the fringes. The majority of economists would impute under income a value for the rent of owner-occupied houses: comparatively few would value the services of wives although they would include a housekeeper's wage: there is no hard and fast ruling on whether the incomes of prostitutes should be included in the national income, although the illegal incomes of such individuals as operators on the black market, and burglars, are generally excluded. For most practical purposes this vagueness at the fringe is not particularly important. When an issue does arise in which precision is required —for example, when the services of unpaid dependants are a factor in determining economic policy towards the industrial employment of women—it can be dealt with separately and on an *ad hoc* basis. What is the fringe in one society, however, is not necessarily the fringe in another. It is convenient in considering the United Kingdom economy to disregard the activities of, say, unpaid dependants. There is room for discussion on the usefulness of including these items and on their importance to the national economy, but it would not seriously be argued that their exclusion robbed the study in general of most of its value. In most primitive communities, on the other hand, women and children play an important part in producing the family's food crops. If an economic survey of an African village ignored the activities of unpaid dependants as being outside the scope of economics, it could not be expected to throw much light on the welfare of the villagers, however narrowly defined that was in terms of material things.

In so far as any activity involves the disposition of limited time and resources which have alternative uses, in relation to a relatively unlimited system of wants, it has an economic aspect.[2] It is the element of

---

[1] A. C. Pigou, *The Economics of Welfare*, London, Macmillan, 1946.

[2] Professor Lionel Robbins' definition of economics as 'the science which studies human behaviour as a relationship between ends and scarce means which have alternative uses' makes this point. See his *Nature and Significance of Economic Science*, London, Macmillan, 1935

choice and the need to 'economize' that characterizes economic activity. Thus, economic value or price, reflects not primarily the amount of satisfaction derivable from a good or a service, but the sum of all the other potential satisfactions which have been foregone in order to obtain it. Or to put it another way, the price paid for a good represents the value of the other goods which could have been bought for that price or the return the producer has received for the resources he has used to that end.

The primary purpose behind the study of the ways in which individuals or communities adapt their resources to their wants is the maximization of their satisfactions. The general object of economic analysis is to provide a basis of knowledge for the formulation of economic policy. Since satisfactions are generally held to be a function of the quantity and quality of the goods and services which become available, it might be said that the chief aim (although never the only aim) of economic policy is to increase the total value of the goods and services which can be produced by the community.

Each good or service can be produced only at the cost of sacrificing other wants. In a community where the relative costs of producing the different goods and services are expressed throughout in terms of money prices, money is the common denominator which is used to sum the costs and reach a figure for the total economic value of the goods and services produced. On the assumption that the sacrifice involved in producing a good is generally correlated with the satisfaction received from it, this aggregate provides us with an index of the level of satisfaction achieved as a result of economic activity. Again, provided that the pattern of wants does not change, and also provided that there is no change in the value of money itself, we can use the changes in the aggregate value of goods and services produced from year to year as a measure of the changes in the level of economic satisfaction or welfare enjoyed from year to year.

This is the best that could be claimed for social aggregates expressed in money terms, and even this claim has to be qualified. The national income of a country is the total value of the goods and services produced by its nationals. It is not even possible to assume that economic value can be regarded as an indication of the measure of satisfaction achieved by economic activity unless it is also assumed that individuals behave rationally. In other words, it is necessary to assume that each individual effectively adjusts the necessary sacrifice to the resultant satisfaction.[1] Even on this assumption it is not necessarily the case that a significant

[1] The use of the word 'rationally' in this context and its interpretation beg the fundamental question of welfare economics.

social aggregate can be achieved by the mere addition of the costs of sacrifice, or of the value of satisfaction, involved in the economic activities of a number of different individuals over an arbitrary period of time. It may be that a few individuals in the community are endowed with most of the goods and services produced by it. In that case, the changes in a simple aggregate are not in themselves a sufficient index of changes in the level of satisfaction enjoyed by the community as a whole. Again, the output of goods and services may fluctuate seasonally, or cyclically, in a community with inadequate storage facilities, so that the people may have more food, say, than they can consume at one period, and be near starvation at other periods. It is thus not enough to know what is the total value of goods and services produced. It is necessary to know, further, how the product is distributed as between groups in the community and how the flow is distributed over time. Economic policy seeks not only to raise the national income, but also to render its distribution more even, both as between persons and over time. Given the two provisos that the pattern of wants and the value of money must have remained the same, a community's level of satisfaction might be judged to have been increased if the national income rose, or if it were more evenly distributed over the community, or if it were more evenly distributed over time.

In fact, of course, it is never possible to assume with confidence that the community's pattern of wants will stay the same, or that the value of money will not change. A community which has been producing for total war, for example, cannot readjust automatically to peacetime production, and national income figures give little or no indication of the sudden slump in the level of satisfactions which comes when the war-intended output is no longer required with the same urgency. The volume of goods and services produced continues to rise although the satisfactions derived from it have fallen. Similarly, a fall or a rise in the value of money produces changes in the money national income which bear no relation to the level of satisfaction. When changes in the pattern of wants or the value of money do occur, all judgments based on national income data must be interpreted and qualified in the light of what is known about the nature of the changes. Generally speaking, however, for an economy that is free from violent change, the year to year movements in national income totals are a useful reflection of changes in the level of economic satisfactions, although comparisons carried over a longer period of time than a few years must be regarded as exceedingly rough.

In so far as it can be assumed that the primitive community has the same broad ends as a modern exchange economy, the information which would be required for an economic study of one would be of a similar nature to that required for the other. In other words, if it can be assumed that the ends of policy for a primitive economy include an increase in the output of goods and services, and an improvement of their distribution as between persons and over time, then it can be fairly assumed that the kind of information which is usually collected by economists is relevant to the special case of the primitive economy. On the face of it the assumption is not unreasonable. The members of a primitive community usually do need more food and better standards of shelter and clothing, and they have a variety of less fundamental but nevertheless pressing needs for other goods and services. Where real income is unequally distributed as between persons it is often desirable that this inequality should be reduced. Where it fluctuates through the year or from one year to another, it is generally reasonable to assume that a more even flow would increase satisfaction in the lean months by more than it decreases satisfaction in the period of plenty. Whether these ends are as important to the primitive economy as they apparently are to the more advanced economy, and what relation they bear to other ends, it is impossible to know without intensive social study of the community concerned. Given that they do exist, however, it is possible to use them as a starting-point for the collection and presentation of economic data.

Briefly, therefore, the economist is interested in all information which throws any light on the pattern of wants in the area concerned, the limits of the available resources, and the ways in which the resources are currently adapted to meet needs. What economic goods and services (i.e. goods and services which involve the disposition of scarce resources with alternative uses) do the people want and with what degree of urgency? What means have they for satisfying these needs and how precisely do they allocate their resources as between one end and another? How successful are they at achieving their ends within the limits of their resources? More concretely, what kind of food, shelter, clothing and other needs, figure among the wants of the villagers and in what order of importance? What is the strength of the labour force, the extent of the land resources and the amount of capital available? What goods and services are produced and how are they distributed as between persons? What are the possibilities of increasing the output of wanted goods and services and how steady is the annual flow?

Much of the information which is sought under these headings is information of a quantitative nature. It is not that the qualitative data are of minor importance. They are the flesh and the form to which the quantitative material is only the skeleton. That the people of a given community will not eat eggs or milk; or that little girls of more than six years of age regularly pound maize; or that manure is used to improve the yield of the land; or that the young men prefer to migrate in search of gainful employment rather than to earn cash locally; or that men would rather accept a low crop yield than labour to make contour ridges to protect their land against soil erosion; all these are economic data of first importance. Facts of this kind, although they are capable of being demonstrated quantitatively, are not primarily quantitative data.

Without a quantitative framework, however, the picture which emerges from the qualitative data is a shapeless affair. It is interesting to find that children pound maize, but the importance of this fact is not clear until the relative contribution of the children has been measured. Any judgment on whether or not the labour involved in contour ridging is efficiently used depends on the knowledge that is available on the actual amount of difference it would make to crop yields and the value of the alternative disposition of the labour. In order to gauge the contribution of the migrant labourer to the net income of the community, it is important to know how much in cash and goods he brings back to his village from work and by how much his absence reduced the flow of goods and services produced in the village.

In short, what is needed as a framework of study is a quantitative account of the way the community lays out its resources and what it gets for its efforts. With this framework as a context and a firm basis of fact it is possible to analyse objectively the direction and causes of change, and the needs for and obstacles to improvement in economic welfare. For the primitive economy, as for more developed economies, a system of social accounts provides a useful tool of economic analysis.

If we start from the assumption that for all communities an increase in the volume of economic goods and services produced, and an improvement in its distribution over time and among persons and groups, are important ends of economic policy, then it is legitimate to focus attention in this way on the physical output of goods and services. It is not necessary to assume that these are the only ends inspiring the community's economic activity. No one who has seen a Central African working party in action can doubt that what is produced is frequently of less importance than the conditions of production. This factor is not, of course, peculiar to the primitive economy. It has never been possible to state categorically that the sole end of production is consumption or that economic activity arises only from its potential return in the form of goods and services produced. A man who is in a position to choose his occupation in the modern state will weigh a variety of factors, of which the material income is only one. In the same way, an African who chooses between migrating to paid employment, growing cash crops locally, or setting out on a roving trade mission will be influenced by many more considerations than can be expressed in a standard profit and loss account.

It has often been remarked that among primitive communities exchange itself has a social rather than an economic significance. The terms of trade may be determined by ties of kinship rather than by the need for or the sacrifice involved in acquiring a particular commodity. Here too, the situation is paralleled in more developed countries. The seller does not always sell for the highest return or the buyer buy the best bargain. The shopper may go to the Co-operative Stores 'on principle' or to Fortnum and Mason's because she likes its 'atmosphere'. What is different for the primitive community is merely the degree to which social and psychological conditions determine economic activity.

In practice, however, the extent of sociological knowledge about the primitive peoples is such that while it is generally safe to assume that an improvement in the supply of physical goods and services produced is universally desirable, it is not possible to define, still less to assess, the other objects of economic activity with any degree of certainty. While it is essential to recognize the existence of, and to attempt to define more precisely, what might loosely be termed the 'uneconomic' incentives motivating primitive economies, it is also useful to be able to examine in detail the more tangible causes and effects of economic activity. In effect, therefore, although an analysis based on the techniques of financial accounting cannot be expected to cover all the relevant aspects of primitive economic activity, a balancing account of the goods and services produced by each group of villagers, and of the goods and services consumed by them, is a useful starting-point in the formulation of economic policy for the rural areas.

The practical problems involved in an attempt to collect the material for a village income and outlay account are discussed in Chapters X and XI, where some experimental surveys are described. In that discussion the conceptual framework is taken for granted. The fundamental assumption is made that it is possible to make a significant evaluation of the village output of goods and services in terms of money.

The first essential in the compilation of any kind of quantitative data is a measuring rod. In order to aggregate all the goods and services produced by the individuals of a community so that they form a meaningful total, it is necessary to be able to apply to them some common denominator, some measuring rod of universal application. It does not mean anything to add weights of maize to weights of monkeynuts (although there could be some point in translating them both into calories first), and it is impossible to add cattle to clothes. In an exchange economy the problem is dealt with by measuring everything in terms of money. As a measuring rod, money has the disadvantage that it is not a fixed standard, since it changes in meaning over time. On the other hand, it is possible to make allowance for changes in the value of money, which has the supreme advantage in an exchange economy that it can be applied to any commodity. In such an economy, economic activity is conveniently defined for working purposes as that part of welfare which can be brought directly or indirectly into relation with the measuring rod of money.

In deciding what can be measured in money terms there is room, of course, for some individual interpretation and there are difficult logical problems involved. For example, the generally accepted interpretation that the services of unpaid dependants should not be evaluated for national income purposes involves the paradox that if a man marries his housekeeper the national income is thereby reduced by the amount of her wages. On the other hand there is no way of evaluating the services of unpaid dependants unless by imputing the average earnings of a few thousand housekeepers to several million housewives. If such problems as these (which are not fundamental for most practical policy purposes) are ignored, the use of money as the universal measuring rod and as the symbol of economic activity proves a prac-ticable proposition in an exchange economy. Goods and services are evaluated at the price paid for them and where, for example, a farmer consumes some of his own produce, it is included in his total output at the value which he receives for his traded output. Since most goods and services produced through the disposition of scarce resources in an exchange economy are either traded, or form such a small part of total output that the value of traded output can safely be imputed to them, it is possible to cover all but a negligible proportion of total economic activity by defining it in money terms. The omissions are important only in special cases and for special problems.

In a pure subsistence economy, on the other hand, every individual produces to satisfy his own needs and there is no exchange of goods and services. There is no universal measure which could be used to sum the costs (either in resources consumed or in foregone satisfactions) of obtaining a particular satisfaction. There are no values which can be imputed to particular activities to indicate their importance in the whole range of activities. In practice, however, the problem of framing economic policy for a pure subsistence economy does not arise. The practical problem is one of assessing the efficiency of adaptation of resources to needs in a *semi-subsistence* economy, that is for a community where a large proportion of wants are satisfied directly by the producer or his family but where barter or money exchange transactions are a potential factor in almost every form of economic activity.

There are few activities in the African village economy that are never exchanged for money. It is almost always possible to cite an instance where a money price has been charged within recent memory and in the same general area. On the other hand, it is probably safe to say that for the majority of economic activities there is no market value as it is understood in the money economies. When goods are not normally traded the prices of the goods that are traded do not reflect the value in resources used or in relative desirability of subsistence output. It might be, for example, that the only trade was seasonal trade. In a village where a small group of careful producers habitually succeeded in retaining a surplus of the principal food crop, say maize, for sale to the inevitable small group of unlucky or inefficient producers who exhaust their supplies before the next harvest is ready, the price of maize would be significant only in relation to the special circumstances of a particular season. To evaluate all maize produced by all households at this, the only known price, would be meaningless.

This is an example of the extreme case. For all the most important commodities there is a price which has some kind of meaning, even if the meaning is irrelevant to the internal economy of the village. For example, the price of maize even in the remoter villages is generally dependent, directly or indirectly, on its value on the urban or world markets. When considering the external aspects of the village economy (its relative contribution to the national economy, for example) there is a certain significance in a figure which corresponds to external valuations. On the other hand, it is well to remember that this external price has only a limited significance and national accounts framed in terms of international valuations do not permit a precise analysis of the national economy in all its aspects.

Even when this relatively low level of significance is accepted as inevitable the problem of valuation is a constant source of difficulty in reporting the economic data for a semi-subsistence economy. The more important commodities tend to have a market value deriving from their value on urban or world markets, provided that they are also important outside the village economy. They have a relatively fixed and recognizable value. In some cases the value is too fixed to make sense by exchange economy standards, as when, for example, a man cites the same price for his maize at place of production as he would at a market some hundred or so miles away.

Commodities which are unimportant on the external market and which may not be as unimportant in the village economy raise an apparently different set of problems because they have no fixed value. One might well find, for example, that pots or baskets have never been sold in a given village over the past year but are frequently bartered. Standard rates of barter do exist, but, generally speaking, the terms of a barter transaction tend to be unique. In any case, standard rates of barter are formulae which tend to apply to standard situations and to show insufficient response to quality variations. In some areas, for example, baskets or pots when exchanged for maize are habitually exchanged for their capacity of maize, although these terms of trade bear no direct relation either to the relative usefulness of different sizes of basket or of their relative costs of production. Thus a woman with a pot to dispose of might be willing to sell it for 6d. or for its capacity of maize meal, or for a sleeping mat, regarding each of these as a standard market 'price' for the pot, although the money which she would expect to pay for the maize or for the sleeping mat might be more or less than 6d.

In effect, although money is used freely and money value is a familiar concept in the semi-subsistence economy, the prices are not necessarily part of an integrated system. Each transaction which does not take place in an organized market tends to be isolated in time and space from all similar transactions or at least to bear only a formal and not a dynamic relationship to them. There is no common standard of value which would make it possible to consider each economic activity as a function of its drain on the community's total scarce resources or of its contribution to the community's total needs.

To look at the matter from another point of view, an attempt to compare the level of incomes in the villages, say, with the level of incomes in the towns (defining income as the flow of economic goods and services described in money terms) is rendered practically meaningless by the fact that the values applied mean different things in different places. For the towns the assumption that money values are a reflection of the relative importance of the different items in terms of each other is roughly true. It is only possible to compare money standards of living in town and village in so far as this is also true in some measure of the villages, after adequate allowance has been made for differing scales of values in town and country. In practice, the village price schedule is often no more than a distorted reflection of the urban price system and has little or no relevance to the village scale of values.

Nor is the problem of valuation the only obstacle in the way of comparing one group with another in terms of relative social incomes. Since resources and needs take a different form in different environments, what is an economic good in one place need not be an economic good in another. More important still in an economy containing within itself widely different types of economic environment, what is an economic good for a man in one place may not be an economic good for him in another place.

Here again, the attempt to compare income levels in town and country illustrates the nature of the difficulties involved in interpreting African social accounts. The Central African in the town is usually a man who was in the village a few months or years ago and who will return to the village before many months or years have elapsed. The urban community is essentially the same as the village community, and it seems reasonable to expect some measure of effective quantitative comparison to be possible. Moreover, this question of whether the African is better off in the towns or in the villages is one of the most important of those to which the policy-maker is seeking a definite, quantitative answer. Nevertheless, the comparison involves almost as thick a smokescreen of qualifications as a comparison of one country's national income with another's.

A concrete example may clarify the point. An African moving into a new village needs sleeping accommodation. He will generally find that there are several vacant huts which he could inhabit if he does not wish to build one for himself. If not he will share a hut with an existing resident until he has finished building one for himself—frequently with the unpaid help of the villagers. In any case there is no question of having to pay any rent in cash or in kind because sleeping accommodation does not come under the heading of a scarce factor and there is thus no economic service imputable to housing. If, on the other hand, he should move to a town location, he can obtain a hut of his own only by renting it or by building one for himself on a rented site. If he builds one of his own, it is logical to impute to it an annual economic value equivalent to the rent which he would have had to pay for the hire of it or for which he could let it. Thus, when the villager moves to the town, his income, for accounting purposes, rises by the rental value of the hut of which he is owner-occupier in the location, although in fact his town accommodation may be of no better quality (may even be worse) than his village accommodation.

Another group of village accounting problems arises from the fact that in practice money payments are not easily attachable to a particular economic good or service. A payment which is not evoked by a distinguishable good or service is not regarded as net income for accounting purposes. Thus gifts, social security receipts and damages resulting from court decisions, to take a few examples, are regarded as transfer incomes. Social accounts which attempt to record total economic activity exclude these payments because they do not actually represent any addition to the total output of economic goods and services, but are simply the transfer of purchasing power from one individual or group of individuals to another individual or group of individuals.

On the face of it this definition of income for net income purposes is simple and straightforward. It is when actual village payments have to be interpreted that difficulties of definition arise. In so far as a man helps a neighbour to pay his tax in the definite expectation of getting a return, even if it is only a claim to assistance in the hour of his own need, the money is not gifted. Where, however, a man helps in the payment of another's tax because it is an obligation of kinship which is not directly related to the expectation of a return, then this could fairly be described as a transfer payment between members of the same family. In practice, the difficulty is one of establishing the existence of a claim or expectation, however indirect it may be, or of defining the limits of the family. All a man's neighbours in the village may be related to him and to argue by analogy with the European-type family may be highly misleading.

The problem, which is primarily a sociological problem, would not be so important were it not that these unattached payments form a significant proportion of the total number and value of village transactions. Anyone who has ever tried to collect family income and expenditure budgets in a Central African village will have been struck by the complications of the gift pattern and the difficulty of analysing it in Western economic concepts. Time and again in answer to the question 'And what did you give in return for such-and-such a good or service?' comes the reply 'Nothing. He did it to help me.' Rarely, it seems, does the average villager build his house alone. It is generally built with the assistance of neighbours and not necessarily always with a beer party to cheer his helpers. Even where a beer party is held it is by no means certain that it is a *quid pro quo* rather than a celebration for which the joint labour provided the occasion. In effect, to decide whether an activity is a gift or represents a contribution to economic output, it is necessary to decide whether or not it is made in reasonable expectation of a corresponding return or whether it establishes a claim (however qualified) to such a return.

The problem is complicated by the fact that the definition of income on which this argument is based implies exchange. In a European-type exchange economy it is logical to maintain that as the services rendered by a man for himself or his family are not generally included as part of his economic activity, so the services which he renders for other people without expectation of return are also excludable. In an African village, however, it is scarcely reasonable to include the value of a hut built by a man for himself and to exclude the value of a hut built by him for another man. In practice, therefore, one would normally include all subsistence output even if it is produced for gift purposes. Thus the practical problem of whether or not to exclude a gift does not arise until it becomes a question of a payment. Then it is necessary to decide whether a given payment represents an additional economic activity (does it bring the payer any consumable return or does it establish any claim for him?) or whether it merely elaborates an existing activity by bringing in a second participant.

For similar reasons, damages paid or received as the result of court proceedings do not in general qualify as income because they are not payments for economic activity. They represent payments between individuals for which no service is rendered. Sociological evidence, however, may suggest qualifications to this rule. It is open to argument, for example, that some men make a 'business' of their court cases. Where the damages for adultery are well established and automatically exacted it might fairly be argued that the damages are merely payment legally enforced and that the service has in fact been rendered.

Marriage payments are particularly difficult to handle logically because of their very mixed nature. If the wife can be regarded as an economic good—which is inconceivable by Western European standards but which might well be in keeping with African concepts—a standard non-returnable marriage payment from groom to father-in-law can be conveniently treated as a straightforward act of purchase. In that case the expenditure payment is matched in the output column by the 'production' of a wife and in the income column by income received from wife-providing activity. A non-returnable marriage payment, apparently varying at the will of the groom, looks very much like a money gift. It might fairly be treated as a payment designed to create a general feeling of good will among a group of relatives-to-be and thus as a transfer payment rather than as a payment for services received or receivable: or, on the other hand, it might be regarded as the fulfilment of a ritual obligation which does not of itself symbolize an economic activity any more than does the payment of a tax.

Finally, if wives can be regarded as economic goods they can also be classed as economic wealth, capable of rendering a flow of services to the possessor in the same way as a horse or a cow. Thus a returnable marriage payment is a form of investment in return for which the groom obtains a claim on the services of his wife and of her children by him. It should be noted, however, that if wives are accounted for in the social income tables by analogy with livestock, there will be some very odd-looking entries in the output column. The output of livestock, for example, logically includes the net increase in the value of livestock held by the community during the year. By analogy it would be necessary to evaluate a man's quiver of female children and to enter the net increase or decrease during the year.

In practice, the solutions adopted to these conceptual problems will tend to be dictated by two main sets of considerations acting together. On the one hand, there is the need to maintain some kind of uniformity with international conceptual standards so that the village social accounts will have some meaning in an international framework. On the other hand, there is the nature of the available data which are generally limited enough to restrict the application of logical principles. For international comparative purposes it would mean little to draw up social accounts which ignored the bulk of the staple food crop production. On the other hand, there are no data which would permit any kind of realistic estimate of the value of services of African women in preparing food, other than beer, for consumption. I found one case where a woman received money payment for cooking for a stranger, and there are doubtless others which could be cited by investigators. But there was no evidence to suggest that there was any ascertainable market value for that service. Thus the net result is that African women are assumed to be performing economic services which should be recorded in the social accounts up to the point at which the food is brought off the field. Beyond that point, unless they are engaged in producing beer, for which there is a readily ascertainable market value in most areas, they are not treated as if engaged in economic activity and their services cease to count in the social income.

In essence, of course, none of the problems which have been discussed above are conceptually peculiar to the primitive economy, although they may emerge there in an unusual form. No attempt to construct a logical and meaningful system of social accounts is free from anomalies and obscurities which severely limit the precise quantitative significance of the results. There are two main reasons why the primitive economy should raise especially difficult problems for the national income investigator. The first is that the problems are often different in degree, if not intrinsically, from the similar problems which attend the construction of social accounts for a Western European economy. The second is that the logical compromises which have to be made in practice are based on an inadequate background of sociological data and are therefore more arbitrary than they would be for an investigator for whom the community's accepted ends of economic and social policy are part of his native background.

Thus, although money is never a completely satisfactory measuring rod, it is a great deal more significant for an economy where production is normally designed for exchange, than in an economy where the standard of living depends primarily on subsistence output. Problems of evaluation which affect the fringe of the exchange economy are at the heart of the semi-subsistence economy. The inadequacies of the price system which make it difficult to compare the United Kingdom national income with that of the United States or to compare one year's national income with that of another, are such as to make it difficult to combine rural and urban incomes, or European and African incomes, into a single meaningful total for a colonial economy.

Nor indeed is it possible to assume at present that the prices of the village economy are anything more than an incompletely understood reflection of the relationship of the village with the urban economy. It may be, for example, that the village price of maize is directly related to the village price for baskets, but the existence of discrepancies between the money exchange value and the barter exchange value of maize and baskets makes it difficult to appreciate the relationship. There are insufficient data to suggest reliable conclusions. It has been easier to find discrepancies in the village price schedules when considered in terms of the European exchange economy model than to detect any pattern in it and thus to understand its origins and significance. Without careful price and barter records covering not only the village economy but also the relevant contiguous urban economies over a period of time it is not possible either to appreciate the role of money in the villages or to attribute to village accounts an intrinsic significance. In evaluating subsistence output for inclusion in national income totals we can suggest in the broadest of terms the relative importance of subsistence income in the national total and particularly in the African total; but it is not possible to claim any strictly quantitative significance for either the whole or the part unless we can attribute a significance to an arbitrary group of prices based on current market conditions in the sector of the economy which is more susceptible to external than to internal influences.

In essence, therefore, the figures for subsistence output in the national accounts are purely token figures and it is important to remember that a revised scheme of evaluation would alter the results radically. So also, of course, would a revised set of definitions. It is not possible, given the gaps in sociological information, to be at all certain about income definitions, and the differences expressed in money terms may be considerable. A system of social accounts which excludes marriage payments, for example, will show quite a different pattern of consumption and quite a different national income total from one which includes these payments as income. On the other hand, if marriage payments are included, the concept of national income takes on a new significance and its effectiveness for purposes of international comparison is correspondingly reduced.

It seems worth while emphasizing strongly in a study of this kind the limitations of a money calculation as an index of economic activity in a community where money plays a subordinate role. The difficulties are numerous. In the first place, there is often no money price which bears direct relation to the other money prices in the economy. As a corollary of this, there are often multiple standards of valuation and there is no fine adjustment of supply and demand. Secondly, money does not have the same power of inspiration in the semi-subsistence

K

economy. Social and psychological considerations frequently outweigh the money factor as a determinant of activity. Men tend to value the medium of exchange not for itself as a generally useful commodity, but directly in terms of what it will buy. Hence, on the one hand, they often work for things directly and not for money in general, and, on the other hand, they often do not even try to make profits from either production or exchange. It is not easy to interpret all this in positive terms. Although it is easy enough to cite instances in which money does not mean the same to the member of a primitive community as it does normally to the member of a highly developed community, it is not possible to define exactly what money does mean to such a community. It is probable that in the context in which a national income calculation is likely to be of any use these qualifications and problems are of comparatively little significance. They should, however, be borne in mind whenever any attempt is made to relate national income figures to real standards of living.

In sum, the village economy is the background against which we should like to set the urban activities of African and other colonial communities. There is, however, apparently no way of measuring its activities except by using the measuring rod of money and the defini- tions which are ultimately applicable to a modern European economy. These alien concepts can be adjusted and adapted to meet some of the principal difficulties involved in applying them to village conditions, but they reflect the village economy only in so far as it can usefully be interpreted in these terms. It may be that this problem is in the long run not as important as it seems, that the semi-subsistence economies are rapidly being drawn within the orbit of the exchange economy and adopting its concepts and standards, that an evaluation of village subsistence output by an urban exchange measure provides all the information that is necessary for public policy purposes. Nevertheless, while the process of developing the semi-subsistence economy into a predominantly exchange economy is still going on, it would be useful to have some standards of measurement and methods of analysis which would be applicable to both types of economy, and which would enable one to measure the changes in the general standard of living for the population as a whole rather than for a particular section of it or in a particular direction. The best that can be said about a social accounting system when applied to a primitive economy, or to an economy with primitive sections, is that it takes all sectors and aspects of the national economy into account and that it provides a very rough and often one-sided indication of their relative contributions to total national economic activity.

CHAPTER X

COLLECTING THE DATA

1. THE DATA REQUIRED

The quantitative material available to form a basis of estimate of the contribution of the rural economies to Central African national incomes is sketchy in the extreme. It amounts in all to a few incomplete compilations of economic material made by anthropologists and other specialists who have amassed it as a by-product of their own studies. A bibliography at the end of this Part describes the available material. It covers only a small proportion of the total rural population of Central Africa and even for this small proportion the information is incomplete. The lack of information on the rural areas in general makes it virtually impossible to judge, on any but the most subjective basis, what degree of reliance can be placed on generalizations from particular areas.

The problem of filling this vast and significant gap in the economic data of the two colonies is formidable. Northern Rhodesia, for example, covers about 290,000 sq. miles and the ecological survey distinguished twenty-one agricultural systems. Its African population has never been properly counted, but provisional estimates based on a sample census would put it at about 1.7 million in 1950. The tribal map of the territory distinguishes over fifty different native tribes. If this lack of homogeneity reaches deep into the structure of economic activity in the rural areas, the construction of even the most approximate estimates of the volume and value of their economic activity requires extensive investigations on an unprecedented scale. Even to make use of the scanty information already available it is necessary to form an opinion of the broad limits of possible generalization, and for this purpose a planned series of sample investigations is essential.

Under the circumstances there was little that could be done by a national income investigator with a limited period in which to study this particular aspect of the colonial economy, beyond an attempt to devise a method of procedure in surveying village economics. This involved drawing up a schedule of information required and conducting practical experiments in the collection of that information. Even this modest objective would have consumed more time than was available

131

TABLE 35. Village Economic Survey Schedule

Area:	Village:	Hut:	Informant:

HOUSEHOLD	Name	Birthdate	Religion	Education	Occup'n	Civil Status
Woman						
Man						

DEPENDANTS	DWELLING HUTS Number of
Sex	
Age	

CROPS
List of crops grown: Maize, cucurbits, groundnuts, beans, kaffir corn, finger millet, rice, sweet potatoes, tobacco, castor oil, sugar-cane, fruit and vegetables

CROPS SOLD	Maize	Maizeflour	Millet	Groundnuts	Tobacco	Other
Quantity						
Value						

MANUFACTURERS	Beer	Pottery	Woodwork	Ironwork	Baskets	Mats	Other
Quantity made							
Quantity sold							
Value sold							

SERVICES	Hutmaking	Bicycle repairs	Distribution	Employment	Doctoring	Other
Earnings from						

LIVESTOCK	Oxen	Cows	Calves	Goats	Pigs	Sheep	Chickens	Other
Owned								
Bought								
Sold								
Killed								
Died								
Given away								

MISCELLANEOUS INCOME	MISCELLANEOUS EXPENDITURE
Sales of: fish	Taxes or fines
wildfood	Gifts
secondhand goods	Transport
	Marriage payments
Marriage payments	Cases
Cases	School or mission
Migrant relatives	Food
Gifts	Tobacco
Other	Soap and other store goods
	Doctors or medicine
	Newspapers
	Other

Article	Nos. owned	Source	Date obtained	Price paid
Huts				
Kitchens				
Granaries				
Cattle kraals				
Goat or pig pens				
Chicken houses				
Mortars				
Pounders				
Grinders				
Sifters				
Pots—drinking				
beer				
water				
porridge				
relish				
other				
Baskets—winnowing				
market				
harvesting				
fishing				
other				
Plates—wooden				
tin				
other				
Spoons—wooden				
metal				
gourd				
Cups				
Basins				
Churns				
Buckets				
Water drums				
Beds				

Article	Nos. owned	Source	Date obtained	Price paid
Chairs				
Stools				
Tables				
Lamps				
Cupboards				
Boxes				
Sewing machines				
Bicycles				
Sledges				
Carts				
Cultivators				
Ploughs				
Hoes				
Axes				
Sickles				
Ox-yokes				
Ox chains				
Shovels				
Flat-irons				
Spanners				
Adzes				
Scissors				
Spears				
Knives				
Guns				
Watches				
Ornaments—earrings				
bracelets				
necklaces				
other				
Books				
Blankets				
Sheets				

Article	Nos. owned	Source	Date obtained	Price paid
Pillows				
Men's long trousers				
shorts				
loin cloths				
shirts				
jackets				
waistcoats				
vests				
overcoats				
belts				
ties				
socks				
hats				
sweaters				
shoes				
other cloths				
Women's cloths				
skirts				
headbands				
baby clothes				
blouses				
dresses				
other cloths				
Children's cloths				
shirts				
shorts				
blouses				
skirts				
dresses				
sweaters				
jackets				
trousers				
Other possessions				

had it not been possible to obtain the co-operation and assistance of anthropologists who were already well acquainted with certain areas.[1] The experiments involved the construction of a schedule of information required from the separate households in each area studied. Table 35 shows the general framework on which the schedule was built up. As can be seen, it might be elaborated to cover every possible form of economic activity or transaction carried out by the household or its members. In practice, however, it proved necessary to reduce the schedule for each area to the necessary minimum which would yield a reliable reflection of its main economic activities.

I visited three areas in experimenting with the schedule contained in Table 35. They were, respectively, in Tonga country in the Mazabuka District of Southern Province; in Ngoni country in the Fort Jameson District of Eastern Province; and in Lozi country in the Mongu District of Barotse Province. The areas are briefly described in Chapter XI. The visits were made in the period April-May 1947.

The principle of procedure was to collect, by questioning the members of each household, such information as would enable the salient economic activities of the village to be interpreted in quantitative terms.[2] Such a procedure implied certain grave limitations from the outset. Its accuracy and comprehensiveness is limited by its dependence on the memory of the individual, on his willingness to tell the truth, and on his ability to interpret his economic activities in quantitative terms. In a primitive economy, where the pattern of economic life is relatively simple and static, the memory of the individual, when suitably jogged by locally appropriate check lists, may be reliable enough to account for all the major transactions and activities without distortion. The process is assisted by the tendency, mentioned in Chapter IX, to work directly to satisfy a need rather than for money in general. Thus a particular sum of money is often linked, in the mind of its spender, both with the activity which produced it and with the transaction which disposed of it. On the other hand, the more primitive the economy, the less likely is it that the individual informant will be able to

---

[1] I am greatly indebted to the anthropologists of the Rhodes-Livingstone Institute for their generous co-operation and valuable guidance in my field researches. They assisted me both in drawing up my schedule of questions and in actually applying them. Without their extensive local background knowledge, the stock of good will they had built up with the villagers concerned and their presence and constant advice throughout my investigations, these field experiments, which were compressed into a few weeks in all, would have taken very many months of field research on my part.

[2] Strictly speaking, an economic activity is any activity which results in the production of a good or service: in practice, however, we should also be interested in all 'uneconomic' transactions which involve money.

describe all his activities in terms of standard units of measurement. Moreover, it is often the case that the closer the individual's relationship with the exchange economy, and the more marked his habit of thinking in standard quantitative terms, the less willing is he to divulge the details of his economic transactions.

For these reasons it is not possible to obtain an accurate and comprehensive quantitative account of village economic activity merely by questioning the villagers. The alternative is for the observer to watch and record each economic activity of every individual as it takes place. This was done by a team of investigators carrying out a nutrition survey in Nyasaland under the direction of Dr B. S. Platt in 1938–9. Valuable results can be obtained in this way. It is a method which, however, requires an abundance of time and manpower even if carried out on an exceedingly small scale. A single observer would usually find it was more than he could do to keep a complete day to day record of the economic activities of a single village of 20–30 households even if the pattern of life was simple and even if he relied on questioning as well as on personal observation. The record would be incomplete if it covered a period of less than a year. It would tell the investigator very little about the colonial economy as a whole, unless he already knew enough about economic conditions in other rural areas to be able to judge which aspects of the village economy were unique to that village and which reflected village conditions in general.

In short, while the permanent value of scientifically accurate intensive surveys of village economies cannot be overestimated, there is an urgent present need for more extensive surveys which, although not so accurate, could provide a national framework for specialized studies and make it possible to draw an undistorted picture of the economy as a whole. It was this less elaborate method of conducting village economic surveys, based on questioning the villagers concerned, that I endeavoured to use. What I wanted was a method which would yield for each household a quantitative description of the principal economic activities of its members over the past year and of the principal types of real wealth owned by its members. To save time and to avoid exhausting the patience of informants it seemed desirable to ask no more questions of each person than could be answered at a single interview, although it would usually be necessary to check or supplement answers by interviewing more than one person in each household.

It is difficult to estimate the time which would be consumed by such a survey. So much depends on the type of economy, the length of the questionnaire, and the availability of the informants. At certain times of the year—harvesting and planting times for example—the villages will be deserted and it will be necessary to search or wait for informants who are free to talk. In some areas informants may go far afield to work —to a farm some miles away or to fishing sites—and may be available in their villages only occasionally. And there is always the funeral or the beer-drink or some other social contingency to prevent the investigator from making full use of his time in interviewing. On the assumption, however, that the questionnaire is such that the average householder and members of his family can provide all the answers required in less than two hours, then it should be possible to complete the work of interviewing a village of not more than thirty households in about a fortnight except in seasons of special pressure of work or social obligations. My own pace was faster but constituted a severe strain on interviewer, informant and interpreter. It was a pace which could certainly not have been maintained, or even reached, had it not been for the fact that the anthropologists had, in each case, already accumulated a considerable stock of confidence and good will among the villagers and also for the fact that mine was known to be a very short visit.

It must be emphasized that the estimated period of a fortnight refers to the work of interviewing alone and assumes that the groundwork of acquiring sufficient background knowledge to be able to frame a suitable schedule, and of establishing good relations with the villagers, has been done already. In my case it had been done for me by the anthropologists who were already in the field. In effect, an economist who had the advantage of using as fields of study areas which were already under investigation by anthropologists who could provide the basic environmental data, could collect returns for something like a hundred households in each of half a dozen widely different areas in rather less than twelve months. The use of African research assistants would, of course, vastly increase the population which could be covered in each type area.

The need to reduce questions to a minimum makes it necessary to abandon altogether the attempt to collect certain types of information by this method. Two main types were discarded readily. First there was the material for which more reliable data for estimate could be obtained from other sources. Secondly, there was material for which it would be difficult and time-consuming to get reliable data by means of questions, and which formed a relatively unimportant section of total economic activity.

It was found, for example, that it was of little value to question the villager on the yield of agricultural crops from his land. Even if the quantity consumed straight off the field were treated as negligible— and it is never so—it is impossible to interpret answers measured in terms of sledges full or baskets full or distances up the wall of the granary when none of these units is standard, even for a single village.

In any case, people who do not either sell a significant amount of their output or store it in standard measures, are ill-equipped to give estimate of their harvests. An Agricultural Department Survey which checked the ability of farmers to recognize the quantity of crops waiting to be harvested on their own lands found that the farmers' estimates varied widely from the actual amount—the discrepancy being in some cases of the order of 100%. Dr Richards, who checked estimates of the amount of grain in granaries by their owners, found discrepancies of a similar order of magnitude.[1] It would seem, therefore, that the problem of calculating the approximate output of African agriculture is largely one of obtaining scientific sample measures by expert agricultural surveyors. So while it was often useful to obtain from each household a list of the crops grown and a rough measure of the amount, it was decided that any attempt to estimate agricultural yield for a particular area should be based on such information as the agricultural department could give on average area cultivated and average yield of the main crops concerned.

Moreover, while the villager could usually remember how many bags of maize he had sold in the past year, his memory probably would not extend a full twelve months in recalling occasional sales of a basin of groundnuts to a visitor or an exchange of one type of relish for another with a neighbour. Where small-scale transactions are frequent but irregular they are almost certain to be understated by most informants and may constitute a significant hiatus in total information. This applies also, for example, to small-scale purchases of such items as salt. Where salt is normally bought by the sackful or is a luxury purchased only rarely, expenditure on it will be remembered for a considerable period. Where, as in many areas, it is bought in small tins-full of say, 1d. or 2d. each in value, and is used regularly in cooking, the informant cannot be expected to know how much has been spent over a period of a year, although in proportion to his total income it may be a significant amount.

Thus the final content of the schedule which it is decided should be applied to any particular area will be dictated by local conditions. These will determine the nature of the check lists, the amount of questioning which can be conveniently undertaken for any one household, the number of questions which should be discarded because the unreliability of the answers would not justify their inclusion, and the variety of the activities which should be investigated. In areas where the range of activities is small and the standard of living does not vary

[1] Audrey Richards, *Land, Labour and Diet in Northern Rhodesia*, published for the International Institute of African Languages and Culture, Oxford University Press, 1939.

greatly in content as between one individual and another the schedule which would emerge from a consideration of the local conditions would be broadly on the lines shown in Table 35. It would cover all the more important economic activities without overloading the interview and would produce results which although not accurate would be free from serious distortion. It is well suited to the semi-subsistence economy which is too far from an organized market to permit frequent small-scale transactions and where there is relatively little specialization of activity as between one individual and another. This type of backward village economy seems to be common in Northern Rhodesia and Nyasa-land. In such communities most economic activities tend to conform to a standard pattern for most households and most cash transactions tend to be memorable events. Unusual economic activities would soon be obvious and need not be included in each formal schedule, while the number of cash transactions which would be omitted after working through a set of simple and brief check lists would not be important in relation to the total of cash transactions.

Wherever the economic life of the community is complex, however, the one interview per person system breaks down and the investigator must either abandon the attempt to collect much of the information of the kind suggested in Table 35 or resign himself to spending a much longer period in the area so that he can observe as well as question informants. This problem emerged markedly when I visited Barotseland and attempted to apply the schedule there. For example, even among the Tonga and the Ngoni, where the range of crops grown by the average villager is relatively small, it was not possible to be certain of obtaining a full list of crops by interview alone. Among the Lozi living on the margin of the flood plain, where there were nine varieties of traditional garden, each with its own crop distribution, and a vast number of potential crops, it was possible only to ask each individual for a list of the types of garden he cultivated.

A further characteristic of the Lozi was the relatively high degree of specialization of subsidiary activity and the consequent complexity and importance of internal trade in small items. A typical Tonga family in the villages I visited normally manufactured for itself a substantial pro-portion of its household requirements in the shape of household goods. A man would make his own bed, sledge and often his stools. A woman might make her own pots, mats or baskets. Among the Lozi ques-tioned, these items would be bought from neighbours or travelling salesmen unless the individual himself specialized in their manufacture, when he would make the household annual requirements, give some away to begging friends or relatives, barter some when attracted by somebody else's products, and sell some to the people of his own and neighbouring villages. All this would be done in a haphazard and irregular way, and he could not be expected to remember twelve months of such informal transactions, although in sum they might involve a relatively considerable volume of output. This kind of difficulty could arise, even in areas less accustomed to specialize and trade, whenever there was an organized market. For example, in an area close to a European settlement there would be a small-scale trade for many individuals in such items as milk, eggs, fruit and vegetables, which although they might be regular for the more productive individuals were also seasonal, and so only an observer who spent some time in the area would be able to interpret the answers of his informants in terms of a year's transactions.[1]

There is no simple solution to the problem of surveying the more complex types of village economy, except that of spending more time in the area. Some idea of the general structure of the economy and of the characteristic orders of magnitude of cash incomes and expenditure can be obtained by applying the kind of schedule shown in Table 35. Except for the most general purposes, however, quantitative data obtained by questioning informants in a complex economy are of little value. On the other hand, the more one has to rely on observation rather than on questioning the more necessary does it become to stay in the one area for the full period of a year. It is quite clear, however, that no measurable progress will be made in this field until trained African research assistants are at work in each type area.

2. CHOOSING THE AREA

Theoretically, if the object of surveying the village economy is to obtain a basis for generalizations covering the whole colonial economy, it is desirable that each area of study selected should be chosen as randomly as possible, and that there should be a sufficient number of samples investigated. Ideally, every village (or every household) should have as much chance of being selected as any other village in the economy. Whether or not a random selection is a practicable proposition depends, however, on the amount and nature of the information which is sought and on the number of samples which can be taken. More concretely, it is a matter of the time involved in completing the data for each household and the personnel and technical equipment available for collecting it.

[1] In practice, of course, the existence of any European investigator in the area is a complicating factor from the point of view of the village economy. Although it is easy enough to obtain accurate records of his disbursements, it is not easy to make any intelligent allowance for the distortion in the normal trend of village life.

If, for example, it is possible to collect the necessary data from three households a day, a staff of fifty investigators could not complete the work of collection of data from a sample of 10% of the households on Northern Rhodesia in less than a full year. The speed with which it could be analysed would depend on its complexity and the availability of machines and machine operators. It could not be started at all without a complete list of villages or households from which the random selection could be made.

At present the position is that parts of the data required have been collected at different periods of time from small groups of households in connection with enquiries of a primarily uneconomic nature. Almost any attempt to collect systematically economic data from any area at all would yield valuable results, both by provisionally confirming or correcting existing stocks of data and by eliciting information covering subjects on which no quantitative data whatever is available. It will be necessary to collect many more samples and reach many more areas before the material collected will permit any quantitative generalizations whose margin of error can be reliably estimated.

In practice, therefore, while the number of samples that the available investigators hope to cover is so small in relation to the whole population that there is no prospect of obtaining material for generalizations which are safe within statistically significant limits, there is much to be said for a policy which subordinates the ideal of randomness to the principles of convenience. The physical accessibility of the area, the degree of good will or hostility with which its inhabitants receive investigators, and the presence and experience of an anthropologist or agriculturist or other trained observer, are all convenience factors which would influence the choice of an area for economic survey purposes. If the investigator is to make the best use of his time he will avoid areas where his own transport and supply problems are most acute and where the dangers to his health are greatest, in favour of other areas within the same broad economic or agricultural divisions where these difficulties are less pronounced. If he is to obtain reliable material on all or most of the points contained in the schedule, he will avoid areas where the inhabitants are hostile or known to be unwilling to divulge the truth on important points. Finally, if he is to obtain the economic information with all speed he will tend wherever possible to choose areas where the background material has already been collected by another observer whose experience of local fact-collecting problems could reduce both the amount of information to be collected and the number of practical blunders which might be made in trying to collect new data.

By making the choice of a survey area depend on considerations of convenience such as these, one introduces elements of bias into the sample. The area which is most accessible to the economist is often an area which is relatively more accessible to the exchange economy in general and differs therefore in economic structure from less accessible areas. A relatively healthy site for a village may produce in its African population a relatively high efficiency of labour. Differences in degree of hostility to European enquiries on economic matters may reflect certain patterns of culture contact which in themselves may be correlated with a particular type of economic organization. Finally, the interest of the anthropologist or the agriculturist is unlikely to have been randomly stimulated. Convenience factors influence other observers also and the social or agricultural bias of the area will almost certainly be matched by an economic bias. The very existence of a European observer in an African rural area is itself a focus of abnormal economic activity. A field worker does not live extravagantly, but he does not live alone. His camp generates a unique flow of incomes which tends gravely to distort the local pattern of economic activity and obscure its normal trends.

Nevertheless, in spite of the inevitable bias involved in any system of selection which permits factors of convenience to influence choice, the practical problems of economic surveying in Central Africa and the acute dearth of economic data of any kind are such that expediency must be a prime consideration. At this early stage in village economic research, the extra expenditure of time and money involved in surveying a relatively inaccessible village is not justified when a more accessible part of the same district or ecological division remains totally undocumented. Similar considerations apply to areas where the hostility of the local population threatens the success of the investigation. While so little is known about the economies in which the investigator could work unhindered by hostility it is not worth spending time and money in trying to build up good will among unwilling informants unless the information they can give is uniquely valuable.

It might be suggested, however, that if one cannot choose a random sample, one can at least aim at finding a 'typical' sample, and that it is unwise to allow physical convenience to be the sole basis of choice. In essence this is another kind of convenience factor which arises when the material is to be used for immediate, if tentative, generalization. For a 'typical' sample is a sample in which the known variations from the universal mean are known to be small. It is a sample for which the adjustments which are known to be necessary in presenting the results in a form suitable for the purposes of generalization are least in number and complexity. The investigator who expects or intends the results of his sample to be generalized may thus find it convenient to reduce the known complications involved in generalization by choosing what he believes to be a 'typical' sample in preference to one which he believes to be a-typical.

It is important, however, to specify in which respects the sample is believed to be typical and how firmly grounded in fact is this belief. For there are few aspects of African economic activity for which one could calculate the area mean with any degree of reliability; and such is our present state of ignorance in most areas and on most economic activities, that we must necessarily place a high degree of faith in the results of each individual investigator. That being the case, it is of immense importance that the reasons for selecting a sample should be as objectively clear as possible. Generally speaking, we start out with almost no overall quantitative information whatever on the economy we are going to investigate, although there may be some reliable general data on particular details. An investigator who, after a preliminary survey of his area, chooses, without quantitative support, what he believes to be a sample typical in most respects, and weights his presentation by what are, after all, largely subjective judgments, is dangerously obscuring the weaknesses of his results and may, if his hunches are not justified, confuse other investigators for a long time to come.

It is probably true to say that at the present stage of knowledge no investigator can fairly claim that he has chosen a typical sample for any rural area in Central Africa. On the other hand, it is possible deliberately to avoid areas which are known to be a-typical in one or more important respects. One might, for example, hold that it is in general advisable to avoid a chief's village because there is, after all, only one chief in an area, and his income, with the income of his immediate satellites, is unique in the area. My own results for the Tonga were reduced in value for generalization because I had included a chief's village. Or again, if we know that a large proportion of the inhabitants of a certain village belong to an occupational group for which we know the total area figures and can state with certainty that the area average is much different to the village average, it would be advisable to exclude this village from our sample.

Beyond such simple and unmistakable evidences of a-typicality it is seldom possible to proceed. For if we pursue the matter there is no village that is typical, if only because there is an observable tendency for particular economic groups to concentrate and because villages are usually so small. In one of the villages I visited there was a carpenter who gave irregular employment to six men and thus accounted for the cash income of about 20% of the households of the village. In another most of the market gardeners of the area had concentrated.

If it is possible to take a large enough sample many of the problems of the a-typical village vanish, as the individual peculiarities are lost

COLLECTING THE DATA 145

in the larger whole. One might either take a large area and select one's informants randomly from that area, without attempting to complete any one village; or one might take a small group of villages and cover every household within that group. If the former method is adopted it is necessary to begin with a census covering a wide area, so that a random sample can in fact be drawn. It has the advantage that it tends to iron out peculiarities which may concentrate in particular villages. In adopting the latter method it may be necessary to allow for a fairly long stay in the area in order to be certain of covering everyone since Africans are notoriously mobile. It has the advantage that it reflects the economic unity of the village. On the whole the former method seems to have most advantages when the purpose is to generalize for a wide area, but it is advisable to survey some villages intensively in each area, since the economic organization of the village does not emerge without that intensive study.

It must be emphasized that these observations on choosing the area and planning the survey are based on the assumption of the kin group village which is to be described in the next section. This kind of village, whose nucleus is the headman and his relatives and which potentially covers the whole range in age distribution, seems to be characteristic in Northern Rhodesia. It would be necessary to adopt a special procedure to account, however, for villages such as those described by Godfrey Wilson for the Nyakyusa.[1] There each village is in origin an age group formed by the hiving off of villages of boys aged 10–12 from the villages of adult men. Thus it would be found that some 'villages' consisted entirely of unmarried young men with no cultivated area attached. Others might consist primarily of old people with no young children left in the village. It might be necessary to cover a very wide area in order to obtain a representative age distribution among informants in such an area.

Considerable economies can be gained by using the results collected by other investigators or by co-operating with them in the collection of joint basic material. Without the necessary background of sociological information it would be impossible to plan the survey or to frame a schedule of the type shown in Table 35. If the economist had to collect this information for himself it would add many months to his work in the field even if he had already the necessary sociological and linguistic training. In an area which has already been or is being sociologically or agriculturally surveyed, much of the groundwork for an economic survey has been completed.

---

[1] See Rhodes-Livingstone Papers No. 1, *Land Rights of Individuals among the Nyakyusa*, by Godfrey Wilson, Livingstone, 1938.

L

More important still than the economies which are to be gained in using material collected by other and specially skilled observers, is the greater breadth and depth which a firm background of sociological or agricultural knowledge can give to the final analysis of economic data. This enlarged viewpoint and the stimulus which can be gained from seeing one's data through the eyes of other observers while they are actually being collected and analysed, are advantages which an economist can give as well as receive. For this kind of reason, as well as for the economy of effort involved in an operation, there is a strong case for organizing economic surveys as part of a wider survey covering also sociological, dietetic and agricultural aspects of the community's life.

3. DEFINING THE VILLAGE

Generally speaking, a Central African village consists basically of the headman and his direct relatives with perhaps a few individuals indirectly related to the headman or his resident relatives and, more rarely, an unrelated stranger or two. Occasionally, villages which are not of this related pattern spring up around men of character and wealth. From the administrative point of view a village is generally a group of at least ten taxpayers and their dependants registered under a single headman.

The villages are situated near their gardens and tend, in this area of shifting cultivators, to be shortlived, the inhabitants of the village moving in a body to a new area every 5–10 years. In addition there is a constant splitting of villages, within the government's prescribed minimum of ten taxpayers. As the villages grow in size, groups of kinsfolk tend to break off and form separate villages. In a survey conducted by the Agricultural Department in Serenje District in 1946 it was found that the average length of time spent on one site is five and a half years and the average distance of each move made is five miles: generally the move is made to go to new garden sites, but occasionally a small move of less than a mile is undertaken because the huts are dilapidated and ant-eaten. In this survey it was found that on an average over the past twenty years a village split every seventeen years, but it was estimated that the rate of fission is greater now and may be nearer 12–15 years.

Over and above this movement of villages and parts of villages there is a constant shifting of individuals between villages. Continuity of residence in a particular village seems to be rare except among the older men and there is a constant movement of individuals within an area. A movement from one village to another of a resident taxpayer is liable to involve the individual concerned in a fine unless he notifies the authorities. In practice, however, the District Administration staff is rarely ample enough to keep the taxpayers' registers up to date annually, and in any case the man who moves within a small area occasionally finds it more convenient to present himself at his village of original registration when the District Officer makes his rounds than to run the gauntlet of officialdom at the Boma. It is thus extremely difficult to take and keep an accurate record of villages and their inhabitants for statistical reporting purposes.

In most of the areas visited the villages consist characteristically of discrete groups of huts a mile or more apart, although they tend to be closer together in Nyasaland, where the population is more crowded, and on the Barotse flood plain margin. The margin villages of the Barotse flood plain are in a special category, however, since most of their inhabitants are people who belong to a mound homestead on the plain to which they move in the dry season and where they live when the flood permits. The margin villages were more or less continuous and it was often impossible to distinguish one from another on the basis of superficial observation.

4. DEFINING THE HOUSEHOLD AND ITS DEPENDANTS

The attempt to define a household in Central African villages raised many perplexing problems. Broadly speaking, each woman and her family were regarded as constituting a separate household. In addition, each man living alone and having a garden of his own was held to constitute a household. This meant that one man with six wives constituted six households. Since a man automatically provides a hut for each wife this corresponded in concept and practice with local custom. On the other hand, it was not always practicable to separate the six households into six economic units. Theoretically, a man made a hut, a garden and a granary for each wife and a garden and granary for himself. In practice, his newest wife probably shared a granary with him and worked on his field. She might even share a granary with another wife. More frequently, household equipment, such as a mortar and pounder, was shared, although there was usually a fairly definite understanding about the actual rights of ownership. Where a man earned a money income from his garden or as wages there was no recognized share for each household. He allocated it as he chose. Where a woman earned income through sale of produce or beer brewing the money was hers to be spent on her household. Sometimes two or more wives would combine households in preparing the day's meals. Hence, in practice the accounts of the six households in a polygamous group were usually so intermixed that for most purposes it was convenient to collect the data and present the accounts together.

More difficult specific problems arose in trying to decide on border-line cases of young bachelors. Many young men build huts for themselves to sleep in before they have gardens of their own, so the possession of a dwelling hut did not necessarily imply independence of status. Nor does an independent person necessarily have a hut of his own. One young man with a garden of his own shared a hut with an uncle also with a garden of his own. Both ate with the young man's mother, who cooked their food. The older man bought his own clothes. The younger man bought some of his own clothes from occasional earnings, and had some provided by his father and some by the older man, apparently in undefined return for help in the garden. Another young man recently returned from the army lived with his new wife in the kitchen of his father. He had no garden (this was in harvest time) because he had had no time to make one. He provided his own and his wife's clothes out of his army pay, but ate with his mother or of food provided by his mother, and worked in his father's garden.

Young men are often more or less indefinitely attached to several households. They might live in the household of one family for whom they herded cattle, eat with any one of a group of families for whom they hoed gardens, earn occasional pocket money with households whose pigs they took to market, and receive gifts of clothes from any one of the households at which they were on call for odd jobs throughout the year. The problem of allocating them to a household would be less difficult if payments were of a *quid pro quo* nature. In practice, however, the boys may stand in the relation of unpaid dependants to each one of the households which they assist, and payment is completely haphazard, taking the form of food, sleeping accommodation, clothes and extras, according to the immediate need of the boy and the prevailing inclinations of his masters or benefactors. In the last analysis the decision as to which household a lad belongs to is often unavoidably arbitrary.

The principal difficulty in surveying was that the sleeping household, the eating household, the income household, the producing household, and the spending household all represented different combinations and permutations within one wide family group. If one travels round the village on a person to person basis and asks each woman how many unmarried children she has she would include in her answer young children living with their grandmother, perhaps in another village. The parents have temporarily handed over responsibility for feeding or housing these children and their responsibility for clothing them is ill-defined. Sometimes the grandmother provides the little vest or dress or cloth. Sometimes the parent sends the money. Frequently there is no hard and fast allocation of responsibility. If one travels on a hut to hut basis and asks each woman how many children she has sleeping in her hut the answer will include such children as those who habitually eat with their grandmother and others who are, say, the children of migrant brothers and have all their clothing sent by their own parents. It is often the case, in dealing with such a mobile population, that no one person can give all the answers in respect of a particular child, and it may not be possible in practice to locate all the necessary informants.

Nor are the different kinds of household or living group fixed from day to day. We have seen that there need be no hard and fast allocation of responsibility for providing clothes. In the same way the sleeping and eating groups are indeterminate. Children may sleep in their mother's house one day and in their grandmother's another. They eat where they are 'called'. If they are not called they do not eat. At harvest time a woman may call to food, besides her own children, all the children of a co-wife and of a son's wife. Another day she will offer food to her husband alone. Another day she and her children will share the food of a co-wife or of a neighbour because she has been too busy to prepare food herself. The bewildering variety of the eating groups in any particular village is one of the first problems which faces anyone who tries to do research on food intake. Like so many aspects of African life the eating pattern is—or appears to be—irregular and haphazard. Even at harvest time a group of persons will eat no definite meal on one day and perhaps three full porridge and relish meals the next day. With whom one eats, whose food one eats and even whether one eats often seems to depend entirely on the circumstances of the moment.[1]

The ideal household for accounting purposes is the group of persons eating and sleeping under one roof and pooling their income. In most villages, however, one has to deal with a considerable number of persons who are attached to more than one household, and the allocation of these intermediate categories to one or other of the households to which they are attached must depend on arbitrary considerations of convenience. In any case, the final allocation of persons to households must depend on the kind of analysis which is made of the results and no one pattern is likely to be satisfactory. If the analysis is concentrated on food intake, for example, it is the eating groups which are most conveniently regarded as the households. If the analysis is concentrated on cash budgets it is the expenditure group that is relevant.

[1] It must be remembered that any conclusions on food intake which are based on observations covering less than a full year (as these are) must be received with considerable caution. There may have been seasonal regularities in the eating pattern which I was unable to observe.

An enquiry which aims at collecting information of the kind set out in Table 35 and which has abandoned the attempt to get quantitative data on subsistence production and consumption of food, can conveniently regard the cash expenditure group as determining the limits of the household. It is, in effect, the cash income and expenditure section of the family accounts for which information is most likely to be complete enough for quantitative analysis. The most important item of personal cash expenditure for the African villager is clothing. Thus a normal household can be regarded as the woman then resident in a given hut, together with her present husband, and the dependants for whom she or her husband had bought the clothes they were then wearing.[1] An unmarried man (or woman) is a dependant of the household which feeds him unless he has a garden in his own right sufficient for subsistence needs, or unless he has enough independent income to supply all his own needs in the way of clothes and taxes.

One of the drawbacks of this *de facto* method of investigation as applied to clothing is that clothes seldom last a full year for an active individual who wears only one set at a time. Since most children and many adults in the rural areas have only one set—often only one article in the case of children—an enquiry which confines itself to clothing now being worn will omit clothing bought during the course of the year and now worn out and discarded. Where the present clothes are less than three months old, enquiries could usefully be pursued into previous sets of clothing, but the results will necessarily be doubtful and will probably lead to long family arguments as to whether the previous set was bought just before this time last year or just after. In practice it will often prove desirable to avoid the additional drain on the patience of the informant by verifying the fact that expenditure on clothing is likely to have been understated and abandoning any attempt to chase up details of old and half-forgotten expenditure.

5. CHOOSING THE INFORMANT

Generally speaking, the most convenient way of beginning the enquiry is to approach first the member of the household who is likely to know the answers to the majority of the questions and to complete the schedule later by enquiries from other members. It was found in experimenting with the schedule shown in Table 35 that it was usually the man who knew most about the family economy, largely because he tends to take the initiative in economic matters. He builds the hut and

[1] It is useful to make each question as concrete as possible and to specify each individual by name in asking questions about the money which was spent on him or of which he was the recipient.

seems to decide on the area of the garden. He owns most of the live-stock and organizes most of the sales of produce and earns the wages. Among the Tonga, however, the woman seemed in most cases to know quite as much. She was usually well acquainted with the financial transactions of the husband, unless he earned wages away from the village, and was always better able than the male to answer questions about her own household equipment. Among the Ngoni, on the other hand, while the man knew most of the economic affairs of the woman, the woman knew relatively little about the man's activities. Frequently she did not even know how much had been spent on the clothes she was then wearing. There it was almost essential to start with the chief male member of the household. Among the Lozi the man again seemed to know most, but there was a substantial section of his wife's activities about which he was ignorant. Her income from beer brewing or from selling pots she had made was regarded as her own business. She received and spent the cash without necessarily consulting her husband.

Which member of the household makes the best principal informant depends, therefore, on the customs of the people studied. Often the most satisfactory form of interview is that in which all the responsible members of the household are present and where they can discuss doubtful points such as dates. Where, however, there is reason to believe that answers to some questions are careless or evasive it may be useful to question the individuals separately so that their answers may be used as a check on each other. For example, there seemed a tendency among the Ngoni men to insist that their wives made beer 'for drinking only', whereas the women, when questioned separately, said they had sold some. Except, however, in a fairly simple case such as this, where the answer of one informant is obviously more reliable than that of another, the fact that two answers have been received does not necessarily mean that the investigator is any closer to the truth. Nor, if there is a desire on the part of one or both informants to evade the question will an attempt to pursue the matter to a point of agreement do much more than exasperate all concerned. On the whole, therefore, a joint inter-view seems to be worth aiming at, wherever possible, without the sacri-fice of too much time for either interviewer or informants, since that offers the best opportunity of reducing errors due to confusion, or ignorance, or memory difficulties.

In choosing one's informant it has to be remembered that children are frequently cash earners and that their incomes may be forgotten by, or unknown to, the man or woman of the household. Older boys commonly take seasonal work for wages: many herdboys earn regular rewards in cash or in kind. Young children own livestock in some areas and sell milk and eggs. Occasionally a young child cultivates a small plot of saleable crops, such as European vegetables, and hawks them for money of his own. For the details of such transactions the child himself is the only suitable informant.

6. FIXING THE PERIOD

One of the chief difficulties encountered in the collection and analysis of data on village income, output and expenditure is the necessity of relating it all to some definite period of time. It is not enough to know what is the nature of the economic activities being carried on at the time the survey is made. If we are to place any quantitative interpretation on the economy it is necessary to know the volume of activity over a period of time. For most comparative and general purposes it is the period of a year with which we are concerned.

For an agricultural people the year is usually the most satisfactory accounting period. A shorter period is inadequate since it does not cover the full agricultural cycle. Income tends to be irregularly spaced over the year, and cash expenditure, which tends to be laid out on postponable or marginal needs (the more urgent needs being satisfied by subsistence output) tends also to follow cash income closely in time.[1] Even subsistence food consumption is irregular within the year since not only does the pattern of the diet depend on the crops, etc., in season, but its quantity varies significantly according to the distance in time from the main harvest. Thus we find a burst of expenditure on clothing, and on beer, at the time of the harvest, when there are crops to spare and money to spend. On the other hand, just before the harvest food tends to be scarce and only the lucky ones have much money to spend.

For the migrant labourer, however, the natural budgeting period is normally longer than a year. A man goes off to the mines for eighteen months or so and returns with money in his pocket and a stock of new clothes. He plans to return to work when the money is exhausted and the clothes worn out or given away. There are no general figures which would show the average length of time spent in the villages between trips to work, but we know that in many cases, perhaps in the majority of cases, it is longer than a year. If a man is still living in his village on income brought from outside the area more than a year ago, it is extremely difficult to draw up a balancing income and expenditure account covering the period of the past year.

This problem of the longer budgeting period of the returned migrant emerged with particular emphasis in the Ngoni survey villages where there were a number of households whose main earner had returned

---

[1] Subsistence output is used throughout this book to mean output produced for one's own or one's family's use, i.e. untraded output.

from the army towards the end of 1945 with anything from £20 to £100 in his possession plus a large stock of new clothes. His budget which was being accounted for in April or May 1947 consisted largely of expenditure of earnings made eighteen months or so ago. Theoretically, one should have found out what was left of the gratuity or savings in April or May 1946, but in the absence of any memorable event by which to fix the time exactly a year ago the question was useless.

In effect, even for specific transactions of a money-exchanging character, which are frequently memorable transactions in a largely subsistence economy, it is extremely difficult to secure accurate time records. The African villager does not space his life into months with the same precision as a European. At best one can expect him to remember, for example, whether a transaction occurred in the last dry season or the last hot season or at the planting season. If one can find and date a memorable event either in the life of the community or in the life of the individual, it is of considerable value in fixing other dates. It is useful, for example, to be able to frame one's questions in terms of what has happened since the last harvest. Nevertheless, there is a good deal of unavoidable confusion about transactions which have occurred between nine months and eighteen months ago, and in any case the time of harvest is a period of weeks which may vary from one year to another. On the most optimistic assumptions concerning the memory of the informant, a question which seeks to discover what has happened since the last harvest has a margin of error of a month. One is on firmer ground when one can relate the question to a particular event in the life of the individual—say, a journey to another area—and when one can say 'did this happen before or after you went to X?' Such a date line, however, occurs relatively infrequently and cannot be relied upon to assist in more than a small proportion of the interviews.

Probably the best time to make a rapid economic survey is the time of harvest or slightly before the harvest. If the interviews are conducted while the harvest is actually in progress, informants will tend to be fully occupied for most of the day and tired when they are at leisure. If they are conducted just after the harvest there may be too many beer brews afoot to make the interviews very satisfactory or to enable the observer to make the best continuous use of his time. In areas where there is a succession of small harvests rather than one main harvest it may be necessary to find another watershed in the agricultural cycle to serve as a date line. In areas such as the flood plain area of Barotseland, for example, the date of the annual migration from plain to margin would be a useful starting-point for enquiries.

CHAPTER XI

EXPERIMENTS IN VILLAGE ECONOMIC
SURVEYING

(1) QUESTIONS AND ANSWERS

In order to illustrate the principal problems of collection and analysis
of village economic survey data, the actual experiments conducted in
Northern Rhodesia within the period April-May 1947 will be described
and discussed in some detail in this chapter. It must be emphasized
that these experiments were not a means of acquiring information
of a kind suitable for generalization in connection with a national
income calculation. They were no more than an attempt to discover the
practical nature of the problems involved in the collection of economic
material from the rural areas of Central Africa. In view of the very
scanty total store of information on village economies it was inevitable
that even these tiny experiments should yield some noticeable addition
to the stock of useable material. They could not, however, of themselves
make any significant improvement in the margins of error involved in
the calculation of Northern Rhodesia's national income.

In experimenting with the collection of data on the lines shown in
Table 35, three areas were visited. In each of these an anthropologist was
already at work so that it was possible to construct the appropriate
schedule and to apply it to the villages without delay.

I. THE AREAS VISITED

The first of the selected areas was a part of Mazabuka District,
inhabited by the Tonga, about fifteen miles from the railway line at
Monze. It lies in the maize belt, which is an area more fertile than most
in Northern Rhodesia, and is free from tsetse fly. Being within easy
walking distance of the railway line, it enjoys a virtually unlimited
market for all the maize, livestock, or eggs which it can produce for
sale. For those who have nothing to sell but their labour, the European
farms of the maize belt offer local employment of a seasonal or permanent nature. The available adult population is a relatively high

154

proportion of total population, since the rate of migration to work outside the area is relatively low (the Tonga Survey put it at 14% in
1945).[1] In addition the area is relatively well stocked with mechanical
aids to production such as ploughs and cultivators, and has a large
livestock population.

Thus the quality and quantity of the productive resources of the area
are in general above average, although the recent development of maize
as a cash crop has led to some overpopulation of the maize-growing
areas and a noteworthy degree of soil erosion; it should also be noted
that the General Tonga Survey found that an appreciable proportion
of the families retained insufficient food for their own consumption.
On balance, however, the Mazabuka area can be regarded as one of the
most prosperous areas in the colony and was described in the Agricultural Department's development plans as having 'perhaps the highest
rural income of the Territory'.

The second of the survey areas is in the Ngoni Reserve of Fort
Jameson District, about eighteen miles (i.e. within walking distance)
from the township of Fort Jameson. It is about three days by lorry from
the railway line, and although there has been a good market for small
surpluses of flour, fruit, vegetables and livestock in Fort Jameson during
the war and post-war years, there is no normal market here for large
quantities of any African cash crop. Generally speaking, the regular
way of earning cash for the men of this area is to go away from the
village to work, and the Ngoni have a strong tradition of migrant labour.
There is a certain amount of scope for wage earning on local farms, and
some men working on tobacco farms in the District return to their
villages at the week-ends and form part of the available village labour
force at busy periods. Most of the Ngoni earners go out of the province
to earn cash, many to Southern Rhodesia or to the Union.

Local productive resources are poor both in quality and quantity.
There are scarcely any ploughs or cultivators. Many villages are almost
denuded of able-bodied men. The area has been selected by the Agricultural Department as being in special need of agricultural improvement. On the other hand, being fly-free it has a livestock population
above the average; and in terms of cash income and European-manu-
factured goods it is one of the richest districts in the colony in view of
the wealth brought back by migrants. This was particularly true of
1945 and 1946, which were abnormal years in that the area received
large sums, first in family remittances from serving Askari and then in

[1] The national average was about 35%. See Table 36. The report which is here-
after referred to as the Tonga Survey or the General Tonga Survey was carried out
by the Northern Rhodesia Agricultural Department assisted by Dr Max Gluckman.
See annotated reference in the bibliography contained in Appendix III.

gratuities and savings brought to the villages by demobilized soldiers. The third survey area was in Loziland, within five miles of Mongu on the edge of the Barotse flood plain. The flood plain area of Barotse-land is unique in Northern Rhodesia. It is rich in game birds and fish. In about a dozen different varieties of gardens the Lozi cultivate a wide variety of grain, pulses, root crops, fruit, cucurbits and vegetables. They are a cattle-owning people. The great variety of products obtainable from the plain is in striking contrast to almost all other parts of Northern Rhodesia and has made the Lozi keen traders, well known for their enterprise throughout the colony.

Against these factors making for a high standard of living must be set the heavy dependence of the Lozi on the annual floods, and the dearth of local wage-earning opportunities. Dr Gluckman points out in his *Economy of the Central Barotse Plain*[1] that 'in many years the Lozi have been seriously short of food since their gardens, dependent on flood conditions, are spoilt not only by high and low floods, but also if the flood comes earlier than usual'. Moreover, the fact that for at least three months of every year (i.e. at the height of a normal flood) most villages in the Plain are under water, means that the plain dwellers have either to move to other huts at the margin every year, or to live in the Plain under conditions of considerable discomfort. Most huts on the Plain need repair or rebuilding every year as a result of the flood. The dearth of local wage-earning opportunities means a high rate of migration to work, and a shortage of able-bodied men which must inevitably reduce the variety of activities which can be under-taken by each household. On the other hand, since many of the plain gardens can be cultivated by women (unlike bush gardens for which male labour is indispensable), the effect of the labour shortage on basic agricultural returns is probably not so great in this area as it is, say, in Northern or Eastern Provinces.

Thus all three of the areas visited were areas which were more prosperous than the average in certain important respects, so far at least as can be judged by general observation. All of the survey villages were close enough to a township to have a market for their surplus. They were all cattle-owning areas. The Tonga were manifestly more fortunate than other Northern Rhodesian villagers in their cash crop, in their proximity to the railway line and in their high proportion of available male labour. The Ngoni were richer in that their share of the remittances and savings of migrants, and of the gratuities of the ex-soldiers, was above the average. The Lozi had a wider variety of re-

[1] Rhodes-Livingstone Papers No. 7, *Economy of the Central Barotse Plain*, by Max Gluckman, Livingstone, 1941.

sources (especially food resources) and a vigorous tradition of internal trade which must tend to raise rural cash incomes.

It seems probable from the little we do know that these advantages raised the average total income (i.e. subsistence income plus cash income) above the average for Northern Rhodesia as a whole in each of the three areas visited. We still do not know, however, whether the survey villages were more or less prosperous than the other villages in the area from which they were drawn. Known features in which they were a-typical can be pointed out as the results are analysed, but only by wider sampling can we draw any firm conclusions on the relationship of mean incomes in the survey villages to mean incomes in the total area from which they were drawn.

In Table 36 some comparative figures are given for the different provinces of Northern Rhodesia. It may be noted that the Tonga Survey villages are in Southern Province, the Ngoni villages in Eastern Province, and the Lozi villages in Barotse Province, but it must at the same time be emphasized again that they cannot be regarded as typical of the province from which they derive. The figures in Table 36 are intended simply as indicators of the provincial variations from the colonial mean in certain significant respects.

TABLE 36. Provincial variations in economic conditions in
Northern Rhodesia

1	2	3	4	5	6
Provinces	Households 1946	Livestock per household 1945	Percentage taxpayers migrant 1944	Adults available per cent available population 1945	Jobs in province per taxpayer 1946	Army payments per household 1946
	Nos.	Nos.	%	%	Nos.	£
Northern	115,000	0.2	34	45	0.14	0.70
Eastern	84,000	1.4	55	42	0.25	0.87
Southern	72,000	4.7	22	47	0.32	0.41
Central and Western	77,000	1.2	27	44	1.27	0.26
Barotse	94,000	1.5	37	46	0.08	0.13
All Provinces	442,000	1.6	35	45	0.38	0.48

Explanatory Notes on Table 36

1. The population figures are estimates based on the figures for registered taxpayers given in the District Commissioners' returns to my questionnaire. It is assumed that there are as many households as there are adult women.

2. The livestock include cattle, sheep, goats, and pigs, as estimated by the Veterinary Department to have been owned by Africans in 1946. Poultry are not included.

3. Estimates of the percentage of taxpayers employed outside their own province (whether in Northern Rhodesia or abroad) were derived from figures published in the 1944 report of the Labour Department.

4. The population available in the villages was estimated on the basis of the District Commissioners' returns for registered taxpayers, the Labour Department's figures for migrants, and censuses of urban locations. It was assumed that men employed in their own province were available in the villages unless they were living in urban locations.

5. The numbers of Africans employed in each province as in October 1946 were collected in the African Labour Census.

6. Payments to or on behalf of Askaris which were made through the District Commissioners (and this includes most payments deriving from war service, with the exception of savings brought back in the hand) were returned in answer to a questionnaire to the District Commissioners.

2. THE POPULATION SURVEYED

Before beginning to describe the questions and answers which were put to the surveyed population, it may be useful to indicate its composition. For the Tonga villages the population figures can be regarded as relatively reliable since Dr Colson had recently taken a census of all the households concerned and the economic survey was in effect partly a check on her figures. For the Ngoni villages, Mr Barnes' figures, which covered a different group of households to those surveyed by me, are given in brackets. It seems likely that my figures understate the number of children even for the households covered by me and certain that they show a lower proportion of children than the average for that small area. It is probable that expenditure, particularly expenditure on clothing, is understated because some children have been overlooked and because the size of family accounted for is smaller than the average. There were no accurate census figures available for the Lozi households covered, since Dr Gluckman's census data were collected during his 1940–2 field tour and were irrelevant to 1947 conditions. Here again I should judge that my figures understate the proportion of children.

TABLE 37. The surveyed population

	Tonga	Ngoni		Lozi
Households	68	60		13
Adults	126	100	(177)	18
Children	131	70	(156)	18
Persons per household	3.8	2.8	(3.2)	2.8

The Tonga population included a chief (Cona), two councillors, a court clerk, a court messenger and five teachers, all of whom received incomes from outside the village. Thus the area was a-typical in respect of the number of employed persons included. The Ngoni population included eleven families whose male head had returned to the village within the past eighteen months with an army gratuity and army savings. This again was above the average for the district. The Lozi population included one induna and one full-time tailor, and the sample was far too small for any generalized conclusions to be drawn with any safety. Indeed, my stay among the Lozi, which lasted less than a week, was too brief for me to do more than gain a fleeting impression of a very varied economy.

3. CROPS GROWN

In a community where subsistence income[1]—and particularly subsistence food—forms a large proportion of total income, the standard of living often depends on the range of crops grown as much as on the amount grown. So far as can be judged from the scanty data already collected in Central Africa the average yield of gardens or the average intake of food per head of the population does not vary greatly between one area and another. What does vary is the range of crops grown and hence the quality of the diet and of the standard of living.[2] Under the circumstances it is useful to know not only the range of crops which could be or are produced in the area, but also the range which is in fact produced by the average household. Further, since the Ecological Survey divides the colony into agricultural districts for which the characteristic crops are known, a knowledge of the range of crops grown in the villages surveyed is to some extent a guide to the degree to which they can be regarded as typical of the area.

In asking for a list of crops grown the first essential is an adequate check list. If the range is very wide a full check list may be difficult to compile and tedious to apply. On the other hand, it is usually possible to draw up a list which, while it does not show the full possible range, covers enough of the significant crops to illustrate the quality of the standard of living.

Table 38 shows the results obtained in asking Tonga households what crops they grew. It will be seen that all of those interviewed grew maize and most grew some kind of pumpkin or cucumber. Most also grew groundnuts, although there were a few men who did not grow groundnuts 'because' they had no wife. On further enquiry into this prohibition it was found that groundnuts were regarded as hard work and so a man without female assistance would not bother with them. In most cases, the men without wives in the village were working for the chief or the local councillors, and were able to buy relish or were fed

---

[1] I.e. income in kind produced for use of the producer or his dependants.

[2] For example, a cassava-producing area where the bulk produced is usually high is an area low in food standard of living unless there is a widespread production of some good protein food to balance the excessive starch of the cassava. Similarly, a community which grows its own tobacco has a higher standard of living in this respect than a community which has to buy its tobacco.

by their employers. Enquiries into eating habits of the villages surveyed
indicated that the staple diet of the Tonga at this season consisted of
maize, groundnuts, and pumpkins or similar cucurbits, with little
variation. This confirms the picture suggested in Table 38. To these
should be added wild fruits and spinach which are important at some
seasons. A check list of crops grown could usefully be followed by a
short list of some of the wild crops of the area, but the compilation of
such a list would involve residence for some time in the vicinity.

TABLE 38. Crops grown by the Tonga

(68 households)

	Percentage growing crops %
Maize	100
Cucurbits	96
Groundnuts	89
Kaffir corn	89
Beans	35
Sweet potatoes	29
Tobacco	5
Other crops	4

The question was not applied to the Ngoni households interviewed,
because Mr Barnes had already made enquiries on these lines and it
was undesirable to question informants twice on the same subject.[1] Nor
was it applied in this form to the Lozi households, partly because the
range of possible crops was so wide as to make the check list very long,
but largely also because it was of at least as much interest to know what
type of garden was cultivated. The villagers of the Barotse flood plain
and margin cultivate a variety of traditional gardens, each with its
own characteristic pattern of crop distribution, and a knowledge of the
range of gardens given in any particular household or village is a useful
indication of the range of crops. The results obtained by questioning
thirteen householders are given below in Table 39.

It should be noted in interpreting the first column of this table that
the reference is to gardens owned rather than gardens cultivated. In
general it would be more useful to know how many of the different types
of garden were actually under cultivation at any given moment of time,
rather than the number that were owned (some of which might be
unused). It should also be noted that this list of gardens is not sufficient
to indicate either the wide variety of fruit trees under cultivation, or the
special crop gardens—such as vegetable gardens, rice gardens, tobacco

---

[1] Mr Barnes' questions did not cover the identical group of persons to whom the
schedule was applied and his results are therefore not analysed here.

gardens—which may be made by the more enterprising villagers in response to local market demands. A satisfactory check list would contain, besides a list of the main types of general gardens, a list of fruit trees, special crop gardens, and wild crops.

TABLE 39. Lozi gardens

(13 households)

Types of garden	Number of gardens owned	Number of households with garden
Maize and kaffir corn mounds	20	5
Rootcrop ridge gardens	7	5
Village mixed crop (dry)	10	8
Village mixed crop (seepage)	4	3
Winter maize (drained)	11	7
Winter maize (lagoon)	6	6
Millet and cassava bush gardens	12	10
Special crop gardens, etc.	5	1

4. LIVESTOCK OWNED AND CONSUMED

The part played by livestock in the rural economy is varied and complicated. Apart from the normal transactions of buying and selling livestock, there are a host of potential minor transactions. A man may pay someone to tend his cattle, or he may pay for the loan of somebody's bull. He may sell grazing rights on his land, and he may buy manure. Animals may die of disease, or be killed by wild animals, or be killed ceremonially, or for food, or because they are raiding the food crops. In most cases, animals that die are eaten as food, although very occasionally certain kinds of diseases may make them uneatable, or the depredations of wild animals will leave nothing for human consumption. A thorough enquiry into all these and related points for all kinds of animals would be a very long process. A simplified form of enquiry, however, produced the results shown in Table 40. It can be assumed that the figures given there tend to underestimate the true averages for the villages concerned, at least as far as chickens are concerned and probably as far as pigs, sheep and goats are concerned. Generally, the death or slaughter of cattle is memorable, but the death of a young calf might be forgotten after a period of six months or more, even though it had provided several meat meals.

The circle of people eating animals killed on funeral or other ceremonial occasions is wider than that of the village in which the beast is killed. It is, however, usually fair to assume that the amount of locally killed meat eaten by strangers is equivalent to the amount of meat eaten in strangers' villages by locals. It could have been expected that the chief's village would be the exception to this rule and would provide

M

more ceremonial and other meat meals for strangers than it obtained from strangers. For most types of livestock, however, the amount owned and the amount killed in Cona's village was actually less than in the other Tonga villages of Cobana and Hanamonga. The exception was in the number of pigs killed, which was slightly higher per household in Cona's village than for the other two villages. This, however, could be accounted for by the special zeal in killing other people's pigs which was shown by one member of Cona's village.[1] Pigeons were excluded from Table 40 because the data collected was not satisfactory and probably showed too many omissions.

TABLE 40. Livestock

(Per household)

	Ngoni	Tonga	Lozi
Cattle owned	2.1	5.3	2.2
killed or died	0.3	0.3	0.2
Sheep and goats owned	0.8	1.5	0.4
killed or died	0.5	0.2	—
Pigs owned	1.2	1.0	—
killed or died	0.3	0.4	—
Fowls owned	2.8	6.6	1.8
killed or died	1.3	0.6	1.8

On the assumption that the average dressed weight of cattle killed was 300 lb., of sheep or goats, 40 lb., and of pigs, 70 lb.—which are the averages generally used by the Veterinary Department—and that fowls provided about 2 lb. of meat apiece, the amount of meat consumed per household was 134 lb. among the Ngoni, 127 lb. among the Tonga, and 63 lb. among the Lozi. In fact, of course, since many of the deaths are deaths among young stock, these averages are too high. On the other hand, errors and omissions combine to make the final total an understatement, while it takes no account of wild animals consumed. Further, it should be remembered that the Lozi sample is too small for it to be fair to draw the conclusion that the consumption of meat in the Lozi area was under half that in the Ngoni or Tonga villages, and that in any case there was a twice-weekly slaughtering at a European butchery in Mongu which is not accounted for in these returns. The higher consumption among the Ngoni relatively to the Tonga could satisfactorily be explained by the existence of a high proportion of returned soldiers who had become used to a meat diet, who had relatively large expendable cash resources, and who had often to buy

[1] Pigs were frequently slain among the Tonga for some act of destructiveness such as the raiding of maize fields or the eating of young chickens. If the owner claimed a pig slain for this reason he could take it away and eat it himself; if not the slayer would eat the pig and the owner had no redress. The Tonga often said that they were not pig-eaters, but there seemed to be no difficulty in disposing of pig meat in the Tonga villages I visited.

their own relish because they had not had time to make their own gardens. These men provided a ready market for meat and fowls. Possibly also the greater abundance of game in the Ngoni area, as compared with the Tonga area, produced a greater tendency to eat meat.

TABLE 41. Percentage of livestock killed or died

	Ngoni %	Tonga %	Lozi %
Cattle	15	6	11
Sheep and goats	55	11	—
Pigs	25	40	—
Fowls	48	9	100

It is interesting to note from Table 41, however, that the percentage of livestock killed or died is a factor which varies much more than the average amount of meat available from animals killed or died. As we have seen, the amount consumed by the Ngoni interviewed was estimated to amount to about 134 lb. compared with 127 lb. among the Tonga. If we assume that the Lozi sample was not a-typical, in the small amount of small stock it revealed, it would be reasonable to account for the apparently slightly smaller consumption of cattle by an undoubtedly higher consumption of fish. It is possible that the total annual consumption per household of meat, or meat and fish together, will be found not to vary greatly as between these three areas, and to be at least as much as 2 lb. per week per household in each of them. This is a great deal higher than any average reached in previous investigations.[1] It has to be remembered, however, that all of these areas were sufficiently fly-free to enable herds of cattle to be kept. The Tonga, the Lozi and the Ngoni are all traditionally cattle owners. There were no cattle among the Bemba studied by Dr Audrey Richards, and Mr Peters' more recent survey of the Serenje Lala indicates that 50% of the villages of his substantial survey area have no livestock at all, excluding poultry.

5. CROPS SOLD

How satisfactory a response one can hope to obtain from a question on the amount and value of foodstuffs sold during the preceding year must depend on the way in which trade is usually carried on in the locality. If there is a ready and easy market for bulk sales of produce, and if crops are usually sold by the bagful rather than by the basinful or the basketful, then each transaction will tend to be memorable.

[1] Dr Richards quotes a survey in Northern Province which found an average village meat consumption of less than 6 lb. per man value per annum. See Audrey Richards, op. cit., p. 40.

This was so among the Tonga, where there was a ready trade in maize at 10s. a bag. Even here, however, one cannot assume that there were no omissions and that the householder invariably remembered all sacks sold over a period of a year.

In areas where local trade usually takes the form of small-scale transactions this question produces much less satisfactory results. Among the Ngoni, for example, of fifty households (or household groups) questioned, forty-two said they had sold none of their crops, while eight admitted to sales totalling nearly £26, of which £20 represented the earnings of a market gardener with a regular weekly or twice-weekly sale in Fort Jameson.[1] It is unlikely that the average household traded much of its crops, but the answers suggested that there was a certain amount of petty local trade, and irregular visits to Fort Jameson which involved transactions in units of perhaps a shillingsworth or even less would certainly not be remembered for longer than a few months. Among the Lozi, on the other hand, although most persons said that they had sold crops and gave figures covering several kinds of crops, these again were in terms of such small sums that they could not be expected to cover a memory span of more than a few months, if as long. Here it would be essential to make enquiries over an extended period concerning crops sold before even the order of magnitude involved could be reliably estimated.

Table 42 below summarizes the information which was collected in three Tonga villages. Cona village is definitely a-typical because it is the chief's village and because a high proportion of its inhabitants earn regular cash incomes. In effect, they are not dependent on their gardens for cash and some are not wholly dependent on them for food. However, there is probably a constant small-scale trade in foodstuffs not only with these local wage earners, but also with the visitors to the chief's court, which would not be memorable. The average value of crops sold per household should probably be scaled up slightly to give a true value even for this a-typical village with so many part-time farmers. The returns from Hanamonga were also biased, but less strongly and in the opposite direction. There was not time to complete the survey of the whole village, and most of the households that were interviewed were male, or male plus female, households. Since very few households without men trade maize by the sackful it is probable that the inclusion of the remainder of Hanamonga's households would have brought the village average down to something approaching the Cobana average.

[1] There were fifty returns collected for the Ngoni of which eleven related to poly-gamous groups and eighty contained more than one household. They covered sixty households of which two were actually living outside the villages visited (i.e. where a man had a wife living in another village).

If any generalizations are to be drawn on this point, therefore, the Cobana returns provide the most useful starting-point.

TABLE 42. Summary of crops sold in three Tonga villages

	Number of households	Quantity of maize sold	Value of all crops sold[2]	Value of all crops sold per household
		Bags[1]	£	£
Cona	34	35¼	19	0.56
Cobana	20	110	60	3.00
Hanamonga	14	97	55	3.93
3 villages	68	242½	134	1.98

In Table 43 a summary of the results obtained among the Ngoni is given. It relates to twelve households out of the sixty that were covered. Thus for 80% of the households no crop sales were recorded. Of these a number could have had no garden in the previous year as they were demobilized after the 1945–6 planting season. On the other hand they are almost certain to have bought small quantities of food locally. The market gardener whose takings account for about 70% of the total was an unusual individual, and his year's takings were calculated on a weekly average estimated by him. They are therefore not accurate, but can probably be regarded as an indication of the order of magnitude involved. It should be emphasized here that there is no reason to assume that the Ngoni sample was representative. In particular, we cannot assume that one in sixty of the households of this area relied for cash income on crop sales as much as the market gardener interviewed. There were others gardening on his scale in his own village, but not in other villages that I visited. On balance, it seems probable that there were fewer than one in sixty market gardeners in the areas as a whole, but that the average household interviewed understated its casual sales of crops over the past year. Some aged women pounded and sold flour on a very small scale (e.g. in threepennyworths) as and when they wanted minor store goods such as salt.

TABLE 43. Crops sold from among sixty Ngoni households

	£	s.	d.
Maize	2	12	0
Groundnuts		4	0
Tobacco		19	0
Vegetables, fruit, flour, other	24	10	9
	£28	5	9

[1] Bags of 200 lb.
[2] To the nearest £.

No attempt is made to summarize the answers collected from Lozi households on this point because it is unlikely that they are a fair index, even of the orders of magnitude involved. The thirteen households, however, reported total sales of a value of £2 6s. 3d., of which more than 75% was accounted for by fruit and vegetables.

6. OTHER FOODS SOLD

Generally speaking, the sale of livestock when it concerned the larger animals such as cattle, sheep, goats and pigs, was a memorable event which could be expected to be remembered with a reasonable degree of accuracy. Here again, of course, sales which had taken place nearly a year ago—perhaps a small litter of pigs sold for 5s. each—might be forgotten, especially by an individual who conducted many such transactions in the course of a single year. Nevertheless, while the recorded income figures from the sale of larger livestock tend to be understatements, they can probably be relied upon to be approximately true. Where the sale of small livestock such as chickens or pigeons are a significant item in trade, however, the degree of understatement may be considerable. This is also true of the sale of livestock products such as eggs or milk or meat. Where the sale is regular—as when a regular milk delivery is made—it is, of course, possible to calculate returns fairly accurately, provided that the degree of seasonal fluctuation is not important and that the dates of commencement and termination of trade are known. Constant irregular sales, especially of such items as eggs, tend to be understated, and there are potentially a large number of occasional transactions which might well be forgotten. For example, when an animal dies, the owner, while keeping the bulk of the meat for himself and his family, frequently retails small quantities to neighbours and visitors. These small-scale casual transactions might be forgotten where the sale of the whole carcass would be memorable. In practice it was found that records of such small-scale sales of meat were uncommon in the income returns and, if recorded at all, usually came to light as the result of some chance statement. On the other hand, they appeared fairly frequently in the expenditure records when a question was asked on expenditure on meat.

Table 44 summarizes the information which was collected on the sale of livestock and livestock products. The figures relating to the Lozi must be interpreted here as elsewhere with considerable caution since they relate to a very small sample. Dr Gluckman thought that this village was poor in cattle, as are most margin villages compared with those in the plain.

TABLE 44. Income from livestock

	Value of receipts per household Livestock shillings	Value of receipts per household Livestock produce shillings	Percentage reporting sales of livestock or livestock produce %
Ngoni	3.7	9.3	28
Tonga—Cona	31.4	0.5	76
Cobana	35.5	4.7	82
Hanamonga	25.0	—	71
Total three Tonga villages	31.3	1.6	77
Lozi	44.8	18.4	75

It is noteworthy that among the Tonga studied the sale of livestock is a source of cash for a relatively high proportion of the population. It is, in fact, the poor villager's standby. Whereas under 63% of the returns recorded income from the sale of crops there were 77% which recorded income from livestock. It must be borne in mind, however, that the occasional sale of crops by the subsistence farmer is generally on a very small scale, and is therefore less memorable than the sale of livestock though the money value over the period of a year may be roughly the same. In effect, the difference in the percentages recording income from livestock and income from crops may not be significant.

The relatively small average return from livestock in Hanamonga village returns is perhaps due, along with the relatively high return from sale of maize, to the fact that all those interviewed in Hanamonga village were men. Women living alone rarely trade maize by the bagful, and their returns from the sale of crops will be at most the results of small-scale transactions which would often escape records dependent on a year's memory span. On the other hand, they frequently keep pigs and chickens, and although sales of chickens might be forgotten, the sale of a pig might fetch at least as much as the price of a bag of maize and would almost certainly be remembered for a fair period. Thus Hanamonga village returns, being overweighted by men and under-weighted by women living alone, would be expected to show a higher relative dependence on income from crops, and a lower relative dependence on income from livestock.

The question concerning the manufacture of beer was asked in all villages with varying degrees of detail, and the results concerning sales of beer are given in summary form in Table 45.

There is reason to believe that the Ngoni records of income from sales of beer understated the true amount for the households questioned. There were occasions when the wife and husband were questioned separately and the former admitted to sales of beer, while the latter maintained that all brewing had been 'for drinking only'. There were other occasions when the interpreter remembered having bought beer at a house where the informant said none had been sold. It seems likely that the recent imposition of the regulations requiring a licence for the selling of beer made people reluctant to admit even to sales before the licensing laws came into operation. Beer brewing seems to be an important activity throughout Northern Rhodesia, and in the three areas visited it accounted for a relatively important proportion of cash income from local sources. In some districts the brewing of beer for sale is illicit, and in others a licence is required. In areas where it is either illegal or licensable it will normally be extremely difficult to obtain a full record of beer sales.

TABLE 45. Income from sales of beer

	No. all brewings per household brews	Value of beer sold per household shillings	Percentage returns reporting sales of beer %	Value of beer sold per selling household shillings
Ngoni	1.3	4.5	34	15.0
Tonga—Cona	n.a.	1.97	32	8.5
Cobana	1.1	1.1	12	11.0
Hanamonga	0.9	0.36	7	5.0
Total Tonga	n.a.	1.38	20	8.5
Lozi	2.8	16.5	75	21.5

The higher proportion of people shown as receiving income from beer sales among the Tonga of Cona's village might have some connection with its being a chief's village, but is probably more closely connected with its relatively large number of wage earners. On the whole, one would expect that where so large a percentage of able-bodied men were drawn from work in the gardens by other occupations, and where the high visitor rate demanded a surplus of food, there would be a large number of beer brews for garden working parties. There seem to be few beer brews from which none is sold, whatever the original purpose. The relatively low proportion shown as brewing beer in Hanamonga village could be partly accounted for by the fact that women living alone have been omitted from the returns collected in this village, and these are just the people who might seek to earn cash from beer brewing.

One of the reasons for the higher record of beer brews found for the Lozi may have been the fact that the answers were more complete. Most of the informants were margin people who spent half the year on the flood plain and half at the margin, so that the question framed thus: 'How many times did you brew (*a*) on the plain, (*b*) on the hill?' was likely to bring a more complete answer than 'How many times did you brew last year?'. Also, it must be remembered that such a very small sample might well have netted all the keen beer drinkers, and thus might reflect a rate of brewing higher than the average for the area. Nevertheless, even allowing for such factors as these, which tend to reduce the significance of the Lozi figure for beer brewing, it seems highly probable that the rate was at least twice that among the Tonga, and perhaps nearly twice that among the Ngoni.

Some informants were able to give the number of 'nongo' (large pots) brewed at each brewing. Among the Tonga, for thirty brewings about which the number of pots could be stated, the average per brewing was seven and a half. Among the Ngoni, the average over thirteen brewings was three. On balance, the Tonga average is more likely to be significant than the Ngoni average, since the latter was derived largely from questioning men. A nongo is by no means a standard unit of measurement, but where beer is sold by the nongo it seems, among the Tonga as among the Ngoni, to fetch a customary price of 1s. per nongo. For the most part, however, it would be sold in smaller units and would probably fetch more.

7. MISCELLANEOUS GOODS AND SERVICES

Cash earnings from miscellaneous goods and services produced locally are extremely difficult to track down, both because the transactions themselves are on so small a scale, and because the number of ways of earning small sums are so many. When a man makes spoons at 1d. or 3d. each, it is not easy for him to remember how many he has sold over a period of a year, unless he deals in bulk orders. A man may earn a few shillings for building a granary, or a woman may get a shilling or two for cooking for a passing stranger. If the cash was earned nine months or so ago, the probability is that it will be forgotten, unless one's check list is very precise and comprehensive. In practice, it is rarely expedient to attempt a very long check list for these items, which are inevitably minor activities for each individual, although for the community as a whole they may be a substantial aggregate.

Information on earnings from doctoring are likely to understate the truth, even if there is no unwillingness to disclose such earnings (and this unwillingness is common in areas where divining is actively discouraged by administration or missions). The reason is that the earnings are irregular, often on a small scale, and sometimes given more as a gift than as a *quid pro quo*. It is clear from the information recorded concerning expenditure on doctoring, and also from the number of known doctors who have no other way of accounting for their income, that the income records on this point are inadequate. Moreover, since the question was framed in terms of doctoring rather than of divining (which may be illegal in some areas) the answers are necessarily incomplete.

TABLE 46. Income from miscellaneous goods and services

	Manufactures		Doctoring		Miscellaneous services	
	Percentage households earning %	Return per head of all households shillings	Percentage earning %	Per head of all households shillings	Percentage earning %	Per head of all households shillings
Ngoni	10	6.3	10	1.0	3	0.3
Tonga:						
Cona	12	0.9	—	—	6	1.0
Cobana	40	12.0	—	—	5	0.5
Hanamonga	7	0.1	—	—	14	4.3
Total Tonga	19	4.0	—	—	7	1.6
Lozi	25	0.3	25	1.2	8	30.0

The Lozi returns were obviously too few to give the figures shown in Table 46 any significance as a reflection of the local average earnings from these sources, and the returns for the other areas were so few as to offer results of very low significance.

8. INCOME FROM EMPLOYMENT AND MIGRANT LABOUR

Income from employment and migrant labour tended to be reliably reported, except in a few cases where the informant was a woman whose husband was earning away from the village but lived in it sufficiently to be counted part of the village. It was not always easy to draw the line between the resident worker and the migrant labourer. Where, for example, a man was working at a tobacco factory and returned to the village at week-ends he was regarded as a resident of the village. Similarly, a teacher who was away for the school term and returned for the holiday was regarded as a local resident if he kept a wife and garden at the village. The difficulty here is, of course, that much of the expenditure of these semi-migrants is not accountable. Many of them have families in their other home. Among the migrant labourers' remittances recorded for the Ngoni were the remittances of soldiers who at the time the record was taken had actually returned to the village. Their earnings while in the army were ignored except in so far as they remitted them or brought them back to the village.

It should be remembered in interpreting Table 47 that Cona village is a-typical in this respect more than any other. The majority of its households earn income from employment either because they are attached to the chief or his court or because they form part of the unusual concentration of school teachers to be found in this village. If an attempt had to be made to generalize for this area, the averages found for Cobana village would probably be nearer to a true reflection of the general average. The Lozi averages are again of small significance, although it may be fair to attribute to the group a benefit from migrant labour which is at least of the same order of magnitude as that enjoyed among the Ngoni. Even this broad conclusion, however, must necessarily be tentative since it is derived from such a small area of observation.

TABLE 47. Income from employment and migrant labour

	Value of income per household investigated shillings	Receiving households as percentage of all %	Value of income per household investigated shillings	Receiving households as percentage of all %
Ngoni	41.3	45	11.9	22
Tonga:				
Cona	108	65	0.3	3
Cobana	5.3	5	—	—
Hanamonga	9.3	7	—	—
Total Tonga	57.5	35	—	—
Lozi	4.6	15	15.4	69

It is interesting to note that receipts from migrant labour among the Tonga were so small as to be negligible. This is the kind of result one would expect for an area where opportunities for earning cash locally or in accessible districts, either by selling crops or livestock, or by taking paid employment, are relatively high. The migrant labourer who comes from a village in the railway belt finds that his friends and relations in the village are less dependent on him for cash than is the case for the migrant labourer from the remoter areas. For most of the Tonga the answer to the question on migrant labour remittances was that the family had relatives working away, but that they did not remit. Frequently they had not even been seen for some years.

9. OTHER CASH RECEIPTS

Amongst the other cash receipts available in these three areas were soldiers' gratuities (which occurred only in the Ngoni sample), receipts from sale of secondhand goods, and such transfer payments as court damages and marriage payments. It should be noted here, that damages awarded by the court and marriage payments often took the form of cattle, or other physical goods, so that total receipts from these sources might greatly exceed cash receipts.

Gratuities and army pay received by soldiers demobilized within the last twelve months amounted to £160 among the Ngoni. This was

equivalent to about £2.7 per household studied and was a large addition to the income of the area. Gratuities received within the past
eighteen months, the bulk of which were available for expenditure
within the past twelve months, amounted to £305 or about £5.1 per
household. The existence of these gratuities greatly complicated the
problem of analysing income and expenditure for the Ngoni villages
because the amount actually available for expenditure within the past
twelve months was unknown. In effect, the savings from gratuities
received more than twelve months ago and carried over into the past
twelve months were not ascertainable. The gratuities were also a
temporary phenomenon, and when considering the village economy
over a wider range of time than the demobilization period, it is necessary
to eliminate the gratuity families, for they involved a serious distortion
of the village accounts. Unfortunately it is not possible to cut them out
altogether, for they are too much a part of the economy. If they were
not returning from the army with gratuities some of these same men
would almost certainly have been returning from the south with
migrants' savings. It is thus not sufficient simply to strike them out and
to regard the families not receiving gratuities as providing a fair reflection of the normal village economy of the region. Moreover, the ex-
soldiers distributed money gifts in an extremely liberal fashion and
bought many local products, and the remainder of the villagers who
had this unusually large local source of cash may well have been induced
to abandon normal habits of seeking cash by casual labour or sales in
more distant areas.

Trade in second-hand goods seems to be common everywhere, but
is difficult to cover because it is easily forgotten. Without long check
lists and a great deal of knowledge of the informant's background
it is almost impossible to frame a satisfactorily concrete question.
Where a concentration of villages is surveyed intensively much of this
information emerges from the expenditure and the property questions.
This, however, involves knowing the informants by name and taking
the time while interviewing to discover and enter the name of the person
from whom each item was bought. It is then necessary to sort out these
cross-references during the analysis. The only group for which any useful
data was collected on this point was for Cona's village among the Tonga.
There it was found that £3 15s. had been received from the sale of
second-hand goods of various kinds, amounting in all to about 2.2
shillings per household. This was almost certainly an underestimate for
this village. Whether it is a fair indication of the results which could
have been obtained for other villages is impossible to say, but it was
clear that they were a factor to be accounted for everywhere. When a
man returns from employment or the army with a large stock of essen-

tial personal possessions from flat-irons to neckties, these possessions are extremely attractive to the villagers. Many of them have never been so far afield themselves, while the returned migrant, when his cash has been dissipated, is glad to trade the now superfluous relics of his town life for the wherewithal to buy a little relish or some tobacco.

Receipts from 'cases' (i.e. damages awarded by the court) are a common source of cash income in many areas. How important they are, and what form they are likely to take, depends greatly on the tribal background. In the interests of making the question as concrete as possible, it is useful to find out in advance what are the commonest types of cases and what are the standard charges involved.

It is even more important to be in possession of the basic facts of the marriage customs, before framing or putting any questions on marriage payments. An orthodox Tonga marriage, for example, may involve five payments by the bridegroom, often spread out over a period of years. The first is a token payment of a hoe, or perhaps about 10s. in cash, which establishes a betrothal. The second occurs when the girl is brought to her husband and her family asks him for gifts: on this occasion he may distribute anything from £1 to £5. The third is paid to the father, generally before marriage, and may be a beast or about 10s. The fourth is paid to the girl's mother and may be anything from 10s. to £1. The fifth is the bride payment itself, which may be in the region of four cattle if it is paid in cattle alone, or between £4 and £10 if paid in money; in one case recorded, this payment was as much as five cattle plus £6 in cash. Finally, if the man had abducted the girl he may have to make a payment that does not come under any of these heads, in order to validate the marriage.

Not every Tonga marriage involves all five forms of payment, nor is the amount of each payment fixed, but a check list on the subject of marriage payments should specify each of them, and it is useful to have some idea of the usual order of magnitude of each payment. Nor are marriage payments simply a matter of a transfer of cash or goods from the husband to the bride's family. The man may be assisted by his own family in making the payments. Or he may actually receive payments from his wife's family if something goes wrong with the marriage, since most of his original payments are returnable. Other communities have their own complex of marriage customs and payments. This is one of the clearest instances of the need for an adequate background of sociological knowledge as a pre-requisite of quantitative economic enquiries.

Court damages, marriage payments and gifts were potential sources of cash in all areas, and the results of questions on this point are given below in Table 48.

TABLE 48. Receipts from damages and marriage payments

	Damages		Marriage payments	
	Value received per household investigated shillings	Receiving households as percentage of all households %	Value received per household investigated shillings	Receiving households as percentage of all households %
Ngoni	2.5	5	2.4	13
Tonga:				
Cona	—	—	6.4	47
Cobana	2.0	10	1.5	15
Hanamonga	2.9	7	—	—
Total Tonga	1.2	4	3.7	28
Lozi	4.1	54	—	—

In interpreting Table 48 it is to be remembered that cases, marriage payments and gifts involve payments in kind probably at least as often as they involve payments in cash. In Hanamonga village, for example, receipts from cases and marriage payments included, in addition to the above cash sums, five cattle, a hoe and a spear which were together worth more than the cash receipts.

The above averages for the Lozi must again be interpreted very cautiously. The sample was small and receipts under the case and marriage payments heading tend to be large per person receiving them, while the proportion of households receiving income from this source in any one year is small. Thus a small sample can easily provide a distorted average. It is probable that the average value recorded as received through damages and marriage payments is too high and that the total omission of cash gifts is a distortion of the general average for the area.

The differences between the Tonga averages for each village can perhaps be explained by the character of the village concerned. For example, the chief's village has an a-typical concentration on the one hand of steady wage earners and on the other hand of destitute old women, which together with the presence of the chief and his officials would tend to produce an economy heavily weighted by money gifts. Hanamonga village, where the main gift receivers (unmarried, divorced, deserted, or widowed women) were omitted from the survey altogether, would tend to give returns showing a lower proportion of gifts. The higher average value of gifts *per recipient* reflected in the Ngoni returns is consistent with the existence of a relatively important group of persons endowed suddenly with unprecedentedly large cash resources. These are the gratuity recipients whose distribution of gifts was on a lavish scale, frequently measured in pounds per recipient rather than in shillings.

10. EXPENDITURE ON SERVICES AND ON GOODS FOR CURRENT CONSUMPTION

The recurrent problem of making questions sufficiently concrete is least troublesome when dealing with expenditure on property. It is practically insoluble when trying to cover cases of expenditure on goods and services for immediate consumption. The question, for example, 'How much do you spend on salt in a week (or a month or a year)?' is most unlikely to produce a satisfactory answer. Even if there is a regularity about the expenditure, informants are generally unaware of it. One can ask 'When did you last buy salt and what did you spend on it?', but except where the informant buys salt in bulk the answer will reveal little about his annual expenditure. He may have spent 3d. last Saturday because he was paying a visit to the town, but his visits might be irregular, so that a record of one purchase is of no significance. Theoretically, of course, the matter can be pursued into previous purchases, but the time consumed by such an exhaustive enquiry is rarely justified by the relative importance of the result in the total return.

Such considerations as these apply to all questions dealing with the purchase of such items as salt, beer, tobacco, soap, sugar, bread, and other minor foodstuffs or relishes, and in some areas paraffin, vaseline, or stationery come into this category. The purchases tend to be irregular and elastic in their response to the supply of cash. In a single village where the basic standard of living was apparently fairly uniform, expenditure on salt, for example, might vary from nothing at all to 15s. in the year. Some poor people manufacture their own salt or habitually beg it from their neighbours. The returned migrant with plenty of money at his disposal is not inclined to be thrifty in his expenditure on such items as salt, and frequently provides a steady supply to his begging relatives.

If it were possible to relate store purchases to any particular store or group of stores, the records of traders would prove a useful check on the totals of entries for store purchases of particular items. This is most likely to be possible for some of the more elusive items of small-scale expenditure such as salt or paraffin, for which the tendency would be to buy in the nearest store. As far as the larger items are concerned, the comparative mobility of the African, even of the non-migrant, and his readiness to walk many miles to obtain the particular piece of cloth he wants, makes it difficult to use particular traders' records as a check.

Whether or not a particular store accounts for a large proportion of village purchases will emerge from the question on source which is included in the property questionnaire. When this has been established, it is then necessary to discover what is the total area served by the store concerned, for it is only by relating sales to population served that one can form any idea of the value of sales to a particular village or group of villages. If the sample investigated is a natural unit, and cut off by distance or customs barriers from other stores and other villages, then it may be practicable to relate the sales of a given store to the population served by it. Alternatively, if the sample is large enough to extend beyond the range of a given store, so that the number of its customers can be estimated from the answers received to the 'source of property' questions, it may again be possible to relate its trade to a specific population. Unless sales can be conclusively related to population it is not possible to use them to check family budget data.

Further difficulties may arise from the unsuitable nature of the shop-keeper's records. Some African storekeepers in a small way of business on their own account do not keep books, so that they have no records which can be examined. On the other hand, their bulk purchases are usually sufficiently memorable for them to prove reliable informants, provided that they do not suspect the enquirer of being a spy for the tax collector or the price controller. African storekeepers in charge of a European or Indian store have to keep some kind of paper records, but these may be very simple and uninformative. In a typical little village store owned by an Indian and kept by an African, for example, the system was that the African turned in his total takings weekly, and the Indian visited the store monthly and revalued the stock. In this case the Indian's records showed details of takings from each type of mer-chandise, or at least of the issue of each item to the store over the period of a year, but the African's records showed only total takings, and total value of stock over a period of weeks.

For none of the three sets of villages for which the economic survey data were collected was it possible to use traders' records as a check on the expenditure answers. In the first place, the sample of households was too small to provide a sufficient market for any one store. In the second place, the villages were all too near a township to depend largely on a village store for their purchases. The township was the market for their produce and contained a group of relatively well-stocked European or Indian stores in which to spend their cash receipts. In no case was it possible to identify a store with a particular group of customers.

For the small and more elusive items of expenditure the enquiries were not exhaustive, except in the case of the Ngoni, from whom information was collected as far as possible on all of them. The results given below in Table 49 contain an appreciable basis of estimate. While not accurate, they indicate the orders of magnitude involved. It must be emphasized, however, that the weight of the expenditure by gratuity families is likely to distort the averages (especially in the smaller items), from what they would be for more normal communities and at more normal times.

TABLE 49.   Estimated Ngoni expenditure on consumable goods and services

	Estimated average per household shillings
1. Salt, soap, tobacco and other consumable store goods[1]	17.5
2. Doctoring and medicine	0.3
3. Transport	2.7
4. Food	6.9
5. Miscellaneous other[2]	6.3

Item 1 in the above table contains a high degree of estimate. Items 2 and 3 are recorded values only and have not been added to by estimate. They are certainly understatements. Some of the items contained in item 5, for example, trinkets, emerged firmly from the property questionnaire; others, such as school fees and mission dues, were small but probably reliably reported; but an appreciable proportion of this item consists of beer, on which expenditure could only be guessed.

In all villages except Cona's, specific enquiries were made as to expenditure on doctors and on transport. The results are shown in Table 50. So far as could be judged, expenditure on doctoring, which should, of course, be taken into account, was not important. The tendency to forget or conceal receipts from doctoring or divining was strong.

TABLE 50.   Expenditure on doctors and transport

	Doctors and Medicine		Transport	
	Expenditure per household	Spending households as percentage of all households	Expenditure per household	Spending households as percentage of all households
	shillings	%	shillings	%
Ngoni	0.3	8	2.7	5
Tonga:				
Cona	0	0	n.a.	n.a.
Cobana	3.5	30	2.4	50
Hanamonga	3.6	14	7.6	64
Total Tonga	1.8	12	n.a.	n.a.
Lozi	4.8	39	0	0

There is reason to suspect a strong bias in the Lozi sample when

[1] 'Other consumable store goods' excludes all more or less durable property such as clothing, household equipment, trinkets and books. In effect, it covers the minor varieties of store goods such as paraffin, vaseline, thread, etc.

[2] This heading includes beer, books, trinkets, church and education fees, newspaper subscriptions, etc.

N

considering expenditure on doctoring. Of the thirteen households questioned, six were living in the family group of a native doctor who was greatly preoccupied by a prevalent hysteric disease. There was not time to enquire into susceptibility of other villages to this disease, but it seemed likely that households in close contact with an active doctor would be more prone to spend on doctors and medicines than those in villages where the mysterious complaints were not so frequently brought to their notice.[1]

No safe conclusions can be drawn about expenditure on transport in general since it varies so sharply with the availability of transport. It should be noted, however, that the area near the railway line showed more households spending on transport and a smaller rate of expenditure per spending household. A small sample in the remote area of Barotseland provided no example of expenditure on transport, which is not surprising. The Fort Jameson area, which is 35s. from the railway line by lorry, showed few persons spending on transport, but those few persons spent relatively large sums. This again is an expected result.

It might be possible in some areas to check transport expenditure answers by collecting material from the transport-providing firms. Here again, however, it is only possible to use general sales statistics to check family budget data if they can be related to a specific population. If all the passengers boarding or leaving a train at a particular station can be ascribed to a particular geographical area, of which the population is known, it is worth while extracting the relevant statistics from the railway company's records, wherever possible. Similarly, it may be practicable to delimit the area which is served by a particular bus halt. If, however, as is the case for most parts of Northern Rhodesia, wide tracts of country are served by a single railway line or main road, the users of trains or lorries may come to each boarding point from villages which are hundreds of miles away.

II. TRANSFER EXPENDITURES

Expenditure on marriage payments, court damages, and fines, being often lump-sum payments of some size, tend to be memorable, and the information collected on these points was probably fairly reliable. Where time can be spared for an examination of court records and tax registers, budget data can be confirmed by obtaining accurate or near-accurate figures for damages, fines and taxes.

Expenditure on gifts, however, was not always memorable. Frequently it took the form of small sums of a shilling or two given casually

---

[1] Dr Gluckman questions this view on the grounds that he found this hysteric disease wherever he went in the area and that all villages were affected by it.

or at a moment of need. Or again, it might form part of the lavish distribution of gifts that characterized the migrant's homecoming, and being one transaction among many was not memorable, though it may have been large in relation to most local incomes. Nevertheless, it is probably fair to assume that most donations of over 5s. were accurately remembered by the donors in most cases. In addition, of course, the migrant makes a large number of gifts in kind. The figures in Table 51 relate to cash gifts only; but if the migrant were asked what goods he brought with him, what he gave away, and to whom he gave, his answers would provide a useful check not only on his own budget and property answers, but also on the answers by other villagers on their property and its source.

TABLE 51. Transfer expenditures

	Taxes and fines		Marriage payments and cases		Gifts	
	Expenditure per household shillings	Spending households as percentage %	Expenditure per household shillings	Spending households as percentage %	Expenditure per household shillings	Spending households as percentage %
Ngoni	4.1	62	4.4	—	8.8	15
Tonga:						
Cona	n.a.	n.a.	n.a.	n.a.	n.a.	n.a.
Cobana	8.0	70	8.3	20	1.9	15
Hanamonga	11.8	86	—	—	n.a.	n.a.
Total Tonga (Cobana and Hanamonga)	9.5	77	4.9	12	n.a.	n.a.
Lozi	1.6	31	3.1	15	n.a.	n.a.

12. EXPENDITURE ON CLOTHING

Expenditure on clothing was recorded in connection with the property survey. Informants were asked, in respect of themselves and each member of their family, what quantity they had of each item of clothing that might be possessed. They were asked, for each item, where and when it was bought and how much had been paid for it. In so far as clothing was worn out in less than a year these records understate the amount spent on clothing; except in the rare instances where the article was bought recently, so that it seemed worth while enquiring into its predecessor, the information collected related only to the clothes then possessed. For the poorer members of the community who had only one set of clothes, this might involve appreciable understatement, since one set of clothes subjected to constant hard wear has a short life on an active individual, even though it may be worn for as long as the rags will hang together. Without keeping records for the full period of a year it is not possible to assess the degree of understatement involved in a questionnaire based on current clothing. In the areas where the schedule was applied the adults of most households had more than one set of clothing annually. Those who had not were commonly the aged poor and old women in particular. Since these led a less active life than most they were often able to make one set of clothing last for more than one year, although frequently they supplemented it by the skin of a domestic animal, and sometimes one set of clothing meant only one article of clothing. For children it was possible that the error of understatement was large in relation to the total village economy. The very young children of a poor household would frequently go naked or in the old cast-off rags of the adults. Older children, however, give very hard wear to their clothes. Boys and girls frequently lead as active a working life in the village as their elders. Herd boys in particular are constantly ripping their clothes on bushes and sharp branches. Nevertheless, on balance, and judging from the dates of purchase given for clothing, it was thought that a questionnaire based on current possessions would not greatly understate the truth.

TABLE 52.   Expenditure on clothing

	Blankets, bedding, etc., per household shillings	Men's clothing per man shillings	Women's clothing per woman shillings	Children's clothing per child shillings	Total blankets, clothing, etc., per household shillings
Ngoni:					
(1) including gratuity families	12.0	39.7	26.1	3.4	66.5
(2) excluding gratuity families	5.6	17.4	21.4	3.0	42.4
Tonga—Cona	7.8	31.1	17.6	6.6	59.5
Cobana	9.3	17.9	19.4	2.7	54.1
Hanamonga	10.1	17.7	25.3	3.8	55.1
Total Tonga	8.8	23.4	19.4	4.6	58.6
Lozi	8.9	31.3	36.6	5.5	65.2

It will be seen from Table 52 that the heaviest expenditure on cloth-ing occurred among the Ngoni, which is not surprising if one takes into account the eleven households enjoying soldiers' gratuities. In fact, a study of the returns relating to the gratuity families shows that in most cases the bulk of the gratuity was spent on clothing. If the gratuity families' returns are excluded from consideration, the average Ngoni expenditure on clothing is, as can be seen, the lowest of the three groups. By excluding the gratuity families, of course, the sample is weighted abnormally in the other direction. If these men were not soldiers, some at least of them would have been migrants, and would have had a rate of expenditure on clothing rather higher than was average for the families not receiving gratuities. On the other hand, returned soldiers with gratuities are, on the average, wealthier, and probably give larger gifts to the rest of the community than if they were ex-migrants. These gifts help to raise the average rate of expenditure of the families not receiving gratuities. Against this, it must be remembered that the returning soldiers were well supplied with stout army clothing which would tend temporarily to reduce the clothing needs of themselves and their beneficiaries.

The relatively high rate of expenditure recorded among the Lozi seems to reflect a relatively high rate of earnings from the sale of beer. As has already been seen, however, the sample may be a-typical on this point. Whether it is characteristic, even of the Lozi of the margin near Mongu, it is impossible to judge without investigating a larger sample. Dr Gluckman comments that the Lozi are well-known for their high standard of dress and that they say themselves that their clothing styles keep them poor.

TABLE 53. Comparative prices of clothing

	Ngoni s. d.	Tonga s. d.	Lozi s. d.
Blanket	17 3	17 9	14 9
Shirts and shorts	18 0	19 0	18 0
Blouse and skirt (or cloth)	13 3	14 0	9 6
	48 6	50 9	42 3
Index of prices	95	100	83
Index of expenditure (a) gratuity families	113	100	111
(b) non-gratuity families	72		
Index of expenditure at Tonga prices (a) gratuity families	120	100	134
(b) non-gratuity families	78		

In Cona's village the expenditure per child seems unduly high. This is largely due to the fact that it contains a large proportion of older children, some of whom give economic assistance in return for clothing and food. It also contains the chief's and councillors' children, and the children of teachers, all of whom seem to enjoy a rather higher standard of clothing than is normal. The probability that the number of Ngoni children has been underestimated (see above, p. 158) suggests that the records of expenditure may have been incomplete also.

Expenditure on clothing is not necessarily a fair index of standard of living in clothing, unless it is considered in relation to prices paid, which vary from one area to another. Average prices were derived from the total recorded transactions in each item and for each area, and these give an indication of the kind of adjustments that should be made in the expenditure estimates given in Table 52. In Table 53 different prices are shown for the different areas in respect of typical clothing needs. From these prices an index of prices is calculated and applied to the results shown in Table 53 to give an index of expenditure on clothing at constant prices. For the Ngoni two indices are shown—(a) including gratuity families, and (b) excluding gratuity families.

13. EXPENDITURE ON HOUSEHOLD AND PRODUCTIVE EQUIPMENT

Like expenditure on clothing, expenditure on household and productive equipment could be investigated relatively easily by the questionnaire method since it was concerned with items of a durable or semi-durable nature and could be discussed in concrete terms. There were, as far as I could judge, no general reasons for hiding expenditure on these items of equipment, although occasionally there were items like petrol tins or buckets which an informant might conceal in the hope of receiving a gift from the investigator.[1] It was also possible that informants might overstate expenditure on productive equipment in order to emphasize the heavy expense of it. On balance, however, it seemed unlikely that many informants were deliberately distorting the facts and it seemed probable that their expenditure under this heading was sufficiently memorable to be relatively accurately expressed. The danger that some items, for example, certain types of axes, were omitted from the check list through ignorance on the part of the investigator should not be overlooked, since a complete check list on household and productive equipment demands a thorough knowledge of the main forms of economic activity in the area and will vary substantially from one district to another.

TABLE 54.   Expenditure on household and productive equipment

	Household equipment (housing, pots, furniture, etc.)		Productive equipment (ploughs, hoes, axes, spears, etc.)	
	Expenditure per household shillings	Spending households as percentage all households %	Expenditure per household shillings	Spending households as percentage all households %
Ngoni	12.8	92	4.1	80
Tonga:				
Cona	7.5	88	9.2	77
Cobana	14.7	95	13.1	75
Hanamonga	9.5	72	4.0	72
Total Tonga	10.0	87	9.3	75
Lozi	12.4	92	0.9	17

[1] An anthropologist's camp is a treasure-house of such possessions and there is always the possibility that informants might deny their own resources in petrol tins and even in clothing, with the hope of receiving a gift.

The results of the enquiries into expenditure on household and productive equipment are given above in Table 54.

Perhaps the most striking feature of the above table is the relatively low expenditure by the Ngoni on productive equipment. The expenditure records of the Tonga families showed an appreciable number of ploughs and cultivators purchased. The Ngoni, in spite of their relatively higher command of cash resources in the form of gratuities, did not record the purchase of one plough or cultivator or indeed of any large-scale purchase of productive equipment. The average of 4s. per household represents expenditure on small-scale items, principally hoes, but also such items as axes and spears. The low expenditure records for the Lozi cannot be regarded as significant in view of the small sample investigated; judging from the small percentage of households which recorded expenditure, the results are almost certainly distorted. On the other hand, very few Lozi use ploughs or cultivators, so that even a larger sample might not include expenditure on the more expensive types of equipment. Unfortunately, no questions were asked about expenditure on dugouts or nets, which might have raised the Lozi totals under this heading.

14. EXPENDITURE ON LIVESTOCK

Questions on the expenditure on livestock were asked of all villages except Cona's. None of the Lozi informants recorded expenditure on livestock, but the sample was too small for this to be significant, and the Lozi are therefore not included in the following table of results.

TABLE 55. Expenditure on livestock

	Expenditure per household	Spending households as percentage of all households
	shillings	%
Ngoni	17.7	40
Tonga—Cobana	12.8	35
Hanamonga	25.6	43
Total Cobana and Hanamonga	17.8	38

It is interesting to note that the results for the total of the Ngoni of whom this question was asked are very close to those from the total of the Tonga covered by it, but the number of cases concerned is too small for this correspondence to be conclusive.

CHAPTER XII

EXPERIMENTS IN VILLAGE ECONOMIC
SURVEYING

(2) COMBINING THE ANSWERS

In the preceding chapter the questions and answers were discussed individually. It is now necessary to consider the problems involved in an attempt to make a synthesis of the answers and to combine them into an intelligible whole. The main difficulty was that both questions and answers were incomplete. Their adequacy was inevitably limited by the interviewer's background knowledge or by his ability to put sufficiently precise questions, and by the informant's patience or by his ability to carry an accurate memory over all of a year's activities. The problem was thus one of manipulating the available material so that all its implications were recognized and to build up from this a coherent picture of the economy concerned.

I. RECORDS OF INCOME AND EXPENDITURE

By applying the schedule to a number of households in each of three different areas there was obtained for each household a sum of recorded incomes and a sum of recorded expenditures. These were not complete, partly because some questions were omitted since they were believed to relate to very minor items which did not justify the time they would take to investigate, and partly because the schedule was developed in the light of experience in its application, so that the framework was progressively changed in the course of the experiment. Broadly speaking, however, the results are believed to indicate the principal orders of magnitude involved, although they do contain a number of errors and omissions. Most of the errors and omissions are on the side of understatement and the recorded figures can usually be assumed to fall short of the truth.

In the tables which follow the main results are given for each area or village separately. These tables will show the magnitude of the discrepancies between the income and expenditure records. It was found that where the informant earned a regular wage, and where his income was relatively high, expenditure records usually fell short of income records. This was to be expected since in such a case income was derived from a few sources and could probably be recorded with a fair degree of accuracy, while for the regular earner or the wealthy man income might be spent on all sorts of minor items such as store goods, purchases which were neither memorable nor regular. It was found, on the other hand, that where the informant was a farmer on a very small scale, who derived his cash income from occasional sales of surplus produce, the expenditure records tended to outweigh the income records. This was because his income was derived from a variety of small unmemorable sales while his expenditure consisted basically of important and necessary items, such as clothing, which were easily recollected.

TABLE 56. Recorded income and expenditure of sixty Ngoni households

Income	per house-hold £	Expenditure	per house-hold £
Sale of:			
1. Crops	0.45	14. Clothing, blankets, etc.	3.33
2. Livestock	0.19	15. Miscellaneous other store goods	0.46
3. Livestock products	0.46	16. Housing and productive	
4. Beer	0.23	equipment	0.84
5. Manufactures	0.31	17. Livestock	0.80
Receipts from:		18. African services	0.60
6. Doctoring	0.06	19. Food (excluding store foods or	
7. Migrant labour	0.59	livestock bought alive)	0.12
8. Employment	2.07	20. Miscellaneous other expendi-	
9. Gratuities	2.67	ture as goods and services	0.32
10. Miscellaneous services	0.12	21. Gifts	0.44
11. Gifts	0.01	22. Savings	0.39
12. Damages and marriage		23. Other payments	1.29
payments	0.12		
13. Total recorded incomes	7.28	24. Total recorded expenditure	8.59

The income column of Table 56 includes only the gratuities received during the past year, although the expenditure column covers substantial purchases made with gratuities received in the last three months of the previous year. Hence there should, strictly, be an item for dis-saving as a source of income, representing expenditure out of the gratuities saved from the previous year. In fact, of course, it was not reasonable to ask men how much they had left of their gratuity at this time last year. The gratuities received during the latter part of the previous year and not included in item 9 of Table 56 were equivalent to a further £2.41 per household.

Table 57 shows the income and expenditure records derived from the three Tonga villages. The records were deficient for Cona's village because no questions were asked on the items contained in the miscellaneous section of the schedule, with the exception of the question on remittances from migrant relatives. (See Table 35.) Some data on these miscellaneous items came to light in discussion of other points in the

TABLE 57. Income and expenditure of sixty-eight Tonga households

Income	Cona £ per household	Cobana £ per household	Hanamonga £ per household	Total villages £ per household
Sale of:				
1. Crops	0.55	3.02	3.93	1.98
2. Livestock and products	1.59	2.01	1.25	1.64
3. Beer	0.09	0.06	0.02	0.07
4. Manufactures	0.04	0.60	0.01	0.20
Receipts from:				
5. Doctoring	—	—	—	—
6. Miscellaneous services	0.05	0.02	0.24	0.08
7. Migrant labour	0.01	—	—	—
8. Employment	5.40	0.26	0.46	2.88
9. Gifts	0.32	0.08	—	0.18
10. Cases and marriage payments	n.a.	0.10	0.14	0.12[1]
11. Miscellaneous other	0.11	0.07	—	0.07
12. Total recorded incomes	8.2	6.2	6.0	7.2
Expenditure				
13. Clothing and blankets	2.98	2.71	2.75	2.85
14. Household and productive equipment	0.85	1.39	0.64	0.96
15. Livestock	n.a.	0.64	1.25	0.89[1]
16. Transport	n.a.	0.12	0.38	0.23[1]
17. Taxes and fines	0.29	0.40	0.59	0.39
18. Damages and marriage payments	n.a.	0.41	—	0.24[1]
19. Doctors and medicine	n.a.	0.18	0.18	0.18[1]
20. African services	0.31	0.19	n.a.	0.26[2]
21. Other property	0.14	0.09	0.09	0.12
22. All other	0.01	0.92	0.17	0.30
23. Total recorded expenditure	4.6	7.0	6.0	6.4

schedule with informants, but in general it can be taken that the records are incomplete on this score. This meant that expenditure records were particularly unsatisfactory since a large number of individuals in Cona's village were regular earners who spent frequently in these miscellaneous ways and it would have been of value to have been able to gauge the order of magnitude of their annual purchases. Nevertheless, even the most meticulous examination would probably have failed to establish all the miscellaneous expenditure items for this village. There was

[1] Cobana and Hanamonga only.
[2] Cona and Cobana only.

reason to believe that the regular earners—several of them men living alone—spent a significant proportion of their money on beer and women, as well as on bread and tea from the stall at the court house and other casual luxuries bought on visits to the railway-line township of Monze, which was within easy walking distance. Without spending a long period in the village it would be impossible to cover these channels of expenditure with any degree of reliability. On the other hand, the income column for Cona's village probably contains a smaller margin of error than is usually the case in these rapid investigations, since it contained so many employed persons the bulk of whose income could be recorded quickly and accurately.

It is stressed that the close correspondence between total incomes and total expenditure of Hanamonga village is not evidence of the comprehensiveness and reliability of the records collected there. It is simply that the sum of the surpluses and deficiencies on the income side of the individual budgets has cancelled out against the sum of the deficiencies and surpluses on the expenditure side. The individual Hanamonga budgets do not balance any more satisfactorily than the individual Cobana budgets.

Table 58 compares income and expenditure records for the thirteen Lozi households. The effect of the small sample is illustrated, for example, by the relatively high average income derived from tailoring. Clearly the presence in the sample of one prosperous tailor has distorted the average and made it impossible to generalize therefrom. It is unlikely that the investigation of a further fifty households would have produced another tailor and the average for this item would have become insignificant. On the other hand, the investigation of a further fifty households in this particular area might well have thrown up another tradesman earning as much if not more than the tailor. Two

TABLE 58.   Income and expenditure of thirteen Lozi households

Income	£ per house-hold	Expenditure	£ per house-hold
Sale of:			
1. Crops, meat, fish, etc.	3.35	10. Clothing and blankets	3.26
2. Beer	0.82	11. Household equipment	0.62
3. Manufactures	0.02	12. Productive equipment	0.05
		13. Other property	0.07
Receipts from:		14. Doctoring	0.24
4. Migrant labour	0.77	15. Taxes and fines	0.08
5. Employment	0.23	16. Marriage payments	0.15
6. Doctoring	0.06		
7. Tailoring	2.00		
8. Gifts	0.20		
9. Total recorded incomes	7.5	17. Total recorded expenditures	4.5

other tradesmen in the vicinity of Mongu were interviewed. One of them had in the past fourteen months earned £55 from hawking and between £5 and £6 from the sale of crops and livestock. The other, a leather worker, had had a total turnover of over £240 in the past twelve months and a net return of at least £120.

2. ESTIMATES OF INCOME AND EXPENDITURE

By taking the household returns separately and examining each individual's budget to discover the possible sources of the discrepancy between the income and expenditure records, it was possible to make estimates of total income and expenditure which are in many ways more satisfactory than the records given in the tables above. For example, it was often possible to use additional qualitative information which had been collected by the anthropologist or became evident in the course of the enquiry. In others it was necessary to deduce errors and omissions from the total picture of the individual's economic activity as illustrated by his return. For example, if it was known that a local widow received assistance from a particular individual and her budget showed some item of necessary expenditure which was not other-wise accounted for, it seemed reasonable to assume that this surplus expenditure was financed by a gift. Or again, if we find that a man whose income exceeds expenditure has recorded no clothing expenditure during the past year it may prove reasonable, after an examination of his other possible channels of expenditure, to assume that his last recorded purchase of clothing was made less than twelve months ago and not more than twelve months ago.

These, of course, are highly arbitrary decisions. They represent guesses based on what general information is available about each household concerned.[1] In each case, unless particular data were available to suggest otherwise, the assumption was made in balancing an individual's budget that the higher figure—whether income or expenditure—was nearer the truth than the lower figure. In other words, it was assumed that the informant is more likely to omit items of income and expenditure, either because he has forgotten or because the question has not been put in a sufficiently evocative form, than to include items which either do not belong to his budget or which belong to the budget of a previous year. This assumption, although not universally reliable,

[1] The source of general and additional information which was used to balance each individual's budget was usually the anthropologist, except where it emerged from the returns from other informants. The necessary adjustments of the balance based on this information was my responsibility, however, and any assessment of the value of the resulting estimate must take into account my limited acquaintance with each area visited.

is a reasonable one for all general purposes, and the estimated average total income or expenditure is almost certainly nearer the truth than the recorded total income or expenditure. Whether or not the estimates for particular items of income or expenditure are more reliable than the records, depends, of course, on the nature and completeness of the additional qualitative information in each case. Generally speaking, the background information collected by the anthropologist and the data collected by observation and indirect questioning during the enquiry was sufficient in most cases to prevent the estimates from distorting the records. It must be borne in mind, however, that although

TABLE 59. Estimates of average income and expenditure for 141 households

Income	Ngoni including gratuity families 60 households £ per household	Ngoni excluding gratuity families 49 households £ per household	Tonga 68 households £ per household	Lozi 13 households £ per household
Sale of:				
1. Crops	0.6	0.7	2.1 ⎫	
2. Livestock and products	0.7	0.7	1.9 ⎭	3.3
3. Beer	0.3	0.3	0.1	0.8
4. Manufactures	0.4	0.4	0.2	0.01
Receipts from:				
5. Migrant labour	0.4	0.4	—	0.8
6. Employment	2.4	2.6	2.9	0.2
7. Miscellaneous services and all other	0.1	0.1	0.3	2.2
8. Gifts	0.1	0.4	0.6	0.2
9. Gratuities	2.7	—	—	—
10. Damages and marriage payments	0.1	0.02	0.1	—
11. Dis-saving	2.5	0.06	—	—
12. Total estimated income	10.3	5.7	8.2	7.5
Expenditure				
13. Clothing, blankets, etc.	3.8	2.5	2.9	3.3
14. Store goods not included elsewhere	0.9	0.8	included in item 18	
15. Household and productive equipment	0.9	0.7	1.0	0.7
16. Livestock	0.8	0.1	0.8	—
17. Food	0.4	0.3 ⎫	2.6	3.3
18. Miscellaneous other	0.5	0.4 ⎭		
19. Transfer payments[1]	0.9	0.4	0.9	0.2
20. Saving	2.1	0.5	—	—
21. Total estimated expenditure	10.3	5.7	8.2	7.5

[1] Taxes, fines, damages, marriage payments, gifts.

the records for each item offer a fairly reliable minimum average per household the estimates offer probable averages only and should be considered in relation to the original records.

3. INCOME DISTRIBUTION

Average figures of income, while they indicate orders of magnitude which are useful for an at-sight comparison of one economy with another, tell us relatively little about the average man's income. Before leaving the subject of total incomes, therefore, it is necessary to supplement these averages by an attempt to illustrate the pattern of income distribution among the households studied. From the original records, since we have different income and expenditure columns, we can derive both a distribution of incomes and a distribution of expenditures. The two distributions are given in Table 60 below. They are given in this form because it may be of interest to see in another aspect the differences between the income and expenditure estimates. Figures for the Lozi are not given in this table because the sample was too small to make the comparison worth while.

TABLE 60. Comparison of recorded income and expenditure distributions

| | Ngoni | | | | Tonga | |
| | With gratuity families | | Without gratuity families | | | |
	Income %	Expenditure %	Income %	Expenditure %	Income %	Expenditure %
No cash income or expenditure	7	7	8	8	I	I
Under £3	32	25	39	31	36	30
£3 and under £6	25	37	31	45	25	41
£6 and under £10	10	8	12	10	15	13
£10 and under £15	I	5	2	6	10	10
£15 and under £30	15	15	8	—	12	5
£30 and over	10	3	—	—	I	—

The correspondence between the two distribution patterns in each case is generally so close that very little comment is required. The samples are too small to permit a fine analysis of the differences. Nevertheless, it might be noted that the distribution of expenditure is more closely concentrated about the mean than that of incomes. This is capable of reasonable explanation. There is a certain minimum level of needs below which expenditure does not as a rule fall, however low the earning power of the individual concerned. The excess needs may be met in case of low income receivers by loans or gifts which do not appear readily in income returns. At the other end of the scale there is a level at which most of the high earners have satisfied their primary needs before they have exhausted their income. Their surplus expenditure may flow partly into exotic channels which have escaped the check lists based on normal purchases in the area, and partly into savings or gifts, neither of which appear readily in expenditure returns.

Finally, in Table 61 is given the *estimated* income distribution pattern which corresponds to the final estimates of average incomes and expenditures given in Table 59.

TABLE 61.   Estimated distribution of incomes in 141 households

	Ngoni		Tonga	Lozi
	With gratuity households	Without gratuity households		
	%	%	%	%
No cash income	5	6	1 ⎫	
Under £3	23	29	18 ⎬ 71	
£3 and under £6	30	37	40 ⎭	
£6 and under £10	17	20	13 ⎫	
£10 and under £15	2	2	12 ⎬ 29	
£15 and under £30	13	6	15 ⎪	
£30 and over	10	—	1 ⎭	

4. PROPERTY RECORDS

The property questionnaire absorbed a large part, often the major part, of the interview. The check list was drawn up in consultation with an anthropologist whose area was being studied, and it was added to as the enquiry progressed and new items were found to be appropriate. Thus it tended to err on the side of understatement. Since, however, the basic possessions varied comparatively little from one area to another and any variation of importance was usually already known to the anthropologist, the relative number and importance of the additions made during the course of the enquiry were small.

For each item the informant was asked how many he possessed, whence he had got them, what they had cost him in cash or kind, and when he had got them. This shed a great deal of light on the nature of the possessions which formed the background to the local standard of living. The basic properties were very much the same from one area to another and from one individual to another. The total range of properties possessed by a significant proportion of the households was very limited. Only a few articles were found to be in the possession of more than 75% of the households in all three areas. They were huts, storehouses, pots, hoes, axes or sickles, and blankets. These can fairly be regarded as universal. Articles owned by more than 50% of the households investigated in all areas are set out in the following list:

Huts	Cups
Storehouses	Porridge stirrers
Pots	Hoes
Sifters	Axes
Baskets	Blankets
Plates	Shirts
Spoons	Blouses

It must be remembered that the check list was not necessarily comprehensive. For example, among the Ngoni it was found that between 25% and 50% of the households had combs or hairbrushes, but since this question was not put to Tonga villagers we do not know whether there were any or many households owning these items. On the other hand it is fairly certain that the check list covered all but a negligible proportion of the goods which were owned by more than half the households.[1]

TABLE 62. Possessions of the average household in three areas
(i.e. property owned by more than 50% of the households in each case)

1. Ngoni	2. Tonga	3. Lozi
Huts	Huts	Huts
Storehouses	Storehouses	Storehouses
Pots	Pots	Pots
Baskets	Baskets	Baskets
Spoons	Spoons	Spoons
Porridge stirrers	Porridge stirrers	Porridge stirrers
Sifters	Sifters	Sifters
Plates	Plates	Plates
Cups	Cups	Cups
Knives	Mortars	Mortars
Chairs or stools	Pounders	Pounders
Bottles	Chairs or stools	Beds
Hoes	Beds	Hoes
Axes or sickles	Ploughs	Axes or sickles
Mats	Hoes	Ornaments
Blankets	Axes or sickles	Blankets
Shorts	Ornaments	Shorts
Shirts	Spears	Blouses
Cloths	Ox yokes	Overclothes
Blouses	Ox chains	Shirts
Headbands	Skins	Child's cloths
	Blankets	Child's shirts
	Skirts	
	Blouses	
	Shorts	
	Shirts	

Table 62 shows for all three areas what can be regarded as the minimum list of possessions for the average household. It will be noted that children's clothes appear in only one list, that for the Lozi. It

[1] Table 35 gives the basic check list and will show what goods are being defined as 'property' in this chapter.

must not be assumed, therefore, that the average child went unclothed. In practice the possession of at least one garment by the child is almost universal as soon as it can walk, and in many cases it has some covering of its own even sooner. Since, however, a child may wear any one of a large range of garments—shirt, shorts, blouse, dress, cloth, etc.—and frequently has only one of these at a time (although it may have several in the course of a year) no one garment is sufficiently common to be found in more than 50% of the households.

A glance at the above table would suggest that in so far as the possession of a wide range of basic properties is an index of the standard of living, the highest standard of living was enjoyed by the Tonga in spite of the larger command of cash resources among the Ngoni. Less than 50% of the Ngoni households had their own mortars and pounders (in spite of the fact that this is a necessary piece of equipment for every woman), and most Ngoni households had therefore to borrow these items from a neighbour. More than half the Tonga households had ploughs of their own, but none of the Ngoni questioned had ploughs. More than 75% of the Tonga had beds, usually made by the men of the household themselves, and a home-made Tonga bed of poles slung with thongs compared favourably with the local carpenter's product retailed among the Ngoni at 25s. or 27s. 6d.

In order further to compare the wealth of the three groups of people their property was converted into money terms. Where the commodity had been bought it was evaluated at the price paid for it—however old it was. Where the commodity was received in gift or by barter or was part of subsistence output it was evaluated at the average price for all the recorded transactions in that commodity for the area concerned. The resulting figures will not permit of precise comparisons, but are useful for broad comparative purposes.

TABLE 63. Value of property owned by three groups of households

	Value of property acquired in last year £ per household	Value of total property held £ per household	Estimated average money income in last year £ per household
All Ngoni households	5.6	13.1	10.3
Ngoni gratuity households	11.5	25.1	18.2
Ngoni, excluding gratuity households	4.3	10.4	5.7
Tonga	5.6	15.5	8.2
Lozi	5.1	11.8	7.5

Probably the most striking feature of this table is the relatively low average wealth of the Ngoni in spite of the high cash resources which the gratuity holders brought to the group. It illustrates the relative poverty of villages whose men go off to work or to the army. There is less

o

subsistence output, and although gifts send money flowing round the villages the cash seems to be dissipated rapidly in current consumption. In so far as the lower figures derived from the small Lozi sample are significant they can be used to illustrate the lower prices of this remote area and the greater dependence on articles of African manufacture rather than on European store goods. It must be borne in mind, however, that my period of stay with the Lozi was too short to enable me to construct a satisfactory property check list for a people with such a varied economy, and the record may be a serious understatement. There will be, of course, a degree of understatement in all these figures, since the check lists could not be completely comprehensive for any group. In fact, the figures in Table 63 cover all the property set out in Table 62 plus a number of usually small items which appeared only once or a very few times in one area only. It does not include livestock and there are a number of other minor items—for example, playing cards—which might make an appreciable difference in the value of property recorded for the gratuity families and indeed for all households with relatively large quantities of cash at their command. On balance, however, it does not seem likely that these additions would raise the above figures very considerably.

Table 64 carries the comparison further for the Ngoni and Tonga by showing the distribution of total property holdings. No figures are given for the Lozi because a sample of thirteen is too small to justify even a rough percentage distribution table. Hanamonga is excluded from the Tonga returns since complete property inventories were not attempted there.

TABLE 64.   Property distribution in fifty-four Tonga households and sixty Ngoni households

Property valued at:	Tonga households %	Ngoni households %
No cash value	—	—
Under £3	2	5
£3 and under £6	11	18
£6 and under £10	17	22
£10 and under £15	22	33
£15 and under £25	39	7
£25 and under £30	—	12
£30 and under £50	9	3
Over £50	—	—

Table 64 illustrates anew the existence of poverty among the Ngoni families who are not migrants. It is interesting to note, however, for both communities the closer and more even distribution of total wealth when compared with the distribution of annual cash income as shown in Table 61. There are no families with no property at all and few with property worth less than £6 or more than £30. This may reflect in part the tendency of differences in annual income to be dissipated in the form of gifts instead of becoming established as a wealth differential. In part also it reflects the tendency of the high earners to spend their surplus incomes not on durable or semi-durable goods, but on goods and services for immediate consumption purposes—such as transport, beer, food, soap, tobacco, paraffin and other rapidly consumed store goods. Another factor is that the budgeting period for a people with a strong labour migration tendency is longer than a year. The returned migrant or the demobilized soldier returns to his village with a substantial amount of wealth and then proceeds to live on his stocks of money and clothes for perhaps eighteen months or more during which he earns very little additional income. During the second year his income and expenditure will be relatively low, although his standard of living and his level of wealth will not be correspondingly depressed.

5. TRANSACTIONS WITHOUT CASH

It is inevitable that a village economic survey devoted to obtaining quantitative results in a very short period of time should be concentrated mainly on collecting the data for cash transactions. It is of importance, nevertheless, to form some idea of the relative contribution of non-monetary activities to the village economy. It is doubtful whether this can be done by a method which relies predominantly on interview by questionnaire. Certainly, as far as goods and services for current consumption purposes are concerned, the probability is that even the most painstaking questionnaire would fail to cover the ground at all satisfactorily since the problem of posing sufficiently specific questions is often insoluble. Some conclusions were inevitably drawn from general unsystematic observation, together with some miscellaneous information that came to light in the course of interviews. It seems, for example, that barter transactions in goods and services for immediate consumption are both common and casual. A man may barter a chick for some beer because he is temporarily short of cash and a beer party is in progress. A woman may barter a few groundnuts for a cupful of salt because she has not time to go to the store for it. A man may prescribe for another's cough and receive a pumpkin in exchange. All these are small and ephemeral transactions, often entirely unconnected with current exchange values, so that even an interviewer with second sight might fail to elicit the necessary information after the passage of about six months or so.

In sum these transactions may be important, yet without direct observation over a considerable period of time it is impossible to say how important. It may be that for some poor households, especially in remote districts, the only means of obtaining salt or beer is by small barter transactions: any cash that comes their way would be immediately absorbed by major essentials such as clothing or tax. One doctor questioned had filled a well-stocked *kraal* with the proceeds of his doctoring over a period of many years; it is more than probable that much of his household's current consumption was derived from the same source, but that the services rendered were so unimportant that they were quite immemorable. A doctor will usually remember that he got a cow for curing a lunatic a year ago; but that a neighbour gave him a chicken for curing his stomach-ache six months ago is a fact that is not likely to remain in his memory sufficiently vividly to be elicited by such a general query as 'Did anybody ever give you anything in return for medicine or for curing sickness?'

In dealing with durable or semi-durable items, however, we are on firmer ground. There is at least one aspect of an activity involving such items which is concrete and there is therefore some hope of asking the appropriate question. When informants were asked about their property they were asked also where they got it. This question gave a fund of background data much of which was unfortunately not measurable in quantitative terms. It gave information on, for example, the localization of village industries, the dependence on European stores or on African pedlars, and of the amount of inter-village exchange. It also illustrated the relative importance of barter exchange, subsistence output and gifts as a source of wealth.

An attempt was made to compare those forms of local economic activity on the basis of imputed values. The prices were those used in evaluating total wealth as described in the previous section. To each commodity was ascribed the average price of the whole series of cash transactions recorded for that commodity in the area concerned. Thus if a man received an overcoat in exchange for a cow, the transaction was valued at the average price for all transactions in overcoats that were recorded in his area.

It is necessary to emphasize the arbitrariness of this method of evaluation and the theoretical complications to which it gives rise if the figures are considered by themselves. One might equally well, for example, evaluate the barter transaction just described at the value of a cow. All that can be said for the evaluation employed is that it applies a common denominator which enables a rough comparison to be made between the different forms of activity. The total or average money value of each form of activity measured in this way has no intrinsic significance.

TABLE 65.   Relative importance of different forms of economic activity
as a source of village wealth[1]

	Ngoni With gratuity families %	Ngoni Without gratuity families %	Tonga %	Lozi %
Value of property:				
Bought	66	61	70	79
Bartered	4	6	8	0.5
Gifted	21	21	9	14
Subsistence output[1]	9	12	13	6.5
Total property	100	100	100	100

A close comparison of the percentages in Table 65 would be unjusti-
fied in view of the small samples and the crudeness of the methods of
evaluation. A few tentative comments on the broad distinctions may be
of some interest, however. The relatively low proportion of Ngoni
wealth which is acquired by cash purchase is interesting, especially
when one remembers the high command of cash resources enjoyed by
the gratuity households. On the other hand, it should be remembered
that the Tonga sample is heavily weighted by full-time wage earners
who would normally buy or barter much of their wealth. Again, it is
interesting to observe the low proportion of gifts among the Tonga
households. This is unexpected from a sample which includes the chief's
village. It is possible, however, that cash gifts are important enough to
redress this balance and that the total weight of gifts as a source of
wealth in the Tonga villages is considerably higher than Table 65
would suggest. (See Table 66, below.)

Finally, the high proportion of things bought by the Lozi households,
matched by a correspondingly low proportion of things bartered or
subsistence products, reflects a lively inter-African trade. In the Tonga
and Ngoni households, and particularly in the Tonga households, much
of the household equipment of the family was made by one of its members or bartered with neighbours. Very few households did not make
some of their household equipment, their pots, say, or their baskets.
Among the Lozi, on the other hand, most of the items in the household's
property record had been bought or gifted. There was greater specialization and more local trade in every kind of commodity. Whether
this is a general feature rather than a characteristic of the small sample
studied it is impossible to tell. So far as could be judged, however, from

---

[1] The items covered in this table are the durable and the semi-durable items
specified on pp. 2–4 of Table 35. Hence crops and current services which constitute
the bulk of subsistence output are entirely excluded.

general qualitative observation, it seems that inter-African trade is livelier in Barotseland than in other parts of Northern Rhodesia.[1]

In order to apply these proportions to total income to obtain some idea of the total value of barter and subsistence output (excluding, of course, subsistence crops) we should have to make the arbitrary assumption that barter and subsistence income have the same relation to cash income as barter and subsistence property to cash property. The results of this assumption are given in Table 66, which also gives the result of adding cash gifts to gifts of property in kind. This, of course, excludes gifts of goods and services for current consumption, but they provide such a wide range of possibilities and doubts that no attempt can be made to estimate their value unless the observer is prepared to spend long periods in the field recording every activity which takes place in the village. Such an enquiry would raise endless problems of definition. Is it a gift, for example, when one man cuts another's hair, or when a child is invited to share another household's food?

TABLE 66. Estimate of monetary and non-monetary income

	Ngoni (excluding gratuity families) value per household		Tonga value per household	
	£	%	£	%
Cash	5.3	68	7.1	73
Barter	0.4	5	0.1	2
Subsistence	0.8	10	1.2	12
Gift	1.3	17	1.3	13
Total incomes (excluding subsistence crops)	7.8	100	9.7	100

The calculation on which Table 66 is based contains a number of highly arbitrary assumptions which would require a great deal of checking in the field before the results could be regarded with any but the greatest of caution. Nevertheless, it is interesting to note that the proportions for each category of income are roughly of the same order of magnitude for both groups. The gratuity earners were excluded from the Ngoni calculation since they impose a special factor which is not only overweighted, but has a peculiarly distorting effect on the activities of the past year. The Lozi were also excluded because the sample was regarded as too small to warrant even such very tentative calculations.

---

[1] This view is supported by Dr Gluckman, whose extensive knowledge, not only of Barotseland, but also of other parts of Northern Rhodesia, gives his qualitative judgments considerable weight in connection with any comparative statements of this kind.

CHAPTER XIII

VILLAGE ECONOMIC SURVEY RESULTS

The surveys which have been described in the preceding pages were
undertaken primarily with a view to evolving a method of economic
survey for the village areas of Central Africa. They were too limited in
scope and they covered too small a sample of people to be of much value
in themselves. Nevertheless, the fact that there is almost a complete
dearth of information on the village economies makes it inevitable that
these and the other tiny surveys which are available should assume a
certain intrinsic value. It is the object of this chapter to consider the
results of the surveys in the light of the other existing material and to
formulate a few tentative hypotheses from a combination of the data.

I. INCOME LEVELS

For the purposes of comparison the results of these and the other
quantitative surveys that are available on the village economies of
Northern Rhodesia can be reduced to a series of collections of cash
income and expenditure budgets. So if we are prepared to accept a
limited definition of income and economic activity, to confine them, in
fact, to cash transactions alone, we can hope to draw from the surveys
some general conclusions on the level of incomes in the areas in which
the enquiries have been conducted.

(a) Tonga budgets

In 1945 a survey was made among the Plateau Tonga by a team of
workers from the Agricultural Department, assisted by Dr Max Gluckman of the Rhodes-Livingstone Institute. This survey, which can conveniently be styled the General Tonga Survey in contra-distinction to
my own Cona Tonga Survey, covered a wide area of Tonga country
and is particularly suitable for comparative purposes since it was sufficiently close in time and space to provide a real check. The team of
workers collected budget data from thirty subsistence farmers, eight
smallholders, five large farmers, and (through an African research
assistant) twenty-four wives of monogamists, eight wives of polygamists,

199

and ten women without husbands. Thus, the results of the survey, which set out to obtain data from each of the main farming groups of the area, could be weighted to give an average which was, on the face of it, more readily generalizable than my data collected entirely from three adjacent villages. On the other hand, the Cona survey was collected from a larger number of people and was altogether more intensive in its approach.[1]

In the following tables the results of the General Survey and of the Cona Survey are given together in comparable form. This necessitated a certain amount of adjustment in the two sets of figures: but the error introduced by these adjustments can be regarded as negligible in view of the general margin of error which must attend any attempt to draw up an individual's budget on the basis of his memory of the previous twelve months. In effect, the General Survey results for each group of budgets were combined into a weighted average, the weights being derived from figures in the General Survey itself. My own figures were converted to a 'per male head of household' basis. In order to bring the figures into a comparative form it proved necessary to cut out the budgets of women living alone: this is not an important omission, but it does mean that there is a tendency to overestimate incomes when converting to a per head basis.

TABLE 67. Comparative Tonga incomes
(per masculine household)

Income from:	General Survey £	Cona Survey £
1. Crops	6.65	2.86
2. Livestock	2.66	2.34
3. Labour	0.98	3.63
4. Gifts	0.27	0.81
5. Manufactured and second-hand goods	0.12	0.33
6. Other	0.70	0.46
7. Total incomes	11.38	10.43

The difference between the two totals here is insignificant in face of the margin of error involved in both sets of estimates. The difference for items 1 and 3 can, however, be regarded as significant. They can largely be accounted for by the differing compositions of the two samples. The General Survey was concerned primarily with the farming population, and may have underweighted the contribution of wage-earning employment to the sum total of rural economic activity. My survey had no examples of large-scale African farmers, for whom the dependence on

[1] The Cona survey covered 126 adults; the General Survey covered eighty-five adults.

crops as a source of cash tends to be absolute, and was known to be overweighted by employed persons since Cona's village contained a chief, two councillors, a court clerk, a court messenger, and five teachers. There is probably never more than one village in any chieftaincy with so many employed persons.

Similar adjustments were made to reduce expenditures to a comparable form, and the results are seen in Table 68.

TABLE 68. Comparative Tonga expenditures

(per masculine household)

Expenditure on:	General Survey £	Cona Survey £
1. Clothing	5.20	3.71
2. Equipment	2.39	1.24
3. Livestock	0.56	1.04
4. All other	3.23	4.44
5. Total expenditure	11.38	10.43

The difference in the two estimates for expenditure on equipment in this table is again largely a function of the composition of the two samples. It can probably be ascribed in large part to the fact that for farmers, expenditure on equipment increases out of all proportion to increases in their income. For a community where cash farming was a less important occupation there would be a greater tendency for higher-income groups to invest their money in livestock or to spend it on 'other items' rather than to buy farming equipment.

On the basis of these two sets of budget data, and of my own crude estimates of the relative representativeness or reliability of the samples in respect of each item, I have drawn up an estimate of average Tonga village income and expenditure which is the nearest we can get, with existing material, to a generalization which would fit Mazabuka District as a whole. This average budget is shown in Table 69.

TABLE 69. Tonga village budgets. Estimated average

(per masculine household)

Income from:	£	Expenditure on:	£
1. Crops (including beer)	5.7	7. Clothing	4.8
2. Livestock	2.6	8. Equipment	1.5
3. Labour	1.6	9. Livestock	0.9
4. Gifts	0.6	10. Other	4.1
5. Other	0.8		
6. Total receipts	11.3	11. Total expenditure	11.3

We might go further and generalize for Mazabuka District on the assumption that there were 20,000 masculine households (i.e. that there were roughly as many masculine householders as there were estimated to be taxpayers).[1] This gives us a total income and expenditure account for Mazabuka District as follows:

TABLE 70. Tonga income and expenditure. Generalized account for Mazabuka District (villages only)

Income from:	£	Expenditure on:	£
1. Crops	114,000	7. Clothing	96,000
2. Livestock	52,000	8. Equipment	30,000
3. Labour	32,000	9. Livestock	18,000
4. Gifts	12,000	10. Other	82,000
5. Other	16,000		
6. Total village incomes	226,000	11. Total village expenditure	226,000

The interesting feature about Tables 69 and 70 from the point of view of the economy as a whole is that they represent estimates of total rural income and expenditure for what is reliably believed to be the area with the highest rural income in Northern Rhodesia. My own impression is that these estimates are more likely to overstate income and outlay for the rural areas of the District as a whole than to understate it. On the other hand, it must be remembered that the method pursued in both surveys relied on the informant's memory of twelve months' transactions and for this reason is more likely to understate than overstate their total value. As far as village income levels are concerned, however, there is good reason to believe that the estimates in Table 69 represented an upper limit for Northern Rhodesia.

If we are interested in the value of village cash economic activity, as opposed to the value of total village incomes from all sources, we should exclude the items for gifts, and other transfer payments (such as marriage payments, court damages, etc.). These transfer payments do not, strictly speaking, constitute economic activity at all. We should also exclude most of the amount recorded for labour, since this derives almost entirely from activities performed outside the village. In effect, therefore, it is estimated that the average village income for Mazabuka District amounted to about £2.6 per head of the population, and that village economic activity was worth about £2 per head.

At the time of final revision of this volume for the press, I received from Dr Colson, who has been working among the Tonga almost continuously since 1946, some preliminary results of the budget data which she has been collecting over the period 1948–50. It is not possible, without seeing her full report, to give results which are precisely com-

---

[1] Estimates collected from the District Commissioners gave a total of 19,981 taxpayers for Mazabuka District as a whole in 1945.

parable with the other estimates in this section, but in a preliminary comment on her results she estimated that the Tonga average income from all sources in 1948 was about £33, with a median income of about £12, and that a good 1950 crop would produce similar income levels. The 1949 crop was abnormally bad, and it is doubtful whether income levels were as much as a quarter of the 1948 standard. These figures can be very roughly compared with those in Table 69.

(b) Lozi budgets

As has been emphasized throughout the preceding pages, the Lozi sample was too small to permit any convincing generalizations to be arrived at, even for the immediate area from which the sample was drawn. It is fairly certain that the Lozi of the flood plain area are more prosperous than the average inhabitant of Barotse Province, and still more certain that the existence of one induna and one tailor in my thirteen-household sample weighted it heavily in favour of the higher-income groups.

In an attempt to arrive at a more generalizable figure I examined a set of budgets collected for Dr Max Gluckman in 1944 by an African research assistant. Dr Gluckman permitted me to see these budgets in their raw state, and before he had had time to analyse or comment on them himself in any way, so that my judgments in this matter are subject to correction by his considerable experience of the area.

The budgets were for the most part incomplete in that they did not balance. The assumption that a difference between income and expenditure meant that some items had been omitted on one side of the account (rather than that too many items had been included) gave an average income over sixty-seven households of about £2.25 per household. It was not quite clear what period had been covered in these budgets, nor how the period had been fixed for the purposes of questioning, but it seemed fairly certain that the answers did not in practice cover the full period of the past year. In fact, the budgeting period may in some cases have been as little as six months.

It seemed fair to assume on what evidence was contained in the budgets and the compiler's notes that they covered a period of between six and twelve months for most items, and that—since they covered the harvest period—they accounted for 75% at least of the total cash income and expenditure. On this assumption the average income was about £3 per household. If my budgets are added to these budgets on the assumption that the latter were insufficiently weighted in favour of the higher-income groups to be found in the immediate vicinity of Mongu township, the average income works out at about £3.7 per

204 COLONIAL SOCIAL ACCOUNTING

household. Of this, between £0.4 and £0.6 could be ascribed to labour, migrant labour, and transfer payments, leaving about £3.2 per household for the value of village economic activity. Thus, in terms of the proportions of population estimated to be available in Barotse Province villages, the average income per head of the village population would be about £1 and the average value of village economic activity per head of the village population would be worth about £0.87.

(c) Ngoni budgets

There are no other budgets available for the population of the Ngoni area in which I collected my data, so that there are no checks, direct or indirect, on the averages contained in Table 56. It is possible, however, to make some attempt to weight the gratuity families in the total population. In August 1945 there were 4,046 Africans in military service from Eastern Province. Assuming that this was roughly equivalent to the number of discharged soldiers in Eastern Province at the time I took my returns (i.e. in April 1947), they amounted to about 5.77% of the number of taxpayers. We have no evidence on the polygamy rate among returned soldiers, but in my sample seven men accounted for eleven households. If this was true on the average, of them all, there were about 6,350 gratuity families, or about 7.56% of the number of households. Weighting the gratuity families on these lines with the data collected in Fort Jameson District, we get an average income of about £7.64 per household, of which as much as £5.52 could be attributed to labour, migrant labour, gratuities, gifts, and transfer payments.

This suggests that village economic activity was not worth more than about £2.11 per household. Converting these estimates to a per-head-of-the-population basis, the average income per head in the Fort Jameson District (judging by the families investigated in the area I visited) appears to be about £2.20, and the average value of village economic activity per head about £0.61. Unfortunately, there are no data of this type for Northern Province, where there is another community with a strong tradition of migration and a low standard of internal resources. It is interesting to note, however, that this area in Eastern Province with a high rate of migration appears to have a very low rate of village productivity in traded output.

(d) Lamba budgets

Finally, there is available a collection of twenty-nine budgets made by a group of research workers under the auspices of the Rhodes-Livingstone Institute. The data were collected among the Lamba of Ndola District in February-March 1946. The results were analysed by

Mr J. C. Mitchell and Mr J. A. Barnes, both anthropologists of the Institute, and their final report on the Survey, with Dr Gluckman's comments, was circulated privately in 1947. Table 71, which is derived from this report (but involves some rearrangement of the material) gives the averaged result for the twenty-nine budgets.

TABLE 71. Summary of budgets obtained from twenty-nine Lamba households

Receipts from:	per house-hold £	Outlay on:	per house-hold £
1. Produce (including beer)	2.40	7. Clothing	1.44
2. Labour	0.68	8. Household goods	1.10
3. Gifts	0.56	9. Implements	0.13
4. Loans and savings with-		10. Food, drink, tobacco	0.68
drawals	1.07	11. Medicine	0.05
5. Unaccountable and miscel-		12. Damages, fines, taxes, etc.	0.88
laneous	0.68	13. Gifts	0.55
		14. Savings and loans	0.14
		15. Miscellaneous and unaccount-	
		able	0.42
6. Total receipts	5.39	16. Total outlay	5.39

No claim is made by the authors that these budgets are in any way typical or representative. At best they are believed to show the more common forms of income and expenditure in the area. Thus the hypothesis that the above averages are an indication of income levels in this area of Ndola District is put forward very tentatively. Nevertheless, it may be worth while pursuing it a little further by expressing it in terms of the volume of village economic activity, and converting it to a per-head-of-the-population basis in terms of Central and Western Province population proportions.

After deducting receipts from labour, and transfer payments and savings, from the receipts side of the Lamba budgets, we get a value for the volume of economic activity which is in the region of £2.82 per household and £0.76 per head. The average total income per head of the population is, on these assumptions, in the region of £1.46.

Table 72 summarizes the results of these calculations from budget surveys in terms of village cash income estimates for four groups of villages in Northern Rhodesia. The results are given per *female* household.

TABLE 72. Village cash incomes and activities

	Tonga £	Ngoni £	Lozi £	Lamba £
Village cash income:				
(1) Per female household	10.9	7.6	3.7	3.4
(2) Per head	2.6	2.2	1.0	1.5
Village economic activity per head	2.0	0.6	0.9	0.8

2. LEVELS OF INCOME AND EXPENDITURE FOR PARTICULAR ITEMS

A further examination of the budgets collected by other observers, and in other areas, throws a certain amount of light on variations in particular items. Figures relating to expenditure on beer, for example, were available for all these areas. The Cona Survey figures for beer sales among the Tonga amounted to about 2s. per household, while the figures collected in the General Survey showed the average for the women interviewed to be between 2s. 6d. and 3s. per household. The difference is not great and it is probably reasonable to assume that the true average lies between 2s. and 3s. per household among the Tonga.

The budgets collected for Dr Gluckman gave an average income per household from beer sales of 4.7s. If we assume that this relates to only 75% of the total, the average was about 6.27s. per household. My own records showed 16.5s., which seemed too high as a general average. Combining the two sets of budgets, the average is not far short of 8s. per household, which is higher than was normal in other areas visited.

Among the Lamba, income from beer sales averaged about 7.4s. per household, and among the Ngoni my estimates show 6s. per household. My estimates allow for a certain amount of understatement by the Ngoni, but it seems probable that 6s. is still an underestimate.

It is interesting to note also the existence of gifts as a source of income in all areas. They varied from about 3% of income per household among the Lozi (where I am convinced that the records are inadequate on this point) to a little over 10% among the Lamba. For the Tonga the average was about 5% and for the Ngoni about 7%.

Expenditure on clothing varied considerably from one area to another. Among the Tonga it was ultimately estimated to be about £4.8 per male household, or 42% of total expenditure and rather more than £4 per female household. Among the Lozi a combination of budgets from all sources suggested at least £1.78 per household or 48.1% of expenditure. This, however, is fairly certainly an underestimate. Among the Ngoni a weighted average amounted to about £3 per household or 40% of expenditure. The Lamba budgets were not strictly comparable, because blankets were included under household expenses instead of under clothing. Expenditure on clothing alone, however, amounted to £1.44 per household or about 27% of total expenditure.

The information on clothing was amongst the most satisfactory data collected in my village income enquiries. It is not accurate as a record of the year's expenditure, largely because clothing does not necessarily last a full year, and it was rarely possible to investigate previous sets of clothing to those now being worn. One must allow also for the inevitable omissions due to a misunderstanding of the question. For example, it was found that some persons had spare sets of clothing packed away in a box as a form of saving, and they did not always remember this reserve when the questions were asked. When the practice came to light, all following enquiries took it into account, but there remains the possibility that earlier informants had failed to give relevant data. Moreover, there was reason to believe that informants occasionally understated their clothing expenditure because they regarded the investigator as a source of gifts of clothing and wanted to emphasize their need.

Nevertheless, the questions on clothing were conveniently concrete. They referred to relatively large expenditures of a memorable nature and expenditure which every individual undertakes at some time or another. Thus the data collected relate altogether to some 463 men, women or children (Ngoni 170, Tonga 257, and Lozi 36).

It could fairly be assumed that, below a certain level, the demand for clothes does not vary greatly with the changes in income and price. In other words, if we assume that there is a certain minimum demand for clothing which on an average is satisfied for the colony as a whole, one might deduce a lower limit for the overall average expenditures on clothing. If, on the other hand, we assume that this enquiry covered representatives of some of the wealthiest communities in Northern Rhodesia (as indeed it must do if we measure wealth by cash resources, since the gratuity receivers are relatively rich men and the Ngoni sample is heavily weighted by them, while the Tonga and Lozi samples are both weighted heavily with high cash earners), then we might attempt to deduce an upper limit for a generalized average.

The results of these deductions are given below:

	Lower limit s. d.	Upper limit s. d.
Blankets, etc., per household	6 0	12 0
Men's clothing, per man	17 6	39 6
Women's clothing, per woman	17 6	36 6
Children's clothing, per child	2 6	6 6
All clothing, per household	40 0	87 6

In effect it seems probable that the true averages for the rural areas lie within these limits, and they are much closer to the lower limit than to the upper limit. These deductions had to be based on some estimates of the overall distribution of the population into the various categories of men, women and children, and since there were no census data for Northern Rhodesia the percentage proportions for Nyasaland's 1945 Census were regarded as giving a fair approximation.

3. GENERALIZATION OF RESULTS

Any attempt to measure these estimates of income levels in four small areas of the colony against the general level of incomes is fraught with considerable difficulty. At best we can make subjective judgments based on qualitative material. It seems fairly certain, for example, that the Tonga levels are well above the average for the population of the railway belt provinces. On the other hand, the Lamba levels are probably slightly below average. The true average for the railway belt provinces may therefore be somewhere in the region of £7.4 per household for village income and £1.4 per head for village economic activity. For the non-railway provinces the Ngoni income levels are almost certainly above average, since their share of the ex-soldier incomes was so high. Lozi incomes are probably relatively low in that they do not reflect the incomes of ex-soldiers (being collected in 1944), but high in that Mongu District was probably more prosperous than the rest of the Province. An average village income of £5 per household and an average value for village economic activity of 16s. per head is probably not far from the true average for the outer provinces, although the complete lack of data for most of the area makes it difficult to speak with any confidence even in the most general terms. On balance the scanty evidence suggests that these averages tend to err on the high side.

On generalizing these crude assumptions for the railway-belt provinces and the outer provinces respectively, we get a total village purchasing power of about £2,300,000. On the same assumptions, the value of village cash economic activity is about £1,466,000. This figure for village economic activity compares with a figure of £1,150,000 which was reached independently on the basis of an approach which involved estimating total sales of the various items entering into village economic activity. On the evidence so far collected, it seems probable that the total value of village cash economic activity for Northern Rhodesia fell between these points, at about £1,300,000.

CONCLUSIONS

It may be worth considering at this point what the village economic surveys and these village income estimates mean in terms of the conceptual problems which were outlined in Chapter II. What has been measured in these experimental enquiries is not the total real income of the villagers, but their cash incomes. In the estimates of village income levels we have some indication of the level of purchasing power in the villages. In the estimates for so-called village economic activity we have a reflection of the value of trade generated by and within the villages.

By confining our attention to cash transactions, however, we overlook two important spheres of real economic activity in the villages—the output which enters into barter trade and the output which never enters into trade at all but is produced by the villagers for the use of themselves and their families. In the village economic survey these aspects of village economic activity were touched on very inadequately in the course of the property survey. There it appeared that the amount of property acquired by cash was between two-thirds and three-quarters of the total value of property acquired during the year. Of the rest, about 18% was acquired by barter or subsistence transaction and the remainder in the form of gifts.

If these figures can be regarded as a fair reflection of the order of magnitude of the contribution of non-monetary transactions to real income (excluding food not purchased by cash) the cash income of the villagers should apparently be increased by something in the region of 25% to cover barter and subsistence output. Moreover, if it is accepted that many of the gift and transfer payments are economic in the sense of indirectly involving a *quid pro quo*, then we must raise cash incomes by between 40% and 50% to give total real incomes exclusive of subsistence and barter food.

P

PART V

CONCLUSIONS

CHAPTER XIV

THE CENTRAL AFRICAN ECONOMY

The three Central African territories of Northern Rhodesia, Nyasaland and Southern Rhodesia form a tropical land-locked mass of about 475,000 sq. miles somewhat south of the centre of the African continent. To the north and west and in the east they are bordered by foreign colonial territories.[1] To the south is the Union of South Africa, to which they are linked by rail and road and with which they have strong cultural and social ties. To the north-east is Tanganyika, which is their contact with British East Africa. There are as yet no rail links with British East Africa, however, and the volume of traffic in goods and people flowing between the East and Central African colonies is insignificant.

The Central African block contains a total population of probably more than six million people, of which about 2% are Europeans, less than 0.2% Asians, and the vast majority Africans. Nearly 80% of the Europeans are in Southern Rhodesia, which is a colony with an elected European government. About 38% of the Africans live in Nyasaland, and about 30% in Northern Rhodesia, leaving rather less than one-third in Southern Rhodesia. About 40% of the Asians live in Nyasaland and about 37% in Southern Rhodesia. Table 73 gives a picture of the area and population of Central Africa in 1948. It will be seen that Nyasaland is the most important of these territories in terms of population although the smallest in area.

TABLE 73. Central Africa. Area and population, 1948

	Nyasaland	Northern Rhodesia	Southern Rhodesia	Central Africa
Area (sq. miles)	38,000	290,000	150,000	478,000
Africans	2,270,000	1,700,000	1,870,000	5,840,000
Europeans	3,000	28,800	103,000	134,800
Asians	4,000	2,300	3,300	9,600
All peoples	2,277,000	1,731,100	1,976,300	5,984,400

[1] The Belgian Congo lies to the north, Portuguese Angola to the west and Portuguese East Africa to the east.

Allowing for the variations between different districts within each of the three territories, the pattern of African life is broadly the same in each. The indigenous peoples are Bantu tribes, most of whom live in mud-hut villages, grow the bulk of their own food, and are relatively free from dependence on the money economy except in relation to their need for clothing. Although the industrial and commercial side of the Southern Rhodesian economy is more developed than is the case further north, the mobility of African labour within Central Africa and between Central and Southern Africa is such that the characteristic pattern of economic life for the African is the same in all three. Thus the main occupation of the African is subsistence farming, the adult male normally makes periodic visits to areas of employment during the prime of his working life, and most people engage in trading produce as a small-scale irregularly practised sideline. There are local variations in the amount of cash earned and in the degree of dependence on migrant labour or trade, but, broadly speaking, the conditions of life described in Part IV are characteristic of the home background of the bulk of the inhabitants of all three territories.

The Asian immigrants also play much the same role in the three countries. They are normally traders (almost exclusively so in Rhodesia) mainly engaged in supplying retail goods for African consumption. The Indian's contribution to the economy is characteristically seen in the dim rural store selling cotton piece goods, salt, soap, hardware and minor manufactured produce generally summed up in the term 'Kaffir truck': it is also reflected in the irregularly timed lorry carrying goods and passengers from urban to the rural areas and (in Nyasaland only) in the stationmasters, artisans and clerical workers employed on the railways.

For the European communities the typical pattern of life is more variable as between the three areas. It is true that in each the Europeans are largely concentrated in skilled and better-paid semi-skilled occupations and thus enjoy an average standard of living which is generally higher than the average for the United Kingdom or even the Union. In Southern Rhodesia, however, the European population is settled and permanent. There seems little doubt about its being a country climatically suitable for European habitation over the greater part of its area. The climate is pleasant and equable by tropical standards, and the country is relatively free from malaria for the most part. There is a substantial farming and mining element and a settled city population. The main towns have most of the material amenities of European civilization. Even the administration, which is the fluctuating feature of most colonies, is a genuinely local administration: it is largely recruited locally or from immigrants who do not have a regular provision for overseas leave added to their real incomes.

In neither of the two northern territories do the majority of the European inhabitants enjoy all the material amenities of the countries from which they originate, although the Northern Rhodesian mining townships are fast building up the essential structure of European material civilization. For the most part they are temporarily immigrant people who aim to retire abroad and who normally maintain extensive commercial, financial and social connections with homelands abroad. This is so even of the relatively urbanized mining townships whose inhabitants are largely drawn from Southern Africa itself. On the other hand, there is a growing nucleus of permanent settlers in both countries and a positive feeling of local patriotism is already a marked feature of European society in both. This tendency to settle has perhaps been accelerated by the war, which broke the practical ties with Europe for most people and which certainly changed the character of the United Kingdom for many of its emigrants.

In Northern Rhodesia the pattern of European life is beginning to approximate visibly to the Southern Rhodesian model as closely as the increasing industrialization of the country permits. In Nyasaland, where there is as yet no significant industrialization, the pattern is still one of European settlement within an African society, although the tendency to settle is already producing a re-orientation of outlook and a will to build up a consciously local variety of European society. Here again the model is Southern Africa rather than the United Kingdom in its inspiration, and the unique influence of the permanently settled missionary, which was one of the characteristics of pre-war Nyasaland, is rapidly being submerged.

In spite of interesting social similarities, the pattern of economic development in the three countries has shown some significant divergences. Table 74 provides a broad indication of the value of economic activity carried on in Central Africa. The figures for Northern Rhodesia and Nyasaland are based on the calculations described in the appendices to this volume, and those for Southern Rhodesia are based on the official estimates.

The presence in Southern Rhodesia of a large European population with considerable capital resources increases the productivity of the African population (measured in money terms), and the average value of African earnings (including the value of subsistence incomes) is more than twice its value in Nyasaland, and about half as much again as its value in Northern Rhodesia. It should be remembered, however, that these differences in African average earnings are in part due to different levels of money wages and prices, and it cannot be assumed that they reflect corresponding differences in real incomes. There is no evidence to suggest that Africans living in rural areas of Southern

Rhodesia (where the majority of Southern Rhodesians live) are any better off in real terms than the rural populations of either Northern Rhodesia or Nyasaland. African wage earners from both the less industrialized territories can migrate freely to the urban areas of Southern Rhodesia, so that in so far as they enjoy a higher standard of living while in employment the benefit is shared by the African communities of all three countries.

TABLE 74. Territorial incomes in Central Africa, 1948

(In millions of pounds)

Earned by:	Nyasaland £m.	Northern Rhodesia £m.	Southern Rhodesia £m.	Central Africa £m.
Africans[1]	10.4	11.5	19.1	41.0
Non-Africans	2.3	10.6	39.1	52.0
Companies	0.8	16.5	12.8	30.1
Government	0.3	0.4	1.5	2.2
Totals	13.8	39.0	72.5	125.3

The greater part of the incomes earned from economic activity in Southern Rhodesia goes to the immigrant communities who together receive more than half. Africans receive rather more than a quarter and companies (mainly European owned) account for 18%. In Northern Rhodesia where there is a high level of investment of European capital, but not a correspondingly high rate of European settlement, the largest share goes to European companies—most of it to companies financed from abroad. High post-war mineral prices exaggerated this feature of the economy, but ever since before the war the companies' share has fluctuated between 24% and 45%. In Nyasaland roughly three-quarters of the value of economic activity carried on in the territory or bringing incomes to the territory is spread thinly over the African population.

One important consequence of the way incomes are distributed among the different sectors of the three economies is seen in the size of the government budget. In 1948 the Northern Rhodesian government was able to contemplate a budget (exclusive of its loan programme) which was equivalent to about 25% of its territorial income. For Southern Rhodesia, with a higher per-head productivity, the proportion was 23%. Nyasaland's 1949 budget amounted to about 23%

[1] There is some overlap between these figures in that the earnings of migrant labourers remitted to their home countries are counted both in the country in which they were earned and in the country in which they were received. Southern Rhodesia's net share of African earnings is therefore rather less than would appear from this table.

of its 1948 incomes, but if the colony had had to dispense with the free grants-in-aid provided by the United Kingdom Treasury, the proportion would probably not have exceeded 14%. All three of the territories are heavily dependent on international trade, although it must be remembered that they are largely self-supporting in foodstuffs. Table 75 gives a very broad analysis of the current receipts and payments made by each country. They are summed to give totals for the Central African area as a whole, but there is some overlap between the figures in that they include inter-territorial trade in goods and services (amounting to about 3% of total merchandise trade) and in migrants' remittances. It will be seen that roughly two-thirds of the territorial incomes of the area are attributable to receipts from abroad.

The area as a whole depends for its livelihood on the production of primary products—agricultural or mineral. In each case the bulk of the population is engaged in producing food for internal consumption, but the mining and urban centres of Northern and Southern Rhodesia are an increasing drain on the rural labour supply of the whole area. As a result, Central Africa is finding it more and more difficult to remain self-supporting in staple foods. Unless a marked increase can be achieved in the productivity of agriculture, further industrial expansion will be severely limited by rising labour costs.

TABLE 75. An estimated balance of payments for Central Africa

	Nyasaland £m.	Northern Rhodesia £m.	Southern Rhodesia £m.	Central Africa £m.
Receipts on account of:				
1. Domestic exports	4.162	28.129	29.325	61.616
2. Investments	—	0.100	0.890	0.990
3. Migrants	1.200	0.600	6.076	7.876
4. Services and other current receipts	0.321	0.300	10.468	11.089
5. Total	5.683	29.129	46.759	81.571
Payments on account of:				
6. Retained imports	4.690	19.000	48.053	71.743
7. Investments	0.400	11.000	4.537	15.937
8. Migrants	—	0.050	1.182	1.232
9. Services and other payments	0.650	1.200	6.926	8.776
10. Total	5.740	31.250	60.698	97.668

The chief domestic exports for the area are copper, valued at over £24 millions in 1948, tobacco at £13 millions, gold at £4½ millions, and asbestos at nearly £3 millions. They accounted for over 72% of the total in 1948. Other exports whose 1948 value exceeded a million pounds were zinc, tea, lead and chrome, in that order of importance. As far as Nyasaland is concerned, tobacco, tea, cotton and migrant labour remittances represent the chief sources of cash income in the colony; internal trade is of minor importance. In Northern Rhodesia the only other important source of cash is the maize sold on the home market. Southern Rhodesia, however, has a more diversified economy stimulated in large part by the substantial weight of European purchasing power in the colony. Its factories and workshops produced a gross output of £9½ millions in 1946, the net contribution to Southern Rhodesian incomes being £7¼ millions. Most of this was sold on the home market, but its export of manufactured goods to the surrounding territories is a factor of growing importance in the Central African economy. In 1948 the value of exports of processed foods from Southern Rhodesia was in the region of £1¼ millions, and of apparel and footwear more than half a million pounds. In producing this wider range of goods and services Southern Rhodesia makes use of labour drawn from the whole Central African area.

To some extent the rapidity and diversity of development expressed in Southern Rhodesian trade and income statistics obscures the fact that the fundamental flow of real goods and services at the disposal of the 1½ to 2 million African inhabitants of the territory does not differ substantially from that available to Africans in the two northern colonies. There is no evidence that rural conditions are any better, if indeed they are as good, when compared with those prevailing in some of the cash-cropping areas of Northern Rhodesia and Nyasaland in a good harvest year. The higher urban money incomes are partly outweighed by higher urban prices. Economic development defined as development of European industry is, however, proceeding spontaneously at a faster and more solid pace in Southern Rhodesia—or at least in certain centres of Southern Rhodesia—than anywhere else in Central Africa.

It is clear that there is some causal relation between this differential rate of progress in Southern Rhodesia and the larger volume of European settlement. It is partly a question of increased purchasing power and the incentive which a sizeable home market provides for industrial development. It is partly also a question of greater political certainty and a greater readiness on the part of investors to put their money in a European-dominated economy than in an economy where African self-government is part of the political horizon. A third factor, closely dependent on these two, but more tangible and more measurable, is the flow of immigrants' capital.

Much of the past investment which has taken place in Southern Rhodesia has arisen in the same way as the investment which has provided Northern Rhodesia with its capital assets—i.e. is financed by externally registered companies and non-resident shareholders. As a result, Southern Rhodesia also remits abroad each year substantial sums to pay for the capital it has borrowed from non-residents. These sums, however (see item 7 of Table 75) have recently fallen short of the annual inflow of capital brought by immigrants (see item 3 of Table 75). Much of the recent rapid advance in industrialization in Southern Rhodesia has been financed locally, either as a cumulative process from the profits earned by local companies, or from immigrants' funds. In considering the general strategy of economic development in dependent areas this difference between the two Rhodesias is significant. Southern Rhodesia's immigrants, being largely composed of permanent settlers, have always tended to bring their capital with them. Like Palestine, the colony has obtained much of its capital for development free of any burden of external debt. The volume of this 'free' capital inflow has reached striking proportions in the post-war years. Table 76 shows the estimated volume of funds brought in by immigrants over the past nine years. The figures for these as for other Southern Rhodesian illustrations in this chapter are from the *Economic and Statistical Bulletin of Southern Rhodesia.*

TABLE 76. Funds brought into Southern Rhodesia by immigrants

£000

1939	309
1940	169
1941	92
1942	101
1943	101
1944	227
1945	468
1946	2,540
1947	4,697
1948	5,671

No comparable official estimates are available for Northern Rhodesia or Nyasaland, but it is clear that the current rate of inflow into these colonies is small by comparison. Indeed, if we set off against the funds of European settlers in Northern Rhodesia the outward flow carried by individuals from the mining townships who are taking their savings to a southern African investment, the net gain is probably entirely negligible. The economic expansion of the two northern territories is thus severely limited by this dependence on outside capital, whereas in Southern Rhodesia expansion seems to be limited more by the current shortages of men and materials and the caution of the local business community.

Partly because of this relatively small degree of dependence on non-resident sources for its capital, and partly because the process of successful industrialization tends to be cumulative, Southern Rhodesia has been expanding since the war at a much more rapid rate than either Northern Rhodesia or Nyasaland. In the two years 1945–7 her national income, which is a better index of local economic progress than the territorial income, rose by about a third, compared with 11% for the two northern territories. The increase in Northern Rhodesia's territorial income over the same two-year period reflects an inflated world price for copper and is not evidence of a corresponding economic expansion.

It is difficult to see an immediate alternative to the dependence on external capital with its heavy burden of recurrent debt charges for either Northern Rhodesia or Nyasaland. Clearly here, as in other African colonies, solid progress depends on the development of local sources of capital. It may be possible to reduce the volume of debt charges to the extent that profitable investment can be financed through a Development Corporation rather than by equity capital; but in so far as the Corporation embarks on speculative projects—and in pioneering development some speculation is essential—the burden of a low permanent rate of interest may in fact be heavier than the kind of burden which fluctuates with profits and can disappear altogether in face of a loss.

Local sources of capital are at present limited, however. The rate of non-native earnings for both Northern Rhodesia and Nyasaland is high, but the population concerned is small, so that their absolute value is also small, and in any case the tendency of the temporary immigrant to take his savings abroad is strong for both Europeans and Asians. The average rate of earnings for Africans is so low as to make the prospects of an increase in savings from native sources very small indeed. Even in Southern Rhodesia, where the relatively high level of industrialization means more opportunity for sale of produce, higher wages (and through higher prices higher cash commitments), the average annual income per head of the African population—including subsistence incomes—seems to be under £9 per head. In Nyasaland it is probably not more than £5 per head, and in Northern Rhodesia it is between £6 and £7 per head. Much of the cash income is earned by Africans in employment who have high prices to contend with and whose incomes are in any case rapidly fragmented by gifts to friends and relatives. The final distribution of income, after allowing for gifts, marriage payments and other transfers, is fairly even, and there are few Africans with incomes large enough to permit appreciable saving even if they were willing to allow their savings to flow into the institutional channels of the capitalist economy.

In principle the practical administrative problems of tapping and making effective use of African small savings should be soluble, provided that the reservoir of true savings is large enough to justify it. The field enquiries which have been described in this book are too slight and superficial to provide any firm conclusions on a point of this kind. It would certainly not be possible to suggest a figure for potential African savings from all sources and the residual figures which can be derived from the social accounts are obviously too flimsy to form a basis for estimate. If the economic development of Central Africa is to be lifted out of the narrow rut of European industrialization, the need for more research into present and potential avenues and sources of African saving and investment, involving family budget surveys of generalizable proportions, is clearly pressing.

These considerations apply as much to the economy with an expanding European sector as to the economy where African activity is the predominant contributor to the national income. The standard of living of the average villager is not necessarily raised by the expansion of secondary industries and mining development. Indeed, the loss of adult male labour to areas of employment may actually reduce the standard of living of the families left behind. The gain from increased opportunities for employment may be offset by the increased cost of food. The gain from increased opportunities to market native produce may be outweighed by a reduction in the amount of food available for subsistence consumption. The community advantage from the existence of local secondary industries depends primarily on their proving themselves to be low-cost industries, and if they result in a loss of agricultural output and increasing labour costs this advantage may well be eliminated.

The general conclusion is that balanced economic progress in Central Africa depends primarily on the productivity of the African and particularly the African farmer. The low output of food, in subsistence as well as in cash-cropping areas, is the fundamental limiting factor to an improvement in real incomes where that improvement is most needed, and even to an expansion of industrial output in general. The contribution of the non-African farmer, valuable though it is to an underfed community, constitutes only a fraction of the total food supply. Even a revolutionary improvement in yield on European farms could not produce an appreciable rise in the basic standard of living. The potential effect of a widespread improvement of only a few per cent in African yields is, however, very great indeed. The present wretchedly low standard of African living can be lifted only by an improvement in the yield of African agriculture. Given the economic backwardness of the African farmer, the responsibility of government in stimulating progress in this sphere is basic.

The importance of the village economy in Central African economic life has been a main theme of this volume. The pattern of economic activity which has emerged from the studies of Part IV is in its essentials the characteristic pattern for most of the inhabitants of Central Africa, if not for the whole of tropical Africa. The pattern is unfortunately blurred because the studies which have so far been made are superficial. It is impossible to describe it with any degree of precision because quantitative data collected on such a small scale cannot be convincingly generalized.

Nevertheless, there is a basic framework of economic activities which differs in important respects from that to which we are accustomed in Europe and on which the European-type money economy has been loosely super-imposed. In this pattern the unit of production and of consumption is the farming family. Usually it can be defined quite narrowly as the woman, her husband and her children; but for some purposes it is extended to include the wider groups of kinsfolk—generally the village, but occasionally the whole tribe. Thus there are certain productive activities—commonly hut building and certain harvest processes—which automatically involve co-operation of the wider groups and which are not necessarily inspired by the prospect of a *quid pro quo*. Similarly there are obligations with regard to sharing income beyond the members of the earner's family which are not necessarily inspired by their consequent 'prestige value' or 'investment value'. For example, a migrant can rely on his kinsfolk in the village to look after his children when he is away and they can expect to share in the wealth he brings back with him, without these acts having a reciprocal association. They reflect the acceptance of mutual responsibility rather than expectation of mutual benefit.

Within the village a unit of production as small as a single individual is a rarity. Even when a man must go far from his village to earn cash he normally remains part of the family and is regarded only as a temporary absentee. His remittances buy the family clothes and when he returns his savings provide for the family's cash needs for as long as they last. Meanwhile it is his garden that his wife has kept going and he aims to return often enough to extend it under the system of shifting cultivation and sometimes often enough to plant it. Thus it is irrelevant to the Central African economy to think in terms of the 'average man' as is conveniently done for a European-type economy. The corresponding concept is the average family or household. Most of the labour for the basic unit of production, the family, is supplied by the woman. She does most of the recurrent agricultural work, most of the planting, the weeding, the fetching and carrying, the routine harvest work and the preparation of food. The man is the dynamic element in the partnership. He chooses and clears the new piece of land, is the 'shock worker' of the planting or harvesting season, supplies the initiative and enterprise in undertaking new activities (e.g. the production of crops for sale, the adoption of paid employment), and is the architect of the hut (whereas the woman muds the wall and stamps the floors) and is the hunter, the fisherman, the trader, the headman, the priest. In effect, therefore, while the man is the spearhead of change the woman is the principal worker and the guardian of the traditional processes. Now, when change is largely a function of the link with the money economy, this means that the woman is the chief earner in the field of subsistence production and the man in the field of production for sale.

The woman, however, is still the main supporter of the family since she is the principal food producer. The man's role as chief cash earner is becoming more important as the money economy extends its range and as more and more goods are produced with a view to their exchange; but it is on food produced by female labour that the bulk of the population depends for life itself.

This fact, which is vital both from the policy and from the accounting point of view, is in some danger of being overlooked in an analysis which starts from an assumption that all economic activities can be expressed in money terms. An attempt to construct a system of social accounts involves the application of a money measure to the economy as a whole. Since the changing, dynamic part of the colonial economy is the money aspect and since it is this part which most reflects and is susceptible to administrative and other external influences, the social accounts can be made to serve the same kind of purpose for which they were originally evolved in the European-type economy. It is not possible, however, as it is in the European economy to ignore altogether the activities that do not normally enter into the course of trade, for these are vitally important activities. The contribution of the subsistence producers, the unpaid female and child labour, is one of the most important factors in maintaining the standard of living. On the other hand, if this contribution is entered into the social accounts it must be evaluated on an artificial basis and it will normally appear as a largely static, unchanging contribution to the nation's total income. It is unchanging partly because there are no revolutionary changes in this sector of the economy and partly because any known method of measuring this kind of output is so clumsy and inaccurate that it would not reflect any but the most startling changes. Thus the result of a severe drought or a striking glut might be recorded very roughly, but gradual increases in yield due to improvements in method and decreases due to soil exhaustion are unlikely to be measurable. It might even be that a government which succeeded in diverting food from the market to subsistence consumption was raising basic living standards, although in money terms the effect of its action might be a fall in the aggregate of money incomes. Certainly it is unlikely that a moderately successful and steady drive to raise productivity among subsistence producers could in practice be reflected in the social accounts under existing conditions of statistical reporting.

CHAPTER XV

THE EXPERIMENT REVIEWED

An interim report of this enquiry into the national income of selected colonial territories was published in 1948 as an Occasional Paper in the series issued by the National Institute of Economic and Social Research.[1] It described step by step the actual process of converting the economic material available for three colonies—Northern Rhodesia, Nyasaland, and Jamaica—into a set of national income accounts on the lines of those which are now familiar to the readers of this book. The base year for these experimental enquiries was 1938, since that was the last year for which, in the difficult conditions of war, sufficiently full material was available in London for even these experimental enquiries. In the case of Jamaica an attempt was made to carry the estimates back over a ten-year period, but the results were too unsatisfactory to constitute a firm basis for any detailed analysis.

These experimental enquiries for the year 1938 were carried out on the basis of most inadequate material and involved a very high proportion of guesswork. It was often impossible, at this distance from the colonies concerned, to form any reasonable estimate of the possible margins of error for some of the items. It was impossible also for an enquirer who had never seen the territories to obtain a satisfactory picture of what these money incomes meant in real terms. Nevertheless, the preliminary stage of the enquiry had some definite results. It established the practicability of the experiment and it suggested the character of the further research that was needed. It also showed by practical illustration the process of manipulating inadequate data into national income accounts so that they yielded up a coherent picture of the economy.

The methodological conclusions of the experiment were fully discussed in the course of and at the conclusion of the interim report. No attempt will be made to go over them again here. Briefly, however, the main problems which remained intractable were those arising out of an attempt to construct national income tables for the Central African economies, and the most intractable of them all related to the treatment of subsistence output. Given that subsistence output could not usefully be excluded from national income, a whole host of problems arose, not

[1] See note, page 11 above.

only in deciding where to draw the line between economic and uneconomic activities, but also in evaluating subsistence output so that it
could be compared with or added to traded output in a meaningful
way. It was concluded that the next stage was to pursue the enquiry
into the field in order to test the framework of accounts which had been
tentatively evolved 'as well as to achieve more accurate and up-to-date
results and to experiment in direct statistical reporting methods for
national income purposes'.

The enquiry which was pursued into the field and which has been the
subject of this volume, confirmed the importance of the conceptual
problems which arose from the existence of a subsistence economy, by
showing that the subsistence economy was in fact the backcloth against
which the economic activities of the majority of the people took place.
Even on the assumption that all migrant labourers found their way to
urban areas, an average of more than 88% of the population of the two
colonies studied were actually resident in the villages. For all but a very
few of those that were away from the villages the severance from the
village economy was incomplete and temporary. They had been brought
up in the rural areas and they would retire to the rural areas: for most
the return would take place within the next two years.

Within the villages the production of goods for personal and family
consumption is the main object of economic activity. Production of
goods for exchange is the part-time activity of a small proportion of the
population and for the remainder the sale of an occasional small surplus
is their contribution to the traded goods and services. It is not that
money is unknown or insufficiently appreciated in the villages. Most
adult males earn a regular cash income either through the sale of crops
and livestock or through migration to temporary employment. Most
women earn an occasional few pence through the sale of surplus flour
or pottery or small livestock. There are very few goods and services
which do not have their price, a price which is directly related to their
value in the nearest market. Money is a major factor in village social
life; it is important to the villager and a matter of great interest to him.
Beyond a certain point, however, a point which is fairly easy to reach in
normal circumstances, it is a luxury.

In effect, the *scale* of living in the villages depends primarily on the
output of subsistence products and only to a small extent on traded
output. The only essential that demands cash is clothing, and even that
can be reduced to a bare minimum which involves very little expenditure indeed. Children and old people without active families can and do
manage by begging and by making a few rags last an indefinite period.
The villager gives his clothes hard wear, but in a year of bad harvest
or if he is lazy he can go in rags all next year.

(*a*) A corner of Nchanga Mine Compound, Northern Rhodesia. The mineworker enjoys a relatively high standard of living in housing as in other forms of income in kind.

I

(*b*) Lusaka Municipal Compound, Northern Rhodesia. This was the new part of the compound.

(*a*) A sanitary worker's home in a Lusaka compound, Northern Rhodesia. This is an example of one extreme in compound housing for Africans.

II

(*b*) A civil servant's home in the African Suburb, Lusaka. This is the other extreme. The African Suburb houses the more highly paid African clerks, etc.

(*a*) An African boatman on the banks of the Luangwa River, Northern Rhodesia.

III

(*b*) A fishing party spearing fish in the Barotse flood plain, Northern Rhodesia.

(a) An African market in Northern Rhodesia. This is one of the most active of the organized African markets outside the Copperbelt.

IV

(b) African sawyers at work, Northern Rhodesia.

(a) A Barotse woman making a pot, Northern Rhodesia.

V

(b) A Tonga woman making a basket, Northern Rhodesia. Note the baby slung on her back while she works.

(a) Small boys assisting at a fishing party on Lake Nyasa. The boy on the right is pulling in the net.

VI

(b) Sharing the catch after the net is landed, Lake Nyasa. The yield from inshore fishing is rarely large and these lads will be lucky if their catch provides them with a small fish each.

(*a*) A grass house in the making, near Livingstone, Northern Rhodesia. The frame for the roof will be lifted on to the grass walls which are being built on the right and then thatched.

VII

(*b*) The finished product. A newly built grass house near Livingstone, Northern Rhodesia. More solid huts are built with mud or, occasionally, with sun-dried brick for the walls.

(a) Women carrying harvest from the gardens. Note the varied shapes and sizes of the baskets which contain the harvest.

VIII

(b) Preparing the ground for planting, Northern Rhodesia. The short-handled hoe is the only agricultural implement in use over the greater part of Central Africa.

It is partly because money is needed for luxuries rather than essentials that it proves such a poor incentive. The constant complaint of the European employer that the African will work for a given amount of money and then stop, so that an increase in wages may reduce output, has a good deal of basis in fact. To this we may add the effects of the natural apathy of ill-nourished people living in the tropics and suffering constant attacks of chronic malaria and begin to see why neither the manpower nor the land resources of the African territories are as fully utilized as they might be even allowing for the absence of capital.

To a semi-subsistence community satisfying its basic needs without the use of cash, money is a commodity for which there is a limited elastic demand. When it is plentiful in relation to the supply of goods the urge to earn more is weak. When it is scarce the demand is strong —strong enough to send workers hundreds of miles on foot to work unwontedly long hours in mines and factories—but limited. Having reached that limit the workers return to their villages and drift back into the traditional rhythm of the subsistence economy until the money, being spent, is scarce again.

It is possible, moreover, to overestimate the contribution of general apathy and ill health to the low national productivity of African labour. Leisure—pleasurable in itself, unstimulated by expensive recreational activities—competes with the desire for other commodities. The African buys with his money the pleasures of fulfilling all his gift obligations, of buying a wife who will produce food and children for him, buying an occasional bowl of beer or a little tobacco and sitting peacefully in his village for months on end without having to worry where the next cloth for his wife or shirt for himself is coming from. At harvest time and at planting time he works very hard indeed. For the rest of the year he need not do more than two or three hours' work a day, and a very small stock of ready cash is often enough to keep him contented given the very low range of wants to which he is accustomed. The leisure itself is particularly attractive. Social accounting systems based on the money measure do not account for the contribution of leisure to social welfare. When wages go up and the African does less work than before, the national income might even fall, although probably his standard of living has risen.

In the village economy, money is important not only in relation to the fringe of luxury needs, but also in relation to certain activities that are not strictly economic. One of the features which emerged most clearly from the village surveys was the significance of the expenditure on such social necessities as marriage payments, gifts, and damages or other court payments. It would probably not be an exaggeration to say that about 10% of the income and expenditure of the villagers went

Q

into these 'non-economic' channels. It is not possible to say much about them without the results of further and more representative village surveys, but it is reasonable to conclude, even from a superficial study of the villages, that the exclusion of such activities as these—on the ground that they do not result in the production of a tangible good or service—would produce a false picture of the village economy.

Ideally, for the characteristic semi-subsistence community of Central Africa it should be possible to draw up a complete system of social accounts in three distinct stages. It should be possible, first of all, to measure the volume and content of activity and consumption in the villages, and to construct a set of village accounts showing how the average villager received and consumed his total income in cash and in kind. Into this account would go a full record of the marriage payments, damages, gifts, etc., which play as dynamic a part in determining the shape and direction of the rural economy as do the needs for clothes or bicycles. Into this account also would go the value of goods and services not traded for money, the goods and furniture that the villager makes for himself and his family or that he gives to his neighbours, or the services that he performs for other villagers—e.g. in hut building—and the goods and services that enter into barter trade.

The village account is not an easy one to construct. Apart altogether from the difficulty of making adequately reliable estimates—and this will be a stumbling-block even with a statistical reporting system that provides for enough trained observers to conduct proper sampling surveys—there are difficult conceptual problems. It is not easy, for example, to decide which of the goods and services people provide for themselves should be included in the accounts. An arbitrary line can be drawn by including all activities which have an ascertainable price; but since these may vary from one district to another and even from one village to another it may be necessary to break this rule if comparable results are to be achieved for each village and if they are to be combined into meaningful aggregates. In any case the process of putting a money value on subsistence output is itself difficult to justify logically for a semi-subsistence economy. Where the bulk of goods in a given category are traded it does not greatly strain the conceptual framework to impute a value to the remainder. Where the bulk are *not* traded it is obviously a highly artificial process which bears no direct relation to the physical facts of the case. The figure for subsistence output can never be more than a token figure.

On the other hand it seems reasonable to insist that some such token figure must be included in the final account if only to give—in the language of the money economy—some indication of the relative 'weight' of subsistence activity in the sum total of economic activity.

If we confined ourselves to goods and services exchanged for money we should include, say, certain marriage payments and the payments to witchdoctors, while excluding the value of staple food produced. This would give a distorted picture of village economic life, and although the introduction of token figures for the various categories of subsistence output does not by any means give a logically complete picture, it does help to redress the balance in important respects.

The second stage is to draw up a set of so-called national accounts which would embrace a consolidated version of the village accounts and set them in the wider context of the population's total economic activity. The national accounts, which would correspond to the normal national income accounts as they are generally interpreted, would cover the transactions of all individuals resident in the country, reflecting the changing content and level of their standard of living and output. For a plural community it would be desirable at this stage to present the accounts in such a way as to bring into relief the relationships between, and the relative progress of, the different racial or national groups.

This in its turn would find a setting in the third stage—the construction of a system of accounts covering all the economic activities carried on within the territory's borders or benefiting the territory's nationals. The territorial accounts would contain a complete record of the transactions entered into by all factors of production operating within the territory, whether the owners are resident or not. For the residents of a dependent economy are usually without capital and are obliged to rely on the co-operation of non-residents to carry out their economic activity. Where the volume of goods and services produced within a country's borders is significantly different to that produced by residents it is clearly desirable to examine the accounts of the wider unit as well as those of the narrower.

This threefold system of accounts, while reflecting the many-sided nature of a semi-subsistence, dependent economy with a plural community, would not be any more effective in illustrating real progress or in measuring real welfare than the national income accounts of an industrial country. To some extent it would be less effective, for a money measure means different things for the different races in a plural community, for the subsistence economy and the exchange economy, for the resident owners of factors of production and the non-resident owners. In so far as these differences exist an aggregate account adds unlike things and the resulting total is correspondingly less significant. It is doubtful whether it would ever be possible to define income so that it meant the same thing to the African villager and the European town dweller, or to the African in his subsistence habitat and the same African in temporary urban employment.

Such qualifications as these, however, apply to every national income calculation, though perhaps with differences of degree. Without a more thorough knowledge of the motives for economic behaviour in the semi-subsistence economy and of the fundamental theories of value which colour the African outlook on economic matters it would not be profitable to do more than recognize the qualification and accept the limitations on the possible economic analysis. Certainly our knowledge of the African economic outlook is not sufficient to permit a more precise analysis designed to measure the significance of the qualifications for particular cases.

In sum, therefore, it must be admitted that this experiment in national income measurement for colonial territories has had a very limited success. It has resulted in the construction of a series of articulated but necessarily incomplete social accounts which within the limits of such crude accounts are as reliable as the existing stock of data will permit. It has set up a framework which can be useful for general descriptive and analytical purposes, as has been illustrated in Chapters V and VIII, in which the bare bones of the social accounts were clothed with a qualitative account related to current economic problems. It is by no means sufficient to form the basis for detailed national budgeting, however. By a deliberate and methodical attempt to use all the evidence this kind of experiment emphasizes both the unreliability of the basic data and the complexity of the concepts which are being applied. On the face of it this is one of the drawbacks of the method adopted. It is a pity to have to qualify the analysis at every step with warnings about the unreliability of the data, and it is a pity to have to admit that there are no clear-cut concepts which can be applied to all aspects of the colonial economy with confidence.

These, however, are the basic truths about colonial social accounting and it is difficult to see how they can honestly be thrust into the background. The statistical material is inadequate for purposes of precise and intelligent analysis, and the concepts which are applicable to a money-exchange economy mean relatively little in the context of a sub-sistence economy. There are no simple economic magnitudes which express concisely the movements in a semi-subsistence economy with any degree of reliability, and there are no economic indicators which could safely be set up as guides without a fairly detailed map of the accompanying economic and social context. It will be necessary to attempt systematic studies of this kind (though by no means necessarily on this particular pattern) in other colonial and underdeveloped terri-tories before more sophisticated analytical tools for the measurement of real welfare and for the interpretation of the dynamic factors in African economic progress can be evolved. Similarly, it will be necessary to complete investigations over a much wider field before a standard form of accounts for colonial territories can usefully be laid down. It cannot be claimed that this particular experiment has done more than collect, sift and discuss the readily accessible evidence for two Central African economies.[1]

[1] Even this claim must be qualified, for the study was completed in mid-1950 and a good deal of evidence relevant to the enquiry has been published since that date.

APPENDIX I

SOURCES OF THE ESTIMATES OF
NATIONAL INCOME, OUTPUT AND EXPENDITURE
OF NORTHERN RHODESIA

Attention has been drawn in the preceding chapters to the fact that the figures used to illustrate a description of the economy of Northern Rhodesia are estimates. They represent an overall appreciation of the total available data. Some are reasonably accurate. Some are mere guesses. Most of them are the end result of a careful sifting of a mass of detailed, unco-ordinated and often incomplete evidence. None of these takes account of data published or otherwise made available since mid-1950.

For the benefit of those who wish to examine further the basis of these estimates and to assess the relative weight that can be put on individual items, this appendix describes the sources of the principal estimates and the process by which the incomplete pieces of the economic jigsaw were re-constructed and the picture completed. Not all the items are described in detail. Those which can be deduced with reasonable accuracy, e.g. from company reports or administrative returns such as income tax data, are largely ignored. Minor items which may have involved much guesswork but which resulted in a very small sum have likewise been passed over. It is the important items which have involved much processing of the raw material of estimate that have been treated in most detail.

One qualification should be borne in mind when these figures are com-pared with those in Chapters III–V. That is the fact that the later refinements which resulted from checking and cross-checking between one set of data and another in the final tables have not all been introduced. It has been thought worth while giving the illustrative figures in full, although a strict comparison will reveal some discrepancies between them and the final results. The discrepancies, however, are within the margin of error of the estimates. Where they are large the reader's attention will be drawn to them, for they are a fair reflection of the weight which can be put on them in considering them individually. They will also indicate the directions in which the basic data need most improvement if they are to provide material for more reliable information in future years.

No attempt has been made to describe the mechanics of estimating in all stages and to explain the process of cross-checking by which the different items in the tables are pulled into relation with one another. These matters have been dealt with in considerable detail in the interim report of this enquiry published in 1948, and it has not been thought necessary to repeat the process here.[1] On the other hand, there will inevitably be some repetition in the appendices of material appearing in the descriptive chapters of this volume, for in order to keep the latter complete there has been some discussion of the reliability of the estimates.

I. POPULATION

Probably the most important set of statistical data on which it is necessary to rely for national income purposes are the population figures, and it is here that the African material tends to be particularly deficient. In Northern Rhodesia, African population figures are in general extremely unreliable. Until 1950 when the Central African Statistical Office attempted a sample census (which has not been taken account of in this study) the last attempt to produce estimates for the whole territory on a systematic basis was in 1931. Between then and 1950, the colony's population figures have been largely based on the estimates for each District which the District Commissioner is able to produce on his official tours on administrative business. Very occasionally a District Commissioner who has the time and the interest to make a special attempt at a census, or an Agricultural Officer or anthropologist or other worker who needs the population figures as a background for his own studies, undertakes a careful and systematic count of a small group of villages. Generally these censuses cover too small an area to be of much use as a basis for generalization, although they may give the District Commissioner some guidance in the framing of his estimates if he has time to consider them.

A District Commissioner's tour count cannot in the nature of things be an accurate account. At best he may have time to spend an hour or two in the village and will in the course of other administrative business bring the taxpayers' register up to date by consultation with the villagers, count the villagers who have been called together for his visit, and enquire after possible absentees. So far as can be judged from personal observation of a District Commissioner's tour count the principal source of error would be in omissions. There may be people in the gardens whom nobody elects to mention. There may be others whom it seems desirable to conceal. There may be temporary absentees whose names on the tax register do not correspond with the names by which they are known to neighbours.

Where a tour count exists, however, it is probably as reliable as a sample census of Africans. Unfortunately, tour counts are few. During the war years regular touring and census work was suspended altogether in the Districts. By 1947 there were still rural areas which had not been visited for some years. Hence a District Commissioner's estimate for the population of his district in 1945 or 1946 is usually found as a function of the numbers on an out-of-date tax register. Moreover, since the factor by which the number of taxpayers is multiplied to reach total population is usually based on precedent or guesswork rather than on actual recent specimen counts, the final result is a very rough estimate indeed.

[1] Op. cit.

A questionnaire which was sent to District Commissioners asked them amongst other things to estimate the population of their district in 1945 and 1946. Not all the District Commissioners gave figures for both years and not all gave figures for each of the four categories required—total population, taxpayers, adult men, adult women. Where estimates were given for one year only they were accepted as a close enough approximation to the figures for the other year. Where some categories were omitted they were estimated on the basis of the figures for other categories and by analogy with areas where actual counts had been made.

The results of the analysis of the questionnaire are given below for the four Provinces in 1945. Adults are defined for this table as persons of sixteen years of age and over. Population is here distributed according to province of registration rather than province of residence. Hence, for example, the resident population of Western Province would include a further 96,000 persons drawn from other districts.

TABLE 77. Population of Northern Rhodesia in 1945. From district estimates

Provinces	Total African population	Tax- payers	Adult men	Adult women
Northern	461,603	92,886	115,817	126,347
Central and Western	251,288	64,150	72,872	74,955
Southern	260,679	60,445	71,583	66,179
Barotse	339,318	77,088	97,456	109,015
Eastern	313,860	66,373	77,321	100,055
	1,626,748	360,942	435,049	476,551

How unreliable these figures are is illustrated by the comment of one District Commissioner when submitting his population estimates. 'I consider that the estimate of population is low by at least 10%, perhaps by as much as 20%. The figures given are the present official ones based on district touring of 1941. On three tours carried out in 1946 the 1941 figures were found to be low by 18% for the areas toured.' When it is remembered that many of the district estimates were submitted before it was possible to carry out any significant check of the 1941 touring results, it can be seen that the margin of error of 20% at least applies to the district estimates as a whole. Nor is it safe to assume that all the errors were on the side of omission. Several District Commissioners after comparing 1946 or 1947 touring results for limited areas with the relevant 1941 figures remarked that in their view the estimates they gave were too high. In the course of a survey undertaken by the Agricultural Department in 1946 it was found that the population was lower than that indicated in the District Administration's estimates by as much as 32% for men, 33% for women, and 35% for children.

If we are considering the District Estimates as a whole, some of this error disappears, since it is due to a high mobility of families between villages and even between districts. Since it is not possible to tour a whole district in the course of one year with existing district staff, and since people and villages shift from one area to another very readily, in spite of the administration's efforts to keep a check on such movements, it is to be expected that tours conducted at intervals of several years are bound to produce substantial changes in the population results. Further, any attempt to check the tour counts with careful censuses based on residence in an area for some weeks or months will reveal discrepancies in the tour counts which are not significant for general purposes. A man who has moved from one village to another some miles away, for example, will often report to the touring District Commissioner at his village of registration rather than at his village of residence, especially if some penalty is normally levied for unnotified removals. In general this will not affect the figures for the colony as a whole, although a local observer might find some differences between his figures of population based on village of residence and the District Commissioner's figures based on village of registration.

Nevertheless, when all allowances have been made for errors cancelling out over the country as a whole it remains true that the District Administration's population estimates are subject to a high margin of error which may well be of the order of 20% on the total population figure. Of the subdivisions in the District Estimates, the category of taxpayers is probably the most reliable, since it is based on a list of actual individuals entered in the registers by name rather than on a count of heads or on a mathematical calculation. Yet even these are by no means firm estimates, since regular touring was suspended during the war years and the registers have not all been brought up to date since.

A glance at the proportions of the three population subdivisions shown in Table 77 does not inspire confidence. Taxpayers are able-bodied males of the apparent age of eighteen years or more. Adult males include in addition men over eighteen who are exempt from tax for reasons of age or infirmity together with youths of sixteen years and over not yet paying tax. It is difficult to believe that in Northern Province this group of youths and the aged and infirm should together constitute about 20% of the total male population of sixteen years and over. Yet that is what the figures suggest. Again, the apparent shortage of adult women in Southern Province is, on the face of it, an odd result. Given the inadequate material for making any kind of population estimates in Central Africa it is not possible to rule these results out as inadmissible. In the absence of a satisfactory explanation, however, they do cast doubt on the proportions of men, women and children reflected in the District Estimates.

In the following table some of the results found in actual counts for limited areas are set out in terms of proportions of men, women and children. None of the counts was sufficiently watertight for its results to be regarded as a model and none of them has any special claim to be suitable as a basis for generalizations. Nevertheless, they are sufficient in number to permit the drawing of general conclusions with regard to orders of magnitude, although they are sufficiently few and uncontrolled to make small discrepancies insignificant.

TABLE 78. Proportions of the population in Central African Censuses

	Men	Women	Children	Rounded Total
Serenje: District administration count	23	26	51	100
Agricultural Department count	19	23	58	100
Lamba Reserve: Agricultural Department count	22	28	50	100
R. L. Institute count	22	32	47	100
District Administration count	31	28	42	100
Nyasaland Census: *de facto* population	19	28	53	100
de jure population	23	26	51	100

In the Nyasaland census the *de jure* population included, besides those Nyasalanders living in the colony (i.e. the *de facto* population), those absentees from the colony who have kept in touch with their villages. Since the rate of migration is high in Nyasaland it is the proportions of the *de jure* population which are most significant in any attempt to generalize for other areas. It is interesting to compare the Nyasaland figures with the Serenje figures and note that the proportions of the *de jure* population in Nyasaland are identical with the proportions found by District Administration count in Serenje, while the proportions of the *de facto* population agree fairly closely with the proportions found by the Agricultural Department count. In fact, since the District Administration generally counts the registered population and other observers generally count the resident population, this would correspond fairly closely to the distinction between the *de facto* and the *de jure* population.

If we assume: (*a*) that the figures for taxpayers are in general the most accurate figures of all the population estimates provided by the District Administration, (*b*) that the infirm, the aged and those omitted from the tax registers accounted for 5% of the taxpaying population, and (*c*) that 23% of the population were men and 26% women, then we might draw up a table of populations based on the taxpayer figures only. It should be noted, however, about these assumptions that (*a*) is reasonable; that (*b*) is highly arbitrary—the best that one can say for it is that it seems to be borne out by very limited observation in the field and that it is unlikely to be too low; and that (*c*) is a generalization which should be received with great caution, more especially when it is carried into detail and applied to provinces which may well have a very different population composition. What may be true of such areas as Serenje, or even of Nyasaland as a whole, may involve distortion for Barotseland or for Central Province, and perhaps for Northern Rhodesia as a whole.

In effect, the assumptions are tenable only if our inadequate stock of data can be treated as though it were not misleading. The results of these assumptions are given in Table 79. No great faith can be put in these estimates. Their claim to be utilized in preference to a summary of the District Commissioners' estimates lies in the fact that the assumptions on which they are based are simple and intelligible, whereas the estimates in Table 77 are based on a variety of assumptions, often unstated, for the most part just as arbitrary, and in many cases not even remotely influenced by the results of actual recent counts. The estimates in Table 79 are superior only in that their weaknesses are inescapably obvious. Their margin of error cannot be put below 10% even in the most optimistic view.

TABLE 79. Estimates of population of Northern Rhodesia based on District Commissioners' Returns of Taxpayers, 1945

Provinces	Taxpayers	Men	Women	Children	Totals
Northern	92,886	98,000	111,000	217,000	426,000
Central and Western	64,150	67,000	76,000	148,000	291,000
Southern	60,445	63,000	71,000	140,000	274,000
Barotse	77,088	81,000	92,000	179,000	352,000
Eastern	66,373	70,000	79,000	155,000	304,000
All	360,942	379,000	429,000	839,000	1,647,000

The distribution of population as shown by the taxpayers' registers is not, however, the same as the actual distribution of population according to its place of residence at a particular time. Many taxpayers are at work abroad or in provinces other than that in which they are registered, and there are a number of aliens (14,627 in October 1946) working in the colony. The Labour Department published for 1944 estimates of the number of taxpayers at work abroad, the number at work in Northern Rhodesia but outside their own provinces, and the number at work in their own province. The estimates are subject to considerable error in view of the fact that the taxpayers' registers were out of date in 1944, since regular touring had been dropped in view of the wartime shortages of staff. For Africans employed in each province (without information on their province of origin) the African Labour Census gave reliable figures showing the position in October 1946. On all this information estimates were made of the number of adult males actually resident in each province in 1945. In addition, information on the urban population was obtainable from the quarterly censuses taken in the Copperbelt towns and from the rough census of non-mining locations made in 1944 for the Commission appointed to enquire into the Administration and Finance of Native Locations in Urban Areas.

Table 80 gives the resulting estimates based on the assumption that there were no considerable and unpredictable changes in the distribution of the male population since the early nineteen-forties and that the Labour Department's estimates were not based on misleading data.

TABLE 80. Distribution of adult males in 1945, Northern Rhodesia

Provinces	Men registered	Men resident	Men in locations
Northern	98,000	74,000	—
Central and Western	67,000	109,000	57,300
Southern	63,000	63,000	5,900
Barotse	81,000	58,000	—
Eastern	70,000	41,000	1,000
Totals	379,000	345,000	64,200

Not all the men resident in a province are available for work in the village agricultural economies. On the other hand, of those employed in their own province most will be able to return to their villages at the busy seasons of the year. Some even of those who are strangers to the province will assist in village agriculture and may have gardens of their own. If we make the assumption that all men employed in their own province were available for work in the villages and that none of the strangers was so available we get figures for available men which are almost certainly on the high side, but can be regarded a fair index of the number of adult males in the villages.

There is no information on the migration of women either within the colony or abroad. The rough census of urban locations and the quarterly Copperbelt censuses make it possible to estimate the number of women and children living in urban locations. We could assume that the remainder of the women were living in the villages and working gardens without greatly overestimating the number of working women in the villages. A similar assumption would enable us to estimate the total number of children in the villages. In both cases our estimates would tend to be on the high side, but the discrepancy is probably small. It is more difficult to break up the urban population into provinces of origin. The estimates in Table 80 are based on the assumption that the urban women and children can be allocated to the various provinces in the same proportions according to the Labour Department's estimates for 1944. This assumption, in effect, involves highly arbitrary assumptions as to uniformity of practice in respect of migrants and their families from the various provinces. As a working basis for estimate, however, and in the absence of definite information to the contrary, these assumptions are not unreasonable.

The results of these assumptions and estimates are shown in Table 81. It should be remembered that the number of men given in the first column as available for work in the villages may be high in that some of them are employed and may not in fact give any assistance. This point is illustrated in the last column of Table 81, which shows the proportion of men available for work in the villages as lying between the number which would be available if all local men employed locally could be included and the number which would be available if no employed men were included.

TABLE 81. Population available in the villages of Northern Rhodesia in 1945

Provinces	Men	Women	Children	Total	Proportion of work—available men in relation to the total available population %
Northern	69,000	100,000	204,000	373,000	16.7—18.5
Central and Western	43,000	67,000	138,000	248,000	11.5—17.5
Southern	52,000	68,000	137,000	257,000	17.7—20.2
Barotse	58,000	86,000	172,000	316,000	16.4—18.4
Eastern	35,000	75,000	150,000	260,000	9.7—13.5
Totals	257,000	396,000	801,000	1,454,000	14.7—17.7

2. INCOMES OF EUROPEAN INDIVIDUALS

There were two main sources of material which could be utilized as a basis for estimating the incomes of Europeans. On incomes over £700 per annum the Income Tax Department's returns gave relatively complete and reliable information for income earned in the year 1944–5 (31st March). For incomes under £700 the returns of the 1946 Census, which had required details of income earned during the calendar year 1945, were utilized. In addition to these two general sources, there were a number of minor sources which supplied details of incomes earned in particular industries or occupations. For example, the incomes paid by the mining industry and by the Government could be reliably estimated on the basis of information obtainable from the Chief Inspector of Mines or the Financial Report.

The inclusion of a question on income in the 1946 Census was an interesting experiment. It is an experiment which has been tried in both the Union and Southern Rhodesia, and the form of the question was based for Northern Rhodesia on the Southern Rhodesia model.[1] Briefly, it required the informant to extract the relevant code numbers for his income and the incomes of

---

[1] The instructions relating to the income question in the 1946 Census were worded as follows:

Income Group: Column D

To fill in column D, take the income of each person for the twelve months 1st January to 31st December 1945, and code it on the following basis (the actual income should not be given):

For nil income write	0
For under £50 write	1
For from £50 to £99 write	2
For from £100 to £149 write	3
For from £150 to £199 write	4
For from £200 to £249 write	5
For from £250 to £499 write	6
For from £500 to £749 write	7
For from £750 to £999 write	8
For from £1,000 to £2,499 write	9
For from £2,500 to £4,999 write	10
For from £5,000 to £7,499 write	11
For from £7,500 to £9,999 write	12
For from £10,000 to £14,999 write	13
For from £15,000 or over write	14

The income of wage or salary earners is defined as the total amount received from all sources during this period. In addition to wages or salary all other income such as interest, dividends, pensions, grants, etc., must be included. If free quarters and/or rations are provided the estimated annual value thereof must also be included.

For farmers, business men, professional men, etc., the income coded should be the gross receipts from all sources during the twelve months, less the expenses incurred in the production of that income.

In addition to cash receipts the value of produce bartered must also be included. If a household grows or receives farm produce for its own use, the estimated money value of this produce used during 1945 should also be included in income.

members of his household from a list of incomes and corresponding code numbers, and to enter them in a column set aside for that purpose. Income was defined to include all cash wages, salaries, rents, profits, and interest, plus the value of produce bartered (less expenses incurred in its production), plus the value of subsistence produce and plus the value of free quarters and rations where provided.

The question was not an easy one to answer and there are numerous sources of error which would arise in coding, apart altogether from purely mechanical errors involved in reading a code number from a closely printed note on the back of the form and entering it in the appropriate space on the front. These mechanical errors can probably be assumed to cancel each other out. So also can some of the errors due to a careless inspection of the instructions.

Two criticisms might be made of the instructions. On the one hand the income group intervals seem unsuited to a territory where the majority of earners have an income exceeding £250 per annum. If the returns are to provide a firm basis for estimates of average and total incomes earned in the territory the group interval in the range £250 to £1,000 (in which range nearly 70% of the earners fall) should certainly not exceed £100.

The second criticism is that the definition of income, while long enough to be complicated, is not precise enough to be watertight. It is not obvious, for example, that it is the *net* income from subsistence output and barter transactions that is wanted and not the total value thereof, although in practice and in most instances the costs of output are probably already debited against cash receipts from produce and so are not included in total income. Nor is it clear whether charitable donations to missionaries are to be included in income since gifts are not income on the income tax definition, and the term 'grants, etc.', while it may be intended to imply such gifts, is vague. Thus the farmer or the missionary may find that income is not sufficiently clearly defined for his purposes. Finally, it is not clear whether the income which is to be returned should include income not actually drawn in the colony. For example, should income from property in South Africa or the United Kingdom which is accumulated and spent through banks abroad be included, or should a recent immigrant enter an income received abroad within the year? These incomes may be an important total in a colony such as Northern Rhodesia, where a large part of the population has close ties with places abroad, and where the European labour turnover tends to be high even for such permanent employees as government servants, since promotion frequently involves transfer to another colony.

On the whole, however, the complexity of the question probably led to an appreciable understatement of the true incomes. The householder has to read for this question alone over 160 words of instruction and examine a list of fifteen code numbers and their corresponding income group equivalents. His tendency would be to define his income in the conventional way as the amount of his salary or wages. Unless he read the instructions with deliberate care he would tend to omit that part of his income which was not received in cash, to forget income earned and drawn abroad (which may be important in a colony where most European residents are temporary residents) and often to omit the incomes of his dependants. If he failed to read the code numbers and their equivalents carefully he might assume that the code number 6, for example, applied to incomes exceeding £600 but less than £700. In this case he would be greatly understating his income, for the code number 6 represents incomes falling between £250 and £500.

These tendencies to understate income owing to an insufficient understanding of the instructions were confirmed by an examination of the actual returns. Some pensioners, for example, stated that they were on pension and so had no income to report. Some missionary groups maintain as a matter of principle that they receive no incomes and entered their income as nil, although the census definition of income specifies such forms of income as free quarters or rations, subsistence, farm produce, and grants. In other cases the incomes of dependants and lodgers were omitted, although they were recorded as having an occupation which would clearly bring in some reward: these omissions may, however, have been due to the unwillingness of the dependant or lodger to give his income or to the fact that a person who was gainfully employed in October 1946 may not have received any income in 1945.

In other cases the income information was withheld or falsely entered because the individual was unwilling to give it at all. Unfortunately it was not possible to enforce a return of income, but this fact was not specifically stated. As a result some individuals were told by the enumerator that they need not answer at all, and others who were unwilling to answer but were intimidated by the announcement: 'Every person is required by law to give to the persons responsible for making the return such information as may be necessary to enable the return to be made', may have been tempted into false entries.

It was frequently obvious that a mistaken or false entry had been made. When the returns were being coded at Lusaka the omissions and obvious errors were followed up by sending a query to the householder concerned. In many instances the error was then rectified.[1] The preliminary results which are given in this paper are the result of a very rapid and unchecked examination of the census forms by a single observer before these errors had been rectified. Where the error could be reduced without query—for example, where the income was deducible from the occupation, an adjustment was

[1] Errors due to a mistaken interpretation of the meaning of income could frequently be eliminated in this check—as for example when a person stated that he had no income, only a pension. There were also cases where the same income was entered against husband and wife separately when the fact that the wife was not gainfully occupied suggested that this might be an error. The error (when it was one) was frequently eliminated by a query. Again, many persons who were unwilling to divulge their income to the enumerator or the householder were willing to send the information under seal to the Census Office. Thus the final results will contain significantly fewer avoidable errors and omissions than the results given in this chapter.

made. Where the entry was palpably false and no alternative estimate could be made it was treated as a complete refusal. Otherwise the entries had to be accepted as they were without any attempt at correction.[1]

On the whole, therefore, the omissions and errors tended to produce an understatement of incomes. The omissions were probably considerable as it was obvious that very few persons tried to evaluate their housing, while many persons, particularly missionaries, omitted subsistence income and probably cash incomes too. A person who had not earned a full year's income in the colony in 1945 was not strictly required to make an entry at his full rate of earnings for the year (although many gave their 1945–6 earnings). On the other hand, there were many persons who had earned an income in 1945 and had since emigrated. Errors of understatement due to mobility of the population are probably important. In 1945 and 1946 no less than 4,751 adult European immigrants were admitted into the colony. In effect, if we assume that all those who entered in 1945 and 1946 were in the colony in October 1946, roughly a third of the adult European population had earned less than a full year's income in the colony during the course of the calendar year 1945. If these had followed their instructions to the letter the degree of understatement would have been very considerable. In fact, many of them entered their 1945–6 income. It seems likely that many other persons entered their 1945–6 income instead of their 1945 income, which would help to counteract the general understatement since 1946 incomes were, on the whole, higher than 1945 incomes.

Deliberate understatements and refusals tended to appear more frequently in the returns of persons working on their own account such as traders and farmers. The motive may well have been a desire to hide such incomes from the Income Tax Department, but it is possible that some traders or farmers with inadequate book-keeping systems or with their accounts in arrears for one reason or another may have been unable to enter an accurate figure for their 1945 income and have preferred to leave the column blank. There was also a general category of individuals who seemed to resent the question on principle, but it is not possible to assume with any confidence that their rate of earnings was any higher than the average for those who did answer. In so far as they wanted to conceal their incomes, they may have disliked revealing an apparently small income as often as they disliked revealing a large one.

The rapid preliminary inspection of the census forms produced the results shown below in Table 82.

The percentage of refusals was probably about 7.5%. It was not always clear at this preliminary examination which were the refusals. A blank might have been left because no income was earned. Occasionally the entry of 0 or 1 was tantamount to a refusal. The number of cases in which arbitrary deci-

---

[1] The results after codification and processing by Hollerith have now been published. I should judge that the published results still contain an appreciable degree of understatement. See *Report of the 1946 Census*, Lusaka, 1949.

sions had to be made as to whether an entry or lack of entry constituted a refusal or not was not very large, however.

TABLE 82. European income distribution in 1945. Derived from 1946 Census

Income group	Number of men earners	Number of women earners	Total earners
Under £50	76	121	197
£50 to £99	102	143	245
£100 to £149	205	205	410
£150 to £199	196	223	419
£200 to £249	270	339	609
£250 to £499	1,675	601	2,276
£500 to £749	2,362	38	2,400
£750 to £999	1,009	29	1,038
£1,000 to £2,499	556	11	567
£2,500 to £4,999	49	1	50
£5,000 to £7,499	8	—	8
£7,500 to £9,999	3	—	3
£10,000 to £14,999	2	—	2
£15,000 and over	1	—	1
	6,514	1,711	8,225

According to the preliminary general Census results there were 7,346 European males over twenty-one and 6,562 European females over twenty-one. Excluding Poles living in camps (figures derived from information supplied by Director of War Evacuees), there remain 6,766 potential male wage earners over the age of twenty-one and 4,962 potential female wage earners over twenty-one. The Census results suggest that after allowing for refusals there were about 7,000 males and 1,840 females earning incomes, which implies that there were about 234 male earners under the age of twenty-one and at least 3,122 adult women not gainfully occupied.

An attempt to calculate total earnings in each income group on the basis of the Census data is complicated by the fact that the income group intervals above £250 are so large. Thus where the interval is only £50 the problem of calculating the average income within each group does not arise, since the mid-point is precise enough for most practical purposes. Where the interval is £250 and the income falls in the groups £250 to £499 or £500 to £649 (in which groups fall the majority of Northern Rhodesian incomes), then one must come to some reasoned conclusion about the distribution of income within the group if the estimated average is to be of any significance at all. For incomes over £700 income tax statistics provide reliable and fairly complete data, although unfortunately they relate to the year 1944–5 instead of the calendar year 1945.

In Table 83 the incomes under £250 have been calculated from the Census data and the incomes over £700 from the Census data combined with the income tax data on the assumption that there was on change in income distribution as between 1945 and 1944–5. The incomes between £250 and

R

£750 have been estimated by plotting a distribution curve based partly on an analogy with the curve for Census incomes under £250 and partly on the basis of the curve for assessed incomes under £700. In general, unless the deliberate understatement to both Census and income tax authorities is extraordinarily high, it may be assumed that the table is broadly true with a tendency to understatement and that it is weakest in respect of the details of income distribution in the groups between £250 and £700. The margin of error in the total, again supposing that deliberate evasion is not very wide-spread or substantial, is probably not greater than 5%. In general it can be assumed that it does not include the value of incomes in kind, of which housing is most important.[1]

TABLE 83.   Estimated earnings of European individuals in each income group, 1945

Income group	Number of earners	Average earnings £	Total incomes £
Under £250	1,976	154	304,300
£250 to £500	2,393	390	933,300
£500 to £600	1,403	558	782,900
£600 to £700	523	654	342,000
£700 to £800	576	752	433,100
£800 to £900	542	851	461,200
£900 to £1,000	406	946	384,100
£1,000 to £1,500	722	1,175	848,400
£1,500 to £2,000	140	1,720	240,800
£2,000 to £2,500	70	2,210	154,700
Over £2,500	90	4,420	397,800
Totals	8,841	£598	£5,282,600

No attempt was made at this preliminary examination to estimate the distribution of incomes between industries and occupations from the Census returns. The final results were published in the Census report.[2] Meanwhile it was possible, by using other sources, to show the distribution of incomes among the principal industries in relation to the total as estimated above. Earnings on the mines and the railways have been obtained from the Chief Inspector of Mines and the Chief Accountant of the Rhodesia Railways Ltd. Earnings in government service can be estimated from the central and local government accounts.

In estimating the total value of incomes paid to persons in government and mining service it is necessary to take account of the employers' contributions

[1] On the whole it does not seem likely that deliberate falsification was very substantial, although it may have been widespread among persons working on their own account and among persons earning irregular sums which escaped income tax. The number of Europeans is so small, however, that it is difficult for most persons, especially employed persons (who form the majority of earners), to falsify their returns on a large scale either to the Income Tax Department or to the enumerator or even to the Census Office.

[2] Op. cit.

to pension and provident funds or the value of pensions and gratuities actually being paid. In terms of actual current receipts these incomes are largely received by persons outside the country and so do not figure in the Census data totals. It is estimated that of the £2,597,800 paid to European mine employees about £337,000 represents the current rate of payment to pension and provident funds or the value of pensions and gratuities paid abroad. The pensions and gratuities paid by government amounted to £116,500 in 1945. Thus, including the value of pensions, gratuities and leave payments the following is the estimated value of European earnings in each of the principal industries. Item 4 is a residual item. The value of housing and other incomes in kind are not included. An arbitrary allowance of 5% has been made to cover pensions, etc., earned on the railways and no allowance at all for other industries.

TABLE 84. Earnings of European individuals, 1945, classified by industries

Industry	Number of earners	Total earnings £	Average earnings £
1. Mines	3,525	2,598,000	737
2. Government	1,070	649,000	606
3. Railways	736	427,000	580
4. Other industries	3,510	1,740,000	496
5. All industries	8,841	£5,414,000	£612

It may be noted that after cross-checking with data from other sources (e.g. data on European expenditure) the final estimate for European individuals' incomes was put at £5,666,000. The margin of error in this total is estimated to be about 6%.

3. INCOMES OF OTHER NON-AFRICANS

The Census of 1946 covered the Asian and Coloured populations as well as the European population and thus provided returns for their 1945 incomes. In both cases the refusal rate was higher than among the Europeans. This was to be expected from the Asians since they are predominantly traders on their own account and the percentage of refusals was generally high for traders. There may also have been an element of racial mistrust inspiring Asian refusals, since the enumerators were European. Generally the Asian population is very suspicious of income enquiries, although apparently not more suspicious than the trading community as a whole. The Census returns provided the material for the following income distribution table. Here again the results were obtained from a rapid preliminary survey of the forms and are subject to correction.

TABLE 85.   Income distribution among Asians in 1945 according to the 1946 Census

		Number of earners	Estimated average £	Total earnings £
Under	£50	19	40	760
£50 to	£99	46	75	3,450
£100 to	£149	88	125	11,000
£150 to	£199	99	175	17,315
£200 to	£249	62	225	13,950
£250 to	£499	128	375	48,000
£500 to	£749	33	625	20,615
£750 to	£999	19	874	16,605
£1,000 to £2,499		24	1,335	32,040
£2,500 to £4,999		3	3,000	9,000
		521	£332	£172,735

The crude income intervals in the groups over £250 made it particularly difficult to estimate average incomes since there was not sufficient data from other sources (e.g. income tax data) to provide a satisfactory guide. On balance, however, the estimates made in Table 85 seem reasonable enough in the light of what little quantitative and qualitative information is available from other sources. It is popularly supposed that the Asian population earns a high average income and it seems true that their level of consumption is a poor index of the level of actual earnings. Further, it may fairly be assumed that the high refusal rate is accompanied also by a relatively high rate of understatement and that the returns shown on the census forms must be scaled up to give actual incomes. On the other hand, it should be remembered that the income level of Indians employed by Indians—particularly for the younger employees serving their first contract in the colony—is extremely low by European standards. Finally, in estimating for each income group allowance has been made for understatement.

The apparent refusal rate was in the region of 17%, but there was some evidence to suggest that the actual refusal rate was as high as 20%. This implies a total earning population of 625 Indian earners (including 3 women) compared with a total male population of 835 and a total female population of 288.

On the assumption that the total number of Indian earners was 625 and that the average income of all earners was £350 (compared with about £330 for those making census returns) and that all the refusals came from individuals earning over £500, we have the following estimates of Indian income. This is probably an overestimate of the incomes of refusers, but there was an element of understatement among those who answered which has probably not been fully accounted for in the high estimated averages for each group, and the result may be regarded as a fair approximation to the truth. A comparison with the income tax data for the higher groups suggests a slight overstatement of the numbers earning £750 to £2,500, but since the latest income tax figures relate to the year to 31st March 1945 and it is reasonable to assume an increase in the calendar year 1945, there has been no attempt to adjust downwards.

TABLE 86. Estimates of earnings of Asian individuals

	Number of earners	Estimated average incomes £	Total earnings £
Under £100	65	65	4,200
£100 to £249	249	170	42,300
£250 to £499	128	375	48,000
£500 to £749	76	625	47,500
£750 to £999	45	875	39,400
£1,000 to £2,499	55	1,335	73,500
£2,500 and over	7	3,000	21,000
	625	£441	£275,900

Similar difficulties arise in estimating the incomes of the Coloured individuals from their census returns. Some 219 individuals answered and apparently a further 30% refused to answer. Estimates of Coloured individuals' incomes were made on the same lines as were followed for Asiatic individuals, except that there did not seem the same reason to assume that the refusals were all in the upper income groups.

4. AFRICANS IN EMPLOYMENT

For employed Africans covered by the Workmen's Compensation Ordinance, i.e. for the majority of employed Africans, the Workmen's Compensation Commissioner compiles statistics of earnings. These are computed so as to include an estimate of the value of food or quarters supplied by the employer and all regular overtime or special earnings. They do not, however, include the value of irregular extra payments such as payment for casual work or intermittent overtime or leave and other bonuses, or cost-of-living allowances. Thus in general the Workmen's Compensation statistics tend to understate the earnings of labour in the groups covered. Furthermore, the allowance for the value of food and quarters is arbitrarily determined and may bear only a distant relation to the actual value of these real earnings.

Workmen not covered by the ordinance and excluded altogether from the Commissioner's statistics include employees of the Crown or the Central Government or the Native Authorities, domestic servants in private employ, and casual employees and outworkers. Since the ordinance did not come into operation until March 1945, the Commissioner's figures of earnings do not specifically relate to the calendar year 1945 but to the year ended 28th February 1946. There is no reason to believe that the difference in earnings between the calendar year and the year March to February was generally significant, but it is possible that in particular industries the difference is important.

Table 87 gives in detail the earnings of Africans covered by the Workmen's Compensation Ordinance (including those employed by exempted firms) as compiled from statistics supplied by the Commissioners.

TABLE 87.   Earnings of employed Africans computed for Workmen's Compensation

Industry	£	Earnings for year ended 28th Feb. 1946 £
1. Agriculture		279,387
2. Mining. Gold	2,787	
Base metal	1,134,533	
Other	8,914	
Total mining		1,146,234
3. Manufacturing. Metal and engineering	15,590	
Woodworking and furniture	96,803	
Textiles and leather	5,074	
Food, drink, tobacco	26,921	
Chemicals, etc.	6,870	
Paper, printing, etc.	1,455	
Other materials	28,428	
Total manufacturing		181,141
4. Building and construction		64,416
5. Transport. Railways	87,778	
Other	21,438	
Total transport		109,216
6. Commerce. Retail and wholesale	88,108	
Finance	1,125	
Other commerce	10,687	
Total commerce		99,920
7. Professional. Medical and dental	17,121	
Religious	10,324	
Education	27,428	
Other	25	
Total professional		54,898
8. Government (municipal)		49,892
9. Personal services (excluding private domestic)		36,270
10. Entertainment and sport		503
11. Other miscellaneous		1,771
12. Total earnings assessed for Workmen's Compensation purposes		£2,023,648

More accurate information, relating specifically to the calendar year 1945 and including cost-of-living allowances, bonuses and irregular payments, is available for the mining industry. Figures supplied by the Chief Inspector of Mines gave the total cash payments made to Africans directly employed, plus the actual value of the rations supplied to them at the price paid by the employers. No figures were available for the value of free quarters and it is necessary to impute a value to them. According to the Commission on Native Locations in the Urban Areas which reported in 1944, African urban rents in Northern Rhodesia varied from 1s. 6d. to 6s. per month for a single man and 3s. to 8s. 6d. for a married man occupying a single room, and up to 15s. for a two-roomed cottage. Unfortunately, actual rents are an unsatisfactory index of the value of accommodation, since they are frequently uneconomic rents made possible only by government grants to the municipal authorities. Simplifying the situation, however, and bearing in mind that Copperbelt rents are the highest in the colony and that mine housing is generally of a higher standard than the average for urban locations, it may be assumed that an imputed value of 6s. per miner employed per month would give a fair indication of the order of magnitude of the value of the miners' housing. Clearly, the value imputed to food and housing on the mines for Workmen's Compensation purposes, amounting in all to 21s. per miner per month, is much too low. The value of rations themselves were in the region of 24s. per miner per month in 1945.

TABLE 88.   Earnings of Africans employed in the mining industry, 1945

	Value of earnings £
Cash receipts	758,939
Rations	482,785
Housing	118,800
	£1,360,524

More specific information for 1945 was also available for the railways. Figures kindly supplied by the Chief Accountant of Rhodesia Railways Ltd. provided a basis for estimating the number of employees, the value of cash payments made to them and the value of the Company's expenditure in rations for Africans in Northern Rhodesia in 1945. In general, the housing supplied to Africans by the railways was of a lower value than that supplied by the mines, partly because some of it was very temporary and partly because it was not all concentrated in high-rent urban areas. In the following table the value of housing was estimated by imputing a value of 4s. per month per employee of the railways.

TABLE 89.   Earnings of Africans in Northern Rhodesia on the railways, 1945

	Value of earnings £
Cash receipts	41,800
Rations	22,100
Housing	7,000
	£70,900

A comparison of this estimate of the earnings of African railway employees with the value computed for Workmen's Compensation purposes reveals a discrepancy of nearly 24%. The size of the discrepancy and its direction are unexpected, but it seems on the whole likely that the estimates in Table 88, which relate directly to the year 1945, are nearer to the truth.

For only one of the other industries covered by the ordinance were there enough data to permit an adjustment of the Commissioner's figures. This was the item called Professional Services. If we exclude Africans employed in professional occupations in the service of the Government or commercial sectors of the economy, since they will appear under the relevant industries, and also Africans employed by doctors, dentists, etc., in domestic service, since these will again appear elsewhere, it appears that all but a negligible number of those earning money from industries providing professional services would be in mission employment. This covers all doctors, nurses and teachers not included in Government or commercial industries, African clergy, and a miscellaneous collection of artisans, general labourers, and others who are employed at mission stations.

Information on the value of wages and rations paid by missions was obtained by means of a questionnaire circulated to the various missions. The results of the questionnaire made it possible to account directly for what was probably rather more than two-thirds of the total. The remainder had to be estimated on the basis of data obtained from the Education Department on the missions concerned and chiefly on the basis of the earnings of teachers whose salaries were financed by government grant. It was more than ever difficult to impute a value to the housing supplied by missions, since mission employees vary from casual labourers working for out-stations who do not require any housing facilities from the mission, to teachers on the Copperbelt, some of whom have housing of a standard far above the average even for that area. There was no general information either on the value of housing supplied by the missions or of the number of persons who were supplied with housing. Any imputed value would thus inevitably be arbitrary, and it was decided that an average of 1s. 6d. per month per African employed by the missions would give a rough indication of the annual value of mission housing. After making this allowance for housing the conclusion was reached that some 9,700 Africans employed by the missions earned a total of £113,300 in 1945.

The wide discrepancy between this estimate and the figure of £54,898 which was the Workmen's Compensation Commissioner's figure for incomes earned by Africans in the professional service industries, can only be explained on the assumption that the figures collected from the missions covered a great many casual and out-workers who would not normally be eligible for Workmen's Compensation and also by the possibility that the allowance made by the Commissioner for rations and housing bore very little relation to actual mission expenditures. That the Commissioner's figures did not cover all mission employees is clear from the fact that the records only show £27,428 earned from African participation in educational services, and in 1945 over £42,600 was granted to the missions specifically for the salaries of Government-approved teachers.

To complete the total picture of the earnings of employed Africans it is necessary to add the incomes received by these in Central Government service, in the employ of the Crown or the Native Authorities and in private domestic service. It is necessary to remember also that we have not so far included the earnings of men doing casual work and out-workers, but there is no specific information on these categories of workers, and it is not believed that their total earnings amount to much in relation to the total earnings of regularly employed workers. It is true that many Africans do not work the full period of a year, but their place is taken by others, and since in such cases it is the worker, not the work, that is casual, their earnings will appear for the most part in the returns made by employers to the Workmen's Compensation Commissioner. Odd jobs performed in private employment will, except in so far as they are seasonal, normally be accounted for in the following estimate of earnings in private domestic service.

Government accounts usually divide expenditure into personal emoluments and other charges, but the distinction is not sufficient for our purposes, since the other charges include a considerable amount of direct expenditure on the wages of labour or on its earnings in kind. For example, the Agricultural Department includes under its 'other charges' a substantial labour vote, while expenditure on the maintenance and construction of roads and buildings by the Public Works Department and other Departments is often largely a question of expenditure on African wages. Expenditure on African rations and uniforms is also included among 'other charges' rather than among personal emoluments.

The proportion of personal emoluments paid to Africans was estimated as a residue after the contribution to European personal emoluments was estimated from the 1945 Staff list. Pensions paid to Africans are given separately in the Estimates. The proportion of 'other charges' attributable to African wages and other earnings was deduced from an inspection of the Government accounts. Expenditure under such headings as 'labour', 'rations' or 'uniforms' could readily be extracted. Where the expenditure on labour was hidden within such terms as maintenance or construction of buildings or roads the relevant amount was extracted either by direct query to the departments concerned or (where the information could not be directly provided) by applying a proportion for the average labour cost of various types of expenditure. The proportions for labour costs were based on information supplied by the Public Works Department.

TABLE 90. African incomes from the Central Government, 1945

	Value of earnings £
Personal emoluments (including pensions)	106,700
Rations and uniforms	51,600
Miscellaneous labour charges, including military	277,200
Housing	21,000
	£456,500

The number of Africans for whom housing was provided, and its annual value, were unknown. The above imputed value for housing supplied by the Government was reached on the assumption that it relates to all employees specifically provided for under personal emoluments or labour votes in the 1946 Estimates together with the average monthly number given as employed by the Public Works Department in 1945 according to the Labour Department's returns. Roughly, therefore, it was assumed that the government provided housing for about 14,000 Africans and that the average value of housing enjoyed by them was in the region of 2s. 6d. per employee per month. The actual total number of Africans in the employ of the Central Government is probably about 24,000, but many of these are employed in rural areas and for short periods and there is often no necessity to provide housing for them, since they can either live at home or borrow accommodation in nearby villages. Even 14,000 may be high as an indication of the number of workers for whom housing is provided. Here, as elsewhere, estimates of the number of Africans employed in different occupations are based on the results of the Native Labour Census in 1946, except where more specific information is available on the numbers engaged in 1945.

The Native Authorities' Accounts, like those of the Central Government, make the distinction between personal emoluments and other charges. Here again, the other charges contain a substantial proportion of direct wage payments, but they are a relatively small part of the total expenditure of the Native Authorities, and the rough estimate of the proportion attributable to labour involved an addition of about 15% to the figure for personal emoluments. The total value of African receipts from the Native Authorities was thus estimated at about £60,000.

It remains to estimate the value of incomes received by domestic servants in private employ. The number of Africans so employed was estimated for each province on the basis of the results of the Native Labour Census taken in 1946 and on the assumption that there had been no great change in their numbers between 1945 and 1946. Their earnings were estimated on the basis of data collected orally from Labour Officers and other Government Officials in the various provinces. They are designed to include the value of food and housing, but the perquisites of domestic servants are so wide in their range and so variable that any attempt to value them must be extremely arbitrary. The total value of earnings by domestic servants in private employ was thus estimated to be in the region of £302,300.

In Table 91 estimates are given of the total value of incomes earned by employed Africans in 1945, including the value of free quarters, rations and clothing. Casual earnings, the earnings of out-workers, and the earnings of Africans employed by Africans (excluding the Native Authorities) are not generally included. Estimates of the numbers engaged in each industry were made partly on the basis of data obtainable for particular industries from the Labour Department or other government sources and from questionnaires to firms and partly on the basis of the 1946 Native Labour Census.

TABLE 91. African earnings in employment, 1945

Industry	Numbers engaged	Total earnings £	Average earnings £
1. Agriculture	27,000	279,400	10.3
2. Mining	33,000	1,360,500	41.2
3. Manufacture	9,500	181,100	19.1
4. Building and construction	6,000	64,400	10.7
5. Transport	5,400	92,300	17.1
6. Commerce	4,200	99,900	23.8
7. Professional	9,700	113,300	11.7
8. Government	29,700	566,400	19.1
9. Personal and domestic services	17,500	338,600	19.4
10. Other	300	2,300	7.7
11. All industries	142,300	£3,098,200	£21.8

According to the Native Labour Census of 1946 there were 139,531 Africans in employment in Northern Rhodesia in October 1946, excluding prisoners. Thus the above figure does not seem unreasonable as an estimate of the numbers employed in 1945. The relatively large number of Africans given as employed in agriculture and building and their relatively low annual income can be explained by the seasonal nature of these occupations and the fact that very few Africans engaged in them work a full twelve months in the year. On the whole it is more probable that the above total errs in the direction of underestimate than that it is an overestimate, and the margin of error in it is probably in the region of 10%.

The Native Labour Census, on which the above totals are based, does not, however, cover Africans employed by Africans. Africans are employed by other Africans to assist them in their businesses or in their fields, or as domestic servants, herdboys, messengers, hut builders, and so on. There is no information relating to this group of employees as a whole, but miscellaneous pieces of evidence were gathered together from a variety of sources. Some of the compound censuses classify residents according to occupations: Godfrey Wilson's survey of Broken Hill gives some information on Africans' employees; and my own enquiries and those of the anthropologists of the Rhodes-Livingstone Institute yielded relevant data on employment and wage rates in a few villages.

It can be assumed that the number of Africans employed by other Africans bears some direct relation to the numbers of Africans earning cash incomes, and it was on this assumption that the following estimates were drawn up, using the generalized data collected from special areas as an index of the quantitative relation involved and of the average rates of earnings. They are thus extremely rough estimates. In particular, the division between cash incomes and incomes in kind must be used with particular caution, since some of the income recorded as cash income in Table 92 may well have been paid in the form of food or clothing.

TABLE 92. Africans employed by other Africans

Employed by:	Number	Cash earnings £	Earnings in kind £
1. Employed Africans	4,300	13,000	⎫
2. African cash farmers	10,000	30,000	⎬ 38,000
3. Independent Africans (urban)	3,500	21,000	⎪
4. Independent Africans (rural)	6,000	18,000	⎭
5. Total employees of Africans	23,800	£82,000	£38,000

5. AFRICAN INCOME FROM MIGRANT LABOUR

The income sent or brought into the colony by Northern Rhodesian Africans employed abroad forms an important contribution to total African incomes. During the war, when the local shortage of labour was acute and there was a demand also for men for the forces, some efforts were made to discourage migration to work centres outside Northern Rhodesia, and the Witwatersrand Native Labour Association ceased recruiting in the colony. Nevertheless, migration to the Union and Southern Rhodesia continued, and the number of men away from the territory in paid employment (including the armed forces) was probably higher in 1945 than in any previous year.

Some migrants become lost to the colony in the course of time and are not heard of again in their villages. Many more, however, keep regular contact with the villages, send home cash and goods to relatives, and return with their savings and a stock of clothing and other goods, after a period of eighteen months or less. Even those who have been away so long that they are removed from the tax registers are not necessarily lost to their villages, since they may return there after an absence of many years.

Migrants contribute to the colony's income either by bringing in cash or goods themselves or by remitting them to relatives. The average amount brought back in gratuities and savings by demobilized Askari in 1945 exceeded £40 per head, and in addition to this they brought many goods acquired abroad. Those still in service continued to send regular family remittances. Africans recruited by Witwatersrand Native Labour Association brought back deferred pay and savings as well as many goods and also remitted considerable sums to their families through the Association.

The Labour Department publishes estimates of the number of Africans employed abroad (distinguishing the place of work and the province of origin) and the numbers of repatriates. In both cases the Labour Department estimates are liable to understate the case, since there was a good deal of clandestine emigration and immigration. In particular, the returning migrant will have good reasons for wanting to avoid the customs authorities and some will in any case find that the shortest way home is not always through a border post. Information on the number of returning Askaris and the number in service was obtainable from the African Recruitment Department.

Information on the deferred pay and voluntary or compulsory remittances reaching the colony through recruits of the Witwatersrand Native Labour

Association was obtained from the Association itself, although as it was not officially recruiting in the colony in 1945 the data could not be provided in a directly applicable form. Family remittances to the families of Askaris and their own gratuities and savings were normally paid through the District Commissioners, and I collected information on these points from the District Commissioners themselves, who also returned, in answer to my questionnaire, information on the migrant labour remittances which passed through them.

It was more difficult to find satisfactory material on which to base estimates of the total amount of money or goods brought back by migrants or Askaris in the hand, and sent through the post. The Labour Department gave the results of small surveys made of the cash and money brought back by repatriates passing through certain customs posts during some months in 1942 and 1944. Professor Schapera's monograph on *Migrant Labour and Tribal Life*,[1] dealing with migrants from Bechuanaland, provides confirmatory evidence. The Bechuanaland native's pattern of migration differs from the Northern Rhodesian's, primarily in that a larger proportion go to the Union where the pay (and cost of living) are in general higher than in other work centres such as Southern Rhodesia, where a large number of the Northern Rhodesian migrants are employed. Nevertheless, in making the estimates it was possible to calculate separately the proportion of Northern Rhodesian migrants in the Union and to use Professor Schapera's figures to check estimates made from Northern Rhodesian data. On the whole, my estimates for Northern Rhodesian migrants were higher than Professor Schapera's for Bechuanaland migrants, but the differences were not large. In view of the fact, however, that there was almost certainly an increase in the average value of goods and cash brought back by migrants in 1945 as compared with 1943 (when Professor Schapera's data were collected), and also that the Labour Department's estimates of the number of repatriates are probably underestimates, it seemed unlikely that my estimates would overstate the totals, although they are more likely to overstate than to understate.

The results of the calculations based on this material are given below in Table 93. It was estimated that there were about 64,000 Northern Rhodesian

TABLE 93. African incomes from migrant labour

Askaris	£
Remittances, gratuities, savings, paid through District Commissioners	176,000
Goods and savings brought back by hand	35,000
Migrants	
Deferred pay and savings brought back	112,000
Cash remittances	118,000
Goods brought back by hand	126,000
Goods sent back	28,000
	£595,000

[1] I. Schapera, *Migrant Labour and Tribal Life in Bechuanaland*, Oxford University Press, 1948.

Africans employed abroad of whom 47,000 were in Southern Rhodesia or elsewhere in Africa, 7,000 in the Union of South Africa, and 10,000 in the forces. It was further estimated that there were about 4,000 repatriates from the Union (2,500 from W.N.L.A.), 2,686 demobilized from the army, and 11,000 returning from other African work centres: an attempt has been made to allow for clandestine returns in these estimates.

It seems on the whole unlikely that the total value of incomes in cash or in kind received from migrant labour and services in the forces would have exceeded £600,000 in 1945 or that it would have fallen below £550,000. Of this £595,000 about £414,000 was estimated to have entered the colony in the form of cash and the remainder in the form of goods. Returning Askaris brought back over £40 per head in cash. Returning migrants were estimated to have brought back about £15.86 per head of the repatriates in the form of cash or goods and to have sent back about £2.7 per head of those employed abroad again in the form of cash or goods. The corresponding figures derivable from Professor Schapera's estimates are £13.97 and £2.55 respectively.

The distribution of incomes from migrant labour is very uneven as between provinces. The railway-belt provinces, which have a nearby labour market to absorb a large proportion of those who want to work for wages, and which also enjoy a market for agricultural and pastoral crops which provides an alternative source of cash for many who would otherwise migrate in search of it, benefit least from the migrants. Incomes (in cash or in kind) flowing to the different provinces from the forces could be calculated with some confidence from the District Commissioners' returns to my questionnaire. Incomes flowing from migrant labour were allocated among the provinces on the basis of the Labour Department's estimates of the numbers abroad from each province. The results are given in Table 94.

TABLE 94. Distribution of African incomes from abroad

Province	Askaris £	Migrants £	Totals £	Per village household £
Northern	79,400	49,900	129,300	1.29
Central and Western	19,100	42,300	61,400	0.92
Southern	26,000	38,400	64,400	0.95
Barotse	11,100	107,500	118,600	1.38
Eastern	75,600	146,000	221,600	2.97
	£211,200	£384,100	£595,300	£1.5

There is, however, an outward flow of income, corresponding to this inward flow. The number of aliens employed in each province of Northern Rhodesia is shown in the 1946 Labour Census as about 14,300. The outward remittances of these immigrants were estimated in part from Godfrey Wilson's figures for Broken Hill and in part from the corresponding wage rates in other provinces. At a rough estimate it seems probable that the immigrants remitted or took abroad about £60,000 of cash and goods. Of this, about 95% came from the railway-belt provinces as a whole and about two-thirds from the Copperbelt.

6. AFRICAN INCOME FROM TRADED CROPS

Apart from maize which is grown on a relatively large scale on the railway belt for the home market, there is no important African cash crop in Northern Rhodesia. A few Africans grow market garden and other crops for sale in the vicinity of each urban settlement; there is a small group of tobacco growers producing under government supervision in Petauke district; a few districts, particularly in Barotseland, produce rubber which is purchased by the Agricultural Department for export. For the most part, however, the African trade in crops represents traded surplus rather than cash crop proper. During the war years all districts had a market for their food surpluses and a considerable amount of food was purchased by Government agencies.

The Maize Control Board and the Civil Supplies Board together purchased the major part of African traded grain and a proportion of African trade in all foodstuffs. A considerable proportion of the African trade, however, goes through the markets, or the traders, or is hawked through the villages and thus never passes into the hands of the central buying agencies. While every township has attached to it a small group of regular suppliers within walking or cycling distance, it has a much larger group of people who bring in small irregular quantities of foodstuffs or tobacco or other saleable crops as and when the seller needs some immediate cash or when he decides to dispose of a very small surplus. Many of these casual sellers trade by the roadside and never reach the market place itself. In the remoter districts there is a small inter-village trade in tobacco carried on by hawkers while at the Chief's court and along the main lorry routes and at all meeting places a small *ad hoc* market in foodstuffs springs up wherever travellers gather. These and the hawkers who travel from village to village need no licence for the sale of home-produced goods, and their number is therefore unknown.

Much of the irregular trade in crop surpluses is carried on in small units of, say, three-pennyworth, and the transactions, which are common in all areas, do not amount to a large proportion of the cash income of most able-bodied villagers, although they may represent the whole of the cash income of some old men and women. Thus, although the total sum involved is by no means negligible, it can be over-emphasized.

For crops bought by the Maize Control Board, the Civil Supplies Board and the Agricultural Department, records of these authorities were used as a basis for estimating the amount of income received by Africans in 1945. For the rest of the trade in crops—most of which was small-scale trade—the volume and value of the trade was calculated on the basis of estimates of the total amounts purchased by dwellers in the urban areas: the margins of error in these estimates are large, but it is believed that the orders of magnitude involved can be safely estimated from such sources. Table 95 shows the results of these estimates.

TABLE 95. African income from traded crops

	Output	Value received by Africans		
	Short tons	Through central buying agencies £	Through markets and by hawking £	Total £
Grain	23,120	126,000	33,000	159,000
Pulses	4,830	53,000	18,000	71,000
Nuts	1,900	8,000	15,000	23,000
Rice	40	1,000	—	1,000
Other food	9,100	—	76,000	76,000
Useful crops	300	18,000	2,000	20,000
		£206,000	£144,000	£350,000

7. AFRICAN INCOMES FROM LIVESTOCK

Figures of the number of cattle, sheep and goats, and pigs, slaughtered at licensed butcheries were available in the annual reports of the Veterinary Department. In addition a small number are slaughtered mainly for European consumption at outstations where there are no licensed butchers; the number of these was estimated on the basis of the returns made by District Commissioners to a questionnaire which asked how many beasts were slaughtered at local markets each month. One District Commissioner estimated the number of cattle slaughtered at funerals in his district during 1945, but otherwise there were no figures for village killings or deaths apart from those I had myself collected for some 120-odd households in Fort Jameson, Mazabuka and Mongu districts. These provided the basis for an estimate of the proportions of total African holdings of the various types of livestock which were killed or which died in the villages during the course of the year. Even for the areas from which the figures were collected these proportions were not a safe basis for generalization, and it is possible that the rates of ceremonial killing and the mortality rates vary greatly as between one area and another. Nevertheless, it is probable that the total estimates arrived at by these generalizations are a fair indication of the orders of magnitude involved.

The resulting estimates for the colony as a whole are given in Table 96. The animals slaughtered for purposes of trade were converted to dressed weight by using averages derived from actual 1945 slaughters at centres on the railway belt. Animals which were killed or which died in the villages were converted by using half the dressed weight averages found for traded stock: this may result in a degree of underestimate, but it must be remembered that many of the cattle which die are part-grown, or underfed, or wasted by disease, and in any case the stock retained in the villages would in general yield a lower weight of meat than stock sent to market.

TABLE 96. Quantity of output of African livestock

	Killed at markets or abattoirs Nos.	Killed or died in villages Nos.	Total killed or died, converted to dressed-weight meat lb.
Cattle	22,300	48,500	16,442,000
Sheep and goats	2,218	24,500	608,000
Pigs	6,568	15,900	1,684,000
			18,734,000

The Veterinary Department gives in its annual report average wholesale prices for livestock slaughtered in 1945. These, however, are prices given for stock delivered at the abattoir and in the majority of cases they are delivered by traders and not by Africans. The Cattle Marketing Board, in fixing controlled prices, allowed about 9% for traders' handling charges on native cattle on the railway belt, but where the stock was brought in from the reserves by the trader the African receipts would be smaller. Generally speaking, £6 per head seemed to be a usual price for African slaughter cattle in the railway belt, which represents about 12% less than the Veterinary Department's average. A similar percentage was deducted from the market wholesale value to give a producer's value for sheep and goats and pigs. It is more likely that these are high estimates of the value received by Africans than that they understate the case.

There is a small village trade in meat so that there is, theoretically, a local market price for the village killings and deaths. No satisfactory data were available to provide an estimate of this village price, however, and the village output was therefore evaluated on an arbitrary basis. It was evaluated as meat by converting the controlled live weight prices (less traders' charges) to equivalent dressed weight values. Conversions of live to dressed weight were made on the basis of material supplied by the Veterinary Department or obtainable from the records of the larger slaughter houses.

Thus it was estimated that the Africans received a total of about £156,000 from cattle, sheep and goats and pigs slaughtered at abattoirs or markets, for which the wholesale value was about £175,000.

There is also a considerable railway-belt trade in dairy products such as milk, poultry and eggs as well as a quantity traded or subsistence-consumed in the villages. Most of the milk drunk by Europeans on the railway belt is produced from European dairy herds, but Africans do supply a proportion of the trade and provide practically all the milk for rural consumption. Their own consumption of milk is an unknown quantity. In the cattle areas milk is certainly drunk in the villages, although apparently not to any very great extent except by herdboys: this kind of conclusion is, however, based on superficial observation and there is no quantitative basis at all for an estimate of African consumption of milk.

The amount of milk produced by Africans for the European market was

s

estimated as a function of European consumption in the urban and rural areas respectively and as a proportion of the Veterinary Department's estimates of the total amount of milk consumed. It was evaluated at 2d. a pint, which seemed to be a fairly general price for milk bought from Africans. The Veterinary Department gave information on which could be based an estimate of the total milk obtainable from existing African herds, which seemed to be not much less than two million gallons. In fact, however, it can safely be assumed that the herds were not milked at this rate and it was estimated that about 1,000,000 gallons were produced for consumption, of which 100,000 went to the European market. Here again, there may be a village trade in milk which would provide a local price for evaluating the village output, but I met no instance of it and have arbitrarily evaluated the milk at the price it fetches when sold to Europeans in out-districts.

Poultry seem to be in evidence in most villages, though the rate of village consumption does not appear to be high. In areas where returned migrant soldiers had money to spend and no gardens from which to get their relish, village trade in chickens seemed to be quite brisk, but I had no means of telling how general this trade was. On the railway belt there is a substantial and growing trade in African poultry railed to the various urban centres; and in all rural areas where there is a European population there is an assured local market. A livestock officer, whose results are quoted in the Tonga Survey, made a count of poultry and eggs railed at stations between Mission Siding and Magoye, and his figures were used as a basis for estimate of the total railway-belt trade. Out-station trade was estimated as a function of the European population, and village output was estimated at about one chicken per household per annum. The average of one chicken per household slaughtered for home consumption was the average I found for the 120-odd households that I questioned. It sounds very low and there is every reason to believe that the killing or death of a chicken is an immemorable event and that the villagers understated their consumption over the past year. On the other hand all these areas were pastoral areas and all of them were near enough to a European market to make the keeping of chickens a useful investment. It may be that in the more remote areas which I did not visit there were fewer chickens and less scraps on which they could feed: some of the Tonga actually fed their chickens regularly. Further, I have included urban households among the total in making the estimate, and although there are chickens in the compounds as well as in the villages, they appear less plentiful. I have assumed that African home consumption of eggs is negligible and this seems to be borne out by the qualitative evidence available.

In effect these calculations resulted in the estimates that 779,000 chickens and 160,000 dozen eggs were produced by Africans, of which the Africans themselves consumed about 429,000 chickens in the villages. The value to the Africans of the railway-belt traded output of chickens and eggs, at the prevailing prices, was in the region of £26,900, and the value of the total rural output, at the prices prevailing in rural areas, was about £28,800.

On balance it seems more likely that the estimates for the rural areas understate the true quantities produced than that they are overstatements. Information on the amount of game killed by Africans for village consumption or for the skin trade is very scanty. There are no quantitative data. Qualitative data suggest that although there are regular seasonal hunting parties in most rural areas the amount of meat obtained is not high in proportion to the numbers of men taking part. At the grass-burning season all sorts of small game from rats to duiker are hunted, but the returns in the form of meat seem to be very low. I would estimate that a token figure of about 2 lb. of meat per adult male in the villages does not in any way understate the total amount obtained from these sources. This gives a total of about half a million lb. for the whole territory. In addition, of course, there is the game slaughtered by the Game and Tsetse Department in its various control activities which amounts, judging from the Department's own estimates, to over $2\frac{1}{2}$ million lb. of meat sold to Africans. This, however, I have excluded, since it does not represent African output.

The results of all these calculations are shown in Table 96, below, which evaluates the African production at the producer's price.

TABLE 97. African income from livestock and livestock products

	Village output £	Marketed output £	Total output £
Cattle, sheep, goats, pigs	253,000	156,400	409,400
Game	4,200	—	4,200
Poultry and eggs	21,500	34,200	55,700
Milk	60,000	6,700	66,700
Hides and skins	3,000	800	3,800
	£341,700	£198,100	£539,800

8. AFRICAN INCOME FROM FISH

On the commercial output of fish from the principal fishing areas there were two main sources of information. The Game and Tsetse Department (which also concerns itself with fish) published in 1942 a *Preliminary Report on the Fishing Industry and its Markets*, by T. Vaughan Jones. Since then the annual reports of the Game and Tsetse Department have included sections on the fishing industry which contain estimates of output. The second main source of information was Mr W. V. Brelsford's study of Unga fishermen, which he permitted me to read in manuscript, but which has since been published.[1] From these sources it was possible to form estimates of the quantity of fish produced for purposes of exchange from each of the main fishing areas, and to be reasonably confident that—except in respect of the Zambesi River area—the estimates were of the right order of magnitude. None of the material related directly to the year 1945, but most of it related to some time within the previous four years, and since there was no reason

[1] See Bibliography, item 10.

to expect any great change in fishing conditions over that period the adjustments I made to relate it to 1945 were slight.
Table 98 shows the results of estimates based on this material.

TABLE 98. Value of Northern Rhodesian fisheries

	Fresh fish tons	Fishermen's return £
Trade from:		
1. Bangweulu and Upper Luapula	2,500	15,600
2. Mweru and Lower Luapula	1,100	6,900
3. Lower Kafue	600	3,800
4. Lukanga Swamp	500	3,100
5. Lake Tanganyika	300	1,900
6. All other areas	700	4,400
7. Total traded output	5,700	35,700
8. Bartered output	500	3,100
9. Subsistence output	1,100	6,900
	7,300	£45,700

In this table the fish is shown as fresh fish, although most of it would be dried before it reached the market, and is evaluated at the average waterside price for fresh fish, which was estimated at ¾d. per lb. The conversion ratio for fresh to dried fish has been taken as roughly 3 : 1. The value of the traded output at the controlled price, which would be 8d. or 9d. per lb. of dried fish, would be rather less than £13,000. At the actual market price, which varied in the Copperbelt from 1s. 6d. to 2s. per lb. and at times was even more, it would be nearer £285,000. Most of the £285,000 would pass to Africans, largely to African middlemen and traders, but a proportion was handled by European firms at some stage on its way to market. It is estimated that about £10,000 went to Europeans, and that African cash receipts from the fishing industry totalled about £275,000.

Margins of error in these estimates are difficult to establish. Since the principal source of error derives from the gaps in our knowledge concerning certain areas, and since we have assumed that the areas we do not know about are not big producers, the estimates are more likely to be underestimates than overestimates. It seems, however, most unlikely that the commercial output would have exceeded 7,000 tons or that the total output would have exceeded 10,000 tons. On the other hand, it is unlikely that total output would have fallen below 6,000 tons. On balance, therefore, and on the assumption that the information which is available is not positively misleading, it is probable that the value of the fisheries fell between £38,000 and £63,000 for the fishermen, and between £250,000 and £370,000 for all those taking part in the industry.

It is impossible to give a useful figure of the total numbers of persons producing this output, since much of it would have been produced casually and on a small scale. From the few figures which are available for the commercial producing areas, however, I would estimate that somewhere in the region of

6,000 men engaged in fishing as a major income earning activity, while perhaps as many as three times this number took part in the fish traffic between waterside and consumer. Most, even of the distributors, were subsistence agriculturalists who spent a considerable proportion of the year at their gardens.

9. AFRICAN INCOMES FROM OTHER INDEPENDENT WORK AND VILLAGE INDUSTRIES

Africans working independently and on their own account perform a variety of full-time or part-time occupations in both the urban and the rural areas. There are shopkeepers, market traders, hawkers, tailors, smiths, carpenters, shoe repairers, prostitutes, doctors, and so on. For the urban areas some idea of the total number of persons engaged primarily in working on their own account can be derived from occupational classifications in urban censuses: for townships where a complete compound census was not available the estimates published by the Commission on Urban Locations (for which a rough census was obtained from each location) were utilized. In general it seemed that the Commission's estimates understated the number of independent workers in the locations, judging by the results for locations for which an up-to-date and relatively full census was available. For the rural areas the District Administration could provide rough figures, but since district touring had been greatly reduced during the war, and since in any case the estimates on these matters were very rough, even where touring was regular or recent, they cannot be regarded with very great confidence.

Moreover, although these figures may provide the basis for a rough estimate of the numbers of Africans engaged full-time in such independent occupations, they give no indication of the number of part-time workers who do such odd jobs as shoe repairing or curio-making or hawking or village shop-keeping as a minor sideline to agricultural work or even to employment. Some men, for example, work on their own account as smiths, or builders or hawkers in the slack season for agricultural work, but drop this independent activity altogether during the planting or harvesting seasons.

The number of men benefiting from these casual independent occupations, and their rate of earnings, are very difficult to measure. On the other hand, the impression I derived from my own enquiries in the villages is that they earned relatively little in cash and that their earnings in kind were also worth little in relation to village incomes in general. Independent workers in the villages who did earn at a significant rate by African standards were well enough known for it to be reasonable to assume that the District Administration's rough estimates would have taken account of them.

Data on the earnings of independent workers were obtained from a variety of sources, including the local Boma files, the files of Labour Officers, Godfrey Wilson's Broken Hill Survey, and my own direct enquiries from Africans in compounds and villages. There was no systematically collected material, so that estimates had to be based on figures which showed, at best, the probable level of earnings in particular districts and occupations.

TABLE 99. African incomes from independent work

	Numbers	Earnings £
1. In urban areas on line of rail	3,200	76,800
2. In urban areas off line of rail	300	5,400
3. In rural areas	23,500	282,000
4. Totals	27,000	£364,200

African incomes from small-scale village industries, including subsistence output, but excluding the output of specialists whose incomes would be included in the previous section, are extremely difficult to measure without conducting large-scale economic surveys in the villages. My own data on the Tonga, Lozi and Ngoni villages which I visited, together with the results of the Tonga and Lamba and other local surveys produced by or with the aid of the Rhodes-Livingstone Institute, provided a mass of detailed data for the limited areas covered without giving much guidance for other areas. The material obtained on beer sales, for example, was sufficiently satisfactory to enable the orders of magnitude involved to be gauged in the areas concerned. For other areas—for example, areas where the sale of beer was prohibited—this material was of very little direct value. Similar considerations applied to any attempt to generalize information collected on receipts from manufactures or medicines or doctoring or other small services. Subsistence output could be estimated at all only by putting quantitative interpretations on qualitative observations.

Thus the entries under this item are in many ways merely token entries based on superficial observation or unwarranted generalizations.

TABLE 100. Value of income from village industries

	Subsistence income £	Cash income £	Total income £
Beer	64,000	43,000	107,000
Manufactures	65,000	64,000	129,000
Miscellaneous sources	22,000	21,000	43,000
	£151,000	£128,000	£279,000

10. AFRICAN INCOME FROM SUBSISTENCE AGRICULTURE

The income derived by Africans from the sale of crops is only a fraction of the total income from agricultural output. The bulk of the income so derived is income in kind, enjoyed by the producer's own family or bartered within the limits of the village economy. Since subsistence or bartered output never reaches a market, there are no sales statistics to give an indication of the orders of magnitude involved. The only way of measuring it is by investigating the yield of land, holding by holding, or the rate of consumption, family by family.

Given a certain homogeneity or recognizable pattern of agricultural practice, it should be possible to make estimates of total agricultural return on the basis of sample surveys in selected areas. In the first of the reports on the ecological survey of the territory,[1] which was carried out in the eight years 1934–42, it was stated that:

> ... the distribution of the staple native crops is so closely related to that of the various soil and vegetation types as to allow of the definition of corresponding agricultural systems ... It will be seen that the distribution of crops is throughout consistent with changes in the type of country and that a distinctive combination of crops is found in each agricultural system ... [Comparison of this map the official tribal map of the Territory] with the vegetational map will show that owing no doubt primarily to the requirements of their staple crops, groups of related tribes tend to occupy regions with common characteristics of soil and vegetation and practise a corresponding agricultural system. Where related tribes are found in different soil systems their agricultural systems generally differ correspondingly, although common factors in custom are generally found.

The survey then went on to describe each of the various agricultural systems, largely in qualitative terms. Theoretically, therefore—given sufficient information for each agricultural area on population concerned, average acreage per head, distribution of crops, and average yields of different crops —it should be possible to make estimates of agricultural output for the colony as a whole.

In practice there are many difficulties. The Ecological Survey distinguished twenty-one different agricultural areas and more than a hundred different kinds of crops. To calculate the volume of agricultural output in detail one would require for each of the areas quantitative data on cultivated acreages per head and the normal pattern of crop distribution. Moreover, since yields of crops would tend to vary with the local soil conditions which produced the prevailing local agricultural system, and perhaps also with the customs of the tribes concerned, one would have to start with more than 2,000 normal yields which would have to be adjusted to approximate to the actual yield of the year concerned. Even if all this basic information were available it would have to be periodically revised, since there would be significant variations in the ground plan within a few years. For not only are the Northern Rhodesian cultivators shifting over the face of the countryside and constantly changing the pattern of land utilization with changes in soil cultivated, but they are also, even in the remotest subsistence areas, in contact both with a world market which exerts an indirect effect on their methods of cultivation and with an agricultural department which exerts a direct effect.

Clearly, therefore, in the existing circumstances, any figures which might be compiled on native agricultural output are bound to be highly approxi-

---

[1] See the reference to the Ecological Survey in Appendix III.

mate. On the other hand, it would be possible to produce estimates which were reliable enough and detailed enough for most practical purposes by drastically simplifying the pattern for the territory as a whole. The Director of Agriculture, in putting forward his ten-year development programme in 1945, reduced the classification of agricultural systems to ten main agricultural divisions or areas of which he could say that:

> Almost all the Areas are separated either by belts of sparsely inhabited country or by pronounced natural features. Generally they contain populations having racial affinities, some very close.

If sample surveys were undertaken in each of these areas to find the population concerned, the average acreage cultivated per head, the normal proportion of land under each of the staple crops and main subsidiary crops, and the average yield per acre of the crops so distinguished, we should have enough information to make useful estimates of total agricultural output in the territory. These estimates could be brought up to date annually by adjusting for yield changes calculated by the agricultural officers in connection with their harvest reports.

At present the information available is inadequate even for this limited aim. There have been a very few local agricultural surveys and the officers of the agricultural department are in a position to make only very rough estimates of yields and crop distribution patterns in the areas which they know well. I approached the problem by circularizing the agricultural officers for information on average cultivated acreage per head, average pattern of crop distribution distinguishing staple crops and major groups of subsidiaries, and average yields of the principal crops. Unfortunately, even if one can rely on the estimates of the experts in cases where there were no systematically collected data to provide a basis for their estimates (and each of the officers concerned emphasized the crudeness of the estimates given) the areas covered by the agricultural department are extremely circumscribed. The Director of Agriculture, in presenting his development plan, explained the situation as follows:

> The policy governing the distribution of the existing Agricultural Staff is one of concentration on the areas most in need of attention. The Staff is thus at present practically confined to the maize area of the Southern Province, the Western Province, the Abercorn and Isoka districts of Northern Province and the Petauke and Fort Jameson districts of the Eastern Province. . . .

The most important gap in the information obtainable from the staff of the department relates to Barotseland. We know from the Ecological Survey that the agricultural system of the Central Barotse Plain, with its nine different types of traditional garden and its very wide range of crops, is the most complex of all the Northern Rhodesian agricultural systems. We know enough, in effect, to be sure that the crop pattern of other areas is quite inapplicable to this area.

One encouraging feature about the information which was available from the few agricultural surveys was the small range of variation in average acreage per head. Among subsistence cultivators proper it varied as between the different surveys from 0.9 to 1.1 acres per head; among the cash-cropping Plateau Tonga, where the great majority of the larger African farmers are found, the average was in the region of 1¼ acres per head for the whole group and 1.1 acres for subsistence cultivators only. To a lesser extent, average yields, wherever calculated for a relatively large area, also fell within a limited range, and the distribution of land as between staple and subsidiary crops was also broadly similar as between one area and another.

Thus if we are content with very broad results we may reasonably hope to obtain results for different provinces which are comparable and which are reliable within about 20% of the truth; and we may obtain results for the colony as a whole which have a margin of error of between 10% and 20% at the outside. For this, however, it would be necessary to have access to very much more complete information than is at present compiled.

Using as basis the estimates obtained from the agricultural officers in answer to my questionnaire, I obtained the following rough estimates of output per head of the African population.

TABLE 101. Estimates of African agricultural output per head

	Meal lb.	Pulses lb.	Rootcrops (excluding cassava) lb.
Western Province	652	10	407
Southern Province	593	55	25
Northern Province:			
(a) Chitimene	561	51	—
(b) Grassland	595	99	—
Eastern Province:			
(a) Fort Jameson	403	116	198
(b) Petauke	495	56	240

For the purposes of Table 101, all grain (even when eaten 'green') and cassava was converted to meal. The conversion factors used were based on returns obtained from agricultural officers. The answers varied, but since they were, in any case, estimates, and it did not seem likely that there would be much variation as between areas in the amount of meal obtained from each variety of grain, I derived the factor of 85% to account for conversion of maize into meal, 95% for millet or sorghum, and 2% for cassava.

In Table 102 I have attempted to evaluate the results obtained for each area, using in the first case the actual local prices as supplied by the agricultural officers, and in the second case a single national set of prices for all the areas based on what appeared to be the normal prices for each of the main crops.

TABLE 102.   Evaluation of agricultural output

	Value of output per head Local prices £	Value of output per head National prices £
Western Province	3.06	3.11
Southern Province	2.90	2.44
Northern Province:		
(a) Chitimene	2.02	2.35
(b) Grassland	2.51	2.73
Eastern Province:		
(a) Fort Jameson	3.32	2.62
(b) Petauke	2.65	2.57
Average for Northern Rhodesia	£2.76	£2.71

It must be emphasized that all the above estimates are very rough and there is not much statistical significance in the differences between provinces, although we may fairly regard the differences within provinces, especially as between Chitimene and grassland areas of Northern Province, as being significant. The average for the territory was weighted by population figures for each province and based on the assumption that the results for Western Province could be generalized to cover Central and Barotse Provinces. This is a very doubtful assumption, but the qualitative evidence suggests that Central and Barotse Provinces have in general a high value of food intake, and the results for Western Province exceed the results for any other province taken as a whole.

The agricultural officers were also asked what they estimated was the annual rate of consumption per head of meal, pulses, and other crops, and their answers to this question were used to check the results derived from their answers on acreages, yields, etc. The result of checking the two sets of estimates suggested that there was a degree of underestimate in the output figures taken as a whole, and it was estimated that the average output of meal per head of the population was about 575 lb., of pulses (and similar relishes) 50 lb., and of other crops (including fruit and vegetables) 250 lb. This underestimate was to be expected since the yield and acreage questions related to a selected list of crops only and the consumption questions related

TABLE 103.   Volume and value of agricultural output

	Quantity		Value	
	Per head	Total Northern Rhodesia	Per head	Total Northern Rhodesia
	lb.	lb.	£	£
Meal	575	836,050,000	1.92	2,791,700
Pulses	50	72,700,000	0.38	552,500
Other food	250	363,500,000	0.52	756,100
			£2.82	£4,100,300

to wide groups of crops. Thus the estimates given in Table 103 were reached for the territory as a whole and for a total population available in the villages of 1,454,000.

If we ignore the general problems of evaluating subsistence output and are prepared to rely on the population estimates, it is fair to regard the total value of agricultural output as falling between £3,700,000 and £4,500,000. In fact, however, the prices from which the above results were derived are local prices, and marketed output brought in a larger average return to the producer.

TABLE 104. Value of subsistence and marketed output

	Value of subsistence or bartered output £	Value of marketed output £	Total value of output £
Meal	2,668,200	159,000	2,827,200
Pulses	479,000	94,000	573,000
Other food	716,600	77,000	793,600
Useful crops	180,000	20,000	200,000
	£4,043,800	£350,000	£4,393,800

In Table 104 an attempt has been made to adjust for the extra value of traded output by combining the estimates reached for the quantity and value of traded crops with the estimates for subsistence crops. An additional crude estimate was made for useful subsistence crops. This gives an average value of subsistence output per person available in the villages of £2.78.

II. OUTPUT OF THE MINING INDUSTRY

The reports of the five principal mining companies and the returns made by them to government, and the information obtained direct from particular companies, or from the Chamber of Mines for all the copper companies, formed the chief basis for an estimate of the contribution of the mineral industry to the total national product. In addition, the small mines furnished figures of their local expenditure to the Mines Department and of their labour force to the Labour Department. It was necessary to adjust all company profit and loss accounts (except those for Broken Hill) to bring them into calendar year terms. Table 105 shows the value of metal sales as derived from the relevant company reports.

Since all these companies are registered in the United Kingdom, the greater part of their balances are held abroad and their dividends paid abroad. Sales are also made abroad. In effect, the system is for the companies to remit to the territory such monies as are necessary to cover operating costs and to retain the remainder of the proceeds in the United Kingdom.

TABLE 105. Metal sales in Northern Rhodesia, 1945 and 1946

Company	Value of sales 1945 £	1946 £
Rhodesia Broken Hill Development Co. Ltd.	1,013,100	1,233,300
Rhokana Corporation Ltd.	5,263,700	5,941,200
Roan Antelope Copper Mines Ltd.	3,027,400	3,330,600
Mufulira Copper Mines Ltd.	2,982,300	3,298,900
Nchanga Consolidated Copper Mines Ltd.	822,600	1,307,600
	£13,109,100	£15,111,600

Out of this operating surplus they meet London Office expenses, Directors' fees, interest charges, and other managerial expenses, and pay taxation. The net profit is then available to swell reserves held in the United Kingdom or to distribute to shareholders. Table 106 shows the proportion of the value of total sales which flows abroad in the form of operating surplus.

TABLE 106. Operating surplus of principal mining companies

	1945 £	1946 £
Total value sales of metal	13,109,100	15,111,600
Production and realization costs	9,818,500	10,415,800
Operating surplus	£3,290,600	£4,695,800

Not all of these production and realization costs are incurred in Northern Rhodesia, however, or are paid to Northern Rhodesian nationals. Royalties are paid to the British South Africa Company, which is a United Kingdom company. Railage as far as Beira is paid to Rhodesia Railway Ltd., a Southern Rhodesian company. Then there are the costs of shipping the metal abroad and freight insurance costs, all of which are paid to concerns outside the colony. Finally, transfers to depreciation reserve, which are included in production costs in Table 106, are, in effect, transfers to reserves held outside the colony.

TABLE 107. External production costs of mining industry

	1945 £	1946 £
Production costs	9,818,500	10,415,800
Less external costs:		
1. Royalties	338,700	621,000
2. Outside refining	648,200	632,100
3. Railage	896,500	889,800
4. Shipping and other realization costs	141,600	188,400
5. Depreciation	861,000	955,200
6. Total external costs	£2,886,000	£3,286,500
Internal costs	£6,932,500	£7,129,300

The estimates in Table 107 were derived from the company reports. Since the accounts were not drawn up on a uniform basis it was not always possible to obtain for each company the exact figure for each item. It is not likely that any item has a margin of error in excess of 5%, and in most cases the error is very much less. Royalties were calculated from the reports of the British South Africa Company, the receiving company, whose financial year ran from September to September, and whose figures had therefore to be adjusted to a calendar year basis. They could also be calculated from the reports of the paying companies, but an estimate from this source was less reliable, since some companies did not distinguish royalties separately. Even so, estimates from the two sources were within a few per cent of one another.

In order to reach a figure for the net output of an industry, it is necessary to exclude from gross output the cost of depreciation of equipment and the value of raw materials and purchased services. The value of the net output of the five large mineral companies is estimated below in Table 108.

TABLE 108. Net output of principal mineral companies

	1945 £	1946 £
Sales of metal	13,109,100	15,111,600
Less raw materials and purchased services	5,294,200	5,103,100
Less depreciation	861,000	955,200
Net value of output	£6,953,900	£9,053,300

In Table 108 purchased services include the external production costs shown in Table 107 with the exception of royalties, which are treated as being part of the output of companies concerned in mineral production, and depreciation, which is included separately above. The value of raw materials and purchased services included imported raw materials and equipment (estimated on the basis of figures supplied by the Chamber of Mines) and payments to contractors in Northern Rhodesia (estimated from figures obtained from the Mines Department). Expenditure on raw materials and equipment and on contractors' services were allocated as between capital expenditure and current production costs in accordance with their relative proportions in total expenditure.

For national income purposes, companies which are registered abroad are generally regarded as being foreign companies, and their income is not included as part of net national income. If we confine our attention to that part of the output of mining which is produced by nationals of Northern Rhodesia, we must exclude all payments flowing abroad.

In effect, the contribution of Northern Rhodesian nationals to the output of the mineral industry is equivalent to the sale of their services to the mineral companies. It can be arrived at by taking the total remittances by the companies to cover operating costs and capital expenditure and deducting that part of the total which represents payments for goods and services to foreigners or to other industries. The results of this calculation are given in Table 109.

TABLE 109. Analysis of output of mining industry

	1945 £	1946 £
Value of metal sales	13,109,100	15,111,600
Less value attributable to foreign companies (i.e. operating surplus and royalties)	3,629,300	5,316,800
Remittances to cover operating costs	9,479,800	9,794,800
Remittances to cover capital expenditure	1,233,900	937,400
Total company remittances	10,713,700	10,732,200
Less imported raw materials and equipments	4,050,900	3,641,800
Less imported services (i.e. realization costs and outside refining)	1,686,300	1,710,300
Less local purchases of goods and services (i.e. payments to contractors)	207,300	180,000
Less depreciation	861,000	955,200
Net national output of mining	£3,908,200	£4,244,900

There is, theoretically, another way of arriving at this total for the net national output of mining and that is to aggregate the receipts of Northern Rhodesian nationals from the mining industry. The Mines Department supplied figures for the year 1945 of the value of local payments made by all the mining concerns, including the small mines. The total reached from these figures amounted to £3,839,600, with the small mines, and £3,822,400, excluding the small mines. This is within about 2% of the results shown in Table 109, which were reached from an examination of the company reports, supplemented by data from the Chamber of Mines. If we assume that the figures obtained from the Mines Department are a precisely accurate record of the disbursement in Northern Rhodesia and that they do not include leave and pension payments made to Europeans not actually in the colony, then we can attribute the difference of £85,800 to such payments and put the total output of the Northern Rhodesian mineral industry at £3,925,400 in 1945 and about £4,238,000 in 1946.

The margin of error in the totals for the net output of mining can be estimated at about 2%. The constituent items in Table 109 have margins of error varying between about 2% and 5%.

Total payments made in 1945 in the colony in connection with mining industry operations, as given by the Mines Department, are shown in Table 110.

In effect, the total net output of the mining industry in Northern Rhodesia consists of the net current output of the mineral companies together with the value of services bought with their capital expenditure. Since the output of

TABLE 110. Payments made by mining industry in Northern Rhodesia

	1945 £	1946 £
European salaries, wages and bonuses	2,597,800	2,620,000
African wages, bonuses and rations	1,241,800	1,300,000
Payments to contractors	207,300	180,000
Taxation	1,193,700	1,094,000
	£5,240,600	£5,194,000

building contractors is included elsewhere in the output column, it is specifically excluded from this section of output. Thus Table 111 gives a final analysis of the output of the mining industry in 1945.

TABLE 111. Output of the Northern Rhodesian mining industry

	1945 £
1. Net value current output	6,746,600
2. Wage payments on capital account	138,700
3. Net value output industry in Northern Rhodesia	£6,885,300
4. Net value output mining industry by Northern Rhodesian nationals	£3,908,200

12. OUTPUT OF EUROPEAN AGRICULTURE

The reports of the Agricultural and Veterinary Departments and the report of the Committee appointed to enquire into the Development of the European Farming Industry together provided details of output and gross value of the main products in 1945. They are shown below in Table 112.

TABLE 112. Principal products of European agriculture

	Quantities	Gross return £
Maize	358,400 bags	286,500
Wheat	27,000 bags	40,400
Potatoes	15,700 bags	19,800
Tobacco	2,904,000 lb.	218,100
Cattle	8,000 head	68,500
Butter	54,533 lb.	7,300
Milk	300,000 galls.	22,500
		£663,100

Unpublished reports of the Maize Control Board and the Cattle Marketing Board contain estimates of the average costs of production for maize and cattle drawn up by individuals in the industries concerned. For the other commodities there are no data on cost of production. Estimates of the output of other crops, other livestock, and poultry were made partly on the basis of output and acreage statistics which were collected by the Agricultural

Department before the war and partly on the basis of consumption estimates. A small proportion of the output of each of the above food products,
together with a large proportion of the output of all other food crops were
consumed on the farm. Where the produce was consumed by labourers or
cattle its value has been included once in the final value of the commodity
provided by labourers or cattle. Where, however, it was consumed by the
farmer and his family, this is a net addition to income and is not part of the
value of any other commodity.

Column 1 of Table 113 contains the following additions to Table 112:
an estimate of the value of cattle consumed on the farm, estimates of the
value of livestock produced (including poultry and eggs), and estimates of
the value of other crops. Gross output has been converted to net output by
deducting for purchased materials, repairs and replacements and depreciation on the assumption that the cost of production pattern for crops in general
approximates to that estimated for maize in a report to the Maize Control
Board, and that the cost of production pattern for livestock in general is
similar to that estimated for cattle in a report to the Cattle Marketing and
Control Board. There is some evidence to indicate that these assumptions
involve an underestimate of the value of net output.

TABLE 113. Value of output of European agricultural produce

	Gross value £	Net value £
1. Crops	587,900	322,500
2. Livestock and livestock products	147,100	100,000
3. Total value all agricultural output	735,000	422,500
4. Less crops used in production	69,600	39,700
5. Value of European agriculture	£665,400	£382,800

The suspicion that net value of output is underestimated in Table 113 is
confirmed by an examination of the material on incomes earned in European
agriculture. From the Workmen's Compensation Commissioner, we learn
that the incomes earned by employed persons engaged in agriculture
amounted to £323,000 in 1945–6 (year ended 28th February), of which
£279,400 was earned by Africans. From the Income Tax Commissioner
we find that assessed incomes earned from farming by persons and companies
farming on their own account in the period 1944–5 was £177,700. Thus
we get a total for incomes derived from agriculture of £500,700, excluding
casual profits, rents, interest, etc., earned by persons not actually engaged
in the industry[1] and farm consumption of owner-farmers.

It should be remembered that the Workmen's Compensation Commissioner includes in his figures allowances for housing and other income in
kind, which may, in fact, overestimate the cost of providing them. On

[1] I.e. persons for whom agriculture is a subsidiary occupation.

the other hand, it is unlikely that the overestimate on this account much exceeds, if at all, the underestimate due to the exclusion of income from agriculture which is earned by persons outside the industry together with the food, etc., consumed on the farms by the families of farmers. In effect, it seems probable that the total incomes earned in the European agricultural industry were in the region of £500,000. Of this a certain proportion was accounted for by incomes earned in capital expenditure rather than in expenditure on costs of production of current output. It was estimated as a result of a questionnaire issued to farmers that capital expenditure amounted to about £300,000, of which perhaps £50,000 went in wages. If this was so, then the total value of incomes earned in the production of current output was about £450,000, making the net value of output equal about two-thirds of the gross value of the return received by farmers. Table 114 gives these results.

TABLE 114. Net value of output of European agriculture

	£
Net value of produce	665,400
Value capital expenditure	300,000
Total expenditure on agriculture	965,400
Less raw materials, purchased services, depreciation and equipment	465,400
Net value of output of industry	£500,000

Another way of reaching a value for the net output of agriculture is to examine the import list for agricultural imports on current account and to reduce gross output accordingly. By this means an estimate was reached of about £140,000 as the value of imported materials used in producing current output. To this could be added our estimate for the value of depreciation and expenditure on repair and replacement service, calculated by analogy with the weight of these items in the cost of production of maize, giving a total of £253,000 for the value of raw materials, purchased services and depreciation involved in the production of the year's output. This would give a net output of about £412,400. It seems probable that the allowances for depreciation and repairs and replacement services purchased from other industries were over-generous and that this figure of £412,400 may be a good deal too low.

If we approach the problem of capital expenditure from the side of imports and assume, as before, that total capital expenditure was in the region of £300,000, of which wages constituted about £50,000, we get a total of about £106,000 for the value of imported equipment, and £144,000 for the value of building, boring and other forms of capital expenditure on local products and services.

The details and the breakdowns contained in the estimates below are subject to considerable margins of error. This is borne out by the later adjustments which were made to the estimate for European agriculture in the course of the cross-checking process. The final conclusion was that the total value of net output of European agriculture and livestock was £600,000.

T

TABLE 115. Summary table for European agriculture

Value of output of:	£
1. Maize	286,500
2. Wheat	40,400
3. Potatoes	19,800
4. Other food crops	23,100
5. Tobacco	218,100
6. Cattle and products	102,500
7. Other livestock and products	44,600
8. Less crops used in production	69,600
9. Gross value of output	665,400
10. Less raw materials, purchased services and depreciation	215,400
11. Net value of output	450,000
12. Value of incomes earned in capital development	50,000
13. Total value of incomes earned in European agriculture	£500,000

13. OUTPUT OF DISTRIBUTION

All traders who deal in imported goods are required to take out a licence. The trading licences issued from the District Commissioner's Office account for all the European and Indian storekeepers, all but a very few of the African storekeepers, and a proportion of the African hawkers. They give no indication of the number of African hawkers of local produce or of the number of African marketeers.

The numbers of licences issued in each main category were supplied by the District Commissioners in answer to a questionnaire circulated to them in 1947.[1] The answers are summarized below.

TABLE 116. Trading licences issued by District Administration

Issued to:	1945	1946
Europeans	554	560
Asians	396	429
African storekeepers	3,171	4,242
African hawkers	939	1,007

Turnover and wage statistics relating to the year 1945 were collected from nineteen European-owned trading concerns on the railway belt, of which seven sold producers' goods and twelve consumers' goods. Four Indian retail stores on the railway line and one wholesale store gave similar data. In addition the Provincial Commissioner of Eastern Province was able to supply turnover figures for 1942 or 1943 for 105 Indian stores and eighteen European

[1] In one case the relevant records had been destroyed and it was necessary to make an estimate with the help of the District Commissioner.

stores which dealt primarily in African goods (Kaffir truck). The Workmen's Compensation Commissioner gave earnings figures for those employed in distribution, and the Income Tax Department's figures distinguished earnings from trade of persons working on their own account.

On the basis of these figures an estimate was formed of the total turnover and value of output of European and Asian distributing concerns. It was estimated that the total value of turnover handled by these concerns was in the region of £8,600,000 and that the net value of their output (i.e. wages, salaries, profits, interest and rent) amounted to about £1,720,000 in 1945. On balance this estimate seems more likely to be too high than too low, and the margin of error may be as much as 23%. The estimate for net output is less likely to be too high, however, than the estimate for gross output. The estimates for African licensed shopkeepers were based on information collected originally by the District Commissioners in Eastern Province and on some material that I had myself collected. The District Commissioners' figures, like my own, were probably based on a few selected cases and have a very wide margin of error. The estimates for African licensed hawkers were rough guesses based on the assumption that their average turnover and earnings did not differ widely from that of the shopkeepers. The results of these estimates are given in Table 117.

TABLE 117. Distribution by licensed traders

	£	Net output £	Turnover £
European and Asian			
Employed Africans	72,000		
Europeans and Asians	1,015,000		
Companies	553,000		
Interest, rent, etc.	100,000		
Total European and Asian trade		1,740,000	8,600,000
African licensed shopkeepers		60,000	200,000
African licensed hawkers		15,000	50,000
Total value for licensed traders		£1,815,000	£8,850,000

An attempt to assess the volume of trade carried on through the markets, by wayside trades and by hawkers involves a high degree of guesswork. It might be possible to survey the activity carried on during a given period along one of the main labour routes, or outside a government post, or on the way to a township, but such a survey would be expensive in time and labour and would be of little general significance since seasonal and area differences are considerable. General appearances would suggest that the habit of inter-village trade is much more highly developed, for example, among the Barotse than among the Ngoni; but it is impossible to say whether this difference is not a difference in velocity of circulation which is perhaps outweighed by the relatively higher command over cash resources enjoyed in recent years by Eastern Province with its high quota of demobilized soldiers. General appearances, in effect, are a poor guide to the quantitative interpretation of something so irregular and unorganized as the internal trade of the territory.

The weather, for example, has an important influence on the weekly or monthly amount of vegetables, eggs, or milk offered for sale in a given area. Supply conditions in the stores selling manufactured goods are also an important factor in conditioning the supply of local agricultural produce. An influx to the local stores of goods which have been in short supply tends to increase the flow of sellers to those places in the vicinity of the stores where buyers pass and congregate. This factor is, no doubt, less important in normal times than it was in the difficult supply conditions of the immediate post-war period, but is always liable to occur in the less accessible areas. Thus a survey which is designed to reveal the volume and importance of the inter-village and wayside trade and all that local trade which does not take place in recognized markets (i.e. the bulk of the internal trade in local produce for all districts not on the railway belt) must be extensive in both time and place if it is to reduce the many seasonal, cyclical and irregular variations to their proper perspective.

Even for the markets themselves there are as yet very few quantitative details of general value. On the Copperbelt markets there is some information. There have been surveys by mine compound authorities of the volume of produce flowing into their markets: a study published by the Government Printer in 1947 gives the result of a survey of Copperbelt markets, with particular reference to Mufulira Market, made by Mr W. V. Brelsford, a District Commissioner, and contains an appendix with estimates of sales contributed by Mr W. Allan, then Deputy Director of Agriculture. Thus it is possible to form a reliable idea of the order of magnitude of the trade in the Copperbelt markets, although the margins of error involved in any actual figures cited are considerable. The importance of this margin of error and its sources are illustrated by the following comment by Mr Allan on the comparison of his own estimates for 1944 with Mr Brelsford's estimates for 1945:

> Where it is possible to make comparisons the quantity and price data used in this calculation generally agree well with Brelsford's estimates, but there is a notable exception in the case of fish. He estimates the total value of fish sold in 1945 at approximately £64,000. My data, based on a lower load-weight and price sampling at Wusikili and Kitwe only, gave a total value of £30,000 for all fish sold in 1944. Considering the higher prices at all other centres, concealed sales on the 'black market' and his own reasons for assuming a higher load weight, I think Brelsford's basis of calculation is the more accurate.

Allan's conclusion, based on his own and Brelsford's conclusions, was that:

> . . . the average annual value of sales of foodstuffs and tobacco on the African urban markets of the Copperbelt, excluding Ndola, is almost certainly more than £100,000 and probably not more than £150,000.

In the questionnaire circulated to the District Commissioners on this topic they were asked to give, so far as they could, estimates of the volume of trade in the principal commodities dealt in at the official or unofficial local markets. In the few cases where there had been some systematic attempt to measure volumes of local trade the results were given. In many cases no figures were given at all. There were figures of a kind for twenty-two out of thirty-three of the recognized markets (including the nine Copperbelt markets for which Allan and Brelsford gave estimates), and for seven out of the twenty districts with no recognized markets. Most of the figures represent the guesses of the District Commissioners, often being no more than an attempt to give quantitative expression to personal, general, observation.

Using the figures and price data collected from a variety of sources and making arbitrary estimates based on miscellaneous specific pieces of information for Districts which offered no information, the conclusions were reached that the total value of the internal trade of the territory at the organized markets or recognized places to which people brought their produce to exchange for money, was between £400,000 and £500,000. In Table 118 the estimates are given by provinces.

TABLE 118. Internal trade in local produce

Provinces	Volume of trade £
Northern	64,000
Eastern	50,000
Barotse	30,000
Southern	56,000
Central and Western	250,000
	£450,000

In interpreting Table 118, whose constituent items have margins of error varying from 25% to 50%, it should be noted that (1) that allowance has already been made for possible double counting in the fish trade by reducing the original estimates for Northern Province, (2) that allowance has been made throughout for the tendency to sell at a price above the controlled price, (3) that no attempt has been made to include inter-neighbour trade in the villages, which accounts for most of the local trade in beer and a number of local manufactures, and (4) that sale of maize in bulk to government or traders is not included.

The low figure for Barotse Province is unexpected in view of the fact that general observation suggests a more lively internal trade than usual in this province. It is impossible to know, however, whether this low figure reflects the lack of information available on a trade which is even less organized or concentrated in this province than in other provinces, or whether it reflects the fact of lower wage-earning opportunities in Barotseland and a relative shortage of cash expendable on local products (except on an inter-neighbour basis).

On balance, after considering such contributory factors as number of local wage earners or of returned migrants, it does not seem that the estimate for any of the provinces is improbable, although the sketchy nature of the available information makes it impossible to place much reliance on the absolute figures. Except in the case of the Copperbelt trade it can be assumed that the vast bulk of the returns from sale of produce go direct to the original producer, although it is impossible to extract a net return for the service of distribution. The net return to persons trading in local produce at the markets or by the wayside is probably not less than about £400,000.

On this evidence, therefore, the conclusion was that the total retail trade turnover (excluding inter-neighbour trade) amounted to about £9,300,000 and that the total net return to persons engaged in trade was in the region of £2,200,000. The final conclusion after cross-checking was that this was an overestimate and that the net output was nearer to £2,072,000.

14. OUTPUT OF TRANSPORT

The principal difficulty in calculating the output of railway transport for Northern Rhodesia was that the accounts of the Rhodesia Railways Ltd. are generally shown as a unity, and it is only in broad categories such as total revenue and total expenditure that one can normally expect to find the figures analysed by territory. In extracting the figures for the Northern Rhodesia section of the line, I was advised by the Chief Accountant of Rhodesia Railways Ltd., who estimated relevant amounts for me on the basis of the detailed accounts for 1944–5 (30th September). I adjusted 1944–5 estimates for calendar year 1945 on the basis of movements in the total accounts of Rhodesia Railways Ltd., except for wages and salaries where Workmen's Compensation statistics could be used as a corrective.

TABLE 119. Revenue and expenditure of the railways, 1944–5

Revenue	£	Expenditure	£
1. Passenger receipts	175,100	4. Working expenditure	1,041,900
2. Other receipts	1,479,100	5. Renewal expenditure on permanent way	47,100
		6. Capital expenditure	50,300
		7. Tax to Northern Rhodesian Government	232,700
		8. Surplus on operations in Northern Rhodesia	282,200
3. Total revenue	£1,654,200	9. Total expenditure	£1,654,200

Table 119 shows one way of presenting the accounts for the Northern Rhodesian section of the line. It does not, however, throw much light on the contribution of the Northern Rhodesian nationals to the net output of the railways, since working expenditure contains much in the way of purchased materials and services, particularly purchased materials and services which were imported from abroad. Table 120 breaks down part of the account in more detail to show the incomes actually generated in the colony by the railway.

TABLE 120. Output of the railways, 1945

	£	£
1. Salaries, wages, rations, etc.:		
(a) European	479,900	
(b) African	87,800	
2. Total net output railways in Northern Rhodesia		567,700
3. Expenditure on locally produced materials		93,000
4. Tax to Northern Rhodesian Government		232,700
5. Total gross output railways in Northern Rhodesia		£893,400

The largest road transport company in the territory answered a questionnaire for me on their operations in the year ended March 1946, and other details of road transport operations were obtained from the Road Board at Lusaka and by collecting information at District Offices that I visited. The Workmen's Compensation Commissioner gave salary and wage statistics. The resulting estimates were rough, but probably of the right order of magnitude. It was estimated that the gross output of the road transport concerns amounted to about £150,000, of which about a third was attributable to passenger traffic and the remainder to goods traffic, including mails. Most of the passenger traffic consisted of Africans and a substantial proportion was accounted for by migrant labourers. The net output of road transport was estimated to amount to about £55,000, including wages, salaries, profits and other direct income items.

It was impossible to make any satisfactory estimate for the number or earnings of Africans engaged as porters, or in carrying goods by barge or canoe, but it is likely that a token figure of £10,000 represents an upper limit. Thus Table 121 gives the estimates for the net incomes received from transport in 1945. Total expenditure on transport was estimated to be in the region of £1,815,000, of which about £225,000 represented passenger expenditure, and the bulk of the remainder would be costs of transporting mineral exports.

TABLE 121. Net output of transport, 1945

	£
1. Railways	567,700
2. Road transport	55,000
3. Other private or commercial transport	10,000
4. Total net output of transport	£632,700

15. OUTPUT OF GOVERNMENT SERVICES

The value of local authority output of government services consists of the wages, salaries, etc., paid to individuals in the service of the local authorities and of profits from trading services and incomes from property. In the case of the Native Treasuries, information was obtainable from the Accountant-General's Department. Information on wages and salaries earned in local government (other than Native Treasury) service was available from the Workmen's Compensation Commissioner for the period to end of February

1946 and could also be calculated from the local authority accounts. The two totals tallied closely, being within 7% of one another even before allowance had been made for the fact that some accounts were 1944 accounts and under-estimated the 1945 position. The final estimate for this quantity had a margin of error of about 4%. The profits from trading services were taken to be the surplus on operations of the electricity and water departments and the native beer-halls and canteens. Abattoirs and housing locations were not treated as trading services, since they were rarely undertaken on an economic basis. Table 122 shows the estimated value of output by local government.

TABLE 122.   Output of local government service

	£	£
1. Wages, salaries, etc.:		
(a) Management Board and munici-palities	86,000	
(b) Native authorities	55,000	
(c) Total incomes of individuals		141,000
2. Profits from trading services:		
(a) Beer-halls and canteens	23,500	
(b) Electricity and water	4,200	
(c) Total profits from trading services		27,700
3. Total value local authority output		£168,700

The Central Government's operations could be deduced from the financial report, although some degree of estimate was necessary, for example where expenditure on labour was not included under personal emoluments or labour votes, but as part of a block item such as 'maintenance'. Table 123 details the constituents of Central Government output.

TABLE 123.   Output of Central Government

	£	£
1. Personal emoluments	721,300	
2. African staff rations and uniforms	51,700	
3. House allowances, war bonuses, etc.	97,100	
4. Labour not under personal emoluments, including military	277,200	
5. Miscellaneous other income payments to individuals, and African housing	25,400	
6. Total value income payments to individuals		1,172,700
7. Interest	104,100	
8. Rent	14,500	
9. Total value income from property		118,600
10. Profits from trading services		39,000
11. Total value net Central Government output		1,330,300
12. Income from abroad		16,600
13. Miscellaneous fees and receipts from sales		128,600
14. Total value gross Central Government services		£1,475,500

In sum, therefore, if we include all these items the total value of government services was in the region of £1,645,000.

16. OUTPUT OF FORESTRY

Information was available on the gross value of output of the Zambesi Sawmills and on wages and salaries paid in forestry and woodworking. Other information was obtained from the Forestry Department and from the annual report of the Customs Department, which gives some details on the firms engaged in wood manufacture. The data were not sufficient to cover the whole industry accurately, but were satisfactory for certain large sections of it.

It was calculated that the gross selling value of output of timber cut under licence was in the region of £350,000. To this must be added about £65,000 for the value of poles and firewood sold, giving a total gross value for commercial forestry of £415,000. The net value of this output was estimated to be about £300,000 with a margin of error of about 20%. The value of exports f.o.r. were £156,100, so that the colony consumed commercial wood to the value of about £258,000, of which it is estimated that about £200,000 was consumed by the mining or the railway companies. Thus non-commercial consumption probably did not exceed £50,000 (wholesale value).

In addition, of course, large quantities of timber were consumed in the rural areas for firewood or building purposes. No reliable estimate could be made of this output, but its order of magnitude could be established by assuming that each family consumed on an average a load of firewood every three days and about twenty poles a year for hut-building purposes. This gave an estimated total value for subsistence consumption of timber of about £600,000 worth of firewood and £40,000 worth of poles. On these assumptions, and allowing for all the other uses to which wood is put in the villages, the total subsistence output of wood products cannot be less than about £700,000.

17. OUTPUT OF MANUFACTURE

The sources for an estimate of the output of manufacture were incomplete. There was information on output collected in the course of a partial census of factory operations, and there was information on the operations of particular concerns collected directly by myself from the owners of factories. The Customs Department collects and publishes output information concerning most Northern Rhodesian factories in its annual report. The Workmen's Compensation Commissioner could give figures for earnings in manufacture. A combination of the material from all these sources provided the basis for the following estimates of manufacturing output.

The chief weakness in the above estimates derives from the fact that the information was rarely adequate on the cost structure of the industry and estimates of the value of materials and purchased services involved were often very uncertain. Nevertheless, it is believed that these estimates are

TABLE 124. Value of manufacturing output, 1945

	Value of gross output £	Value of net output £
Food, drink and tobacco	200,000	80,000
Textiles, leather, rubber	25,000	10,000
Paper, printing, etc.	11,000	7,000
Metal and engineering	150,000	75,000
Chemicals, soap and other	233,000	100,000
	£619,000	£272,000

within about 20%–25% of the truth. Later consideration of these estimates in relation to the total evidence of other estimates suggested a degree of underestimate, and it was eventually concluded that the net value of manufacturing output was nearer £300,000, and the gross value in excess of £680,000.

18. OUTPUT OF BUILDING

Information was obtained from the Public Works Department and from the Chief Inspector of Mines on the value of building contracts fulfilled for government and the mining companies respectively in 1945. This amounted in all to £247,300. My questionnaire to building companies covered something in the region of a third of the industry's output and provided information on wages and output. The Workmen's Compensation statistics gave reliable data on incomes earned by those employed by the industry and the Customs Department's annual trade returns gave some data on imported materials. Other information on the cost structure of the industry was obtained in direct evidence from owners of building concerns and numbers employed had already been estimated for the income column.

A combination of these sources suggested that the gross value of the output of the building industry fell between £300,000 and £400,000. Wages, etc., earned in the industry were about £78,000. By deducting estimates of the materials used, the conclusion was reached that the net output of building was about £125,000. Later evidence suggested that the total net output was about £150,000 with a margin of error of about 15%.

19. OUTPUT OF MISSIONS

The chief difficulty in the way of making a money assessment of the output of missions is that many of them are not centrally controlled or administered. Twenty-two denominations were in receipt of government grant in 1945, but of these there were several which belonged to a group of partly or wholly autonomous stations. In terms of the value of government educational grant the fourth in importance was the Christian Mission in Many Lands which, to quote from a letter received from one of them, is

. . . not, in fact, a missionary society at all. We are a company of individuals, each independent, very really so, both in regard to control and finance. We have no central organization and no central fund on which one could check up. I do not know what income or expenditure any one of my colleagues, even on this station, has. . . . This is a point of honour with us and no one ever enquires about it.

There were thirteen stations in this group which acknowledge no head and whose members may be maintained partly from their personal sources abroad, partly from charitable organizations, and partly from sale of produce. In addition, of course, many denominations, of which the most important are the Roman Catholic orders, maintain all their members but do not pay cash incomes as such.

A questionnaire sent out to the different missions brought returns covering probably about two-thirds of the output, although less than 60% were complete enough to permit a reliable estimate of each mission's total output. Estimates were made for the remainder on the basis of their educational activities, which could be assessed from the African Educational Department's report, and on the assumption that educational activities were an index of total activities.

It was estimated that the total value of expenditure plus subsistence consumption of the missions in 1945 was in the region of £275,000. Of this, about £140,000 was derived from abroad, and about £100,000 from government grant. The remainder came from local contributions or sales or subsistence produce. Table 125 shows an income and expenditure account for the missions which has a margin of error in the totals of about 20%. Of the individual items, 2 is near accurate, while 3 and 4 have a margin of error of between 50% and 100%. Item 7 is residual and items 1 and 6 have margins of error of under 20%. The net output of the missions can be regarded as equivalent to the salaries, wages and rations and other income in kind received by their members, i.e. at about £188,000. The estimates are given to the nearest £1,000.

TABLE 125.   Income and expenditure of missions

Income from:	£	Expenditure on:	£
1. Abroad	140,000	6. Salaries, wages, rations and	
2. Government	100,000	all income in kind (including	
3. Subsistence output	28,000	subsistence consumption)	188,000
4. Local contributions and sales	7,000	7. Other expenditure	87,000
5. Total incomes	£275,000	8. Total expenditure	£275,000

20. OUTPUT OF MISCELLANEOUS SERVICES

Finally, there is a group of miscellaneous services, most of which are rendered to the European section of the community and to the railway-line settlements in particular. Banking is carried on by two banks—the Standard Bank of South Africa and Barclays Bank—which have branches in each of the principal line of rail townships and in some other settlements. A large number of insurance companies do business in the territory and some of them answered a questionnaire relating to premiums paid from Northern Rhodesia and expenses incurred in the territory. It was not possible to be at all confident, however, of the relative importance of the business done by the concerns who did not reply, and the estimates under this heading are very approximate. For both banking and insurance companies the value of wages earned (under £950 per annum) were obtainable from Workmen's Compensation Statistics for the year ended February 1946. These did not, however, throw light on commissions earned by insurance agents, and these had to be estimated very roughly indeed.

Professional incomes consist mainly of those incomes earned by doctors and dentists not in government or mission service. These were estimated partly on the basis of the numbers concerned and the estimated average wage supplemented by Workmen's Compensation Statistics of wages paid by professional persons, and partly on the basis of assessed incomes for the year 1944-5, which was the last year for which the figures for professional earnings had been distinguished.

Incomes of employed persons engaged in the provision of services connected with hotels, boarding houses, clubs, entertainment, etc., were derived from Workmen's Compensation sources. For hotels it was possible to make an estimate of gross output on the basis of the returns received to a questionnaire. The returns were not sufficient to give a reliable basis for estimating profits and the estimates in this connection are again very rough. The incomes of domestic servants (excluding those employed by hotels, boarding houses, clubs, etc.) were estimated for the income column and have been carried over from there into Table 126. The figure for other services consists largely of such items as earnings in labour recruiting and must be regarded as a token figure, since it is possible that there are other services which have not been taken into account. Table 126, which summarizes these estimates, has a margin of error of about 20%. Personal services, which would be included as part of distribution as estimated above, have been excluded.

TABLE 126. Output of miscellaneous services

	Value of net output £
1. Financial:	
(a) Banking	100,000
(b) Insurance and other	83,000
2. Professional	70,000
3. Personal:	
(a) Hotels and boarding houses	64,000
(b) Clubs, entertainment, sport	59,000
(c) Cleaners, laundries, etc.	6,000
(d) Domestic servants	305,000
4. Other	15,000
5. Total output of services	£702,000

21. IMPORTS INTO NORTHERN RHODESIA

There are no retail sales statistics as such for Northern Rhodesia, but since all but a very small proportion of the manufactured or processed goods sold in the colony are imported it is possible to assess the volume of an important section of the internal trade by using the import statistics. Unfortunately, the external trade statistics of the colony are collected and presented in such a way that a substantial degree of estimate must be introduced in order to convert them to a form in which they have any local significance at all for national income and outlay purposes.

Imports into Northern Rhodesia are valued for statistical purposes at their f.o.b. price in the country of origin, except in the case of goods breaking bulk in Southern Africa, which are valued f.o.r. at place of despatch in Southern Rhodesia or the Union. For customs purposes, duty is charged on all goods at the actual or estimated f.o.b. value in country of origin, which means that for goods which have broken bulk, a percentage deduction is made from f.o.r. value by the customs authorities in order to arrive at an estimate of the chargeable or f.o.b. value.

This method of presentation makes it extraordinarily difficult and complicated to arrive at any firm figure for the value of goods on arrival in the colony and after levy of customs duties. It is first of all necessary to calculate, for each item, the value of shipping, handling, insurance and railage charges for the proportion which is imported direct from country of origin: and also the value of insurance and railage charges on goods which have broken bulk and are therefore valued at an unspecified station of despatch in the Union or Southern Rhodesia. It is then necessary to calculate the duty levied on each item by applying the customs tariff to the published value in the case of goods imported direct, and to the published value less the relevant percentage in the case of goods which have broken bulk. The Customs Department publishes figures of duty charged on the principal imports and was able to give me a list of the percentage deductions used to arrive at chargeable value of imports which have broken bulk. The calculation of shipping and railage charges is further complicated by the fact that freight rates are generally charged according to weight, and not all imports are described by weight, while for a number of categories quantities are not even shown in the published lists.

The estimates of landed cost which are given in the second column of Table 127 are the result of long chains of calculations in which the links are frequently averages and estimated averages. They are thus very much less accurate than one might reasonably expect for import statistics. They are primarily based on a systematic application of railway rates to all items for which quantities were available, after converting volume and other quantities to weight on the basis of conversion factors given in or extracted from the *Annual Statement of the Trade of the United Kingdom*, 1944. Estimated percentages were applied to items for which quantities were not given and to cover shipping and insurance charges. These percentages were arrived at partly on the basis of detailed data extracted from the Stores and Transport

Department's records showing the various charges incurred by government imports in 1945, and partly on the basis of specific information on particular commodities, or groups of commodities, gathered from a variety of sources. For example, the Price Controller supplied figures of value margins for piece goods and blankets.

The margin of error in the total for landed cost and in the more important constituent items was probably less than 10%, with a greater probability of underestimate than of overestimate, since the disorganized nature of war-time transport of freight made it difficult to estimate the actual expense of movement on the basis of standard charges per lb. The estimates made of duties levied on the main classes of goods were more satisfactory. The total was approximately correct, while reliable details were available for items which accounted for about 75% of the total. The results for each class of imports are thus fairly firm in respect of the more important categories.

TABLE 127. Imports into Northern Rhodesia, 1945, valued at entry

		F.o.b. or f.o.r. value (i.e. published value) £	Estimated landed cost £	Duty as percentage of landed cost %	Estimated landed value inclusive of duty £
Class I.	Food	820,744	986,000	5	1,036,000
Class II.	Drink	233,840	273,000	49	407,000
Class III.	Tobacco	185,595	200,000	49	298,000
Class IV.	Textiles	1,434,760	1,740,000	11	1,923,000
Class V.	Machinery and metals	2,191,674	3,164,000	2	3,229,000
Class VI.	Minerals, etc.	485,326	782,000	3	802,000
Class VII.	Oils, waxes, paints	315,550	518,000	13	584,000
Class VIII.	Drugs and chemicals	205,070	242,000	5	254,000
Class IX.	Leather and rubber and manufactures	234,440	260,000	7	277,000
Class X.	Wood and wood manu-factures	97,786	161,000	2	165,000
Class XI.	Books, paper, stationery	100,388	114,000	1	115,000
Class XII.	Jewellery, clocks, sport	49,397	55,000	5	58,000
Class XIII.	Miscellaneous	564,714	710,000	7	757,000
All classes		£6,919,284	£9,205,000	8	£9,905,000

The goods imported into the colony consist in part of producers' goods destined for industrial consumption and in part of consumers' goods destined for personal consumption. Producers' goods may be divided into two main categories for national income purposes. They may be paid for in the current working costs of the industry concerned and they then figure in current output as part of the value of goods and services produced: or they may be included in the industry's capital expenditure, when they figure in its accounts as investments. Imports for industrial consumption are not entered separately in a national outlay account except in so far as an analysis of investment expenditure distinguishes imports on capital account. Goods imported for personal consumption will, for the most part, be retailed to the final consumers at a price which includes costs of transport and distribution within the territory.

It is possible by a process of inspection of the import list to distinguish a number of important items of which all but a negligible proportion is intended for industrial consumption. If there is any personal consumption of blasting compounds, or of certain types of machinery, for example, it can safely be ignored. Similarly, most categories of food, drink, tobacco and clothing flow straight into the channels of process and distribution for final consumption. The majority of imports can be allocated to one category or the other without significant error. For the remainder it is possible to estimate the proportions going to industrial or personal consumption on the basis of information concerning the consumption habits of the people and the needs of the more important industries. Such estimates are less uncertain than might otherwise be the case in a field for which there is so little reliable statistical material, because the range of imports which Africans consume to a significant extent is so limited and, further, because the pattern of European consumption is so homogeneous and fixed: this means that orders of magnitude in the realm of personal consumption of most important imports can be reliably estimated even where the data for accurate estimate is lacking. There remains, however, a category of imports covering such items as motor spirit, where the line between personal and industrial consumption cannot be drawn with any conviction on the basis of the scanty available data and where the estimated proportions are subject to a very considerable margin of error.

In order to use import data in combination with family budget data as a means of calculating personal consumption for the colony, it is necessary to go yet a further stage in analysing imports. Europeans, Asians and Africans live at three widely different levels and enjoy three widely different patterns of consumption. If family budget data is made the basis of estimates of personal consumption for the colony as a whole, it is necessary to have one set of budget data for each community, since the consumption habits of one group are no direct indication whatever of the consumption habits of the other two. In effect, it is convenient to think in terms of three categories of personal consumption, since aggregate personal consumption figures for the colony have only a limited meaning.

Here again, it is possible to go part of the way in analysing imports without other specific quantitative data as a guide. The imports of some of the more expensive groceries, for example, can safely be attributed to Europeans without significant error, while the Asian population probably absorbs the bulk of the ghee imported. African consumption of petrol, on the other hand, although it exists, was probably negligible in 1945. However, for most imports of consumption goods it is necessary to make some estimate of the volume consumed by each community on the basis of quantitative data on consumption habits. These data were gathered from a variety of sources, being most complete for the European population in relation to which a number of investigations into cost of living had been made during the war years. There was very little quantitative information on Asian standards of living, but the small size of the population concerned made the resultant error, though intrinsically large, unimportant in the national context. Information was least satisfactory for the African population, for although there were considerable quantities of data of one kind and another, they rarely covered a large enough or a representative enough section of the community to be useful for purposes of generalization. Thus the estimates for the African share of imported consumption goods entering into the budgets of all communities were largely residual after making allowance for European and Asian consumption.

The results of the analysis of imports are given in Table 128. The retail values are based on controlled price wherever prices were controlled and unless the black-market price was known to be general (as, for example, in the case of fish). Hence they are more likely to underestimate than to overestimate the value of consumption.

TABLE 128. Analysis of imports by destination

		Industrial consumption (landed cost including duty)	Retail value of personal consumption by: Europeans	Asian.	Africans
		£	£	£	£
Class I.	Food and pastoral products	48,300	911,000	34,000	545,000
Class II.	Drink	—	490,000	—	—
Class III.	Tobacco	—	420,000	—	7,000
Class IV.	Textiles	52,800	275,000	10,000	2,858,600
Class V.	Metals and manufactures	2,990,200	197,000	10,000	175,000
Class VI.	Minerals, earthenware, cement	784,000	19,000	1,000	—
Class VII.	Oils, waxes, paints	344,000	189,800	10,000	160,200
Class VIII.	Drugs and chemicals	190,000	85,000	1,000	10,000
Class IX.	Leather and rubber	94,200	165,000	2,500	107,500
Class X.	Wood	99,000	86,600	13,700	5,300
Class XI.	Books and paper	40,200	111,000	—	1,200
Class XII.	Jewellery and sport	—	87,000	200	5,600
Class XIII.	Miscellaneous	643,500	45,400	18,100	118,100
		£5,286,200	£3,081,800	£100,500	£3,993,500

It might be noted that an analysis of duty made at the same time as the analysis of destination of imports showed that the duty paid on industrial imports amounted to about 20% of total duty paid, on imports for European consumption about 47%, on imports for African consumption about 32%, and on imports for Indian consumption to about 1%.

22. EUROPEAN PERSONAL CONSUMPTION

Although the high concentration of expenditure on imports makes it possible to rely on the colony's trade statistics as a guide to consumption on many items for Europeans, the fact that they have such strong roots abroad makes it doubly difficult to trace certain other channels of expenditure. Most South Africans aim to spend a couple of months in the Union every two years. United Kingdom immigrants go home less often, probably no oftener than once every three years for the most part, but they tend to stay longer, from three to six months. In both cases a large proportion of the shopping for clothes and other normal equipment, such as household goods, tends to be saved up for the period of leave. In general, the European community is heavily insured, since there is no social security, employment and trade prospects are dependent on copper, which is very vulnerable to world market fluctuations, and tropical diseases are a factor to be taken into account in most areas: insurance has to be taken out with foreign companies. In addition, educational facilities of secondary school standard and above have to be sought abroad, as also does specialist medical advice. Many people hold bank balances outside the colony, and many support or assist dependants abroad. Since these transactions take place in another country there is no way of including them in market data collected in Northern Rhodesia. In effect, therefore, family budget data are an essential basis for any estimate of European personal consumption.

In the estimates which follow in Table 129, European personal consumption has been estimated partly on the basis of import figures, partly on the basis of a family budget and cost-of-living survey carried out by Mr J. R. H. Shaul in 1940, and partly on the 1945 cost-of-living standard budgets compiled monthly by the four copper-mining companies to illustrate the basis of their cost-of-living allowances. In addition to these general sources of information there were a number of specific sources for particular items. For example, the Income Tax Commissioner was able to supply data on insurance payments made by the assessed population and also on the numbers of dependants maintained abroad by assessed persons, while I myself collected information from a number of individual and institutional sources on family budgets in general and on particular kinds of expenditure, such as holidays abroad or education of children.

TABLE 129. European personal consumption [1]

Expenditure on:	£
1. Food	1,101,000
2. Drink	490,000
3. Tobacco	420,000
4. Clothing and footwear	350,000
5. Fuel, light, rent, etc.	320,000
6. Servants	328,000
7. Household expenses	170,000
8. Medical, etc., services	123,000
9. Donations and subscriptions	62,000
10. Books, stationery, etc.	47,000
11. Other locally purchased goods and services	259,000
12. Total local expenditure	3,670,000
13. Insurance	198,000
14. Education	200,000
15. Dependants abroad	175,000
16. Holidays, leave, pension, gratuities	874,000
17. Total expenditure abroad by Europeans	1,447,000
18. Total value European personal consumption	£5,117,000

[1] For notes on the table see next page.

U

Notes on Table 129

1. Food expenditure was estimated on the basis of the data collected by Mr Shau and on the schedules of expenditure drawn up by the mining companies. Imports of foodstuffs were estimated to have a retail value of about £909,000, so that the expenditure on locally produced foods was estimated residually to be about £192,000. On the whole it seems more likely that expenditure on foodstuffs is underestimated here than that it is overestimated.

2–4. Expenditure on drink and tobacco was deduced from the import figures and is probably fairly reliable as European consumption accounts for almost the whole of these imports. Expenditure on clothing and footwear was also deduced from the import figures but involved also certain estimates based on family budget data to distinguish non-European consumption. As a reflection of total expenditure on clothing this is probably low since a significant proportion of the expenditure made while abroad is clothing expenditure.

5. Expenditure on fuel, light, water, rent and rates was partly deduced from family budget data and partly also from specific sources of data such as the local government accounts which gave revenue from electricity, water and rates.

6. Expenditure on servants was calculated on the basis of family budget data amended by the results of my own enquiries into this type of expenditure.

7–11. Expenditure on household equipment, doctors, dentists, opticians, club and trade union and other subscriptions, donations, books, stationery, transport and other miscellaneous goods and services, which are included in items 7, 8, 9 and 10 of Table 129, was estimated from a variety of sources of which the most important were the import returns and family budget data.

13. Expenditure on insurance was estimated on the basis of details of insurance paid by the assessed population in 1943, the relevant information being obtained from the Income Tax Department.

14–15. The Income Tax Department was able to give numbers of children and other dependants of assessed persons abroad in 1943. I collected data on the cost of educating children and maintaining dependants from a variety of individuals and organizations and used these data to calculate averages.

16. The item for holidays, leave pay, pensions, gratuities, and similar expenditure abroad includes a sum of about £215,000 which went to pension and gratuity recipients, the vast majority of whom were not resident. It is a composite item which includes expenditure on food, clothing and household equipment as well as entertainment, transport, etc. The estimate was made on the basis of information contained in mining company reports, the Civil Service staff list and material collected from individual Europeans in the colony. It may include outlay on saving as well as outlay on personal consumption.

23. ASIAN PERSONAL CONSUMPTION

There is very little information of any kind which would enable an estimate to be made of expenditure by the Indian community. The vast majority of the Indians are traders. Some of them live at a comfortable level, but there are others who live at a very low standard either because they are paid low wages or because they are saving to set up a business. The following table represents a very rough attempt to indicate the probable orders of magnitude involved.

TABLE 130. Asian personal consumption. Rough estimate

Expenditure on:	£
1. Food	40,000
2. Clothing	10,000
3. Other imports	50,000
4. Other local goods and services	20,000
	£120,000

24. AFRICAN CONSUMPTION OF TRADED GOODS AND SERVICES

There are no general statistics of the African retail trade except those which can be estimated from the import trade statistics and some miscellaneous data on particular items. For example, the value of beer sold by officially recognized beer-halls was obtained from the accounts of these institutions, but this figure was no guide to illicit beer sales in the locations or to the amount of beer sold in the villages. Hence the main basis for an estimate of African consumption had to be family budget data or similar material, such as the details of employers' expenditure on rations which were obtainable from the Chamber of Mines and other sources.

Unfortunately the budget data available were inadequate to form the basis of reliable estimates. Very few studies of African family expenditure have been made in Northern Rhodesia, and those that have been made cover such small groups that no safe generalizations could be made from them. Moreover, prices and wages have changed so much over the past six or seven years that only 1945 enquiries could reasonably be expected to throw much light on 1945 patterns of expenditure. The difficulty of using existing data on small samples would be less if more general information were available on the population as a whole. It is possible to think of all sorts of a priori reasons why any one group of households for which budgets have been collected is a-typical, but since there have been no systematic and reliable collections, covering the population as a whole, it is impossible to make even the crudest type of allowance for most of the distortions which might be expected in an a-typical sample. The main difficulty, of course, whether one is interpreting or generalizing family budget data, is the complete lack of even the most elementary population statistics.

Since the pattern of a family's expenditure on traded goods and services depends largely on its access to subsistence output, the African community falls into two main groups for family budget purposes. There is the urban population which depends for its livelihood on sale of its services and the rural population which depends for its livelihood on its subsistence production. The personal consumption of the first group consists almost entirely of traded goods and services. The second group produces for itself most of its consumption of goods and services of local origin and spends its cash resources largely on imported goods.

The two groups overlap, of course. On the one hand, it should be remembered that there is a constant movement of population between them: an

African resident in the location this year may be resident in the village next year, and vice versa. On the other hand, the location dwellers may have their own food-producing gardens or their own chickens, while some of the villagers concentrate most of their energies on producing goods for sale and there is a significant local trade in articles of local produce.

For budget purposes the population was divided into three classes. First of all there were the dwellers in the urban locations who purchased (or received as wages) the greater part of their personal consumption. Secondly, there were the employed men not resident in the locations; these men often received rations and were generally as dependent on cash purchases as the location dwellers, with the difference that their families were often self-supporting and the cost to them of local produce was accordingly lower. Thirdly, there were the villagers proper, including the families of many men who were resident in the locations or otherwise employed at home or in other parts of the colony. Thus these three groups included about 135,000 persons resident in the locations of which 64,000 were men, about 77,000 employed men living outside the locations, and some 396,000 female households available in the villages.

There was very little information available on family expenditure in urban areas. Godfrey Wilson's budgets collected in Broken Hill in January 1940 were a valuable guide to the general pattern of urban expenditure, but it was impossible to say just how a-typical was the Broken Hill population and, more important still, the steep rise in prices since January 1940 made it difficult to interpret these budgets in terms of 1945 conditions. The two most important items in the urban budget, however, are food and clothing. For food (including beer) a set of budgets covering 279 households was collected in two Lusaka locations early in 1947 by the Nutrition Officer. For clothing, the import figures provided a useful check. In addition there were a number of very small-scale and unsystematic collections of budget data made in connection with cost-of-living statements and memoranda during the years 1942–6: of these the most useful were those which emanated from the Labour Department.

For the rural areas the budget data were just as inadequate and probably even less suitable for generalization. The chief difficulty was that only a small proportion of the many Northern Rhodesian tribes were touched at all by such data, and even where there was information for a particular tribe or district the number of households covered was so small and the method of selection generally so unsatisfactory that any kind of generalization, however small the scale, was necessarily suspect. A general account of the available budget data for rural areas is given in Part IV and Appendix III, and it is on a combination of these data that the rural expenditure estimates were based.

Table 131 gives estimates of the African consumption of traded goods and services in 1945. In making these estimates, urban expenditure was largely calculated on a per-head basis from the relevant budget data. The expenditure of the 77,000 men employed but not resident in locations was estimated as though their pattern of expenditure could be regarded as similar to the pattern of expenditure of single men in urban locations, though generally of a lower level. The expenditure of the remainder of the population was calculated on a per-household basis as a function of the number of adult women estimated to be available in the villages. This grouping was convenient and probably roughly reliable, but it was certainly not watertight. Given the crudeness of this method of handling, the inadequacy of the budget data, and the margins of error in the basic population statistics, it will be obvious that the following estimates of African consumption are highly tentative and can be relied upon to offer only the broadest indications of actual expenditure.

TABLE 131. African consumption of traded goods and services

	Urban and employed population £	Rural population £	Total population £
1. Meal	495,000	5,000	500,000
2. Meat	292,000	8,000	300,000
3. Fish	125,000	15,000	140,000
4. Groundnuts	32,000	3,000	35,000
5. Beans	66,000	2,000	68,000
6. Fruit and vegetables	135,000	1,000	136,000
7. Sugar and tea	50,000	—	50,000
8. Salt	31,000	46,000	77,000
9. Bread	118,000	2,000	120,000
10. Beer	179,000	21,000	200,000
11. Other food	76,000	4,000	80,000
12. Total foodstuffs	1,599,000	107,000	1,706,000
13. Clothing	950,000	1,584,000	2,534,000
14. Tobacco	36,000	3,000	39,000
15. Household and productive equipment	96,000	317,000	413,000
16. Fuel and light	54,000	—	54,000
17. Rent	82,000	—	82,000
18. Livestock	—	158,000	158,000
19. Gifts, damages and other transfer payments	32,000	99,000	131,000
20. Other	224,000	792,000	1,016,000
21. Total personal consumption of traded goods and services	£3,073,000	£3,060,000	£6,133,000

Notes on Table 131

1. The estimate for urban and employed consumption of meal is probably fairly reliable since much of this consumption of meal is accounted for by rations about which the information is more satisfactory here than for any other item of African consumption, and since in any case there is not a great deal of variation as between one individual and another. The estimate of £5,000 for the rural population's meal purchases is, however, little more than a guess and the actual internal trade in meal amongst the villages may be more than double this. It might vary a good deal from year to year according to the harvest.

2. There were considerable discrepancies in the estimates for this item from the different sets of family budget data. Expenditure on meat shows a high income

elasticity among Africans and purchases are too irregular to be satisfactorily reported unless the family budget data is collected on a week by week basis over a period of several months. It seems probable, however, that total expenditure on meat falls between £250,000 and £400,000 with a bias towards the lower figure.

3. It is extremely difficult to make any kind of estimate of rural purchase of fish, which is probably considerable in certain seasons and in certain areas. Urban expenditure, however, is probably between £80,000 and £100,000.

4, 5, and 6. These items are largely calculated from family budget data for Lusaka and the Copperbelt and from ration data. To some extent they tend to be substitutes for each other and the total is probably more sound than the breakdown. Here as elsewhere in this table, the rural expenditure can only be guessed at and no attempt has been made to calculate rural barter trade for this kind of produce.

7. It was assumed that expenditure on sugar, jam, tea and similar items by the rural population, other than employed men in rural areas, was negligible in 1945. This assumption was based on budget enquiries in general, and superficial observation in 1946–7, but there may be some areas where consumption was not negligible. The estimates are derived from a combination of family budget and import data.

8. Consumption of salt is probably a fairly constant item per household but expenditure on salt is difficult to estimate by generalizing from small-scale budget enquiries since this is an item which is frequently 'begged'. The estimates given here are based on a combination of family budget and import data.

9. Expenditure on bread was estimated on the basis of a combination of ration data and family budget and import data. Nevertheless the ration data probably over-estimated the actual amount of bread supplied by employers if current consumption of bread bore any relation to current imports of flour.

10. About £100,000 was spent on beer through the recognized beer-halls in 1945. In addition it was estimated that about £17,000 was spent by the urban population on illicit beer brewed in the urban compounds or in adjacent rural areas. Expenditure by employed men in the rural areas was estimated at £62,000 and may be high but this is one of the principal channels of expenditure of wages in the villages. These estimates were based on family budget data.

11. Other foodstuffs include saladine, groundnut oil, fats and miscellaneous relishes (e.g. caterpillars). The item has been estimated on the basis of family budget and ration data and is more likely to be an understatement than an overstatement.

12. The total for foodstuffs probably has a margin of error of about 10%, being highest in respect of the expenditure of the rural population. Except in the case of a few items, such as meal, however, the breakdown is generally very much less reliable than the total. On the whole it seems unlikely that the value of consumption of traded food and beer fell much short of £1,700,000 or exceeded £1,800,000. On these estimates the average value of expenditure on food by (or for) the urban and employed population amounted to between £7.5 and £8 per head as compared with a figure of just over £8 reached from the Nutrition Officer's data on the Lusaka locations.

13. The estimates for expenditure on clothing (which includes blankets) were based in part on cost-of-living studies and the budgets basic to them, in part on imports and in part on other budget surveys. Estimates of minimum clothing *requirements* by Mr Lynn Saffery, and others by officials of the Labour Department, agreed fairly closely on an average expenditure in the region of £4.75 per head. Mr Godfrey Wilson's budget figures, adjusted upwards for price changes, suggested an actual average expenditure of about £4.5 per annum which was the figure taken as the average for expenditure by the urban and employed population on clothing. Budget

data on the rural population varied fairly widely but a combination of the available data with the results obtainable from import statistics suggested an average of about £4 per female household available in the villages. These estimates, which are fairly generous on the basis of available budget data, suggest that the estimates of the increase in the f.o.b. or f.o.r. value of textile imports as shown in Table 128 may be too high.

14. A note by Mr Trapnell, the Government Ecologist, provided the basis for this estimate of tobacco expenditure, but here again the estimate for rural expenditure (excluding employed persons) is little more than a guess and does not include barter trade.

15 and 16. Household and productive equipment was estimated from family budget data as also were the figures for fuel and light.

17. Rent was estimated from the data contained in the report of the commission to enquire into the finance of urban locations which reported in 1944. It represents cost of accommodation rather than actual rent paid since in most cases the housing on urban locations was let at an uneconomic rent. No cash rents are normally paid or payable in the villages.

18. Expenditure on livestock (as opposed to expenditure on livestock for meat) was estimated from family budget data. No entry has been made for expenditure on livestock by the urban or employed population but in fact much of the expenditure attributed to the rural population was made on behalf of the urban or employed population by their relatives in the villages.

19. Gifts, damages, and other transfer payments, are a common feature of the villager's budget but rarely enter into the urban resident's budget except as money or goods remitted to relatives. The employed man in the villages, however, probably spends at least as much as the normal village household on these items.

20. This item is derived from family budget data and includes all kinds of miscellaneous payments such as store goods not elsewhere included (e.g. soap), transport, medicines, education, books, stationery, etc. It may be overestimated for the rural population but is probably not too high for the town population.

25. PUBLIC FINANCE

In making the entries for government in the national accounts the object is to bring out as far as possible the nature of the relationship between the governmental and private sectors of the economy. Government's activities as a factor of production, for example, can usefully be distinguished from its activities as pure agency of the taxpayer, and when national income is measured at factor cost, as it is throughout this study, Government's activities as a purchasing agent for the taxpayer have to be specifically excluded from the final total. This means in practice that the value of indirect taxes should be included once only in the total national expenditure—either when they are spent by the private and commercial sectors of the economy or when they are spent by Government. Table 132 is an arrangement of the Central Government Accounts which is designed to bring out the features important for national income purposes. Tables 133 and 134 rearrange the local government accounts and Table 135 combines all three.

TABLE 132. Revenue and expenditure of Central Government, 1945

Revenue	£	Expenditure	£
1. Direct taxes and fines	2,109,700	8. Transfer incomes	29,900
2. Indirect taxes	786,500	9. Subsidies	135,600
3. Revenue from trading services	128,700	10. Expenditure financed from borrowing, disinvestment and reimbursements	144,800
4. Income from property and from sales of goods and services	247,200	11. Expenditure abroad	390,800
5. Income from abroad	16,600	12. Central Government grants to local government	116,300
6. Receipts from borrowing, disinvestment and reimbursements	144,800	13. Expenditure on trading services	89,700
		14. Net current expenditure on goods and services in Northern Rhodesia (including imports of merchandise)	1,542,500
		15. Net investment	983,900
7. Total government revenue	£3,433,500	16. Total government expenditure	£3,433,500

Notes on Table 132

Direct and indirect taxes. Direct and indirect taxes have been distinguished according to the criterion that direct taxes are those which are charged on income while indirect taxes enter into costs of production. Tax payments which are not deducted from current receipts as a cost before determining income are direct taxes: of these the income taxes and the native poll tax are the most important examples for Northern Rhodesia. Taxes which are deducted from current receipts from market sales before determining incomes are indirect taxes: of these the most important in Northern Rhodesia are customs duties. Stamp and licence duties may be either, according to the precise nature of the taxes. In practice, they were classified arbitrarily here as indirect taxes because not enough information was available to permit a precise analysis. Fines are treated as equivalent in effect to direct taxes.

Revenue from trading services. This item 3 includes the total receipts in respect of the Post and Telegraphs Department and the Lusaka Electricity and Water Undertaking.

Income from abroad. This item is largely composed of a share of the surplus on currency board receipts but includes also £1,000 in respect of Colonial Development and Welfare grant to the Social Welfare Department.

Reimbursements, etc. Item 6 contains revenue which is not genuine income for accounting purposes since it represents such monies as reimbursements for expenditure incurred for other organizations (e.g. expenditure on behalf of other governments in joint activities), and the realization of investments.

Transfer incomes. Various payments made to the needy and the sick.

Subsidies. The greater part of the expenditure incurred under this heading consisted of a subsidy to the Maize Control Board which enabled it to keep down the selling price of maize.

Expenditure abroad. This item includes expenditure on such matters as public debt, pensions and gratuities, maintenance of representatives abroad, scholarships held abroad, payment for services rendered by foreign bodies and individuals residing abroad, subventions to foreign institutions and travel abroad by government servants. It excludes a sum equivalent to the value of government stores imported from abroad and valued f.o.b. at £316,000.

Grants to Local Authorities. Grants to the value of £116,300 were made to local authorities of which £56,400 were granted to the Native Treasuries and consisted largely of their share of the Native Tax.

Net current expenditure. Item 14 is the residual item after analysing the government accounts to extract the other details in this column.

Net investment. This consists of expenditure on Public Works Extraordinary plus budget surplus.

TABLE 133. Revenue and expenditure of European Local Government, 1945

Revenue	£	Expenditure	£
1. Indirect taxes	12,000	6. Trading services	153,000
2. Revenue from trading		7. Other goods and services	75,000
services	191,000	8. Investment	30,000
3. Government grants	60,000	9. Budget surplus	30,000
4. Revenue from property and			
from other sales	25,000		
5. Total revenue	£288,000	10. Total expenditure	£288,000

Notes on Table 133

Table 133 was compiled from the accounts of the management boards and municipalities. The trading services concerned are the provision of beer-halls (which accounted for about 60% of the total revenue from trading services) for the African population, and the provision of electricity and water services for the European population. The provision of native housing was not regarded as a trading service since the huts were always let at an uneconomic rent. Abattoirs and sanitation were also treated as public services rather than as trading services. In these matters and in the decision on what should constitute investment expenditure the definitions adopted tended to be *ad hoc* and arbitrary. The greater part of the investment expenditure represented expenditure of the beer-hall profits on amenities for the African population. The municipalities which are European-elected bodies were two in number—Livingstone and Ndola. They accounted for 38% of the total revenue of local authorities. The four Copperbelt townships accounted for a further 39% between them and Lusaka and Broken Hill for 19%. The remaining 4% is attributable to the minor townships on the line of rail (Mazabuka, Kafue, Choma, Monze, Emmasdale, Pemba and Fort Jameson).

TABLE 134. Revenue and expenditure of the Native Treasuries, 1945[1]

Revenue	£	Expenditure	£
1. Government grant	56,000	4. Current expenditure	71,000
2. Other revenue		5. Investment expenditure	6,000
(licences, fines, etc.)	33,000	6. Budget surplus	12,000
3. Total revenue	£89,000	7. Total expenditure	£89,000

[1] For notes on the table see next page.

Notes on Table 134

There are forty-five Native Treasuries in all, of which thirty-one had a revenue of less than £2,000 in 1945 and only one, the Barotse Native Treasury, had a revenue of over £10,000. The smallest Native Treasury in 1945 was the Bwila Treasury of Mporokoso with a revenue of £243 and an expenditure of £191. Most of the Native Authority income comes from government grant which is largely a redistribution of the receipts from the native tax. Other revenue includes licences, fines, etc., obtained from the African population. They have been regarded as direct taxes because they were not generally included in costs of production when African incomes were being assessed or as part of African personal expenditure. Investment expenditure is equivalent to the expenditure listed in the summary Native Treasury Accounts as Extraordinary Expenditure.

TABLE 135. Combined net revenue and expenditure account for Central and Local Government, 1945

Revenue	£	Expenditure	£
1. Direct taxes and fines	2,143,000	7. Transfer incomes	30,000
2. Indirect taxes	799,000	8. Subsidies	136,000
3. Profit from trading	77,000	9. Expenditure abroad	391,000
4. Revenue from property and other sales	272,000	10. Expenditure on goods and services in Northern Rhodesia	1,689,000
5. Income from abroad	17,000	11. Investment	1,062,000
6. Total net revenue	£3,308,000	12. Total net expenditure	£3,308,000

Notes on Table 135

In constructing Table 135 disinvestment, reimbursements and expenditure on trading services have been excluded. The 'other revenue' of Native Treasuries has been treated as direct taxation, which for the most part it is, and Central Government grants have been eliminated from the income side of the local authority accounts in order to avoid double counting.

26. INVESTMENT

Investment expenditure and saving are always difficult items to calculate independently in national accounts and it is generally necessary to estimate them jointly as a residual item. Nevertheless, some estimates can be made of the more important items based on company and institutional financial accounts, questionnaires sent out to the commercial sector of the economy, savings bank data and family budget data. The information for the mines, railways and government is fairly reliable because financial accounts were available, but for other industries where estimates had to be based on questionnaires and the industrial imports, the estimates were necessarily very rough indeed. Generally speaking, it is to be expected that estimates based on questionnaires would overstate the case, since answers to questionnaires generally came from the larger, more progressive, institutions: on the other hand, there were probably many important omissions. The figures for savings by individuals are based on family budget and savings bank data and on what was known about saving and spending habits for the relevant communities.

TABLE 136. Investment and saving

Investment by:	£	£
1. Mines	1,234,000	
2. Government	1,062,000	
3. Agriculture	250,000	
4. Railways	50,000	
5. Other	400,000	
6. Total investment expenditure		2,996,000
Savings by individuals:		
7. Europeans	100,000	
8. Africans	311,000	
9. Asians	50,000	
10. Total saving by individuals		461,000
11. Total investment and saving		£3,457,000

It seems likely that the total in Table 136 approaches the upper limit for the value of saving and investment in 1945, but it seems unlikely that the total could fall below about £3,000,000.

27. BALANCE OF PAYMENTS

The Balance of Payments is, unfortunately, one of the most difficult of all tables to construct for Northern Rhodesia because of the practice of valuing imports and exports f.o.b. or f.o.r. at place of despatch. This means that estimates of border value have to be made by adding costs of transport.

TABLE 137. Territorial balance of payments, 1945[1]

Receipts from abroad		£000	Payments abroad		£000
1. Value at border of merchandise produced in Northern Rhodesia		12,285	8. Value at border of retained merchandise imports		9,000
2. Expenditure by tourists		40	9. Expenditure abroad:		
3. Income from abroad:			(a) Europeans	1,360	
(a) Migrant labour	595		(b) Africans	13	
(b) Missions	140		(c) Government	219	
(c) Government	17				1,592
(d) European property	50		10. Commercial remittances:		
		802	(a) Mining companies	3,629	
4. Capital items:			(b) Other	1,174	
(a) Expenditure by mining and railway companies	1,284				4,803
(b) Expenditure by other foreign companies	400		11. Investment abroad:		
			(a) Government	808	
			(b) Other	112	
		1,684	(c) Specie	71	
					991
5. Total accountable receipts		14,811			
6. Residual item (capital transfers)		1,575			
7. Total receipts from abroad		£16,386	12. Total payments abroad		£16,386

[1] For notes on the table see next page.

There is, furthermore, the additional problem of re-evaluating the most important group of Northern Rhodesian exports which are declared for export purposes at London market price less an estimated percentage for railage, insurance and realization charges. Since the declaration is made before either the actual realized price or the costs of transport and realization are known exactly, the adjustment is often considerable.

In Table 137 the mineral exports have been revalued on the basis of the relevant company reports and a small addition has been made for local transport costs incurred on other exports. Imports have been revalued on the lines described in earlier sections of this report by adding transport costs as far as the Northern Rhodesian border. For the purposes of this table it is assumed that the foreign companies operating in Northern Rhodesia are part of the Northern Rhodesian national economy. This will be referred to as the Territorial Nation in contradistinction to the Resident Nation, which excludes all foreigners except in so far as they are actually resident in the colony. Most of the items in Table 137 have already been calculated in the course of this and previous reports, but some adjustments have been made to the original estimates on the basis of later findings and to prevent overlap.

Notes on Table 137

1. *Exports.* The following lists show the effects by principal classes of re-valuing exports according to the company reports and after the addition of transport charges:

	F.o.b. or f.o.r. value (re-published value) £	Estimated border value £
1. Food	96,775	97,000
2. Tobacco	225,136	231,000
3. Metals and minerals	10,903,287	11,725,000
4. Oils, waxes, paints, etc.	36,417	37,000
5. Leather and rubber and textiles	29,335	30,000
6. Wood and other	163,986	165,000
	£11,454,936	£12,285,000

2. *Tourists.* The number of visitors to the colony was estimated from the Immigration Department's report but their average length of stay and expenditure, and also the number and expenditure of the day-trippers to Livingstone who escape examination by the Immigration Department had to be estimated on the basis of what was known from personal observation. The figure is thus very rough but probably indicates the order of magnitude involved fairly well.

3. *Income from abroad.* These items have been covered in other reports in the course of estimating national income, output and expenditure, and no revision has yet been found necessary in the estimates—with the exception of item 3 (d) which has not been adequately covered. In so far as the income of Europeans from foreign property is drawn in the colony and in so far as it is faithfully recorded for income-tax purposes

it has been covered already and the sum concerned is estimated to amount to about £20,000. Even if we assume, however, that all Europeans drawing income in the colony from property abroad have honestly returned it and that the tax assessments cover all this type of income, it is necessary to allow for the fact that some Europeans have property holdings abroad whose income they do not draw in the territory but which they are liable to draw upon abroad either to finance their own holidays or to help maintain dependants and other commitments abroad. Since European expenditure abroad has been included in the outgoing section of the accounts it is necessary to allow also for income received abroad even if not drawn in the colony. It was impossible to make a reasoned estimate of this item, however, and the figure of £30,000 is merely a token entry.

4. *Capital expenditure.* Capital expenditure by mining and railway companies was reliably calculated from company reports and from information obtained direct from the companies and their agents. Item 4 (*b*) is a much less reliable figure and is largely based on an estimated proportion of income.

6. *Residual item.* This residual should be considered in relation to item 10 since it is largely a matter of transfers of dividends, interest, balances, etc. between foreign companies and their foreign banks or shareholders. In effect, the net receipts of foreigners seem to have been in the region of £3,228,000.

8. *Imports.* This figure (which includes government stores) represents a revision of that calculated in the first section of this report since all later evidence pointed to the fact that there had been a degree of overestimate.

9. *Expenditure abroad.* The estimate relating to European expenditure abroad has also been revised downwards to give the present item 9 (*a*). Item 9 (*b*) is based on the assumption that alien African workers in Northern Rhodesia remitted at the same rate as Northern Rhodesian emigrant labourers. Item 9 (*c*) is adjusted so as to prevent any overlap between it and item 9 (*a*).

10. *Commercial remittances.* This consists largely of dividends, transfers to balances, etc., made by the foreign companies which do not in general either hold their balances or raise their capital in the colony. The figures for the mining and railway companies are fairly reliable but for other companies estimates based on estimated income had to be used together with information contained in the Taxation Review Committee's Report. These remittances are calculated to exclude tax paid to the Northern Rhodesian Government but include tax paid to foreign governments.

11. *Investment abroad.* This is largely accounted for by government operations but includes also estimates for the value of investment or savings sent abroad by Europeans and Asiatics.

In order to construct a Balance of Payments in a more usual form, however, it is necessary to treat foreign companies as if they were foreigners and confine the accounts to transactions between resident nationals and non-nationals. This involves radical changes in the content and form of the accounts shown in Table 137. Where a foreign company produces goods which it afterwards exports, all that can be regarded as Northern Rhodesian produce is the goods and services contributed to their production by Northern Rhodesian nationals. Similarly, imports purchased by foreign firms are treated as re-exports unless they enter into the value of goods and services which are actually retained and sold in the colony.

Transactions of the mineral companies, which export all their produce, do not enter into the residents' balance of payments for the colony except in so far as they buy goods and services in the country: their expenditure on imports is excluded in calculating retained imports. The railway company is in a half-way position. Those of its imports which provide a service for Northern Rhodesian residents are genuine retained imports: those which provide a service for the exporters of copper are re-exported.

Table 138 shows the results of re-drawing the accounts in Table 137 to exclude re-exports as thus defined.

TABLE 138. Balance of payments of the resident nation

Receipts from abroad		Payments abroad	
	£000		£000
1. Exports of Northern Rhodesian produce	410	8. Retained imports	4,815
2. Sale of goods and services to foreign companies	4,500	9. Expenditure abroad	1,592
3. Government receipts from taxation of foreign companies	1,620	10. Investment abroad	991
4. Income from abroad	789		
5. Tourists	40		
6. Residual	39		
7. Total receipts	£7,398	11. Total payments	£7,398

Notes on Table 138

1. *Exports.* These include only those exports which were produced by Northern Rhodesian concerns although they may have been assisted by foreign capital.

2. *Sale of goods and services.* The figures for the railway and mining companies could be estimated fairly reliably on the information contained in their reports or obtained directly from them. The estimates for the other companies were less reliable.

3. *Government receipts from taxation.* These were estimated from the material contained in Government reports, particularly the Financial Report and the Taxation Review Committee's report, together with information on particular industries obtained from the companies concerned.

4 and 5. *Income from abroad and tourists.* These items correspond to items 3 and 2 in Table 137.

6. *Total receipts.* No information was obtained on capital investment by foreigners in Northern Rhodesian concerns. This may account for the residual item but it is not large enough to be significant in view of the margins of error involved.

8. *Imports.* Figures for imports by the mining and railway companies could be obtained directly from the companies or their reports. Information on industrial imports in general could be deduced from an inspection of the import list. It was not possible to do more than guess at the value of imports received by other foreign companies, producing for export, but they were estimated to be worth not more than £50,000.

9. *Expenditure abroad.* This item corresponds with item 9 of Table 137.

10. *Investment abroad.* This item corresponds with item 11 of Table 137.

APPENDIX II

SOURCES OF THE ESTIMATES OF THE NATIONAL INCOME, OUTPUT AND EXPENDITURE OF NYASALAND, 1945

In this appendix the process of making the estimates of income, output and expenditure for Nyasaland is described in some detail. Should it prove necessary to compare the figures which follow with those given in Chapters VI–VIII, it should be remembered that the following are provisional estimates, many of which were revised when the total available evidence had been passed in review. The figures in Chapters VI–VIII are the final estimates.

I. POPULATION ESTIMATES

A Census of the African population of Nyasaland was taken in 1945. The count was at best a rough count, since it did not deal with individual Africans separately. Each village was treated as a separate entity and the count was undertaken by 167 African enumerators, each of whom had to visit on an average 72 villages and count approximately 12,250 persons. The time taken by the African Census was about four months. European field supervision was impossible, and not all the enumerators had the level of education and intelligence necessary to avoid major errors in their returns.

Clearly, therefore, the results do not attain a high standard of accuracy. Africans are highly mobile between villages. One man may have cattle, huts and gardens in each of two or more villages. Women, especially women living alone, often visit from one village to another, fitting into the economic rhythm of a new village for periods of days, weeks or months, before returning to their own village. Children are frequently boarded out with relatives for periods of years, even. Most of these people can be logically attached to one particular village if the enumerator has the time and patience to pursue the matter individual by individual. If the count is a count of heads made on a brief visit to the village and supplemented by discussion with the headman and other knowledgeable villagers, then there is considerable risk of errors of double counting and of omission.

It is probable that many of the errors of double counting and omission will cancel each other out, especially in the broader classifications of the census. For example, it is probable that the total provincial figures are accurate enough for all practical purposes. Nevertheless, without specimen counts, individual by individual, for randomly selected samples of the population of each major area, it is not possible to be certain that errors of double counting, for example, do not outweigh errors of omission, or vice versa, in this rapid village by village count. Nor can we observe whether the errors introduce a bias into the proportions of the various groups and what allowances should be made for such a bias. For example, it is possible that in a polygamous community men may be double counted more often and omitted from the record less frequently than women. On the other hand, the effect of attempts to evade tax may be to reduce the recorded number of those liable to pay tax (i.e. of adult males). Or again, it may be that in some areas children under five are omitted more frequently than children over five. Finally, we have to take into account the possible errors of the unskilled enumerator. It may be that the average enumerator enters people twice more often than he forgets to enter them at all, or that he finds it easier to remember to enter people who are on the spot than temporary absentees. All these are merely suggestions of possible sources of error. Until the village by village census can be checked by sample local counts of a high standard of accuracy over an appropriate number of type areas, it is not possible to allow for the errors and omissions. One has simply to recognize their existence as an incalculable qualification to all conclusions based on African population statistics. Counts of the European and Asian populations, which were also taken in 1945, can be relied upon to be reasonably accurate.

2. EUROPEAN INCOMES

At the 1945 Census there were recorded 1,948 European individuals of whom 359 were under the age of twenty. There were just under 500 married households in the community and probably as many as 550 single households. The number of gainfully occupied Europeans was 1,162. Table 139, which is extracted from the 1945 Census report, shows the industrial grouping of the European occupied population.

TABLE 139. Europeans classified by industries, 1945

	Males	Females	Total
Agriculture	225	30	255
Armed Forces	84	4	88
Building	7	—	7
Commerce and finance	83	49	132
Entertainment and sport	5	2	7
Government service	183	49	232
Manufacture	12	3	15
Mining	2	—	2
Professions	178	146	324
Personal services	8	21	29
Transport and communications	70	1	71
Total	857	305	1,162

For the majority of European individuals the Income Tax Department could supply reliable and relatively complete data on earnings. On the one hand it assesses a high proportion of the earning population for income tax purposes (over 80% in 1945); and on the other hand, it obtains from employers annual returns of the amount paid out by them to Europeans in wages and salaries. It also collects data on interest payments made locally. Through the courtesy of the Nyasaland Government I was permitted to examine these returns in 1946 and the estimates given in this section are thus largely based on reliable and relatively up-to-date information, although the assessments of 1945 income were not available when I left Nyasaland.

There were some difficulties in interpreting the returns accurately and allowing for certain omissions. For example, there was no direct information on the earnings of the eighty-eight persons recorded in the census as being in the armed forces. The incomes of missionaries are often paid largely in kind and are not then always entered among the returns made to the Income Tax Commissioner: occasionally 'no income' is returned when the mission con- cerned pays no formal salary, although it does in fact provide for the main- tenance of its workers. Further, no record was made in the income returns for free housing or any other incomes received in kind, although a housing allowance was often included. Since the majority of persons working on their own account are owner-occupiers, it is necessary to add an imputed rent to the majority of incomes.

The estimates of earnings given in Table 140 below are based upon material collected from the Income Tax Department's files, supplemented where necessary with information on particular occupations or groups of payments recorded in other sources. The estimates of numbers in each group were calculated from the census data, since there is a sufficient mobility of labour between employers (particularly for clerical staff) to make it impossible to attempt to interpret the aggregates of employers' returns to the Income Tax Department in terms of numbers receiving incomes over the colony as a whole. The item relating to pensions and gratuities covers payments made by the Nyasaland Government generally to persons living outside the country, and it was abstracted from the 1945 Financial Report.

Since 1945 was the year in which the war ended there was a good deal o change in personnel over the course of the year, and it is not easy to calculate with any certainty the average number of persons employed in each occupa- tion. At the beginning of the year the numbers of those belonging to the colony who were away on active service was near its peak, while the numbers of those away on leave was particularly low in view of the acute staff problem. By the end of the year many individuals were back from the army and, on the other hand, many who had spent the war in the colony were taking a much- delayed leave.

Judging from the staff list drawn up at the end of 1945 there were in the region of 260 civil servants at the end of the year, of whom forty-seven were away on leave and thirteen were still on active service. In the month of April 1945, however, the census showed that 232 persons in government

v

service were in the colony. It was estimated, therefore, that over the year as a whole there were some 260 civil servants of whom an average of twenty-eight were on leave or on active service. Unfortunately it was not possible to make similar calculations for other industries, although it is probably true that for no other industry did such a large proportion of earnings flow outside the country as was the case for government service. There was estimated to be an average of about 1,162 gainfully occupied Europeans in the colony throughout 1945, and it was estimated that there were some thirty-eight individuals away on leave or on active service who were drawing wages and salaries from local employers.

TABLE 140. Incomes of European individuals, 1945

	Numbers gainfully occupied	Receipts £
Persons working on own account in:		
1. Agriculture	87	125,000
2. Trade and other industries	70	76,000
Employed persons in:		
3. Civil service	260	182,000
4. Armed forces	88	35,000
5. Missions	275	56,000
6. Agriculture	170	88,000
7. Trade and other industries	250	168,000
Unearned incomes from:		
8. Interest	—	9,000
9. Pensions and gratuities	—	62,000
10. Housing	—	80,000
11. Total European individuals	1,200	£881,000

As shown in Table 140 it is estimated that about £881,000 was paid to European individuals in, or from sources in, Nyasaland. Of this, some £81,000 was paid to individuals abroad in the form of leave pay, pensions, gratuities, etc., and about £94,000 was paid in kind. Income in kind took the form of earnings in kind received by missionaries or members of the forces, or of free housing enjoyed by the majority of employed persons, or of the rent of owner-occupied dwellings. Thus the cash income of residents was in the region of £706,000 out of a total residents' income of about £800,000.

The files of the Income Tax Department also provided enough material for an estimate of income distribution in Nyasaland in 1945. For the higher income groups a distribution table for assessed incomes earned in 1943 formed the principal basis of estimate, while for the lower income ranges a rapid examination of the 1945 employers' returns gave a basis for estimate.

3. COMPANY INCOMES

The full assessments for 1945 company incomes were not complete when I consulted the Income Tax Department. What were available were the 1944 income records in some detail and the 1945 incomes for a few companies. With this material as a basis and with the import and export figures for 1945 as a background the following estimates were made for 1945 company incomes. For comparative purposes it should be noted that 1943 incomes were in the region of £590,000 and 1942 incomes £593,000, so that in effect it was estimated that 1945 incomes had recovered from the 1944 drop, but not to the 1942-3 level. It is estimated that the margin of error in the 1945 estimates was in the region of 6%.

TABLE 141. Company incomes in Nyasaland, 1945

	1944 incomes £	1945 incomes £
United Kingdom companies	462,000	500,000
Nyasaland companies	75,000	83,000
Total companies	£537,000	£583,000

4. ASIAN INCOMES

It is difficult to construct a convincing estimate of the earnings of Indians in Nyasaland. This is partly because such a large proportion are engaged in trade on their own account (or as members of an extended family) and incomes of independent traders are notoriously difficult to assess accurately: and it is partly because there is such a wide range of variation in Indian income.

The principal sources for an estimate of Indian incomes were the income tax assessments for the 139 persons assessed in 1945 together with employers' returns for 1945. The employers' returns covered most Indians in the employ either of European concerns or of the larger Indian concerns. The income tax assessments gave 1944 incomes for the upper income group. The Census returns gave some details of occupations, but these were not precise enough to permit an accurate allocation of individuals as between occupations. In particular, it was not possible to draw any firm conclusion from the Census as to the number of persons working on their own account. The term 'planter', for example, or 'trader or storekeeper', covered independent workers as well as employed persons, as was clear from information derived from other sources.

TABLE 142. Indian incomes, 1945

Industry	Numbers	Earnings £
1. Agriculture	35	15,000
2. Commerce	1,005	503,000
3. Government service	21	5,000
4. Manufacture (including tailoring and shoe-making)	45	9,000
5. Personal and professional	29	11,000
6. Transport	98	27,000
Total	1,233	£570,000

Thus the estimates given in Table 142 have a higher margin of error than is the case for the estimates made for European incomes, but the aggregate is probably within about 10% of the truth. On the whole it seems more likely that it would overstate than that it would understate Indian incomes.

In interpreting Table 142 it should be noted that the classification by industries is according to persons engaged rather than source of earnings. The actual earnings of Indians from agriculture were, for example, probably nearer £20,000, since there were a number of Indian estate owners whose main occupation is trade and whose incomes are included in full under earnings of people engaged in trade.

In view of the scarcity of data on Indian incomes, only a very rough attempt can be made to estimate the distribution of incomes. This is shown below and is based on information in the Income Tax Department's files. Since only 139 persons were assessed to tax in 1945 and the 1944 assessments were very unreliable, the income tax data are not very satisfactory, while the return of employed Indians is not complete. The broad picture indicated in Table 143, with the concentration of earnings at both ends of the scale, is, however, probably a fair guide to the Indian income distribution pattern.

TABLE 143. Distribution of Indian incomes

Income group	Numbers	Earnings £
Under £400	889	209,000
£400 to £599	105	52,000
£600 to £999	59	41,000
£1,000 to £1,499	40	48,000
Over £1,500	140	220,000
	1,233	£570,000

5. COLOURED INDIVIDUALS' INCOMES

The Census showed a total of sixty-four Coloured persons gainfully occupied, of whom eighteen were engaged in transport, twenty-six in commerce, sixteen in agriculture, and four in professional occupations. Accurate information was available on only eight of these in the returns made by employers to the Income Tax Department, while for the remainder the data were indirect and concerned probable average incomes. A series of rough estimates produced the following table of earnings for Coloured persons. It is impossible to guess an income distribution table, and the margin of error in the estimates is considerable.

TABLE 144. Incomes of Coloured individuals

Industry	Numbers	Earnings £
Commerce	26	1,300
Transport	18	1,500
Agriculture	16	1,200
Professional occupations	4	600
Total	64	£4,600

6. AFRICAN INCOMES FROM EMPLOYMENT

a. Government service

If we include the pay and allowances of Africans in the armed forces, and the earnings of Africans employed in local Government, as well as the earnings derived from the Central Government, one of the principal sources of African income in 1945 was the Government. The bulk of the Central Government's disbursements in African wages are included in the expenditure accounts under the heading of personal emoluments. African emoluments, since they were not separately distinguished, were calculated as a residual after deducting European and Asian emoluments as returned to the Income Tax Department. In addition, however, there were substantial disbursements to casual labour which were not accounted for under personal emoluments, but were included under 'labour' or under certain composite headings such as building, re-afforestation, maintenance, etc. Most departments made some wage disbursements of this nature not already included under personal emoluments. For the Public Works Department, which is the heaviest spender on casual labour, the figures of all wage payments to Africans were obtained direct from that department. For the other departments the payments were estimated from an inspection of the 'other expenditure' charges in the Financial Report.

Altogether it was estimated that direct wage payments to Africans by Central Government amounted to £142,500, a figure which has a margin of error of about 6%. The number of Africans in receipt of wages from the Central Government was deduced from a variety of sources, of which the 1946 Estimates were the most important. Since the work is often casual it was impossible to calculate the total number of Africans concerned, but it was estimated that an average of about 10,500 Africans were in Central Government employment throughout the year. This estimate, however, has a margin of error of about 11%.

Information on the distribution of government employees by various income ranges was collected in respect of the more permanent employees for the African Cost-of-living Committee. For the lower income ranges there were few firm figures and the estimates of income distribution among civil servants are thus more satisfactory for the upper income groups than for the lower income groups.

The local government institutions in Nyasaland include Native Authorities whose accounts are obtainable in summary form from each provincial headquarters; the Sanitary Boards, which also come within the jurisdiction of the District Commissioners from whom information on revenue, expenditure and direct wage expenditure was collected; and the three town councils of Blantyre, Limbe and Zomba from whom copies of revenue and expenditure accounts were obtained direct.

As in the case of the Central Government, the Native Authority expenditure on personal emoluments does not cover all wage expenditure, and there is some unspecified expenditure on wages in the other charges and under the additional heading of Extraordinary Expenditure. The proportion attributable to wages under these other headings had to be estimated from an inspection of the summary accounts available in the provincial headquarters, and the resulting estimates for Native Authority expenditure on wages has an error of about 10%.

Table 145 summarizes the income of Africans from government sources and includes also an estimate of the incomes derived by soldiers, and civilians in the pay of the armed forces. This last was calculated as a residual after deducting the estimate for earnings of Europeans in the armed forces from the figures supplied by East African Command. No Asians were recorded in the employ of the armed forces at the 1945 Census.

None of the available sources gave any indication of the numbers of Africans employed in local government service or in the armed forces, but on the assumption that average income was equivalent to the average in the civil service (which is probably low for the armed forces, but certainly high for local government) there were about 29,000 Africans obtaining wages from government sources throughout the year. The margin of error in total estimated earnings was thought to be about 7%.

TABLE 145. African incomes from government service, 1945

	Earnings £
1. Central government	142,500
2. Armed forces (including civilian employees)	206,400
3. Total central government and armed forces	348,900
4. Native authorities	36,200
5. Town councils	4,900
6. Sanitary boards	1,700
7. Total all government sources	£391,700

b. Mission service

The missions are another important source of wage-earning opportunities for Nyasaland Africans. They employ a considerable number of relatively educated men as teachers, a lesser number as clerks or hospital orderlies, and a much larger number as casual labour in the vicinity of the missions. The numbers and earnings of African graded or certificated teachers could be reliably estimated from material provided by the Education Department. Their salaries were largely financed by government grant. In all there were 1,400 graded and grant-aided teachers earning a total of about £24,000 in 1945. In addition there were 1,379 teachers trained by missions, but without a government certificate, and a further 386 untrained teachers.

Information on the total wage bill of each mission was collected by means of a questionnaire circulated to the various missions. This also provided enough material for a rough estimate of income distribution among the non-teaching employees of missions. An income distribution table for teachers could be drawn up, reliably for the graded teachers, from information provided by the Education Department. The total estimated earnings of teachers was about £35,600.

c. Agricultural employment

There was no recent census of African labour available for Nyasaland, and it was necessary to estimate the number of employees engaged in industries where the unit of production is relatively small. This is particularly true of agriculture, which is the most important industry employing local labour. The Agricultural Department had record in 1945 of over 250 European- or Indian-owned estates ranging in cultivated area from less than 10 acres to over 3,000 acres. In all, the European estate owners cultivated over 48,000 acres, but they also employed labour in tobacco and tea factories and in handling crops (tobacco, for example) grown by Africans on their own estates.

A questionnaire circulated to owners of some of the more substantial estates produced enough information to suggest the order of magnitude of the average labour force in agriculture and the average rates of wages in cash and in kind. These estimates were, however, extremely rough and are in some ways a poor reflection of the actual labour situation. Agricultural labour is not only highly seasonal, but also very erratic in attendance. Labour in tobacco increases by more than 100% in the busy season. Estate owners draw their labour partly from seasonal migrants (there is an appreciable migration from north to south), and partly from the Africans resident on their own and neighbouring estates. At the 1945 Census there were 211,394 Africans resident on private estates, i.e. probably about 43,000 males over the age of eighteen and between 50,000 and 60,000 households. This is a considerable potential reservoir of labour, since not only the adults but also the children can find employment in the fields and factories and grading sheds.

On the other hand, most farmers complained about erratic habits of their labour force. The residents on the private estates have their own gardens and they do not need to work except for cash. Although they are paid by the month their 'tickets' are marked by the day and they do not have to work their month in consecutive days. They are thus able to drift from farm to farm or from work to rest according to the relative attractiveness of the work offered or their need for money. In the later war years and immediate post-war years the stores catering for the native trade were almost bare of goods, and money proved a poor incentive. A half-worked ticket was not a very liquid form of capital, but it was said that some Africans preferred to leave their wages unrealized for considerable periods of time. In order to ensure an effective labour turnout at seasons when work was urgent—for example, at the tobacco planting season—it was usually necessary to offer some special bonus to labour, often a meat ration.

Consequently, estimate of the average number of Africans in agricultural employment gives little indication either of the total number of individuals or households concerned or of the actual current rate of earnings. The rate of absenteeism is high, and there are a large number of children employed, not only at peak seasons, but throughout the year, at low rates of wages and for short periods of time. On the whole it seems probable that the estimates in Table 146, based as they are on the information collected from large estates, are an overstatement not only of total earnings, but also of the average numbers of Africans employed throughout the year. They include earnings in the tobacco, cotton and tea factories, and similar primary processing industries. The margin of error in the earnings estimate is probably about 25% and in the numbers employed about 20%.

TABLE 146. Africans employed in agriculture

	Numbers	Earnings £
Tobacco	12,000	80,000
Tea	30,000	210,000
Other	22,000	129,000
	64,000	£419,000

d. Transport and distribution

Transport and distribution concerns were also circularized on the subject of their African labour, and the following estimates are based on the returns that were received. The most important single employer was the Nyasaland Railways, whose African wage bill, including all income in kind, amounted to about £45,200. The distribution estimates cover also those Africans employed in rural stores, including Indian- and African-owned stores.

TABLE 147. Africans in transport and distribution

	Numbers	Earnings £
Transport	5,400	62,000
Distribution	16,400	102,400
Hotels and clubs	600	5,000
	22,400	£169,400

e. Miscellaneous and other employments in Nyasaland

Domestic service is the only other important source of wages for Africans, and there are also a number of small-scale concerns including several sawmills, a soap factory, a fishing station, and a mineral factory. These latter were circularized and gave information on their labour force. The number of domestic servants employed was calculated as a function of the estimated average number employed per European or Indian household and includes an allowance for domestics employed by Africans. Wage rates were estimated on the basis of a questionnaire on wages circulated to District Commissioners, on other enquiries among individual Europeans and on data collected by the Labour Department. The resulting estimate of earnings includes an allowance for incomes in kind and is unlikely to underestimate the total, although the numbers employed may be underestimated since there is a good deal of casual domestic employment with a low rate of output and of wages. Table 148 summarizes these estimates.

TABLE 148. Miscellaneous employments

	Numbers employed	Earnings £
Domestic service	4,500	38,000
Other	900	6,000
	5,400	£44,000

In sum, therefore, it was estimated that there was an average of 135,000 Africans (including children, who may have numbered 20,000) in employment in Nyasaland in 1945. Their aggregate incomes from employment were estimated to amount to a total of about £1,129,000 in cash or in kind. On the whole it is more likely that this overstates the value of earnings: but it significantly understates the number actually receiving incomes from employment during the course of the year, since there were so many seasonal workers.

f. Migrant labour

According to the 1945 Census there were 133,300 Nyasaland Africans absent from the Protectorate, of whom 25,236 were in the forces and 32,144 had left before September 1939. The Labour Department, basing its estimates on information from the countries in which the migrants were working, gave a total of about 142,000 migrant labourers, of whom 33,200 were in the Union, 78,500 in Southern Rhodesia, 5,300 in Northern Rhodesia or Tanganyika, and 25,000 in the forces. Judging from the results of the Northern Rhodesia African Labour Census, which showed a total of 5,677 Nyasalanders in Northern Rhodesia in 1946, the Labour Department's figures are more likely to understate than to overstate the case. Census figures of migrants are notoriously unreliable, and Labour Department figures tend to omit those migrants who prefer to cut their connections with their country and its representatives while away at work.

Migrant labour remittances are of three main kinds. First there is the cash brought back by repatriates. In some cases this includes deferred pay and voluntary savings made available by the employer at the time of return. Often this is collected from the District Officers by the migrant after he returns to his district. The most important groups of workers in this category were the returning soldiers and the workers repatriated by the Witwatersrand Native Labour Association Ltd., an organization which recruits labour for work on the Rand Gold Mines. Workers who bring back deferred pay, etc., may also bring back small savings which do not pass through their employer's hands at this stage. Other workers bring back cash sums that they have saved for themselves. Secondly, there are the cash remittances to families. Again the army authorities and W.N.L.A. handle a large volume of both compulsory and voluntary family remittances on behalf of their recruits. Other remittances are made by postal or money order and occasionally sent by friends. Thirdly, there are the goods—mainly clothes—which are brought back by repatriates, or sent through the post (when they appear in the parcel trade statistics).

The value of remittances made by or through the military authorities and W.N.L.A. were obtained from the organizations concerned. Figures were also available on postal and money orders remitted from the Union and Southern Rhodesia respectively. The budget data collected by Godfrey Wilson in Broken Hill were used as a basis of estimate for remittances in cash or kind from Northern Rhodesia. The average value of goods brought back per repatriate was estimated on the basis of small-scale surveys made for migrants returning to other countries. The Northern Rhodesian Labour Department had made a study covering some 700 repatriates, and Professor Schapera had evaluated the baggage of a small group of migrants returning to Bechuanaland.[1] Table 149 summarizes the estimates made on all this data.

TABLE 149. Receipts from migrants

	Numbers away	Value remitted or brought back: Cash £	Goods £
Union of South Africa	33,200	284,600	146,500
Southern Rhodesia	78,500	73,000	129,006
Other African territory	5,800	3,500	5,900
Forces	25,000	218,800	39,700
Total migrants	142,500	£579,900	£321,100

The weakest group of estimates in Table 149 is the section on goods remitted or brought back. It may be that these have been too highly valued, but judging from the available evidence and from the current prices of clothing in Africa the margin of error in this item is probably within about 20%. That is to say, goods brought or remitted back by migrants were probably worth between £256,000 and £385,000 in value. The estimates for cash remittances are very much more reliable. Reliable figures were obtained from the military authorities and W.N.L.A. and these showed a total recorded amount of £254,300 remitted or brought back in cash by their employees. In addition, £252,700 was remitted through the Post Office from the Union and Southern Rhodesia. It is probable that the figure for cash receipts is within about 6% of the truth, and that the total of £901,000 for receipts from migrant labour in cash and in kind has a margin of error of about 11%.

7. AFRICAN INCOMES FROM INDEPENDENT ACTIVITIES

a. Economic crops

In so far as these crops were sold to government buying agencies or throughout native produce markets, as was the case for all but a negligible

[1] op. cit.

proportion of the tobacco, and cotton output and for the vast bulk of the sales of wheat, potatoes, rice and coffee, the Agricultural Department was able to provide figures of volume and value of sales. The first eleven items of Table 150 are estimates based on material made available by the Agricultural Department and are fairly reliable. In addition, however, there are quantities of maize, groundnuts and pulses sold to estates to feed their labour, and small quantities of all foodstuffs are hawked direct to Europeans, Asians and other Africans. Only the most arbitrary allowance can be made for trade which does not pass through the organized markets, but it is unlikely to make a substantial difference to the total output of cash crops. In addition also there is a small proportion of sub-standard tobacco which does not pass the standards set by the European produce markets and is sold to Africans: this, however, was very small in the year under review, since tobacco of all kinds was very much in demand. In bad years it may be from 10% to 15% of the total crop. Finally, there is an extensive local trade in the native nicotine tobacco, which is produced on small village plots and usually sold as snuff tobacco. Allowance is made for these items in the last three items of Table 150. The total value of African income from economic crops is thus estimated to be about £488,000.

TABLE 150. African output of cash crops

In organized markets	Output	Value £
1. Tobacco	18,352,851 lb.	292,300
2. Cotton	11,322,567 lb.	60,800
3. Groundnuts (shelled)	2,342 tons	39,000
4. Pulses	3,713 tons	38,700
5. Maize	7,500 tons	16,700
6. Rice	{ 1,352 tons paddy / 272 tons clean }	11,600
7. Wheat	606 tons	6,300
8. Potatoes	489 tons	3,100
9. Coffee	5¼ tons	300
10. Pyrethrum	13,819 tons wet	100
11. Total in organized markets		£468,900
12. Tobacco (including native tobacco)		4,500
13. Food crops		15,000
14. Trade not passing through markets		£19,500

b. Livestock

African livestock is slaughtered regularly for sale at most of the established market places in the colony and for the urban markets they pass through the three municipal abattoirs of Zomba, Blantyre and Limbe. The Veterinary Department was able to give figures for slaughterings at the Central Province market and at a number of other markets; the municipalities provided information on their own abattoirs; for the remaining markets estimates were made on the basis of information collected from the District Commissioners (each of whom was asked the average number of beasts slaughtered

weekly in the markets in his area) and also, where the District Commissioners' figures were inadequate, on the basis of market information collected
by the Nutrition Adviser in her travels from market to market in 1942. Prices
were based on those supplied by the District Commissioner, and the European contribution to the slaughtering was estimated on the basis of European
livestock holdings. On the basis of all this material it was estimated that some
8,000 sheep and goats and some 2,400 cattle were slaughtered for African
owners in 1945 and that the African return from these slaughterings was in
the region of £19,000.

c. Fishing

It is extremely difficult to make any estimate of the cash return from
fishing since there is no hard and fast distinction between commercial and
subsistence fishing. In the off seasons most of the catch is divided up on the
lake shore among the helpers and families and little, if any, is traded. In the
good seasons a great deal of casual fishing is done for sale. Moreover, the
fishermen are not the only group of persons obtaining cash from the industry.
A considerable number of middlemen buy on the lake shore and dry and
carry away for sale. There is also a European firm which caters primarily
for the fresh market, but which in the full season dries its surplus for sale
to the African middlemen to carry away on their bicycles. In addition there
is a constant barter trade in fish for bananas, flour, vegetables, etc.

Estimates made by Miss Lowe of the Fisheries Survey and based on
returns of the Native Authority tax on fishing gears, and also on the information collected by the Fisheries Adviser to the Nutrition Unit, suggested that
there were about 6,000 men regularly fishing the lake and that the total value
of their output was about £30,000. Of this, perhaps 50% was sold to middlemen for transport and sale inland, and perhaps a third of the remainder was
sold or bartered on the lake shore. This suggests a total of about £20,000
for the value of African cash or barter incomes from fish, the proceeds being
shared among about 6,000 men. This may be high as a reflection of the economic return from fish, but after taking into account the number of small
subsistence fishermen living thoughout the lake shore area it seems probable
that the figure of £30,000 may well be too low as an estimate of the total
value of the industry.

d. Sale of miscellaneous goods and services

In addition to the sources of cash income already discussed there are a
number of other ways of earning money, concerning which there are almost
no data at all and certainly no data satisfactory enough for generalization.
For these channels of income, estimates can at best be token estimates which
will serve to indicate the order of magnitude of the items concerned when
considered in relation to the national income as a whole. It must be emphasized that such estimates have no intrinsic value and no relative significance
in respect of each other. They have meaning only as a general reflection of the
importance of these activities in the sum total of economic activity.

Generally speaking, the basis for estimate consisted of (1) an estimate of numbers concerned, derived originally from official records (for example, the District Commissioners could give the number of trading licences issued to Africans, while the number of households could be estimated from census returns); and (2) estimates of average income per unit or household, based upon personal observations collected during the second half of 1946, together with some of the raw material of the Nutrition Survey conducted by Dr Platt in 1938-9. Dairy products, which include ghee, hides and skins, poultry, eggs, and a little milk, are based partly on figures obtained from the Veterinary Department and partly on estimates of the amount purchased by Europeans and Indians.

Where numbers engaged are given they are highly approximate estimates of the earners (including child assistants and other employees of Africans) believed to have been in receipt of income from this particular source and not of numbers engaged in a full-time capacity. Table 151 summarizes the estimates. To this total of £195,000 estimated to have been received from miscellaneous economic activity, a sum of about £38,000 could be added to represent receipts from gifts, marriage payments and other transfers of income which are not made against what can strictly be called economic activity.

TABLE 151. Miscellaneous African incomes

	Numbers	Earnings £
Distribution	10,000	90,000
Handwork	14,000	20,000
Dairy produce	—	27,000
Beer	—	35,000
Other goods and services	—	23,000
Total miscellaneous incomes		£195,000

8. AFRICAN SUBSISTENCE AGRICULTURE

On the assumption that the average cultivated acreage per family in Southern Province was 2 acres and in Northern and Central Provinces 3 acres, and also that the number of families was equivalent to the number of married or widowed women as shown in the 1945 Census, the total acreage under cultivation in Nyasaland in 1945 was in the region of 1,400,000 acres and the average cultivated food area per hut was 2½ acres. On the whole it seems more likely that this erred on the low side than on the high side, but it seems unlikely, so far as one can judge from the scanty evidence available, that the cultivated acreage under food crops fell below 1,250,000 acres or exceeded 1,750,000 acres.

A good yield of maize in Southern Province under native conditions of agriculture would be 1,200 lb. per acre, and in Northern Province about 1,000 lb. per acre. As a general average, however, it is unlikely that the yield exceeded 900 lb. per acre in Southern Province and 700 lb. in the rest of the country. Less is known about the yield of groundnuts or beans than about the yield of maize. The range of yield of groundnuts is 200 lb. to 800 lb. under native conditions. Probably a fair average would be about 400 lb. For beans the average probably would not exceed 300 lb. For root crops the average might be about 1,000 lb. per acre, dry.

To obtain a rough estimate of the value of crops reaped from this 1,400,000 acres it has been assumed that maize or its value equivalent was grown on about 75%, groundnuts, beans or their value equivalent on 20%, and cassava or its value equivalent on 5%. This gave a total value of about £1,860,000 made up as follows.

TABLE 152.   Estimated food-crop yields or yield equivalents

	Acreage acres	Yield lb.	Value £
Maize	1,050,000	810,600,000	1,125,800
Pulses	280,000	98,000,000	685,500
Root crop	70,000	70,000,000	48,600
	1,400,000		£1,859,900

In addition to the maize crops there are fruit trees in most villages and the women collect green leaves and wild fruit of various kinds for relish. It is, of course, impossible to estimate the amount of these goods produced without extensive village surveying. If we assume, however, that each individual consumed in a year an average of 10 lb. of fruit, green leaves, etc., not grown on the cultivated acreage, the total output was in the region of 20,447,000 lb. Valuing this at 2 lb. for 1d. gives a total value of about £42,500. This seems a generous estimate.

Thus the total value of the output of African food crops calculated in this highly speculative fashion is estimated to be about £1,903,000. This can scarcely be classified as a direct estimate, since it involves so many arbitrary assumptions on averages. Nevertheless, it is probably a fair indication of the order of magnitude involved. Of this £1,903,000 some £15,000 has already been estimated to have been traded otherwise than through the organized markets. The remainder of the traded foodstuffs is estimated to have been grown on additional acreages to the above.

If maize is valued as a finished product rather than a grain, i.e. as flour and coarse meal, there is a loss of some 17% in weight and the remaining 675,500,000 lb. of foodstuffs is worth about £2,189,100 by 1945 prices. This means an addition of £1,063,300 by the value of agricultural incomes, bringing the total up to about £2,966,000 and the total for subsistence crops to £2,951,000.

9. OTHER SUBSISTENCE INCOME

In addition to the crops obtained from the land the Nyasaland family produces for itself a variety of other products. Beer is produced for home consumption. Probably at least as much fish as is traded is consumed by the Africans who catch them in the lakes and rivers. They make their own houses, pots, baskets, beds and mats. Livestock is slaughtered for consumption on ritual and festive occasions, and the remains of an animal which dies or is killed by wild animals are usually consumed by the owner. Small game is regularly hunted in most areas at the bush-firing season.

Here again there is no basis for direct estimate of the quantities and values involved. It is not possible to do more than produce token figures by means of such calculations as the estimated proportion of livestock slaughtered or killed in the villages; or the relative proportion of fish consumed by fishermen and their families; or the estimated average quantity of poultry or game, or value of untraded handicrafts, consumed per family. The estimated proportions and averages had in each case to be based on a very few actual instances and superficial observation. The results are thought to be useful as a reflection of the orders of magnitude involved, but have no intrinsic value. They are given below in Table 153.

TABLE 153. Rough estimate of value of other subsistence incomes

		£
1.	Livestock and livestock products (including game and poultry)	76,000
2.	Fish	30,000
3.	Beer	35,000
4.	Housing (building only)	50,000
5.	Other village industries	50,000
		£241,000

10. INCOME OF GOVERNMENT

The only local authorities which supply trading services on a strictly commercial basis are the Blantyre and Limbe municipalities; the former provides water and electricity, and the latter electricity. The profits from these services are in the region of £2,700. The principal other service provided by the local authorities is sanitation, and that has been regarded as a public service.

The Central Government's income from property, profits from trading services (i.e. Post Office and Telegraph), and income from abroad, were calculated from the 1945 Financial Report. Table 154 shows the net income of government as defined for this purpose.

TABLE 154. Net income of government

		£
1.	Receipts from sale of goods and services	60,039
2.	Profits	90,784
3.	Rent and interest	7,781
4.	Colonial development and welfare	22,117
5.	Total net government income	£180,721

TABLE 155. National taxable income of Nyasaland

I. AFRICAN INCOMES
1. *From employment:*   £   £
   (a) Agriculture   419,000
   (b) Government   392,000
   (c) Distribution and transport   169,000
   (d) Missions   105,000
   (e) Miscellaneous other   44,000

   (f) Total in Nyasaland   1,129,000
   (g) Emigrant labour   901,000

   (h) Total incomes from employment   2,030,000
2. *From independent agriculture:*
   (a) Crop sales   488,000
   (b) Subsistence crops   2,951,000
   (c) Livestock sales   19,000
   (d) Livestock products and poultry sales   27,000
   (e) Subsistence livestock   76,000

   (f) Total incomes from native agriculture   3,561,000
3. *From miscellaneous independent activities:*
   (a) Distribution   90,000
   (b) Traded handicrafts   20,000
   (c) Beer sales   35,000
   (d) Fish sales   30,000
   (e) Other traded goods and services   23,000
   (f) Other subsistence incomes   165,000

   (g) Total miscellaneous incomes   363,000

4. Total African incomes from all sources   5,954,000
II. ASIAN AND COLOURED INDIVIDUALS' INCOMES
From:
5. Commerce   504,000
6. Transport   29,000
7. Agriculture   16,000
8. All other   26,000

9. Total incomes of Asian and Coloured individuals   575,000
III. EUROPEAN INDIVIDUALS' INCOMES
From:
10. Agriculture   213,000
11. Government   217,000
12. Missions   56,000
13. Trade and other occupation   244,000
14. Property and pensions   151,000

15. Total incomes of European individuals   881,000
IV. COMPANIES' INCOMES
16. Nyasaland companies   83,000
17. United Kingdom companies   500,000

18. Total companies' incomes   583,000
V. GOVERNMENT INCOMES
19. Profits from trading services   91,000
20. Sale of goods and services   60,000
21. Property income   8,000
22. Colonial Development and Welfare Grants   22,000

23. Total government income   181,000

24. Total national taxable income of Nyasaland   £8,174,000

NATIONAL TAXABLE OUTPUT

II. EUROPEAN AGRICULTURE

The Department of Agriculture compiles figures of acreage and yield for the European-produced crops from the returns obtained to an official questionnaire. Generally speaking, farm management standards tend to be high in Nyasaland, so that the returns are likely to be relatively reliable, although they cannot be regarded as accurate. For most crops the Department was able also to provide the necessary information on values, but for tea the relevant price information was obtained from the Tea Commissioner, for rubber and sisal it was obtained direct from the principal producers, and for tung and for chillies and capsicums the export value was taken as the basis for estimate.

The results of the calculations based on this material are given in Table 156, which gives the acreage and yield of European crops as supplied by the Department of Agriculture and values them at their farm or factory value. It is a complete record in that it includes crops produced from animal fodder (i.e. part of the oil seed and the legume crop). The miscellaneous crops item includes small acreages of nut-bearing trees, coffee, cotton, wheat, rice and essential oils.

In addition to the information on crops obtained mainly from Department of Agriculture sources, Table 156 gives estimates of the gross value of output of European livestock. There is thus an element of double counting in that fodder items are included among some crops, and meat slaughtered for African wages is included in the value of output of the various crops.

TABLE 156. Gross output of European agriculture, 1945

(a) Crops	Cultivated area acres	Yields lb.	Values £
Tea	19,807	13,639,491	750,000
Tobacco	6,154	2,230,018	104,072
Tung oil	10,132	590,659	70,000
Oil seeds	2,342	1,605,441	13,379
Fruit trees	1,680	n.a.	18,840
Rubber	1,431	142,250	6,200
Maize	2,014	1,843,077	2,560
Legumes	1,427	405,183	2,110
Chillies and capsicums	149	55,706	1,400
Miscellaneous	372	—	1,906
Total crops	45,508		£970,467
(b) Livestock			
Meat			19,000
Milk			14,000
Hide and skins			1,200
Poultry and eggs			9,000
Total livestock products			£43,200

There was very little information on European livestock products, and the material which did exist was often in such a form that it was difficult to distinguish between the African and European share of the trade. Thus

w

while the margin of error in the total for the value of European crops is probably under 6%, the total for European livestock cannot be held to have a margin of error less than 25%.

To convert this gross total of £1,013,700 to the net value of the output of agriculture it is necessary to reduce for items which have been counted twice and to eliminate the value of purchased materials and services obtained from other industries or by import. The value of fodder items included under crops was estimated to be about £1,500, and of the meat included in wages of agricultural labourers about £3,000. The Agricultural Department was able to supply figures of fertilizers used and the Customs Department provided data on the value of imported packing materials, tools, agricultural machinery, etc. It was necessary, however to make an arbitrary judgment on what proportion of agricultural machinery imports represented replacement expenditure and what proportion represented new investment. These calculations gave the following results with an estimated margin of error of at least 9%.

TABLE 157. Net output of European agriculture and livestock

		£
	1. Gross farm or factory value	1,014,000
Less—	2. Fodder and food included in wages	5,000
	3. Fertilizers	47,000
	4. Current imports of materials	56,000
	5. Machinery replacements	40,000
	6. Other purchased materials and services	6,000
Leaves—	7. Value of net output	£860,000

12. GOVERNMENT

The net output of government is defined for national income purposes as the value of the salaries and wages and other incomes paid by government, together with the government's own income in the form of profits from trading services, revenue from sales, and receipts from abroad. The total includes the output of Central Government, Local Government and the Crown (in the form of the output of the armed forces supported in Nyasaland). All the items in government output have already been calculated for the purposes of the national income table. They are summarized below in Table 158.

TABLE 158. Net output of government

	£
1. Incomes of civil servants and local government employees	390,000
2. Pensions and gratuities	62,000
3. Profits and revenue from sales	151,000
4. Rent, interest and receipts from abroad	30,000
5. Income from military employment	241,000
6. Total net output of government	£874,000

13. DISTRIBUTION

The distribution industry in Nyasaland can be classified into three main categories. First, there is the licensed retail trade flowing through shops owned by Europeans, Indians and Africans respectively. Secondly, there is the retail trade carried on by Africans in markets, in unlicensed stores (or stores licensed by the local authority only) or as hawkers. Thirdly, there is the handling of export crops, primarily tobacco, organized mainly by Europeans and occasionally by Asians.

As far as the second of these sections was concerned—that is, the unlicensed or Native Authority licensed African trade—there was no means of making an independent calculation which would check the very rough estimates already made for the income column. For the third section—handling of exports—estimates of output were based on the difference between the amount received by farmers (Europeans, Asian and African) for their produce and the f.o.r. value of exports after allowing for other known charges such as transport. The estimate was necessarily rough, but indicated the order of magnitude.

Estimates of the output of the licensed retail trade were based partly on information collected from the District Commissioners by means of a questionnaire (this information covered the numbers of licences issued to each racial group) and partly on turnover and cost information collected directly from certain distributive concerns. For European concerns the information collected covered the bulk of the trade involved, but for both the Asian and African concerns the information covered only a small haphazardly selected sample of cases.

The results of all these estimates concerning the output of distribution are summarized below in Table 159. The margin of error in the total is believed to be of the order of 10%.

TABLE 159. Output of distribution

	Number of concerns	Turnover £	Net output £
1. Licensed retail trade:			
(a) European shops	344	810,000 ⎫	657,000
(b) Asian shops	1,139	1,140,000 ⎬	
(c) African shops	1,988	200,000	60,000
2. Other African trade	—	—	63,000
3. Handling of exports	—	—	350,000
4. Total value of distribution industry			£1,130,000

14. TRANSPORT

Estimates of the value of output of the Nyasaland Railways were based on information collected from the railway company. Information was also collected from the more important European road transport concerns, but it was inadequate. Details of the number of vehicles licensed for commercial purposes were obtained from official sources. The result of the estimates for transport are given below, and it should be noted that the railway figures include lake transport services provided by the railway company.

TABLE 160. Output of transport

	Gross output £	Net output £
1. Railway and lake	262,000	190,000
2. Road	125,000	55,000
3. Total transport	£387,000	£245,000

15. MANUFACTURE, FORESTRY, AND BUILDING

Only very rough estimates could be made for the output of these industries. Information on the number and nature of the factories involved is collected by the Chief Factory Inspector and those factories whose output was not included in the other industries (for example, tea factories) were circularized. The response to the circular was not complete and many small concerns were omitted. It was therefore necessary to generalize for the whole on the basis of the returns that were received. There were 138 factories within the meaning of the Factories Act of which not more than twenty-five were included elsewhere (e.g. as tea factories, sisal factories, etc.). They produced soap, oils, cotton, minerals, furniture, and the value of their total net output was estimated to be in the region of £75,000.

Estimates of the amount and value of the output of the forests in Nyasaland varied widely, particularly in respect of the value of firewood produced. The Forestry Department had made estimates of average quantities and values produced annually in the five years ending in 1939, but these seemed greatly to underestimate native consumption of firewood, judging by later information obtained from the Department. The final estimate, which was based on the assumption that each African family consumed on the average 600 cu. ft. of firewood and twenty poles each year, gave a total of about £700,000 for the value of timber output. This figure is very rough indeed and and is little more than a token estimate.

The building industry in Nyasaland makes a very small contribution to total output. The normal procedure in most areas is for the individual or concern for whom the building is made to organize the whole process, even to the extent of hiring and supervising the brickmaking labour. To a large extent, therefore, the output of building is provided for in this column under other industry headings, e.g. under government service or missions. It seems unlikely, on the scanty evidence available, that the net addition to output not already included would exceed £10,000, or that the gross output would be much in excess of £25,000.

16. MISSIONS

Missions play an important part in Nyasaland life, but their low cost of production—in particular the low value of the income received by their European employees—makes the money value of their output appear disproportionately low in relation to other forms of primarily European organized activity. The basis for an estimate of their contribution to national output was obtained from the answers to a circular to which the majority replied to the best of their ability. In addition information was obtainable from the Education Department which showed Government grants to each mission (distinguishing between grants in respect of European salaries and grants in respect of African wages). Finally, the Income Tax Department could provide information which accounted for a substantial proportion of incomes earned by Europeans. The value of subsistence incomes was calculated very roughly as a fraction of the acreage cultivated by missions, a total which was derived from the records of the Agricultural Department.

A summary of the estimates made is given in Table 161. It should be noted that no separate allowance has been made for local charitable contributions to mission funds since it seems most unlikely that they would exceed a few hundred pounds and there is no satisfactory basis for estimate. Items 8 and 9, subsistence consumption and expenditure on goods and services, may actually contain some items which should be included under European incomes, but an effort was made to allow in full under item 7 for the substantial incomes in kind received from some of the missions (excluding food).

TABLE 161. Combined account for missions

Revenue	£	Expenditure	£
1. Revenue from the sale of goods and services	30,000	6. African wages and salaries	96,000
2. Subsistence incomes	24,000	7. European wages and salaries	44,000
3. Income from abroad	93,000	8. Subsistence consumption	24,000
4. Government grant	57,000	9. Expenditure on goods and services	40,000
5. Total revenue	£204,000	10. Total expenditure	£204,000

The net value of mission output was thus estimated to be in the region of £164,000 with some possibility of an underestimate, but the margin of error is probably in the region of 8%. Expenditure covered investment estimated at about £30,000.

17. MISCELLANEOUS SERVICES

Table 162 summarizes the value of net output for a miscellaneous group of services. The estimates for hotels and clubs were based on the results of circulars and questionnaires and are probably correct within about 10%. The estimates for the other items are fairly reliable, but are largely based on the same sources of information as were relied upon for the corresponding entries in the income column. To that extent, therefore, they are not an independent calculation and do not provide an opportunity for cross-checking estimates. It was estimated on the basis of the questionnaires and circulars that expenditure on hotels in Nyasaland amounted to approximately £50,000, and on clubs and entertainments about £24,000, of which £4,000 was spent on cinemas and £16,000 on bars, and the remainder was largely composed of club and sport subscriptions and similar payments.

TABLE 162. Net output of miscellaneous services

	Net value of output £
1. Banking and insurance	36,000
2. Hotels	25,000
3. Clubs	8,200
4. Other personal services	39,600
5. Other professional services	19,000
6. Total value miscellaneous services	£127,800

18. AFRICAN AGRICULTURE, LIVESTOCK, FISHERIES, ETC.

Estimates of the output of African agriculture and livestock and of other rural activities of Africans have already been made in connection with the income column. There is no separate basis of estimate for these items and the

TABLE 163. National output of Nyasaland

	£	£
Agriculture and livestock		
1. Non-African agriculture and livestock	860,000	
2. African agriculture	3,439,000	
3. African livestock and products	122,000	
4. Total agriculture and livestock		4,421,000
Manufacture, forestry, building, and village industry		
5. Non-African factories	75,000	
6. Forestry products	700,000	
7. Fish	50,000	
8. Beer	70,000	
9. Building (including African huts)	60,000	
10. Village industry and handicrafts	93,000	
11. Total manufacture and industry		1,048,000
Distribution and transport		
12. Distribution	1,130,000	
13. Transport	245,000	
14. Total distribution and transport		1,375,000
Government and missions		
15. Government	874,000	
16. Missions	164,000	
17. Total government and missions		1,038,000
Miscellaneous output		
18. Emigrant labour	901,000	
19. Miscellaneous services	128,000	
20. Total miscellaneous output		1,029,000
21. Total national output		£8,911,000[1]

[1] Includes subsistence income valued at £700,000 and not included in national income as shown in Table 155 above.

relevant items in Table 163 are merely rearrangements and summaries of estimates which have been described in the previous chapter. It should be noted in comparing the national income and national output tables that the former does not include the value of subsistence forestry products, which are estimated to amount to about, or rather less than, £700,000.

NATIONAL EXPENDITURE AND THE BALANCE OF PAYMENTS

19. EUROPEAN EXPENDITURE

The two principal general sources of information on European expenditure were the trade statistics and the various 'standard' needs budgets drawn up for cost-of-living enquiries by Government committees or the Nyasaland Council of Women or other private organizations. The trade figures provided data on certain classes of foodstuffs and tobacco, and on clothing, household wares, and miscellaneous luxury expenditure. The cost-of-living budgets supplemented this information and were the principal basis of estimate of total expenditure by Europeans on foodstuffs.

In addition there were a number of specialized sources which gave bases of varying reliability for estimates of the value of particular items. For example, expenditure on insurance could be deduced from information made available by the Income Tax Department. Expenditure on electricity, water, rates, sanitation, cinemas, subscriptions, club, sports and drinking were estimated from such sources as the annual reports of municipalities or clubs. The Census gave the number of scholars then being educated abroad and with some additional data on costs of education abroad provided the basis for an estimate of expenditure on education.

The results of all these estimates are given below. Some are extremely crude estimates (for example, expenditure on transport, expenditure on leave or dependants abroad, and saving). Others, for example direct taxation or expenditure on drink and tobacco, can be regarded as reasonably reliable. The use of standard budget figures as a guide to the general pattern of expenditure is more justifiable in Nyasaland than it would be in, say, Northern Rhodesia, since the standard of living of the small European population is more uniform, especially in such essentials as food, servants, and miscellaneous household expenses. For these items the various standard budgets varied very little.

It is unlikely that the total arrived at below for value of European outlay is more than 10% in error, although some of the items may be as much as 20% out. In general, however, the table probably reflects fairly reliably the main essentials in the pattern of European expenditure.

Of the amount expended on food and tobacco it is estimated that about half or £75,000 was spent on locally produced foodstuffs, and about £11,000 on locally manufactured tobacco products. Of the amount expended on insurance and education it was estimated that £61,000 flowed abroad which, together with expenditure on leave and dependants, represented a total invisible expenditure abroad of about £211,000.

TABLE 164. Estimated pattern of European expenditure[1]

	Value of expenditure and consumption £
1. Food and tobacco	150,000
2. Drink	102,000
3. Clothing	60,000
4. Insurance	35,000
5. Rent, rates, etc.	33,000
6. Education	32,000
7. Servants	35,000
8. Household expenses	60,000
9. Transport (including private cars)	50,000
10. Direct taxes (individuals only)	52,000
11. Miscellaneous luxury expenditure	70,000
12. Leave and dependants and other expenditure abroad	150,000
13. Total value consumption	£829,000

No independent estimate of the value of savings is possible, but except in so far as saving is made for expenditure on leave (when it is included above under item 12), it did not appear that the European community in Nyasaland had much surplus after providing for the relatively high standard of living that is the socially accepted norm.

20. ASIAN CONSUMPTION

There was no information available for an estimate of Asian budgets, apart from some minor details (e.g. club expenditure). The following table is therefore very crude indeed and is only a most tentative assessment of the pattern of Asian consumption.

TABLE 165. Estimated pattern of Asian consumption

	£
1. Food	48,000
2. Clothing	42,000
3. Household	17,000
4. Servants	25,000
5. Taxes	53,000
6. Other	65,000
7. Total expenditure and consumption in Nyasaland	£250,000

It was estimated that most of the basic food of Asians was Nyasaland produce, sometimes grown by the consumer. To some extent this table contains underestimates and Table 164 overestimates, because it was impossible to distinguish European and Asian expenditure in certain items. The estimates in Table 165 may be as much as 50% too low, but it is unlikely that any of them are overestimates.

---

[1] Some adjustments were eventually made in this table and the final estimates are given in Chapter VI, p. 80, above.

21. AFRICAN CONSUMPTION

African expenditure and consumption had to be deduced in the main from a variety of incomplete data relating to small and not necessarily representative sections of the community. The detailed nutrition survey which was carried out under the direction of Dr B. S. Platt in Kota-Kota district in 1938-9 was one of the most important and valuable experiments of its kind in Africa. The report of the survey has not been published, but I was allowed, through the courtesy of Dr Platt, to see the manuscript in an unfinished form. It deals with rather more than a hundred families in three villages each of which was in a different ecological context and provides a systematic and comprehensive account of their economic activity. Nevertheless, as a source of quantitative income generalizations for the whole of Nyasaland in 1945, and particularly for the areas of Southern Province, where the bulk of the African people live and where the major part of the national income is earned, the survey is clearly of limited usefulness. Its value for national income purposes lies largely in the background of reliable qualitative material which it provides on African rural life and particularly in the systematic way in which it investigates every type of economic activity in the villages concerned.

In addition to this careful study there have been a few agricultural surveys covering small groups of families and illustrating particular aspects of the pattern of consumption and expenditure, and some miscellaneous small collections of family budget material. There are, for example, estimates of the way in which the students at the Jeanes school spend their money, there have been odd budgets collected for cost-of-living enquiries, and I also collected examples from persons in different walks of life. Finally, Miss J. Barker, a nutrition officer who worked in Nyasaland for several years following the nutrition survey itself, produced a number of valuable reports and articles providing largely qualitative, but some quantitative, data on food intake over the whole of the territory.

All these materials are primarily descriptive and it has been necessary to improvise boldly in converting the mass of qualitative data to quantitative terms. Except in a few instances—for example, in connection with African expenditure on taxation, or on certain imports, the quantitative estimates that are made in this section are based on reliable qualitative information or on generalizations from small-scale collections of quantitative data. Thus, while they may indicate the general orders of magnitude involved without serious distortion, they are extremely unreliable in themselves and may be positively misleading if extracted from their general context.

An additional difficulty was that the information on prices was by no means satisfactory. Price data were collected from the District Commissioners of each district, but in many cases these were the controlled prices which might differ widely from the actual price in rural areas and in the unsettled economic conditions of 1945. On that we have little knowledge, and it was necessary to assume that the prices reported from the districts were a fair reflection of the prices actually prevailing in those districts.

The following summary table gives the result of the estimates of African consumption. It includes subsistence consumption as well as cash consumption.

TABLE 166. Estimate of value of African consumption

	£	£
1. Cereals	1,520,000	
2. Green leaves	134,000	
3. Other relish (including pulses, meat, fish)	1,433,000	
4. Salt	87,000	
5. Sugar and other food (largely imported)	105,000	
6. Total value of food consumption		3,279,000
7. Beer	1,250,000	
8. Tobacco	30,000	
9. Total value of beer and tobacco consumption		1,280,000
10. Clothes	2,080,000	
11. Household goods	369,000	
12. Housing	200,000	
13. Education and churches	12,000	
14. Other goods	692,000	
15. Other services	150,000	
16. Total goods and services, excluding food, drink and tobacco		3,503,000
17. Tax		212,000
18. Total value African consumption and expenditure		£8,274,000

22. GOVERNMENT EXPENDITURE

The Central Government's part in the national economy is illustrated by the following table derived from the 1945 Financial Report. Total gross revenue of Government in 1945 was £1,916,205, and total gross expenditure was £1,771,184. Table 167 gives a net rendering of the contribution of the government sector by excluding from both sides of the account all reimbursements and the cost of producing post and telegraph services. The most substantial reimbursement was the sum of £789,552, which represents a loan from H.M. Government in payment of the interest charges on the Trans-Zambesia Railway and the receipt of debenture interest from the railway for payment to H.M. Government. In addition, the Nyasaland Government received a grant-in-aid of interest and sinking fund payments which amounted to £127,320. In effect, therefore, Nyasaland contributed out of its own revenue a sum of £75,703 to the service of its debt, which absorbed a total of £203,023.

The European local authorities in Nyasaland, i.e. the municipalities of Blantyre, Zomba and Limbe, and the Sanitary Boards, play a very small part in the national economy, and their net contribution, after allowing for Central Government grants, would raise the totals in Table 167 to little more than £950,000. For the Native Treasuries the net addition to national outlay amounted to about £31,000.

TABLE 167. Central Government revenue and expenditure

Revenue	£	Expenditure	£
1. Direct taxes, fines and gifts	446,217	9. Net expenditure on public debt charges	75,703
2. Indirect taxes	249,120	10. Other expenditure abroad	100,533
3. Receipts from the sale of goods and services	60,039	11. Net expenditure on goods and services in Nyasaland	570,770
4. Profits from posts and telegraphs	87,984	12. Investment	44,598
5. Rent and interest from local sources	7,781	13. Budget surplus	145,021
6. Interest from railways and unexpended loan funds	63,367		
7. Colonial Development and Welfare grants	22,117		
8. Total net revenue	£936,625	14. Total net expenditure	£936,625

Table 168 gives a combined revenue and expenditure account for all central and local government authorities.

TABLE 168. Combined revenue and expenditure account for government and local authorities

Revenue	£000	Expenditure	£000
1. Direct taxes, fines and gifts	454.3	6. Expenditure abroad	176.2
2. Indirect taxes	276.7	7. Net local expenditure on goods and services	601.8
3. Profits from trading services, revenue from property and other income for services	227.8	8. Saving and investment	202.9
4. Income from abroad	22.1		
5. Total net income	£980.9	9. Total net expenditure	£980.9

23. INVESTMENT

There were no satisfactory sources of estimate for investment and saving, although there were miscellaneous data covering parts of the field. They included, for example, the returns of the Post Office Savings Bank, information derived from the Income Tax Department on the capital position of companies, a few balance sheets for companies, the Government accounts and the trade returns of capital goods imports. These data were processed so far as possible to produce an estimate of saving and investment, but the final result contains a large measure of guesswork and should be received with the greatest caution. In sum it was estimated that the net saving and investment made in Nyasaland amounted to about £780,000 in 1945. It should be remembered, however, that part of the expenditure abroad of European or Asian individuals and a large part of the remittances flowing abroad on behalf of foreign companies are actually savings. Moreover, African saving proved impossible to calculate with any degree of reliability. On the one hand, the saving may have taken the form of cash buried in the floor of a hut; on the other hand it may have been effected through the purchase of durable

332 COLONIAL SOCIAL ACCOUNTING

goods (e.g. bicycles and sewing machines) or through the purchase of stocks of consumers' goods (clothing kept in a box). None of these channels of saving could be assessed without budget surveys, and no systematic budget-taking has been done for Nyasaland in recent years. African saving, exclusive of savings through the Post Office Savings Bank (which did not exceed a net increment of £50,000 for all peoples) was put at £178,000, which may well be an understatement. Government saving and investment amounted to £203,000 (see Table 169).

24. TOTAL EXPENDITURE

A summary of the expenditure estimates arrived at in this section is con-tained in Table 169. The total amounts to considerably more than the total of estimates for the income and output columns. This is not unexpected, since in so far as the expenditure and consumption figures were built upon a basis of family budget data they tended to be based on unrepresentative examples which were biased in the direction of overspending and over-consumption in relation to the average. The sources of the discrepancies will be picked up in the next section, which deals with the balancing of accounts for Nyasaland. It should be noted here, however, that the expendi-ture and investment estimates are the weakest of the three sets of estimates and must be corrected by reference to the more reliable information accu-mulated for the other two sets.

TABLE 169. National outlay of Nyasaland

Personal consumption by:	£000	£000
1. Europeans	566	
2. Asians	197	
3. Africans	8,062	
4. Total personal consumption in Nyasaland	8,825	
5. Less indirect taxes	277	
6. Total value personal consumption and expenditure in Nyasaland at factor cost		8,548
7. Government expenditure on goods and services in Nyasaland		602
Expenditure abroad by:		
8. Europeans	211	
9. Asians	30	
10. Companies (net)	155	
11. Government	176	
12. Total expenditure and remittances abroad		572
Investment:		
13. Private	576	
14. Government	203	
15. Total		779
16. Total national outlay of Nyasaland		£10,501

25. BALANCE OF PAYMENTS

The construction of a balance of international payments involves no new additions to the estimates already made, and Table 170 merely sets out in a new form results obtained in earlier sections of this chapter. Item 9 is a residual item.

TABLE 170. Balance of payments of Nyasaland

Income generated by receipts from abroad	£000	Current expenditure and investment abroad	£000
1. Domestic exports	1,831	6. Retained imports	1,576
2. Migrant labour	580	7. Expenditure abroad by individuals and government	417
3. Government	22		
4. Missions	93	8. Remittances abroad on behalf of foreign companies	320
		9. Other	213
5. Total income generated by receipts from abroad	£2,526	10. Total expenditure and investment abroad	£2,526

APPENDIX III

NOTE AND BIBLIOGRAPHY ON
VILLAGE ECONOMIC SURVEYING IN
CENTRAL AFRICA

I. NOTE ON THE SURVEYS

As is already abundantly clear, the small experiments described in Chapters X–XIII, while they have thrown up a mass of detail on the kind of problems which must be faced in any attempt to collect systematic economic data for rural Central Africa, have scarcely scratched a part of the surface of the extensive field of information that is to be exploited. What they have done is to indicate a practical method by which a useful basis of essential information can be acquired without long residence in the villages and without fundamental long-term research into the conceptual problems of economic activity in Africa. This limited standpoint is not taken up with a view to minimizing the importance of accurate collections of data or of fundamental research and the conceptual problems which it covers. On the contrary, nothing could be more important than the kind of research which seeks to illuminate the motive forces of economic—or 'uneconomic'—behaviour in African society, and to relate the basic concepts of the African producer and the consumer to the general framework of economic theory which has emerged from the needs of modern industrialized society in the west. Without such information it is impossible to comprehend the trends and determinants of economic purposes in African society.

Nevertheless, given the scarcity of all kinds of economic data, and in view of the administrative and immediate practical responsibilities for the formulation and implementation of economic policy, it is permissible to begin by setting more modest objectives. Nor is it simply that any systematic collection of data, however superficial, is at a premium in the present state of ignorance. More fundamental research should itself be planned in relation to a general framework of systematically ascertained fact. A few incomplete observations on this or that handful of households drawn haphazardly from an uncharted 'universe' is no adequate starting-point for a plan of research into the whole basis of Central African economics. We must know broadly and simply what kind of economy we are dealing with, what are its superficial economic variants, and what are the approximate limits of a convenient 'universe'. It may be that the economic concepts and behaviour patterns of the Tonga and those of the Lozi differ from those of the European in similar ways, and that a solid piece of fundamental research pursued in the one group will give data that can be applied without important qualifications to the other. We cannot be in a position to form this kind of hypothesis, even tentatively, however, unless we have a basic and reliable set of facts about both groups, and unless we can form some idea of the limits of generalization in the more obvious spheres of economic activity.

Economic research in the rural areas of Central Africa has so far been a by-product of other disciplines, more particularly of anthropology. Anthropologists, and to a lesser extent other observers such as agriculturists and nutrition experts, have been driven at times to collect economic data for their own use. Generally speaking, they have collected as much economic information as they felt they could spare time for, and as little as they felt was essential to a satisfactory interpretation of their own specialized studies. In so far as they have related their findings to economic structure in general and to the concepts of economic theory, they have done so tentatively and by the way. This is so for almost the whole of Africa, so that the economist who comes to consider the contribution of the African villages to the economy as a whole starts, at best, with a few incomplete scraps of information for a few places in an economically unmapped continent. There are obviously a great many pieces in the economic jigsaw of Africa, but there is scarcely a clue as to where the few pieces that are available belong in relation to each other and to the unidentified many.

The first task, therefore, is to undertake an extensive but systematic survey which will give some indication of the main outlines of the total economy under consideration. The second is to choose some particular point or points within the whole and to examine them so intensively that it is possible to draw firm conclusions on the dynamic nature of the economy and of its underlying forces.

Systematic budget taking is a convenient form of approach to the extensive survey. The kind of information which could be collected in this way is set out in Table 35. By applying such a schedule to a given area it would be possible, in a relatively short period of time, to obtain a stock of basic and reliable (though not accurate) data on levels and patterns of cash income, output and expenditure, on the relative importance of non-monetary activities, on the localization of village industry and on the relative contribution of internal trade. At the same time it should be possible to gather, less systematically but still continuously, a store of qualitative information on problems of productivity and value, the problems which are at the heart of an understanding of primitive economics, Finally, a series of budget surveys carried out over an extensive area would provide up-to-date information of immediate usefulness on certain features in the standard of living in different areas and on other of the more superficial aspects of economic progress.

In effect, therefore, the budget survey would form a useful starting-point for further research in three main ways:

(1) It would provide the kind of information that would permit a classification of each sample of observation in relation to the other samples for which data were available.

336   COLONIAL SOCIAL ACCOUNTING

(2) It would suggest some of the most fruitful lines of approach to more fundamental problems. For so inadequate are the data on African concepts of wealth and welfare, and on their significance in relation to economic activity in general, that we do not even know the right questions to ask because the specific local nature of the problem is obscure.

(3) It would, especially if kept up to date, provide the kind of current material on incomes and outlay which would illustrate the obvious effects of current economic policy. Budget data of a reliable, though not necessarily accurate, kind are essential to any rational policy decisions on labour, migration, minimum wages, cost-of-living allowances, distribution of industrialization, agricultural development, taxation, and so on.

How many points should be plotted in this rough but suggestive fashion before the main significant outlines of the economy could be said to be evident, it is difficult to say. Broadly speaking, it depends on the ecological content of the area conserved. The ecological survey of Northern Rhodesia distinguished twenty-one main agricultural systems, but there were many sub-variants. The Director of Agriculture's report on his Department's ten-year development plan reduced it to more manageable proportions and to a total of ten agricultural areas.[1]

These ten divisions, however, are open to the objection that they are selected for their administrative convenience rather than their ecological unity, and it is by no means certain that the twenty-one divisions of the ecological survey can in fact be telescoped at all, if the main features of the Northern Rhodesian economy are to be distinguished. In practice it might be more convenient to begin by reducing the twenty-one divisions to five or six main sub-divisions based primarily on broad agricultural features. They would be as follows:

TABLE 171. Agricultural areas of Northern Rhodesia

	Estimated number of families in villages 000
1. Kalahari Sands	52
2. Flood plains	65
3. Plateau regions	138
4. Valley regions	144
5. Lake Basin areas	61
6. All regions	460

Since these divisions are completely unrelated to political boundaries it is not possible to give reliable estimates of the population involved. However, there are probably about half a million African families in Northern Rhodesia at the present time and of these perhaps 460,000 are living in the villages.

[1] See Table 15 on p. 39.

Table 171 gives a very rough indication of their probable distribution averages in the main agricultural divisions. Within these divisions it would probably be convenient in practice to subdivide further for survey purposes. The valley regions, for example, can be subdivided into Upper, Central and Lower Valley systems of agriculture. It might be appropriate to subdivide some areas according to the staple crop grown, which might be maize, fingermillet, kaffir corn, cassava or bulrush millet. A further useful distinction might be made within the third and fourth of these broad categories in Table 171 to show the differences resulting from proximity to the railway line. As the use of the bicycle for carriage of saleable produce becomes more general, however, and as the number of those having access to a bicycle increases, the area within the influence of the permanent market which the railway belt provides becomes more and more extensive.

In order to determine the number of households which it would be necessary to cover in order to obtain a sound basis of material for a study of the Northern Rhodesian village economy, the essential subdivisions must first be decided upon. These require further examination in close consultation with the administrative and technical officers who know the country. On the basis of a very general survey of the problem, however, it seems probable that a total sample of about 5,000 families, selected in groups of about a hundred or of two or three villages, from fifty different subdivisions within these five main areas, would be sufficient for immediate practical purposes. An economist attached to the Rhodes-Livingstone Institute and having the inestimable advantage of anthropological advice and co-operation could organize a survey covering 5,000 to 6,000 households in less than two years of field work, i.e. in a normal tour, provided that he had half a dozen African research assistants who could be trained as effective independent collectors of data. In Nyasaland where the area and the range of agricultural variation are both smaller, a much smaller sample would probably be adequate for all practical purposes.

2. BIBLIOGRAPHY ON VILLAGE ECONOMIC SURVEYS

In the bibliography which follows I have tried to give some idea of the nature and extent of the source material available for a study of rural economic conditions in Northern Rhodesia at the beginning of 1950. I have included unpublished material only in so far as it has been written into report form. There is, of course, a considerable amount of uncollected material in the District and Agricultural Stations of the colony, much of which I have not been able to reach, but which would form part of the essential background data for anyone attempting a study of a particular area. So far as I have been able to discover, however, there have been no systematic collections of economic data in the rural areas, even on a very small scale, other than those mentioned in the following list.

Family budget data have been collected from the Tonga, the Lamba and the Lozi in Northern Rhodesia, and from three villages of the Kota-Kota District in Nyasaland in the course of Dr Platt's survey. No property inven-

x

tories have been taken, although Dr Margaret Read has collected some material on the possession of certain capital goods by some Nyasaland tribes, particularly the Ngoni.

The agricultural background which is essential to any economic survey has been sketched for the whole of Northern Rhodesia in the Ecological Survey. Specific quantitative data on yields and acreages in particular areas are, however, lacking, except in the few cases where Agricultural Officers have made special studies. The sociological background is most complete (from the point of view of the economist) for the Bemba of Northern Province and the Lozi of Barotse Province. There is some sociological background material for the Lamba of Ndola District, the Tonga of Mazabuka District, the Ngoni of Nyasaland, and the Unga of the Bangweulu swamp; and anthropologists from the Rhodes-Livingstone Institute have worked in Northern Rhodesia amongst the Tonga of Mazabuka District, the Ngoni of Fort Jameson District and the Luapula of Northern Province; and in Nyasaland amongst the Yao of Liwonde District.

It will be seen that, where income and expenditure data have been collected, it is on too small a scale even to provide the foundations for safe generalizations about the area from which the information was drawn. The population of the Lamba area, from which budget data were drawn, was probably about 9,000 and the number of budgets collected was twenty-nine. The population of the Tonga area surveyed was about 51,600 and the number of budgets was eighty-five. In neither case was a random sample taken. In other Northern Rhodesian cases the samples are even smaller and less informative. Dr Platt's survey for three different types of villages in the Kota-Kota District of Nyasaland covered 111 huts out of about 25,000 existing in the district.

Briefly, therefore, the available data were at best sufficient to enable tentative and very rough conclusions to be formed on the level of cash incomes in three small areas of Central Africa, covering, on the most optimistic assumptions, about 136,000 persons out of the total of more than 3½ million African individuals living in the villages of the two colonies. For the Lozi and the Unga we could probably form still rougher estimates of the level of cash incomes, and bring the total rural population for which there are quantitative data on cash incomes, to about a quarter of a million. For the remaining 3¼ million African villagers we have no specific data on village income levels.

NORTHERN RHODESIAN MATERIAL

GOVERNMENT REPORTS

1. *Report of the Ecological Survey of Northern Rhodesia.*
This was published in two parts: (i) *The Soils, Vegetation and Agricultural Systems of North-Western Rhodesia*, by C. G. Trapnell and J. N. Clothier, Government Printer, Lusaka, 1937; (ii) *The Soils, Vegetation and Agriculture of North-Eastern Rhodesia*, by C. G. Trapnell, Government Printer, Lusaka, 1943. The survey contains a comprehensive description of the agricultural

systems of the territory, but includes very little quantitative data except that of a purely descriptive and general nature; for example, it gives the normal size of some types of garden without throwing any direct light on the average acreage cultivated per family, or even on the numbers of the population cultivating according to each agricultural system.

2. *Annual Reports of the Departments of Agriculture, Veterinary Services, Game and Tsetse Control, and Labour.*

These contain such current information (rarely of a quantitative nature) as is reported by officers of the Departments concerned in the course of their duties. They include, for example, annual harvest reports in qualitative terms from those areas in which agricultural officers are stationed; and there are occasional reports of small-scale local measurements of gardens and yields made by officers of the Agricultural Department. Some information on traded crops, livestock, etc., is contained in these reports, but it refers in general to the transactions with European sectors of the economy and often to export trade only. The Labour Department provides the latest estimates of the numbers of migrants, and so gives a basis for estimating the available village population and its composition. It also gives some data on incomes in cash and in kind brought back by migrants.

3. *Departmental Development Plans* printed in Lusaka for official circulation in 1945 include:
(i) *Agricultural and Forestry Development Plans for Ten Years*, by C. J. Lewin, Director of Agriculture; (ii) *Livestock Industry Development Plans, 1945–55*, by J. H. N. Hobday, Director of Veterinary Services; (iii) *Game and Tsetse Control Development Plan, 1945–55*, by T. Vaughan Jones, Acting Director of Game and Tsetse Control. These contain very little quantitative material except of the most general kind, but they provide a useful general picture of agricultural conditions in rural areas on the basis of existing material.

4. *Annual Reports of Government Buying Agencies.*

Annual Reports of the Maize Control Board are obtainable from the Board's office in Lusaka. They give figures of total maize bought from and total payments made to Africans. Other government buying agencies, such as the Civil Supplies Board, can provide details of total purchases made for various crops. These figures are accurate, but it is rarely possible to relate them to any particular group in the community. Except in the case of the Maize Control Board's operations, it is even impossible to distinguish transactions with Africans from transactions with Europeans. In any case, the purchases of the official buying agencies account for a small proportion only of total trade in agricultural crops.

5. *Agricultural Department's Reports.*

The economic material provided by agricultural surveys, whose results have been published from time to time in the annual bulletins and reports of the Agricultural Department, is largely qualitative, except in so far as it relates to such matters as yields and acreages and population composition. See also items 8 and 12 below.

6. *Nutrition Committee of Northern Rhodesia*, unpublished reports. These include quantitative data on food intake and agricultural output in Northern Province. The field material was largely collected in 1932–3.

7. Brelsford, W. V., *Copperbelt Markets*, Government Printer, Lusaka, 1947. This is a social and economic study of the urban markets of the Copperbelt, with particular reference to Mufulira. The study was carried out in 1945 and contains a considerable amount of quantitative data. As a guide to rural economic conditions it is only of indirect value, i.e. as and when it refers to incomes of persons moving from village to town.

8. Allan, W., *Studies in African Land Usage*, Rhodes-Livingstone Papers No. 15, Livingstone, 1949.

OTHER PUBLICATIONS AND REPORTS

9. Allan, W., Max Gluckman, C. G. Trapnell, and D. U. Peters, *Report on Land Holding and Land Usage among the Plateau Tonga*, Rhodes-Livingstone Papers No. 14, Livingstone, 1947.
The survey which provided the material for this report (referred to in the text as the Tonga Survey) was carried out in 1945 and involved the systematic collection of family budget data for forty-three men and forty-two women. The report also contains valuable background material on economic conditions in the area covered and quantitative data on cash-crop production and capital investment.

10. Brelsford, W. V., *Fishermen of the Bangweulu Swamps*, Rhodes-Livingstone Papers No. 12, Livingstone, 1946.
This is a descriptive account of the lives of the fishermen of the Unga Tribe. The material was gathered while the author was District Commissioner of Luwingu District and contains a quantity of miscellaneous data on income, output and expenditure of fishermen.

11. Gluckman, Max, *Economy of the Central Barotse Plain*, Rhodes-Livingstone Papers No. 7, Livingstone, 1941.
This paper is based mainly on material collected in a field expedition to the Lozi of Barotse Province made in March–November 1940, and is a valuable source of information on economic conditions. It contains a direct attempt to assess the income of Barotseland from external sources. In addition, Dr Gluckman has kindly made available to me the raw material obtained for him by an African research assistant who collected budget data in 1944 among the Lozi.

12. Peters, D. U., *Land Usage in Serenje District*, Rhodes-Livingstone Papers No. 19, Livingstone, 1950.

13. Richards, Audrey I., *Land, Labour and Diet in Northern Rhodesia*, published for the International Institute of African Languages and Cultures, London, 1939.
This is a thorough economic study of the Bemba tribe of Northern Province. Quantitative data on economic activities, except for occasional examples where quantities or values are given, is confined to data on food intake. The field material was collected in 1930–1 and 1933–4.

14. Wilson, Godfrey, *An Essay on the Economics of Detribalization in Northern Rhodesia*, Parts I and II, Rhodes-Livingstone Papers Nos. 5 and 6, Livingstone, 1941 and 1942.
This is the first attempt to collect systematic family budget data in Northern Rhodesia. It contains the results of a house-to-house survey of the urban population of Broken Hill in 1939–40. As such it is concerned with an urban rather than a rural population, but in so far as the town dwellers are only temporary town dwellers, and in so far as they maintain income and outlay links with the rural areas, this study provides quantitative data applicable to village economic conditions.

15. Rhodes-Livingstone Institute, unpublished report, circulated privately, on a *Survey of Some Lamba Villages* carried out by a team of research workers in March 1946.
The survey is largely anthropological in scope, but it contains budget data for twenty-nine households. Brief results of the enquiry were published in the Rhodes-Livingstone Journal, *Human Problems in British Central Africa*, VIII, in an article by J. C. Mitchell entitled 'The Collection and Treatment of Family Budgets in Primitive Communities as a Field Problem'.

NYASALAND MATERIAL
GOVERNMENT REPORTS

16. *Agricultural Surveys.*
(i) *Agricultural Survey of Central Nyasaland*, by A. J. W. Hornby, mimeographed report; (ii) *Agricultural Survey of the Five Most Northerly Districts of Nyasaland*, Government Printer, Zomba, 1938. These agricultural surveys are not constructed on the same scale of comprehensiveness and detail as the Ecological Survey for Northern Rhodesia, but they are sufficient to give a general background of the pattern of agriculture.

17. *Annual Departmental Reports of the Agricultural and Veterinary and Native Affairs Departments.*
These give general data largely consisting, for example, of figures compiled by agricultural officers in connection with crops or by administrative officers in routine administrative duties.

18. Smith, Eric, *Direct Taxation of Africans in the Nyasaland Protectorate*, Government Printer, Zomba, 1937.
A brief description of economic conditions in each district based on figures currently collected by the administration.

19. *Nutritional Review of the Natives of Nyasaland*, Government Printer, Zomba, 1938.
Contains some yield and food intake data based on superficial or particular observation rather than on systematic quantitative studies.

20. *Report of a Commission appointed to enquire into the Tobacco Industry of Nyasaland*, Government Printer, Nyasaland, 1939.
Includes general figures and descriptive data on the African tobacco industry.

21. *Agricultural Department*, unpublished Agricultural Surveys, including (i) *Agricultural Survey of a Village in Mlanje*, by A. P. S. Forbes; (ii) *Village Survey of Ntaja Village, near Zomba*, by E. E. Carrall Willcocks; (iii) *Survey of a Village near Blantyre*; (iv) *Memorandum on Agricultural Survey Methods*.

OTHER PUBLICATIONS AND REPORTS

22. Barker, Jessie, *Nyasaland Native Food*.
This valuable little article on food habits among Nyasaland Africans was published in the *Nyasaland Times* and later reprinted. The author was Nutrition Officer with the Nutrition Unit, and her unpublished reports to the Government are a mine of information on local variations in food customs and on local markets.

23. Mason, T., *Improved Standard of Living for Rural Africans*.
This article was published in the *Nyasaland Agricultural Journal* of April 1944 and contains budget data for the community workers who were attending a course at the Jeanes Training Centre at which the author was an instructor.

24. Read, Margaret, *Native Standard of Living and Culture Change*, supplement to *Africa*, Vol. XI, 1938.
A qualitative account of the trend in village living standards in the Ngoni Highlands of Nyasaland.

25. Read, Margaret, *Migrant Labour in Africa and its Effects on Tribal Life*, article in the *International Labour Review*, June 1942.
Contains some quantitive data on ownership of cattle, furniture, and bicycles and machines relating to six areas in the Mzimba, Kasunga, Dowa, Kota-Kota, Dedza and Ncheu Districts of Nyasaland.

26. Schapera, I., *Migrant Labour and Tribal Life in Bechuanaland*, Oxford University Press, 1948.

INDEX

NOTE. The single alphabetical series contains detailed entries under the headings NORTHERN RHODESIA and NYASALAND. In consulting the index for an item which is likely to occur under either of these headings the reader should use these entries as well as the main alphabetical series. *Example:* 'African earnings' appears both as a main entry in the alphabetical series and also under NORTHERN RHODESIA and NYASALAND.

Accounts, 4, 5, 15
  balancing, 14
  basic, 4, 8
  design of, 9, 10, 13
  international, 14
  standardized, 229
  triple-entry, 8
  see also Social accounts
African agriculture, 139, 219
— behaviour patterns, 10, 334, 335
— clerks, wages of, 83
— consumption, 212, 334
— distribution, 211
— earnings, 213–14
— employment, 212
— expenditure on equipment, 67, 183, 205
— gardens, 140, 146, 150, 151, 160, 161, 220
— hawkers, 31, 51, 52, 196
— income, 214, 218, 335, 336
— internal trade, 335
— military service, 204
— miners, diet of, 31
— mobility, 145, 212
— non-monetary activities, 335
— output and expenditure, 335
— productivity, 219, 335
— property, 192; schedule of possessions, 132–5
— saving, 218, 219
— standard of living, 219, 335
— values, 335
— village economic problems, 116
— village industry, 335
— women, social income of, 128
Age distribution, 145
Agricultural output, 11
— production, 215
— productivity, 215
— work done by women, 220
— yield, 138, 159
Allan, W., 276, 277
Angola, 17

Annual Statement of the Trade of the United Kingdom, 1944, 285
Asbestos, 215
Asian employment, 212
— population distribution, 211, 304
Askari, *see* Northern Rhodesia, armed forces; Nyasaland, armed forces

Balancing account, 121, 152
Bantu, 17, 212
Barclays Bank, 283
Barker, Miss J., 329
Barnes, J. A., 158, 160, 205
Barter, 122–4, 195–8, 209, 226
  see also Internal trade; inter-village trade *under* Northern Rhodesia *and* Nyasaland
Baskets, 123, 129
Bechuanaland, 17, 253
Beer
  expenditure on, 175, 195, 206, 225
  income from, 167–8, 181, 185, 186, 187, 201
  205
Beira, 17, 54, 95, 96
Belgian Congo, 17, 40, 48, 52, 54, 211
Bemba, 163
Bicycles, 67, 226
Brelsford, W. V., 259, 276, 277
British East Africa, 211
British South Africa Company, 36, 54, 268, 269
Budget(s)
  family, 126, 201, 204, 205
  government, 214
Budget data, 202, 203; surveys of, 176, 178; use of, 336
— period, 152, 195
— surveys, 11
Building, 20, 126

Cape Town, 17
Capital (external), dependence on, 218
Caprivi, 17
Cash, demand for, 225

Cash crops, 155, 156
— earner, importance of, 221
— earnings, 155, 212
— expenditure, 150, 152, 201
— gifts, 174, 197
— income, 29, 141, 171, 198, 202, 205, 208, 224
— transactions, 149, 199
— wages, 41; see also Wages
Cassava, 161, 337
Cattle, see Livestock
Central Africa, 199, 211–15
Central African Airways, 54
Central African Statistical Office, 231
Children
clothing of, 180, 192
earnings of, 151, 225
labour of, 121, 221
living arrangements of, 149
proportion of, 158
Christian Mission in Many Lands, 282
Chrome, 216
Clothing, 148, 212, 224, 226
Colonial Development and Welfare, 6–7, 56, 67, 296
Colonial economy
lack of basic concepts, 228
need for social accounting systems, 7–9
Colson, Dr Elizabeth, 41, 158, 202
Companies, 214, 217
Construction, see Building
Consumption, 226
expenditure for, 175
production for, 224
subsistence output as form of, 15
Copper, 215
Cotton piece goods, 212
Court cases, 127
— damages, 225
Crops, 152, 164
cash, see Cash crops
children's, 151
discrepancies in estimation data, 139
garden, 161
income from, 189
range of, 140, 159
sales of, 167, 224
Cucurbits, 159, 160

Damages
accounts record of, 226
definition of, 127
expenditure on, 205
receipts from, 174, 185, 189
significance of, 225
Deane, Phyllis, *The Measurement of Colonial National Incomes*, 11, 13, 61, 223, 230
Debt charges, 218

Dependants
economic importance of, 116
services of, 122, 148
Development Corporations, 218
Development plans, 6, 7
Diet, 31, 149, 152, 160

Economic activity, 15, 121, 136, 182; definition and constituents of, 122, 199, 226; forms of, 197; framework of, 126, 140, 220; general survey of, 200; in the villages, 136, 137, 202, 204, 208; index of, 15; motives for, 120; national accounts of, 227; non-economic objects of, 121; small-scale, 139, 164, 166; territorial accounts of, 227; value of, 196, 204; variations in, 131, 144; volume of, 205
— groups, tendency to concentrate, 144
— output, definition of, 126
— planning, 1, 4, 5, 8
— policy, 4, 334; aims of, 120; effects of, 336; responsibility for, 6
— progress, needs of, 219
— survey, 335
— value, 117
— wealth, definition of, 127
— welfare, 120
Eggs, 141
Emigration, records of, 18
Equipment, expenditure on, 186, 187, 189, 201, 202, 205
Equity capital, charges on, 218
European farms, employment on, 154
— goods, dependence on, 194, 196
— personal consumption, 23
— trade, 141
Europeans, 19, 211–14, 217
Exchange
manufacture of goods for, 224
primitive, 121
see also Barter
Exchange economy, effects of, 129, 137
Expenditure, 14, 139, 141, 225; see also Cash expenditure

Family, the, 126, 150, 220–1
Farmers, 220
budget data, 199
expenditure by, 185, 201
Field work
problems of, 143
time taken by, 145
Flour, sales of, 224
Food, 148, 221
cost of, 219
expenditure on, 175, 185, 189, 195, 205
low output of, 219
per head, 159

Food—*continued*
  preparation of, 128, 215, 220
  processed, 216
  production of, 128, 215, 225
  retained for consumption, 155
Fruit, 141
Fundamental table, 13, 14
Furnishings, 226

Game, *see* Livestock
Gifts, 126, 218, 226
  definition of, 198
  significance of, 225
Gluckman, Dr. Max, 155, 158, 166, 178, 181,
    198, 199, 203, 206
  Economy of the Central Barotse Plain, 156
Gold, export of, 215
Government expenditure, impact of, 6
— income, 214
Grants in aid, 215

Hardware, 212
Harvest, 139, 152, 225
Headmen, 145, 146
Household equipment, 147; schedule of, 132-5
— interviews, 136, 137, 141
Householders, 138
Households, 136, 140, 150
  definition of, 147
Huts, 125, 147, 148, 150

Immigrants, 214, 218
Incentives
  money, 225
  primitive, 121
Income distribution, 118, 218
— -output-expenditure table, 13, 14; *see also*
    Fundamental table
Industrialization, effects of, 218
Internal trade, 7, 10, 126, 140, 141
Interviewing, methods of, 137, 138, 140, 151,
    175
Investigators, influence of, 144
Investment, 216-17

Jamaica, 223

Kaffir corn, 337
— truck, 212
Kin group villages, 145
Kinship, 121, 126

Labour, 143, 220
Labour costs, 215
Land utilization, 225
Lead, exports of, 216
Leisure, 225

Livestock, 224; *see also* Poultry
Lobito Bay, 17
Lowe, Miss R., 316
Lupa, 40

Maize, 129
Manpower, utilization of, 225
Manufactures, 212
Markets, 141
Marriage payments, 127, 225, 226, 227
Migrants, 212, 213, 215, 220
Milk, 141
Mineral prices, 214
— production, 215
Mining, 213, 217, 219
Missionary influence, 213
Mitchell, J. C., 205

National accounts, 3, 7, 129, 227
— groups, 227; *see also* Racial groups
— income, 2, 118, 130, 223; accounts, 8, 223;
    changes in, 225; conceptual problems, 2,
    4, 9; definition, 15, 117; distribution, 3,
    118; measurement, 228
— output, definition of, 15
NORTHERN RHODESIA
  abattoirs, 257, 297
  Abercorn, 39, 48, 54, 55
  absentees and the tax register, 231
  Accountant-General's Department, 279
  accounts, *see* social accounts
  acetylene, 49
  acreage cultivated per head, 38, 264-5
  Administration and Finance of Native Loca-
    tions in Urban Areas, Commission on,
    235
  adults, definition of, 232
  Advisory Committee on Industrial Develop-
    ment, 49
  African agriculture, 19, 21, 38-9, 42, 45, 46,
    159, 236, 255, 262-7, 337
  — cash crops, 22, 38, 43, 68, 70, 155, 156,
    252, 255
  — cash income, 22, 25, 27, 28, 29, 32, 40,
    155, 171, 174, 197, 198, 199, 202, 205,
    208, 247, 251, 252-3, 254, 262, 292
  — clothing, 26, 250-1, 292
  — consumption, 22, 26, 42, 257-8, 287-8,
    291, 292, 293-4
  — cost of living, 27, 245, 288, 292
  — earnings, 25, 26, 27, 246, 247, 248, 249,
    250, 251, 252
  — employment, 26, 27, 35, 154, 245, 248,
    249, 250, 251, 252, 261
  — expenditure, 26, 67, 183, 201, 205, 293-5,
    299
  — gratuities, 253

Northern Rhodesia—*continued*
African hawkers, 31, 51, 52, 196, 255, 256, 261, 274, 275
— housing, 55, 85, 247, 249, 250, 251
— incomes, 25, 26, 83, 250, 251, 254, 256, 259, 262; in kind, 25, 250, 251, 262, 291
— investment, 25, 258
— Labour Census, 235, 313
— medicines, 295
— migrants, *see* migrants
— miners, 26, 27, 31, 35, 246, 247, 251
— nurses, 248
— occupations, 22, 251, 261
— population, 17, 18, 21, 26, 28, 65, 74, 157, 231, 232, 288, 293
— purchasing power, 25
— rations, 27, 31, 32, 37, 42, 55, 246, 247, 248, 249, 279, 280, 283, 291, 293
— repatriates, 252
— savings, 25, 299
— subsistence, *see* subsistence . . .
— wage rates, 21, 26, 27, 37, 248, 254, 251, 271, 279
African Education Department, 283
African Labour Department, 252, 294
Agricultural Department, 38, 39, 155, 232, 234, 249, 255, 263, 264, 271
agriculture, 20, 38–46, 54, 66, 69–70, 263, 276, 299, 336
methods, 30, 38, 43, 337
output, 28, 35, 48, 63–4, 67, 263–6
yield, 38, 43, 68, 69, 159, 263–4
see also African agriculture
air traffic, 54, 58
aliens, 235, 254
area and population, 211
armed forces, 66, 155, 157, 170, 204, 252, 253, 254
army payments, 157, 170; *see also* gratuities
Asian capital, 21
— consumption, 244, 287–8, 291
— employment, 21, 51, 81, 274, 290
— expenditure, 22, 290, 291
— incomes, 244, 245
— population, 18, 21, 22, 243
— propensity to work, 22
— savings, 22, 299
— standard of living, 22, 24, 287
Askari, *see* armed forces
balance of payments, 66, 215
construction of, 299
of the resident nation, 63, 302; *see also* territorial balance of payments
Balovale, 39
Bangweulu, 30, 48, 260
banking services, 283, 284
Bantu, 17

Barotse Province, 19, 40–1, 44, 70, 136, 157, 160, 198, 203, 204, 298
agriculture in, 28, 38, 264
communications, 54
development plans, 70
Economy of the Central Barotse Plain, 156
fishing in, 47, 48
in survey-making, 140, 153, 156
incomes in, 28, 29, 254
population of, 28, 147, 204, 232, 235, 236
rubber production in, 255
barter, 25, 195–8, 209, 238, 260, 262
baskets, 31, 49
beds, 31, 49
beer
consumption of, 30
expenditure on, 175, 195, 206
income from, 29, 30, 167–8, 181, 185, 186, 187, 189, 201, 205, 291
village production of, 49
beer halls, 31–2, 280, 291, 297
bicycles, 31, 48, 55, 67
black market, 276, 288
blankets, 30, 31, 180, 181, 186, 187, 189, 207, 286
bonuses, 245, 246, 280; *see also* wages
book-keeping system, 240
books, imports of, 286, 288
branch trading, 50
bread, 175
bricks, production of, 49, 55
Broken Hill, 34, 36, 48, 54, 57, 261, 297
surveys, 251, 254, 292, 314
budget collections, 32, 176, 178, 195, 201, 202, 203, 204, 205; *see also* family budget data
building, 19, 20, 35, 47, 55, 56, 63, 64, 66ff., 281, 282
maintenance accounts, 249
output, 67, 271
questionnaire to companies, 282
butter, 44
capital, 66
need for, 44, 53
raised abroad, 301
capital equipment
expenditure on, 269–70, 273, 286, 301
investment in, 60, 302
shortage of, 20, 66
cash expenditure, 63, 64
— incomes, *see* African cash income
cassava, 161
cattle, *see* livestock
Cattle Marketing and Control Board, 257, 271, 272
cement, 48, 288
census, 17–19, 21, 22, 49, 56–7, 233–6, 240–1, 243–4

Northern Rhodesia—*continued*
Central and local government, combined net revenue and expenditure of, 298
Central Government, employees of, 56, 245, 280, 298, 296
Central Office of Statistics, 49
Central Province, 28, 29, 34, 39, 40, 42, 157, 205, 232, 235–6, 254, 266, 277
Chamber of Mines, 267, 269, 270, 291
charities, 58, 238, 283
chemicals, 282, 286, 288
Chief Inspector of Mines, 237, 242, 246
Chilanga, 48
children, 21, 31, 151, 158, 180, 192, 235, 236
Chingola, 57
Chitimene, 28, 265–6
Choma, 297
cinemas, 31, 58
Civil Service, 290
Civil Supplies Board, 255
clocks, 286
clothing, 26, 30, 31, 64, 150, 153, 179, 180, 181, 182, 185, 186, 187, 189, 192, 201, 202, 203, 205, 206, 207, 250–1, 287, 292
clothing factories, 49
clubs, 58, 284
coal, shortage of, 37, 47, 66
cobalt alloy, 35
Cobana village, 164, 165, 174, 180; expenditure, 177, 179, 182, 183, 186; income, 167, 168, 170, 186
Coloured persons, 17, 18, 22, 243, 245
Commission on Native Locations in the Urban Areas, 246, 261
Committee on Development of the European Farming Industry, 271
Committee on Native Land Tenure, 38
companies, 61, 62, 65, 275, 298, 300, 301
competition, 53
Cona Survey, 180, 200, 201, 206
Cona Tonga Survey, 199
Cona village, 162, 164, 174, 201; expenditure, 177, 179, 182, 186, 187; income, 165, 168, 171, 186, 187
consumption, 22, 23, 32, 43, 63, 70, 175, 272, 287
consumption goods, 195
copper, 35, 36, 37, 65, 67, 267, 289
Copperbelt, 21, 27, 34, 44 ff., 51 ff., 235, 247–8, 254, 276–8, 297
cost of living, 24, 29, 287
— survey, 289, 292
cotton piece goods, imports of, 62
court cases, 186
— damages, 171, 173, 178

court—*continued*
— fees, 57
— records, 178
crops, 22, 24–5, 29–31, 38–46, 159, 160, 164, 165, 167, 185, 186, 187, 189, 200, 201, 202, 263–4
cucurbits, 38, 159, 160
cups, 31
curios, production of, 50, 261
dairy products, trade in, 42, 257
damages, 174, 185, 189, 205, 293, 295
deferred pay of migrants, 252, 253
deforestation, 39
demobilization receipts, 29
dentists, incomes of, 284
Department of Agriculture, *see* Agricultural Department
depreciation of mineral industry, 268, 269, 270
devaluation, effect on copper prices of, 37
development, 33, 36, 37, 39, 40, 56, 67, 68, 69, 70, 109
Development Centre, 71
diet, 28, 30, 160
direct taxes, 296, 298
distribution industry, 35, 52, 53, 54, 63, 64, 66, 263, 275, 287
District Commissioners, 28, 56, 232, 253, 256, 275, 276
licences issued by, 51, 274
returns of, 235, 254, 256
dividends, transfer of, 301
doctoring, 169, 170, 177, 178, 185, 186, 187, 196, 205
doctors, 49, 248, 261, 262, 284
domestic produce, exports of, 52, 63, 64, 66
— servants, 23, 58, 245, 249, 250, 251, 284, 289, 290
drink, 26, 49, 64, 205, 282, 287, 288; *see also* beer
drugs, imports of, 286, 288
duiker, 259
Eastern Province, 19, 28, 29, 40, 41, 43, 54, 136, 157, 204, 232, 235, 236, 254, 274, 275, 277
Ecological Survey, 159, 253, 336
economic activity, 164, 166, 182, 196, 197, 199, 200, 202, 204, 205, 208
Economic and Statistical Bulletin, 49
economic development, 70
education, 24, 32, 58, 80, 282, 289, 290
Education Department, 248
eggs, 30, 42, 257, 259
electrical machinery, imports of, 67
electricity, 24, 280, 297
emigrants, *see* migrants

Northern Rhodesia—*continued*
  Emmasdale, 297
  employment, 19, 20, 22, 25, 27, 28, 35, 44, 56,
    170, 185, 186, 187, 200, 247, 249, 284
  engineering, 69, 246, 282
  entertainment, expenditure on, 290
    output of, 284
  equipment, expenditure on, 67, 183, 186, 187,
    189, 201, 202, 205
  Estimates (1946), 250
  European agriculture, 38, 43, 44, 77, 257,
    271, 272, 273, 274
  — consumption, *see* European expenditure
  — employment, 19, 20, 21, 35, 238, 242
  — expenditure, 20, 23, 24, 26, 50, 80, 256,
    257, 288, 289, 290, 297, 299, 301
  — goods, dependence on, 194, 196
  — Income Census, 237–43
  — incomes, 22, 23, 24, 238, 242, 243, 272, 273
  — investment, 273–4, 297, 301
  — population, 18, 20, 21, 23, 46, 48, 49, 66
  — saving, 23, 24, 290, 299, 301
  — standards of living, 23, 24
  — townships, 24, 56
  — trade, 21, 289
  — wages, 24, 37, 279
  Europeans, 19
  expenditure, 139, 175, 183, 185 ff., 190, 199,
    201, 202, 225
    accountability of, 170
    at harvest time, 152
    average estimate, village survey, 158, 180,
      188, 189
    by returned migrants, 195
    distribution of, 190
    magnitude of, 141
    non-economic, 225
    of army gratuities, 176
    on clothing, 179, 181, 182, 206, 207
    on doctoring, 177
    on equipment, 67, 182
    on food, 175, 185, 189, 195, 205
    on livestock, 166, 183
    on meat, 166
    on transport, 177
    patterns of, 22
    tables, sources for, 14
    transfer, 179
    see also cash expenditure
  exports, 35, 44, 49, 63, 66, 70, 299, 300,
    302
  external trade, statistics of, 285
  factories, 48–9
  family budget data, 28, 32, 41, 90, 201, 203,
    204, 205, 287, 289, 291, 292, 293, 294,
    295
  farmers, questionnaire to, 24, 32, 42, 238, 273

ferro-concrete, 49
fines, 186, 187, 189, 205; *see also* court
  damages
fingermillet, 337
firewood, 281, *see also* fuel
fish, 22, 25, 28, 29, 30, 32, 39, 40, 47, 48,
  163, 187, 259, 260, 261, 276, 277, 293,
  294
fish-farming experiments, 48
fishing, 35, 40, 47–8
*Fishing Industry and its Markets, Preliminary
  Report on*, 259
floods, 147, 203
flour, 165, 294
food, 22, 27, 32, 42 ff., 46, 51–2, 64, 69, 155,
  159, 245, 255, 272, 276, 286–8, 290, 300
food relish, 159 175
footwear, 26, 64
foreign capital, 301–2
— companies, 270, 299, 300–1
forestry, 35, 61, 63, 64, 67, 281
Fort Jameson, 39, 48, 54, 57, 256, 265–6, 297
  District Survey, 136, 155, 164, 178, 204
Fort Rosebery, 39
fruit, 40, 44, 160, 165, 166, 266, 293
fuel, 47
funerals, 30, 256
furnishings, 46, 49, 193, 246
game, 30, 42, 259
Game and Tsetse Department, 48, 259
gardens, cultivation of, 27, 38, 41, 160, 161,
  236, 292
General Tonga Survey, 199, 200–1, 206
geographical description, 17
— product, 60, 65, 67, 69
ghee, imports of, 287
gifts, 126, 174, 178, 179, 181, 182, 185, 194,
  196, 197, 201, 202, 204, 205
  receipts from, 186, 187, 189, 198, 200, 206
goats, 42, 162, 163, 256, 257, 259
gold, 35, 36, 246
Government
  expenditure of, 19, 56, 63–4, 249
  income from, 64, 249, 299
  income of, 27, 45, 56, 57, 63, 65, 302
  investment by, 298, 299
  output of, 35, 63, 64, 67, 279–81
  see also Central Government, Central and
    local government, local government
grants, accounting treatment of, 57, 58, 247,
  248, 282, 283, 296, 297
gratuities, army, 153, 156, 158, 171, 172, 174,
  180, 185, 189, 193, 197, 204
green leaves, 29, 41
groceries, imports of, 287
groundnuts, 29, 70, 293, 294
Hanamonga Survey, 164, 165, 180

Northern Rhodesia—*continued*
  Hanamonga village, 167; expenditure, 177,
    179, 182, 183, 186, 187; income, 168,
    170, 171, 186, 187; payments in kind, 174
  hand-made goods, 50
  hardwood, 46
  harvest, 21, 30, 43, 203
  hawkers, *see* African hawkers
  hides and skins, 259
  holidays, 24
  hotel industry, 20, 58, 284
  household equipment, 147, 182, 192, 205; *see
    also* furnishings
  — income questionnaire, 30, 238
  — transactions, 174, 177, 179, 196, 203, 204,
    205, 206
  households, 165, 200, 202
    per province, 157
    size of, 158
  housing, 24, 27, 28, 32, 55, 56, 69, 84, 243,
    247, 248, 280, 297
  huts, village, 30
  hydro-electric project, Kariba Gorge, 48
  immigrants, 18, 19, 33, 40, 57, 238, 254
  immigration data, 19
  Immigration Department, 300
  import goods, consumption, 62
  imports, 23, 36, 52, 61, 62, 67, 285–91, 299–
    302
  income
    distribution of, 41, 45, 65, 190, 191, 243
    from abroad, 35, 63, 64, 66, 67, 298, 300,
      302
  income census, 243
  — groups, 238
  — levels, 199, 208
  — -output-expenditure table, 13, 14, 63
  — tax, 37, 296, 300
  Income Tax Commissioner, 272, 275, 289, 290
  Income Tax Department, 240
  industry, concentration of, 54
  infant mortality, 31
  insurance, 24, 58, 284, 289
  internal trade, 40, 276, 277, 285
  inter-village trade, 22, 53, 196, 197, 198, 208,
    255, 275, 276
  investment, 42, 55, 64, 67, 68, 286, 296–9
    abroad, 63, 301
  iron, 49
  irrigation, 45
  ivory, 50
  jewellery, imports of, 286, 288
  journey to work, 22
  Kaffir corn, 160, 161
  Kafue, 48, 57, 70, 260, 275, 297
  Kalahari Sands, 336

Kariba Gorge, hydro-electric project, 48
Kitwe, 57, 276
labour, 21, 22, 29, 39, 40, 42, 56, 200–2, 204,
    205, 215
  drain of, 43
  migration of, 39, 40
  recruitment of, 284
  shortage of, 66, 156
Labour Census, 1946, 254
Labour Department, 235, 236, 250, 254, 267
  surveys by, 253, 292, 314
Labour Officers, 250, 261
Lamba, 204, 205, 206, 234
land, 36, 39, 40, 41, 43, 44, 68, 155, 263, 264
land hunger, 39
— shortage, 40
— utilization, 263
Land Tenure Committee, 38
laundries, 284
lead, 35
leather, 49, 282, 286, 288, 300
Legislative Council, 69
licences, trading, 52, 57, 296, 297, 298
licensed traders, 275
limestone, 35, 36
livestock, 26, 28–31, 35, 39, 41, 42, 63, 64,
    151, 157, 161 ff., 166–7, 183, 185, 186,
    189, 200–2, 256, 257, 258, 271, 272, 273,
    274, 280, 293, 295; *see also* agriculture
living conditions, survey of, 32
Livingstone, 32, 46, 48, 56, 57, 73, 297, 300
local government, 56, 57, 70, 247, 279, 280,
    290, 295, 297, 298
Lozi, 28, 70, 140, 151, 158, 160, 203, 262
  clothing, 180, 181
  consumption, 162
  country, 136
  economic resources, 156–7
  expenditure, 177, 181, 187, 189, 206
  gardens, 161
  income, 164, 166, 167, 168, 170, 171, 187,
    189, 191, 205, 206, 208
  prices, 194
  property, 192, 193, 197
    transfer payments, 174, 179
Luanshya, 57
Luapula, fish trade, 260
Lukanga Swamp, fish trade, 260
Lusaka, 32, 39, 40, 48, 54, 55, 57, 58, 279,
    296, 297
luxuries, 187
machinery, 51, 286, 287
Magoye, 258
maize, 21–2, 28, 29, 30, 38, 41, 43, 44, 45,
    154–5, 159–6, 164–5, 216, 225, 255, 264,
    271, 272, 274, 277, 296, 337
malaria, 31, 68

Northern Rhodesia—*continued*
  malnutrition, 68
  manufacturing, 20, 48, 49, 276, 277
    earnings in, 27, 170, 186–7, 189, 200, 246, 251, 262
    export trade in, 49
    imports, 285, 288
    in village income, 29
    output, 35, 49, 63, 64, 67, 262, 281, 282
  market fluctuations, 289
  — garden crops, 255
  — surveys, 276
  marketing organizations, 44
  markets, 22, 28, 36, 42 ff., 48, 51 ff., 66, 254 ff., 261, 275 ff., 277
  marriage payments, 171, 173, 174, 178, 179, 185, 186, 187, 189
  Mashonaland Railway Company, 54
  Mawiko, 40
  Mazabuka, 38, 39, 40, 57, 136, 154–5, 201–2 256, 297
  meal, 41, 265, 266, 267, 293, 294
  meat, 161, 162, 166, 187
    consumption of, 31, 42, 259
    expenditure on, 294
    in rural diet, 30
    in the Barotse flood plain, 30
    in urban diet, 32
    industrial rations of, 42
    markets for, 42
    production by Europeans, 44
    village trade in, 257
    see also livestock
  medical services (mission), 58
  medicines, receipts from, 262
  metals
    exports, 300
    imports, 286, 288
    output, 282
    value of sales, 267, 268, 270
  migrants, 15, 18, 20, 25, 28, 29, 30, 35, 39, 40, 42, 68, 75, 77, 115, 120, 152, 155, 157, 170, 173, 175, 179, 185, 186, 187, 189, 195, 204, 236, 252, 253, 254, 258, 279, 299, 301
  migration, rate of, 156, 234
  milk, 30, 42, 252, 257–8, 271
  milled grain, 49, 265
  millet, 29, 161, 265, 337
  mineral companies, 36, 267
    accounting treatment, 61
    and housing, 55
    as income distributors, 28
    as taxpayers, 45
    capital expenditure by, 299, 301
    imports by, 302
    operating surplus of, 268

mineral companies, *continued*
    remittances of, 299
    reports of, 290
    sales of, 302
    use of timber by, 46, 47, 281
  — industry, 19, 20, 34, 35, 36, 267–9
    and world prices, 36
    expansion of, 66
    expenditure by, 37
    exports, 17, 279, 300
    investment by, 298, 299
    investment demands of, 60
    market surveys, 276
    output, 35, 63, 64, 67, 270, 271
    payments by, 237, 246, 270, 271
    price trends, 65
    production costs, 35, 63, 64, 67, 270, 271
    rations for workers, 42
    recreational facilities, 31
    returns, 267
    transport costs, 37, 268
    value of, 35
  — wealth, concentration of, 68
  minerals, 37, 61, 67, 286, 288, 300
  miners, 27, 28, 31
  Mines, Chief Inspector of, 282
  Mines Department, 267, 269, 270
  miscellaneous services, 284
  missionaries, missions, 35, 58, 63, 64, 79, 177, 238, 282, 283, 299
  Mongu, 39, 40, 55, 156, 181, 188, 203, 256
  Mongu District, 36, 208
  monogamists, budget data on, 199
  Monze, 154, 187, 297
  motor spirit, 287
  — vehicles, 67
  Mporokoso, 298
  Mufulira, 57
  Mufulira Copper Mines, Ltd., 268
  Mufulira market, 276
  Mweru fish trade, 260
  Mweru Lake, 48
  national accounts, 295, 298
  — expenditure, 295
  — income, 37, 50, 59, 60, 62, 63, 65, 66, 286; and outlay, 63, 285; -output-expenditure estimates, 300
  — output, 34, 53, 63
  — product, 65, 267
  — (territorial) income, output and outlay, 64
  — (territorial) output, 57, 58
  Native Authorities, 245, 250, 280, 298
  Native Labour Census, 250, 251
  native reserves, overpopulation of, 39
  — taxes, 296, 297, 298
  Native Treasuries, 57, 279, 297, 298

Northern Rhodesia—*continued*
Nchanga Consolidated Copper Mines Ltd.,
  268
Ndola, 32, 39, 48, 55, 56, 57, 204, 205, 276,
  297
net output, 61, 269, 270, 279
Ngoni, 75, 140, 152, 155, 158, 262, 275
  army receipts, 171
  budgets, 204
  children, 181
  clothing prices, 181
  country, 136
  earners, 155
  expenditure, 176, 177, 180, 182, 183, 185,
    189, 206
  income, 167, 168, 170, 171, 185, 189, 191,
    198, 205, 206, 208
  interviews with, 160
  meat consumption, 162
  property, 193, 194, 197
  resources, 193
  savings, 156
  transactions, 164, 165
  transfer payments, 174, 179
  villages, gratuity income in, 172
Northern Province, 19, 22, 28, 29, 39, 41, 43,
  48, 70, 157, 204, 232, 235, 236, 254, 264,
  265, 266
oils, 51, 286, 288, 300
outer provinces, 18, 54, 63, 208
output, 34–58, 230–302
  agricultural, 28
  increase of, 70
  subsistence, *see* subsistence output
  see also net output
overcrowding, 32
overploughing, 68
overpopulation, 39 ff., 155
oxygen, 49
paints, 286, 288, 300
paper, 282, 286, 288
paraffin, 175, 195
parquet flooring, 49
payments abroad, 299, 302
pedlars, *see* African hawkers
Pemba, 297
pensions, 20, 243, 249, 296
personal consumption, 286, 287, 288; *see also*
  African consumption, Asian consumption *and* European consumption
— services, 20, 27, 35, 58, 246, 251, 284
Petauke, 255, 265, 266
petrol, 287
pigs, 42, 162, 163, 256, 257, 259
Plateau regions, 336
Plateau Tonga, *see* Tonga
ploughing, 31, 38–41

ploughs, 183, 193
plywood, 49
Polish nationals, 241
poll tax, 296
polygamy, 199, 204
population, 17–25, 28, 39, 41, 59, 67–8, 115,
  131, 157, 158, 200, 202, 204, 207, 208,
  231–6, 243, 264, 336
Post and Telegraphs Department, 296
potatoes, 271–4
poultry, 30, 31, 42, 162, 163, 257, 258, 259,
  271
price control, 52
— data, 277
— index, 182
— stabilization, 45
Price Controller, 286
printing, 282
private contracting, 55
processed goods, imports, 285
producers' goods, 51, 286
production factors, 60, 295
productive equipment, 155, 182–3
productivity, 31, 60, 68, 204
professions, 20, 27, 35, 57, 246, 248, 251,
  284
profits
  local government, 280, 298
  mining, 65
  on capital, 60
property, 175, 176, 191–4, 196
— incomes, government, 298
public debt, 296
— services, 19, 20, 297
Public Works Department, 32, 53, 97, 250,
  282
Public Works Extraordinary, 297
pulses, 27, 29, 41, 90, 256, 265, 266, 267
purchasing power, 46, 49, 50, 53, 62, 208
quarrying, 20
questionnaires
  to agricultural officers, 265
  to District Commissioners, 254
  to missions, 58, 248
racial groups, 17, 18, 22, 34
railway belt, 24, 26, 42–3, 54, 68–9, 70, 254–
  7, 258, 274, 283
— line, 18, 22, 38, 40–4, 48, 53–5, 67–8, 70,
  283
Railway provinces, population of, 18, 208
railways, 55, 242, 243, 247, 278–9, 281, 298–
  9, 301, 302
  see also under railway *and* Rhodesia Rail-
    ways, Ltd.
ranching, 45
rates, 23, 56, 290
rations, *see* African rations

Northern Rhodesia—*continued*
raw materials, 269–70
re-afforestation, 47
real earnings, 245
— incomes, 62
receipts from abroad, 299, 302
remittances
abroad, 64
of Askaris, 253
rents, 23, 246, 247, 289, 290, 293, 295
repatriates, 253–4
reserves, *see* native reserves
resident nation
balance of payments, 302
definition, 300
residents' incomes, 60, 63, 68
resources, shortage of, 68
retail trade, *see* trade
— distribution, *see* distribution industry
retained imports, 299, 302
Rhodes-Livingstone Institute, 234, 251, 262
Rhodesia Broken Hill Development Company Ltd., 268
Rhodesia Railways, Ltd., 37, 54, 55, 242, 247, 268, 278
Rhokana Corporation Ltd., 268
rice, 256
Road Board, 279
roads, 54, 69, 249
Roan Antelope Copper Mines Ltd., 268
root crops, 41, 161, 265
royalties (mining), 36, 61, 268, 269
rubber, 255, 282, 286, 288, 300
rural areas, 21, 27, 31, 32, 45, 50, 51, 69, 70, 71, 250, 262, 291, 292, 293, 294
— communities, 50, 62
— diet, 30
— incomes, 27, 29, 202
salaries, *see* wages
salt, 31, 175, 293, 294
sanitation, 24, 297
saving, 20, 24, 26, 63–4, 67, 185, 189, 205, 253, 298–9
sawmilling, 46, 64
school fees, 177
second-hand goods, trade in, 172, 200
secondary industry, 40, 50, 66
self-government, 19
Serenje, 39, 146, 163, 234
services, 22, 29, 64, 269, 284
Sesheke, 39, 46
settlers' funds, 217
sewing machines, 31
shareholders, transfers by, 301
sheep, 42, 162, 163, 256, 257, 259
shopkeepers, 51, 261, 274, 275
shops, 21, 24, 51

silver, 35
sleeping sickness, 31
smallholding, 51
budget data, 199
smiths, 31, 49
soap, 31, 49, 175, 195, 282, 295
social accounts, 9, 59–71
— security, 289
— services, 69, 70
Social Welfare Department, 296
soil, *see* land
soldiers, *see* armed forces
sorghum, 265
South Africans, expenditure abroad of, 288
Southern Province, 22, 29, 38, 39, 40, 42, 48, 136, 157, 232, 235, 236, 254, 264, 277
specialization of labour, 22, 140, 197
spending habits, 298
sport, 284, 286, 288
standards of living, 18, 19, 22, 24, 28, 29, 30, 31, 32, 43, 50, 53, 61, 64, 71, 159, 181, 191, 193
stationery, 175, 286
stores, *see* shops
Stores and Transport Department, 286
subsidies, 44, 45, 46, 63, 64, 296, 298
subsistence activities, 28, 291
— agriculture, 21, 22, 38, 261, 263, 265, 267
— consumption, 63, 64, 219, 221, 257, 281, 283
— farming, 199
— fishing, 47, 48, 260
— food production, 22, 28, 42
— incomes, 25, 28, 29, 198, 262
— output, 29, 42, 43, 58, 194, 196, 197, 238, 262, 267, 283
— producers, living standards of, 50
sugar, 175, 293, 294
surplus produce, disposal of, 51, 52
surveys, 154, 232, 263; *see also* village surveys
swamps, 47
sweet potatoes, 160
tailors, 49, 187
Tanganyika, 40, 48, 70, 260
tax register, 178, 231, 235
taxation, 24, 37, 55, 65, 66, 67, 179, 186, 187, 189, 205, 271, 302
indirect, 63, 64, 286, 295, 296, 298
see also direct taxes, income tax, native taxes *and* taxpayers
Taxation Review Committee, 301, 302
taxpayers, 17, 21, 45, 202, 204, 232, 233, 235
tea, 293, 294
teak, 46
Ten-Year Development Plan, 39, 67, 69, 70, 264, 336

Northern Rhodesia—*continued*
territorial balance of payments, 62, 299
— income, 62, 64, 65
— nation, definition, 300
— outlay, 64
— output, 64, 67
textiles
    exports of, 294, 300
    imports of, 286, 288
    output of, 246, 282
timber, 46, 47, 49, 281
tobacco
    consumption of, 23, 26, 293, 295
    earnings from, 246
    expenditure on, 64, 175–195, 205, 289, 290
    exports of, 66, 300
    farming of, 40, 44, 54, 155, 255
    imports of, 286, 287, 288, 290
    output of, 43, 49, 160, 271, 282
    sales of, 165, 274, 276
    trade in, 51, 255
    Turkish, 43, 44, 45
    Virginia, 44
Tonga, 38, 43, 186, 193, 200, 208, 262, 265
    beer trade, 168, 206
    cash crops, 156
    cash incomes, 28, 186, 201, 205
    clothing, 180, 181, 206
    crops, 38, 41, 159, 160, 165
    damages, 174
    equipment, 193
    expenditure, 177, 179, 181–3, 186, 189–90, 201–2
    furniture, 193
    income, 167, 170, 171, 186, 189–91, 198, 200–3, 206, 208
    maize trade, 31, 164
    marriage customs, 173
    meat consumption, 162
    population, 158
    standard of living, 193
    survey, 140, 144, 154–5, 199–201, 206, 258
    wealth, 197
tour counts, 231, 233
tourists, 63–4, 299, 300, 302
towns, 21, 24, 27, 29, 31, 32, 36, 42, 50, 51, 54, 55; *see also* urban areas
trade, 21, 22, 23, 24, 25, 28, 40, 51, 52, 53, 157, 166
    in agricultural produce, 43, 267
    in dairy products, 42
    in fish, 30, 39, 48, 70, 260
    in food, 51
    in livestock, 26, 42, 256
    in tobacco, 51
    local, 164, 197
    retail, 21, 51, 246, 278, 285, 291

second-hand, 172
small-scale, 166
statistics of, 62
wholesale, 51, 53, 246
traders, 52, 257
    incomes of, 24, 243
    records of, 176
    roadside, 52, 276
trading concerns, 274
— licences, 274
— profits, government, 298
— services, 297; government expenditure on, 296; government profit from, 280; local authority, 56, 279, 280
— sites, 'second-class', 51
transfers, 189, 202, 204, 209, 293, 295, 296, 298, 301
transport, 19, 20, 35, 47, 48, 54, 55, 63, 64, 66, 67, 177–8, 186, 195, 268, 279, 286, 287, 337
tribes, distribution of, 263
triple-entry account, 59
tsetse fly, 30, 39, 41, 42, 68
underdeveloped areas, 67, 68
Unga fishermen, report on, 259
United Kingdom immigrants, expenditure abroad of, 288
unskilled labour, 23
urban areas, 29, 32, 42, 48, 262, 292; expenditure in, 291, 292, 293, 294
— locations, 21, 32, 236, 292
— markets, 68, 276
— population, 235, 236
— settlement, 255
    see also towns
valley regions, 336–7
vanadium, 35, 36
vaseline, 175
vegetables, consumption of, 293
    production of, 44, 266
    sales of, 165, 166
veneer, 49
venereal disease, 31
Veterinary Department, 162, 256, 257, 258, 271
Victoria Falls, 53
village consumption, 29, 30, 258–9
— economy, 140, 172, 180, 195, 199, 236, 237
— housing, 28, 250
— incomes, 28–30, 209, 251, 261
— industries, 22, 35, 43, 49, 50, 61, 62, 64, 67, 196, 262
— population, 21, 236, 292, 336, 337
— standard of living, 28, 29, 31, 32
— surveys, 28, 29, 155, 176, 184, 199, 200, 208, 262

Northern Rhodesia—*continued*
　village trade, 25, 257, 258, 291, 292, 293; *see also* inter-village trade
　wages, 40, 41, 250, 271, 273, 279, 281–4
　war, effects of, 252
　water, expenditure on, 290
　waxes, 286, 288, 300
　wealth, 155, 193, 194, 197
　welfare amenities, 31, 32
　— analysis, national income concept of, 60
　Western Province, 28, 29, 34, 36, 40, 157, 205, 232, 235, 236, 264, 265, 266, 277
　wheat, 271, 274
　wholesale trade, *see* trade
　women, 22, 31, 38, 180, 199, 200, 232, 235, 236
　wood, 46, 50, 281, 286, 288, 300
　Workmen's Compensation Commissioner, 245–9 *passim*, 272–81 *passim*
　Workmen's Compensation Ordinance, 245, 246
　Workmen's Compensation statistics, data from, 284
　Wusikili, 276
　Zambesi, 54, 70
　zinc, 35, 36
Nutrition experts, 335
— survey, 137
Nyakyusa, 145
NYASALAND
　abattoirs, 315
　acreage cultivated, 90, 317, 318, 321
　African cash crops, 90, 91, 96, 315
　— cash incomes, 77, 83, 89, 95, 101, 103, 216, 311, 313, 314, 316
　— cash needs, 84, 311
　— cash savings, 331
　— census enumerators, 303, 304
　— consumption, 84, 85, 98, 329, 330
　— earnings, 83, 101, 309, 310, 311, 312, 313; margin of error in estimates, 310, 312
　— employment, 82, 98, 309, 310, 311, 313
　— incomes, 98, 101, 309, 310, 311, 313, 315, 316, 317, 318, 320, 329
　　distribution of, 82, 309, 310
　　in kind, 313
　— migrants, *see* migrant labour
　— residents on estates, 311
　— wages, 83, 93, 94, 96, 102, 309, 310, 312, 313, 325
　　children's, 76
　　in kind, 311
　　migrants', 101
　　women's, 76
　Agricultural Department, 90, 102, 105, 112, 139, 311, 315, 321, 322, 325
　agricultural surveys, 89, 102, 329

agriculture, 88, 90, 93, 103, 104, 322
　African, 77, 89, 101, 326
　employment in, 83, 311, 312, 320
　European, 75, 91, 92, 95, 304, 306, 321
　income from, 98, 312, 320, 322
　output of, 89, 98, 103, 322, 326
　price of produce, 93, 113
Annual Report on the Nyasaland Protectorate, 113
area, 211
armed forces, 77, 78, 304, 305, 306, 309, 310, 313, 314, 322
Asian consumption, 82, 315, 328, 332
— employment, 212
— expenditure, 328, 331, 332
— incomes, 81, 320
— population, 74, 75, 76, 78, 304
— servants, 328
— shops, 323
— taxation of, 328
　see also under Indian . . .
Askari, 75; *see also* armed forces
balance of payments, 105, 107, 108, 215, 332, 333
bananas, 316
banking, output of, 326
banks, 87
Barker, Miss J., 329
barter, 316
bauxite, 88
Bechuanaland, 314
beds, 87, 319
beer
　consumption of, 319, 330
　local trade in, 76, 82, 87, 317, 320
　output of, 89, 95, 318
Bell report, 74
bicycles, 86, 332
blankets, 85
Blantyre, 55, 76, 81, 96, 97, 309, 315, 319, 330
brickmaking, 76, 324
budget surveys, *see* family budget data
building, 76, 95, 304, 309
— output, 89, 98, 324, 326
bus service, 81
bushfiring season, 319
capital investment, 103, 108, 112
— resources, 111
capsicums, 321
cash crops, cash incomes; *see under* African . . .
cassava, 318
cattle, 303, 316
census, 75, 78, 234, 303, 304, 310, 311, 313, 317
Central Government, 96, 309, 310, 319, 322, 330, 331
Central Province, 90, 92, 101, 102, 315, 317

Nyasaland—*continued*
cereals, consumption of, 330
Chewa, 75
Chikwawa district, 91
children, 76, 303, 311, 312
chillies, 321
Chinteche, 101, 102
Chiromo, 73, 96
cinemas, expenditure on, 325, 327
civil servants, incomes of, 309, 322
clothing, 84, 85, 327, 328, 330, 332
clubs, 312, 325, 326, 327
coal, 88
coffee, 315, 321
Colonial Development and Welfare Act, 109;
   grants, 107, 109, 319, 320, 331
Colonial Development Corporation, 92, 93,
   97, 108, 109
Colonial Research Fellowship, 63
Coloured persons, 18, 19, 78, 308, 320
companies, 331
   income of, 98, 100, 306, 307, 320
copper, 88
corundum, 88
cost of living, 94, 309, 327, 329
Cost of Living Committee, 309
cotton, 90, 91, 92, 93, 111, 312, 315, 316, 321,
   324
— ginneries, 88
— growers, 83, 91
— piece goods, 85
Council of Women, 327
Customs Department, 322
dairy products, 317, 321
deferred pay, 313
Department of Agriculture, *see* Agricultural
   Department
development, 108, 109, 110, 111, 112
distribution, 77, 78, 79, 89, 95, 98, 104, 312,
   317, 320, 323, 326
District Commissioners, 309, 312, 315, 317,
   323, 329
District Officers, 313
domestic servants, 77, 80, 83, 312, 313, 327,
   328
education, mission provision of, 96
Education Department, 311, 325
eggs, 317, 321
electricity, 81, 319, 327
emigrant labour, *see* migrant labour
employment
   abroad, 194
   agricultural, 311
   casual, 83, 309, 310.
   local, 94, 102
estate owners, 308, 311
Estimates, 1946, 309

European consumption, 80, 98, 315, 322, 327,
   328, 332
— employment, 78, 306, 324
— estates, 75, 91, 311
— expenditure, 80, 327, 328, 332
— incomes, 79, 80, 98, 305, 306, 320, 325
— industries, 78, 304, 306
— investment, 322
— occupations, 305
— pensions, 80, 305, 306, 320
— population, 74, 75, 76, 77, 78, 80, 304; *see
   also* census
— retirement, 75
— saving, 80, 327, 328
— settlers, permanent, 76
— shops, 323
— standard of living, 79, 80, 81, 327, 328
— taxation of, 80, 305, 327, 328
— townships, 76, 97
Europeans, 213
expenditure, 106, 108, 332, 333
   abroad, 98, 107, 331
exports, domestic, 93, 107, 323, 333
   handling of, 95, 323
factor cost of personal expenditure, 98, 332
factories, output, 89, 95, 311, 322, 326
Factories Act, 324
family budget data, 327, 329, 332
Financial Report, 305, 319, 330
fines, 331
firewood, 324
Fiscal Survey of Nyasaland, report of, 86
fish, 77, 82, 87, 88, 95, 103, 312, 316, 319
   consumption of, 318, 330
   output of, 89, 97, 98, 316, 320, 326
Fisheries Adviser, 316
Fisheries Survey, 316
flour, 316, 318
forestry, 95
   output of, 89, 97, 98, 324, 326
Forestry Department, 324
Fort Johnston, 97
fruit, 318
furniture, 324
game, 319
ghee, 317
gifts, 84, 87, 317, 331
goats, 316
gold, 88
Government, 95, 96, 97, 103, 305, 314, 330,
   331, 333
   African income from, 77, 309, 310, 320
   expenditure of, 96, 97, 98, 105, 325
   income of, 96, 98, 101, 110, 319, 320, 322,
   331
   output of, 89, 98, 104, 326
   grants in aid, 113, 330

Government—*continued*
  gratuities, 322
  Great Rift Valley, 73
  green leaves, African consumption of, 318, 330
  groundnuts, 76, 90, 315, 317, 318
  handicrafts, 95, 103, 317, 320, 326
  harvest season, 76, 102
  hawkers, 77, 95, 323
  hides, 317, 321
  hoarding, 86
  hospital orderlies, 310
  hotels, 312, 325, 326
  housing, 87, 318, 319, 330
  hunting, 319
  huts, 303
  immigrants, 74, 104, 112
  imports, 85, 107, 113, 306, 322, 333
  income, 104, 214, 306, 324
    from abroad, 325, 331, 332, 333
    in kind, 325
    see also under African . . ., Asian . . ., European . . ., Government *and* subsistence . . .
  income distribution, 81
  -output-expenditure table, 13, 14, 303
  Income Tax Department, 305, 306, 308, 325, 327, 331
  Indian agriculture, 78, 307, 308, 311
  — Chamber of Commerce, 81
  — employment, 78, 307
  — incomes, 81, 82, 307, 308
  — investment, 81
  — occupations, 78, 307, 308, 323
  — saving, 81
  indigenous community, 307
  insurance, 326
  inter-African trade, 87
  interest, government, 322
  interest charges, 330
  intermarriage, tribal, 75
  internal trade, 216
  inter-village trade, 82, 86, 87, 97
  investment, 87, 104, 105, 106, 107, 331, 332
    abroad, 333
    by missions, 325
    financed abroad, 105
    government, 331, 332
  investment charges, 108
  iron, 88
  Jeanes School, budget survey at, 329
  Kasungu, 92, 101, 102, 108
  Kota-Kota district, 329
  labour, 74, 92, 309, 311, 312, 315
    drain of, 93, 94
    mobility of, 303, 305
    seasonal, 83, 311, 313
    shortage of, 93, 101

Lake Nyasa, 73
  fishing on, 97, 108
  level of, 96
  transport on, 96, 324
lead, 88
leave pay, 306
legumes, 321
Lilongwe, 76
Limbe, 76, 81, 97, 309, 315, 319
livestock, 82, 315, 316, 319, 320, 321, 322, 326
local government, 309, 310, 319, 322, 330
Lomwe, 75
mahogany, 47
maize, 90, 92, 113, 315, 317, 318, 321
Maize Control Board, 112
manufacture, 88, 98
  output of, 89, 304, 324, 326
manuring, 93
markets, 90, 103, 314, 315, 316
marriage payments, 317
mats, 319
meal, 319; *see also* flour
meat, 84, 87, 314, 330, 321, 322
migrant labour, 77, 83, 85, 87, 89, 94, 98, 99, 101, 102, 104, 107, 216, 313, 314, 320, 333
milk, *see* dairy products
minerals, 88, 103, 324
missionaries, 75, 305, 306, 320
missions, 77, 82, 89, 95, 96, 98, 104, 107, 310, 320, 324, 326, 333
municipalities, 327, 330
Murchison Rapids, 73, 96
national accounts, 100, 223, 332
national income, 98, 104, 111
  definition, 100
  distribution, 101, 316, 329
  government share, 110
  tables, 98, 327
national income, output and expenditure, 98
  — outlay, 98, 332
  — output, 98, 103, 326
  — output tables, 327
Native Authorities, 309, 310, 316
Native Tobacco Board, 91
Native Treasuries, 97, 330
Native Trust Land, 90, 91
Northern Extension (railway), 96
Northern Province, 93, 94, 96, 101, 102, 108, 317
Northern Rhodesia, comparison with, 63
  migrants in, 313, 314
Nutrition Adviser, 316
Nutrition Survey, 90, 137, 317, 329
Nutrition Unit, 316
Nyasaland Railways, *see* transport
oil seeds, production of, 92

Nyasaland—*continued*
oils, production of, 321, 324
omnibus company, 95
output, 88–98, 303–33
overgrazing, 90
parcel trade statistics, 314
passenger traffic, 95
pensions, 322
personal consumption, 98, 104, 332
  see also under African . . ., Asian . . . and
  European . . .
— services, output of, 326
planting period, 102
poll tax, 78
polygamy, 204
population, 74, 75, 76, 112, 115, 303, 304; see
  also census
Port Herald area, 92
Portuguese East Africa, 74, 95
Post Office and Telegraph Department, 319,
  331
Post Office Savings Bank, 331, 332
potatoes, production of, 44, 90, 315
pots and pans, 86, 319
poultry, 317, 320, 321
price level, 80, 329
private estates, 90, 311
professions
  output, 104, 326
  training for, 112
public corporations, 103
Public Debt, 108, 330, 331
Public Works Department, 307
pulses, 315, 318, 330
pyrethrum, 315
railways, see transport
rates, 80, 327, 328
re-afforestation, 309
relish, food, 84, 318, 330
remittances abroad, 331, 332, 333
rents, 80, 305, 319, 322, 328, 331
research funds, 109
retail trade, 95, 323
retained imports, 333
revenue, government, 97, 322
Rhodesia, movement to, 94
rice production, 90, 93, 315, 321
roads, 81, 96, 324
root crops, 318
rubber, 321
rural population, predominance of, 76
Salima, 96
salt, consumption of, 85, 330
Sanitary Boards, 97, 309, 310, 330
sanitation, 81, 319, 327
saving, 80, 86, 105, 110, 313, 327, 328, 331,
  332

saving, government, 331, 332
sawmills, 312
secondary industry, output of, 98
service industries, 95
services, output of, 89, 98, 326
sewing machines, 86, 332
Shiré River, 73, 74, 75, 91, 96
shop assistants, 83, 312
shopkeepers, 307
shops, 81, 87, 94, 95, 311, 323
shortages, 80
sinking fund, government, 330
sisal, 88, 321
skins, 317, 321
soap, 88, 324
social accounts, 9, 99; see also national
  accounts
— investment, Agricultural Department, 105
— services, 109
soil erosion, 90
soldiers, 85, 87, 310, 313; see also armed
  forces
Southern Highlands, 73, 74, 75, 85, 89, 91,
  92, 94, 95, 97, 101, 102, 108, 112
Southern Province, 101, 317, 329
standard of living, 79, 82, 83, 84, 102, 103
storekeepers, see shopkeepers
stores, see shops
subsidies, outlay on, 98
subsistence activity, non-agricultural, 99
— agriculture, 76, 77, 82, 87, 89, 318,
  320
— consumption, 325, 330
— fishing, 316
— forestry, 327
— income, 79, 82, 325, 326
— livestock, 320
— output, 83, 89, 96, 97, 111
sugar consumption, 330
Tanganyika, 96, 313
taxable income, 85
taxation, 78, 80, 85, 328, 330
taxation, direct, 78, 331
  distribution of, 110
  evasion of, 304
  indirect, 80, 98, 327, 328, 331, 332
taxpayers, 234, 304
tea, 74, 88, 92, 93, 96, 216, 312, 321, 324
Tea Commissioner, 321
tea factories, 77, 311
teachers, 310, 311
technicians, training of, 311
Ten-Year Development Plan, 109
territorial balance of payments, 107
— income, 88, 106
— output, 89, 95, 100, 106
timber, 88, 97, 98, 324

Nyasaland—*continued*
  tobacco, 76, 77, 88, 90 97, 101, 111, 216
    expenditure on, 327, 328
    exports of, 93
    income from, 77, 83, 311, 312
    Kasungu scheme, 108
    production of, 91, 92, 311, 315, 321
    trade in, 103, 315, 323
    transportation of, 96
  tourist industry, 103, 107
  township authorities, 97, 309, 310
  trade, licensed, 317, 323
  trade statistics, 327
  trading services, 319, 320, 331
  transfers of income, 317; *see also* gifts
  transport, 77, 95, 96
    by steamer, 73, 96
    employment in, 312
    incomes from, 320
    lake to railhead, 96
    output of, 89, 95, 104, 324, 326
    railway, 96, 312, 330; finance, 95; freight
      rates, 95; output of, 323, 324; receipts
      from, 331
    road, 323
  Treasury, 108
  tsetse fly, 90
  Tumbuka, 75
  tung, 88, 92, 93, 108, 321
  United Kingdom companies, 307
  United Kingdom Government, grants and
    loans from, 95, 97, 108, 109, 110, 113,
    330
  urban conditions, 95, 102
  vegetables, 316
  Veterinary Department, 315, 317
  villages
    census of, 303
    economic activities in, 95
    economy of, 140, 329
    industries in, 82, 89, 98, 103, 319, 326
    shops in, 87, 94
  wages, *see* African wages
  water, 327
  wealth, 111
    distribution of, 101, 108
  welfare amenities, missions, 96
  wheat, 315, 321
  white settlement, 73
  woollen piece goods, 85
  Yao, 75
  Zambesi bridge, 95
  — delta, 73
  Zomba, 73, 76, 81, 97, 315, 330

Occupational groups, 144
Occupations, distribution between, 7

Orde Brown, Major, 32
Ownership, concept of, 147

Peters, D. U., 163
Pigou, A. C., *The Economics of Welfare*, 116
Platt, Dr B. S., 90, 137, 317
Ploughs, expenditure on, 183, 193
Polish nationals, 241
Polygamy, 199, 204
Population, 211, 224, 234
Portuguese Angola, 211
Portuguese East Africa, 17, 73, 211
Portuguese West Africa, 17
Pottery, 123, 124
Poultry, 162, 163, 258, 292; *see also* Livestock
Price evaluation, 122
— index, 181
— system, 128
Prices, 124, 181, 224
Primary products, 215
Primitive communities, 119, 121, 130
— economies, 128, 335
Production
    costs of, 124
    factors of, 6, 227
    for sale, 221
Productivity, 222
Property, 132–5, 175, 176, 191–4, 196
Purchasing power, 208

Racial groups, 227
Rand gold mines, 68, 313
Real incomes, 213, 219
    distribution of, 119; *see also* Income distribu-
      tion
Remittances abroad, 64
Rent, 15, 116, 125
Research, expenditure in connection with, 143
Residents
    definition, 170
    national output of, 15
Rhodes-Livingstone Institute, 11, 12, 199, 204,
    234, 251, 262, 337
Richards, Dr Audrey I., *Land, Labour and Diet
    in Northern Rhodesia*, 139, 163
Robbins, Professor Lionel, 116
Rural areas, lack of economic material, 131
— labour, drain on, 215
— populations, 214

Saffery, Lynn, 294
Salaries, *see* Wages
Salisbury, 55, 70
Salt, 175, 212
Sample Survey (1950) of African Population,
    18

Samples
  bias of, 143
  choice of, 141, 143, 144
  use of, 142
Savings, 217, 220
Schapera, Professor I., *Migrant Labour and Tribal Life in Bechuanaland*, 253–4
Secondary industries, 219
Self-government, 19
Semi-subsistence community, 225, 226
— economy, 123, 124, 140, 226, 228; accounts of, 227; definition of, 122; exchange in, 130; purchasing power of, 129–30
Shareholders, non-resident, 217
Shaul, J. R. H., 289, 290
Soap, 212
Social accounts, 3, 7, 9, 12, 115, 125, 127, 128, 225, 226
  construction of, 10, 221, 228
  subsistence output in, 126
  transfer payments in, 12
  use of, 7, 120
  see also Accounts
Social development, costs of, 9
— policy, 119
Soil deterioration, 221
South Africa, *see* Union of South Africa
South Africans, 19
Southern Africa, migrants from, 213
Southern Rhodesia, 17, 211–22, 237
  administration, local, 212
  area and population, 211
  balance of payments, 215
  development of, 216
  Economic and Statistical Bulletin, 217
  economy of, 212, 216
  European immigrants in, 19, 213, 216
  farming in, 212
  Government of, 54
  home market, 216
  immigrants, 212; capital brought in by, 216, 217; from Northern Rhodesia, 254; origin, 19
  income, 212, 214
  industrial development of, 216
  labour in, 19, 215
  manufactures, 216
  mining, 212
  national income, 218
  Northern Rhodesia, contact with, 20
  postal statistics, 314
  purchasing power, 216
  rate of expansion, 218
  remittances abroad, 217
  rural conditions, 216
  standard of living, 214
  trade and income statistics, 216

Southern Rhodesia—*continued*
  urban population, 212
  wages in, 94
  Standard of living, 115, 124, 130, 224, 227
  changes in, 225
  effects of industry on, 219
  in a subsistence economy, 128
  Statistical material, collection of, 8
  Stone, Richard, *Definition and Measurement of the National Income and Related Totals*, 11
  Subsistence consumption, 152
  — economy, 153, 224; applicability of economic analysis, 116; definition of, 122
  — farming, 9, 212
  — output, 7, 15, 128, 209; accounting problems, 223; definition of, 152; evaluation limitations, 129; in the social accounts, 126; value of, 226
  — production, 221; measurement of, 10
  Surplus produce, trade in, 123, 224

Tanganyika, 17, 211
Tax registers, 147, 234
Taxes, 127
Taxpayers, 234
Tea exports, 216
Territorial accounts, construction of, 227
— borders, national output, 15
Tobacco, 225
  expenditure on, 195, 205
  exports, 215
  sales of, 165
Trade, 212, 224
  international, 215
  seasonal, 123, 141
  terms of, 121
  see also Internal trade
Transfer incomes, 125
— payments, 126, 127
Trapnell, C. G., 338, 340
Triple-entry account, 3, 13

Undeveloped economy, problems of, 9
Union of South Africa, 19, 20, 94, 211, 237, 254, 313, 314
United Kingdom Treasury, 215
United Nations Organization, 3
Universities Mission to Central Africa, 96
Urban community, 115, 125

Value, theories of, 228
Vaughan Jones, T., 259
Vegetables, 141
Village(s), 145, 335
  chiefs, 144
  definition of, 146
  mobility of, 146

Village(s)—*continued*
  selection for survey, 141
Village accounts, 226, 227
— census method, 145
— economic survey, 153
— economy, 123, 141, 225; importance of, 115, 130, 219; nature of, 123, 140, 224, 226; specialization in, 140
— fission, rate of, 146
— income and outlay account, 121
— output, 121
— survey(s), 137, 142–3, 148, 152
  see also Internal trade, *and* internal trade, inter-village trade *under* Northern Rhodesia *and* Nyasaland

Wage earners, 185, 197
Wages, 218
  boys', 151
  increase in, 225

Wages—*continued*
  men's, 151
Welfare, 117
Wilson, Godfrey, 251, 254, 261, 292, 294, 314
  Land Rights of Individuals among the Nyakyusa, 145
Witch doctors, 227
Witwatersrand Native Labour Association, 252, 313, 314
Wives
  as economic wealth, 127
  purchase of, 225
  work done by, 220–1
Women
  clothing of, 180
  destitute, 174
  single, budget data of, 200
  see also Wives

Zinc, 216

PUBLICATIONS OF THE
NATIONAL INSTITUTE OF ECONOMIC
AND SOCIAL RESEARCH

published by

THE CAMBRIDGE UNIVERSITY PRESS

None of the Institute's publications is sold direct by the Institute. They are available through the ordinary booksellers, and enquiry can be made of the Cambridge University Press.

ECONOMIC & SOCIAL STUDIES

*I   *Studies in the National Income, 1924–1938*
Edited by A. L. BOWLEY. Reprinted with corrections, 1944. pp. 256. 15s. net.

*II   *The Burden of British Taxation*
By G. FINDLAY SHIRRAS and L. ROSTAS. 1942. pp. 140. 15s. net.

*III   *Trade Regulations and Commercial Policy of the United Kingdom*
By THE RESEARCH STAFF OF THE NATIONAL INSTITUTE OF ECONOMIC AND SOCIAL RESEARCH. 1943. pp. 275. 15s. net.

*IV   *National Health Insurance: A Critical Study*
By HERMANN LEVY. 1944. pp. 356. 18s. net.

V   *The Development of the Soviet Economic System: An Essay on the Experience of Planning in the U.S.S.R.*
By ALEXANDER BAYKOV. 1946. pp. 530. 37s. 6d. net.

VI   *Studies in Financial Organization*
By T. A. BALOGH. 1948. pp. 328. 30s. net.

*VII   *Investment, Location, and Size of Plant. A Realistic Inquiry into the Structure of British and American Industries*
By P. SARGANT FLORENCE, assisted by W. BALDAMUS. 1948. pp. 230. 18s. net.

VIII   *A Statistical Analysis of Advertising Expenditure and of the Revenue of the Press*
By NICHOLAS KALDOR and RODNEY SILVERMAN. 1948. pp. 200. 18s. net.

IX   *The Distribution of Consumer Goods*
By JAMES B. JEFFERYS, assisted by MARGARET MACCOLL and G. L. LEVETT. 1950. pp. 430. 40s. net.

X   *Lessons of the British War Economy*
Edited by D. N. CHESTER. 1951. pp. 260. 25s. net.

OCCASIONAL PAPERS

*I   *The New Population Statistics*
By R. R. KUCZYNSKI. 1942. pp. 31. 1s. 6d. net.

II   *The Population of Bristol*
By H. A. SHANNON and E. GREBENIK. 1943. pp. 92. 12s. 6d. net.

*III   *Standards of Local Expenditure*
By J. R. HICKS and U. K. HICKS. 1943. pp. 61. 4s. 6d. net.

IV   *War-Time Pattern of Saving and Spending*
By CHARLES MADGE. 1943. pp. 139. 10s. 6d. net.

*V   *Standardized Accountancy in Germany*
By H. W. SINGER. Reprinted 1944. pp. 68. 6s. net.

VI   *Ten Years of Controlled Trade in South-Eastern Europe*
By N. MOMTCHILOFF. 1944. pp. 90. 10s. 6d. net.

*VII   *The Problem of Valuation for Rating*
By J. R. HICKS, U. K. HICKS and C. E. V. LESER. 1944. pp. 90.
7s. 6d. net.

VIII   *The Incidence of Local Rates in Great Britain*
By J. R. HICKS and U. K. HICKS. 1945. pp. 64. 10s. 6d. net.

IX   *Contributions to the Study of Oscillatory Time-Series*
By M. G. KENDALL. 1946. pp. 76. 10s. 6d. net.

X   *A System of National Book-keeping illustrated by the Experience of the Netherlands*
By J. B. D. DERKSEN. 1946. pp. 34. 8s. 6d. net.

XI   *Productivity, Prices and Distribution in Selected British Industries*
By L. ROSTAS. 1948. pp. 199. 25s. net.

XII   *The Measurement of Colonial National Incomes: An Experiment*
By PHYLLIS DEANE. 1948. pp. 173. 18s. net.

XIII   *Comparative Productivity in British and American Industry*
By L. ROSTAS. 1948. pp. 263. 25s. net.

XIV   *The Cost of Industrial Movement*
By W. F. LUTTRELL. 1952. pp. 104. 18s. net.

XV   *Costs in Alternative Locations: the Clothing Industry*
By D. C. HAGUE and P. K. NEWMAN. 1952. pp. 73. 12s. 6d. net.

* The publications marked with an asterisk (*) are out of print.

Register of Research in the Social Sciences and Directory of Institutions

Editor: FEODORA STONE

No. 5. 1947/48. pp. 104. 12s. 6d. net.
No. 6. 1948/49. pp. 155. 15s. net.
No. 7. 1949/50. pp. 175. 15s. net.
No. 8. 1950/51. pp. 174. 15s. net.
No. 9. 1951/52. pp. 188. 15s. net.

The annual issues of the *Register* are available direct from the Cambridge University Press, Bentley House, 200 Euston Road, London, N.W.1, or from the U.S.A. Branch, 32 East 57th Street, New York 22, N.Y.

Some Accounting Terms and Concepts—A Report of a Joint Exploratory Committee. pp. 46. 3s. net.

Published jointly for the Institute of Chartered Accountants and the National Institute of Economic and Social Research.

For EU product safety concerns, contact us at Calle de José Abascal, 56–1°,
28003 Madrid, Spain or eugpsr@cambridge.org.

www.ingramcontent.com/pod-product-compliance
Ingram Content Group UK Ltd.
Pitfield, Milton Keynes, MK11 3LW, UK
UKHW042211180425
457623UK00011B/150